# 56th Annual Meeting of the Association for Computational Linguistics (ACL 2018)

Student Research Workshop

Melbourne, Australia
15 – 20 July 2018

ISBN: 978-1-5108-6707-9

ACL 2018

# The 56th Annual Meeting of the
# Association for Computational Linguistics

## Proceedings of the Student Research Workshop

July 15 - July 20
Melbourne, Australia

ROAM

Google



Order copies of this and other ACL proceedings from:

Association for Computational Linguistics (ACL)
209 N. Eighth Street
Stroudsburg, PA 18360
USA
Tel: +1-570-476-8006
Fax: +1-570-476-0860
acl@aclweb.org

ISBN 978-1-948087-36-0 (Student Research Workshop)

# Introduction

Welcome to the ACL 2018 Student Research Workshop!

The ACL 2018 Student Research Workshop (SRW) is a forum for student researchers in computational linguistics and natural language processing. The workshop provides a unique opportunity for student participants to present their work and receive valuable feedback from the international research community as well as from selected mentors.

Following the tradition of the previous years' student research workshops, we have two tracks: research papers and research proposals. The research paper track is a venue for Ph.D. students, Masters students, and advanced undergraduates to describe completed work or work-in-progress along with preliminary results. The research proposal track is offered for advanced Masters and Ph.D. students who have decided on a thesis topic and are interested in feedback on their proposal and ideas about future directions for their work.

We received 66 submissions in total: 12 research proposals and 54 research papers. We accepted 26 papers, for an acceptance rate of 39%. After withdrawals, 22 papers are appearing in these proceedings, including 6 research proposals and 16 research papers. All of the accepted papers will be presented as posters in lunchtime sessions as a part of the main conference, split across two days (July 17th and 18th).

Mentoring is at the heart of the SRW. In keeping with previous years, students had the opportunity to participate in a pre-submission mentoring program prior to the submission deadline. This program offered students a chance to receive comments from an experienced researcher, in order to improve the quality of the writing and presentation before making their submission. Eleven authors participated in the pre-submission mentoring. In addition, authors of accepted SRW papers are matched with mentors who will meet with the students in person during the workshop. Each mentor prepares in-depth comments and questions prior to the student's presentation, and provides discussion and feedback during the workshop.

We are deeply grateful to our sponsors whose support will enable a number of students to attend the conference, including the Don and Betty Walker Scholarship Fund, Roam Analytics, Google, and the National Science Foundation under award No. 1827830. We would also like to thank our program committee members for their careful reviews of each paper, and all of our mentors for donating their time to provide feedback to our student authors.

Thank you to our faculty advisors Marie-Catherine de Marneffe, Wanxiang Che, and Malvina Nissim for their essential advice and guidance, and to the members of the ACL 2018 organizing committee, in particular Claire Cardie, Yusuke Miyao, and Priscilla Rasmussen for their helpful support. Finally, thank you to our student participants!

**Organizers:**

Vered Shwartz, Bar-Ilan University
Jeniya Tabassum, Ohio State University
Rob Voigt, Stanford University

**Faculty Advisors:**

Wanxiang Che, Harbin Institute of Technology
Marie-Catherine de Marneffe, Ohio State University
Malvina Nissim, University of Groningen

**Program Committee:**

Roee Aharoni, Bar Ilan University
Fernando Alva-Manchego, University of Sheffield
Bharat Ram Ambati, Apple Inc.
Jacob Andreas, University of California, Berkeley
Isabelle Augenstein, Department of Computer Science, University of Copenhagen
Petr Babkin, Rensselaer Polytechnic Institute
Fan Bai, The Ohio State University
Kalika Bali, Microsoft Research Labs
Miguel Ballesteros, IBM Research AI
David Bamman, University of California, Berkeley
Yonatan Belinkov, MIT CSAIL
Yonatan Bisk, University of Washington
Facundo Carrillo, Buenos Aires University
Arun Chaganty, Stanford University
Kuan-Yu Chen, NTUST
Tanmay Chinchore, M S Ramaiah Institute of Technology
Grzegorz Chrupała, Tilburg University
Daria Dzendzik, ADAPT Centre Dublin City University
Kurt Junshean Espinosa, University of the Manchester
Tina Fang, University of Waterloo
Silvia García Méndez, AtlantTIC Center - University of Vigo
Matt Gardner, Allen Institute for Artificial Intelligence
Marjan Ghazvininejad, University of Southern California
Hila Gonen, Bar-Ilan University
Alvin Grissom II, Ursinus College
Vivek Gupta, Microsoft Research
He He, Stanford University
Mohit Iyyer, Allen Institute for Artificial Intelligence
Ganesh Jawahar, IIIT Hyderabad
Vasu Jindal, University of Texas at Dallas
Sudipta Kar, University of Houston
Alina Karakanta, Saarland Univesity
Eliyahu Kiperwasser, Bar-Ilan University
Thomas Kober, University of Edinburgh
Alexandar Konovalov, The Ohio State University

Alice Lai, University of Illinois at Urbana-Champaign
Wuwei Lan, The Ohio State University
Eric Laporte, Université Paris-Est Marne-la-Vallée
Haixia Liu, The University of Nottingham
Haijing Liu, Institute of Software, Chinese Academy of Sciences & University of Chinese Academy of Sciences
Edison Marrese-Taylor, The University of Tokyo
Prashant Mathur, eBay
Brian McMahan, Rutgers University
Paul Michel, Carnegie Mellon University
Saif Mohammad, National Research Council Canada
Taesun Moon, IBM Research
Maria Moritz, University of Goettingen
Nihal V. Nayak, Stride.AI
Denis Newman-Griffis, The Ohio State University
Dat Quoc Nguyen, The University of Melbourne
Vlad Niculae, Cornell University
Suraj Pandey, The Open University
Mohammad Taher Pilehvar, University of Cambridge
Daniel Preoţiuc-Pietro, University of Pennsylvania
Emily Prud'hommeaux, Boston College
Avinesh PVS, UKP Lab, Technische Universität Darmstadt
Sudha Rao, University Of Maryland, College Park
Will Roberts, Humboldt-Universität zu Berlin
Stephen Roller, Facebook
Julia Romberg, Heinrich Heine University Düsseldorf
Farig Sadeque, University of Arizona
Enrico Santus, MIT
Shoetsu Sato, Graduate School of Information Science and Technology, The University of Tokyo
Sabine Schulte im Walde, University of Stuttgart
Sebastian Schuster, Stanford University
Vasu Sharma, Carnegie Mellon University
Sunayana Sitaram, Microsoft Research India
Kevin Small, Amazon
Katira Soleymanzadeh, Ege University
R.Sudhesh Solomon, Indian Institute of Information Technology
Richard Sproat, Google
Gabriel Stanovsky, University of Washington, Allen Institute for Artificial Intelligence
Shang-Yu Su, National Taiwan University
Sandesh Swamy, The Ohio State University
Ivan Vulić, University of Cambridge
Olivia Winn, Columbia University
Zhou Yu, University of California, Davis
Omnia Zayed, Insight Centre for Data Analytics, National University of Ireland Galway
Meishan Zhang, Heilongjiang University, China
Yuan Zhang, Google

# Table of Contents

# Conference Program

**Tuesday July 17, 2018**

*Towards Opinion Summarization of Customer Reviews*
Samuel Pecar

*Sampling Informative Training Data for RNN Language Models*
Jared Fernandez and Doug Downey

*Learning-based Composite Metrics for Improved Caption Evaluation*
Naeha Sharif, Lyndon White, Mohammed Bennamoun and Syed Afaq Ali Shah

*Recursive Neural Network Based Preordering for English-to-Japanese Machine Translation*
Yuki Kawara, Chenhui Chu and Yuki Arase

*Pushing the Limits of Radiology with Joint Modeling of Visual and Textual Information*
Sonit Singh

*Recognizing Complex Entity Mentions: A Review and Future Directions*
Xiang Dai

*Automatic Detection of Cross-Disciplinary Knowledge Associations*
Menasha Thilakaratne, Katrina Falkner and Thushari Atapattu

*Language Identification and Named Entity Recognition in Hinglish Code Mixed Tweets*
Kushagra Singh, Indira Sen and Ponnurangam Kumaraguru

*German and French Neural Supertagging Experiments for LTAG Parsing*
Tatiana Bladier, Andreas van Cranenburgh, Younes Samih and Laura Kallmeyer

*SuperNMT: Neural Machine Translation with Semantic Supersenses and Syntactic Supertags*
Eva Vanmassenhove and Andy Way

*Unsupervised Semantic Abstractive Summarization*
Shibhansh Dohare, Vivek Gupta and Harish Karnick

# Towards Opinion Summarization of Customer Reviews


**Samuel Pecar**
Slovak University of Technology in Bratislava
Faculty of Informatics and Information Technologies
lkovičova 2, 842 16 Bratislava, Slovakia
`samuel.pecar@stuba.sk`



## Abstract

In recent years, the number of texts has grown rapidly. For example, most review-based portals, like Yelp or Amazon, contain thousands of user-generated reviews. It is impossible for any human reader to process even the most relevant of these documents. The most promising tool to solve this task is a text summarization. Most existing approaches, however, work on small, homogeneous, English datasets, and do not account to multi-linguality, opinion shift, and domain effects. In this paper, we introduce our research plan to use neural networks on user-generated travel reviews to generate summaries that take into account shifting opinions over time. We outline future directions in summarization to address all of these issues. By resolving the existing problems, we will make it easier for users of review-sites to make more informed decisions.


## 1 Introduction

In recent years, amount of available text corpora has been growing rapidly with increasing popularity of web. Users produce a huge amount of text every day. With a larger amount of text and information included within it, it becomes impossible for people to read all the texts and it leads to information overload. For a common human, it is not possible to read all the available text even if he reads only all the most relevant ones. The task of text summarization is known for a very long period. In late 50s Luhn (Luhn, 1958) tried to create abstract of documents automatically. Over decades there have been many summarization systems dealing with different forms of summarization. This task belongs to one of the most chal-

lenging tasks in natural language processing. The task of text summarization can be particularly important for decision making or relevance judgments (Nenkova and McKeown, 2011).

Automatic text summarization became very useful and also important tool to help the user obtain as much information as possible without the necessity to read all the original documents. Many definitions of text summarization exist. Text summary can be defined as a text produced from one or more texts that contains the same information as the original text and is no longer than half of the original text (Hovy and Lin, 1998). Mani (Mani, 2001) defined the goal of summarization as a process of finding the source of information, extracting content from it and presenting the most important content to the user in a concise form and in a manner sensitive to needs of user's application.

We can divide techniques of summarization into two categories: abstractive and extractive summarization (Gambhir and Gupta, 2017). Extractive summarization aims to choose parts of the original document such as sentence part, whole sentence or paragraph. Abstractive summarization wants to get paraphrase content of the original document with respect to cohesion and concise of output summary. Selection of the text section in extractive summarization leads to a partial loss of an output cohesion, which abstractive summarization tries to accomplish.

In last few years, approaches based on neural networks became very popular for summarization task (Rush et al., 2015). A specific branch of text summarization is a summarization of opinions from the human-generated text. We can summarize opinions from customer reviews or comments on social networks. This problem differs from a standard summarization task due to a number of repetitive and redundant information. There can be also a problem with polarity of opinions be-




*Proceedings of ACL 2018, Student Research Workshop*, pages 1–8
Melbourne, Australia, July 15 - 20, 2018. ©2018 Association for Computational Linguistics

tween different users. This types of summary can be very useful for both a customer of products and a product owner. Opinion summarization can be particularly important for decision making (Yuan et al., 2015). This summarization type can also show trends in opinions collected from comments on social networks, especially when a number of text entries grows very fast.

In this work, we also discuss analysis of specific aspect of opinion summarization: sentiment analysis of customer reviews. In summarization task, sentiment information can be viewed as one of the inputs along with text corpora itself. A difference between sentiment of text fragments and sentiment of whole summarization is a very interesting aspect to consider.

The expected contributions of our research are: (1) overview of a recent development in opinion summarization, (2) assembly of a reasonably big dataset for opinion summarization (from travel based portals), (3) a novel method for opinion summarization based on state-of-the-art neural network architectures.

The rest of this paper is structured as follows. Section 2 explains recent advances in text summarization. In Section 3, we focus on possibilities in the area of opinion mining and summarization of opinions. Future directions in summarization are drawn in Section 4. The research proposal including opinion summarization along with a possible dataset and a planned experiment are described in Section 5. Final observations and conclusions are mentioned in Section 6.

## 2 Text Summarization

In recent years, text summarization has been focusing on the abstractive summarization with a use of neural models. In (Rush et al., 2015), the authors showed a way to use a neural network based on encoder-decoder architecture for creating abstractive summarization on the sentence level. Using this type of model originates from a task of machine translation where these models were used before. The approach presented in (Chopra et al., 2016) can be considered as a follower of the previous work. Instead of a feed-forward neural network a recurrent neural network (RNN) was used. RNN emphasizes the order of input words. The authors presented conditional RNN with convolutional attention-based encoder.

Ferreira et al. presented a sentence clustering algorithm to deal with the redundancy and information diversity problems (Ferreira et al., 2014). The algorithm uses the text representation to convert input text into graph model along with four types of relations between sentences.

A specific yet not very widely used technique is Abstract Meaning Representation (AMR). For text summarization, a framework for abstractive summarization based on the recent development of a treebank for AMR (Liu et al., 2015) can be employed. This framework parses source text into a set of AMR graphs, then the graph is transformed into a summary graph from which the output summary is generated.

The use of neural architecture from machine translation became widely popular and many authors made research in this area. Nallapati et al. (Nallapati et al., 2016) presented a neural model for abstractive summarization along with the introduction of a whole new dataset for evaluation of summarization.

The use of attention mechanism in neural networks became widely spread and very popular. Many works showed usefulness of this mechanism in other tasks. In summarization task, a work proposed by See et al. (See et al., 2017) introduced a method based on the principle of encoder-decoder along with attention distribution of input text. They used hybrid pointer-generator architecture with a use of the coverage. The pointer mechanism tries to solve problem of choosing words either to use original word or generate a new one. The coverage part ensures minimizing repetition during the text generation in the later parts of the output. Interesting modification was introduced by Paulus et al. (Paulus et al., 2017). Their mechanism modifies standard attention mechanism and also objective function with a combination of maximum likelihood and cross-entropy loss. This mechanism is used in a phase of reinforcement learning. Tan et al. (Tan et al., 2017) proposed another modification of attention mechanism and their graph-based attention mechanism was used in a sequence-to-sequence framework. The goal of the encoder is mapping the input documents to the vector representation. Then decoder is used to generate the output sentences. Novelty of their method lies in using graph-based attention mechanism in a hierarchical encoder-decoder framework.

Neural models are widely used for both abstractive and extractive summarization. Nallapati et al. (Nallapati et al., 2017) presented a neural sequential model for the extractive summarization of documents. Visualizing impact of a particular parts of the input text to output summarization we can consider as other contribution of this paper.

Similarly to other tasks of natural language processing, convolutional neural networks can be used for summarization. Yasunaga et al. (Yasunaga et al., 2017) incorporates sentence relations using Graph Convolutional Network on relation graphs along with the sentence embeddings obtained from RNN, which were taken as input node features. This system tries to exploit a representational power of neural networks and sentence relation information which can be encoded in the graph representation of document clusters.

Much research has been conducted in this field in recent years. Other interesting modification can employ latent structure modeling presented in a framework based on sequence-to-sequence oriented encoder-decoder model which incorporates a latent structure modeling component (Li et al., 2017). This model generates abstractive summary of the latent variables but also of the the discriminative deterministic states.

All aforementioned summarization works were primarily aimed at summarization of news articles. There can be also other summarization types like a summarization of emails (Carenini et al., 2008; Yousefi-Azar and Hamey, 2017), event-based summarization (Glavaš and Šnajder, 2014; Kedzie et al., 2015), personalized summarization (Díaz and Gervás, 2007; Moro and Bielikova, 2012) and also sentiment-based or opinion summarization described in the next section.

## 3 Opinion Mining and Summarization

Summarization of opinions is a special type of summarization. Product and services along with comments on social networks could consist of hundreds of entries and could lead to information overload. Repetition of opinions is one of the major differences that contrasts with the summarization of news. User-generated text often remarkably differentiate from news text which is commonly widely revised.

### 3.1 Summarization of Customer Opinions

Summarization of opinions from product reviews is the most common example of opinion summarization. These reviews often come from stores of electronics like Amazon. Yuan et al. (Yuan et al., 2015) presented user study how opinion summarization can help in decision making before consumer purchase.

One of the first works in opinion summarization could be considered the work of Hu and Liu (Hu and Liu, 2004). They proposed a set of techniques for mining and summarizing product reviews. The main goal of their opinion summarization system is to provide a feature-based summary.

Tadano et al. proposed method based on evaluative sentence extraction where aspects are judged by their ratings, tf-idf value and number of mentions with similar topic (Tadano et al., 2010).

Summarization approach based on the topical structure was introduced by Zhan et al. (Zhan et al., 2009). They presented a topical structure as a list of significant topics related from a document set. To reduce redundancy of sentences they implemented a method of maximal marginal relevance.

The Opinosis project presented a graph-based summarization framework (Ganesan et al., 2010). This framework tries to generate abstractive summarization of highly redundant opinions. Authors showed that their summaries have better agreement with human summaries compared to the baseline extractive methods.

Dalal and Zaveri presented application of a multi-step approach for automatic opinion mining consisting of various phases (Dalal and Zaveri, 2013). Authors showed that this multi-step feature-based semi-supervised opinion mining approach can be successful in identification of opinionated sentences from user reviews.

Aspect-based sentiment analysis can help to produce a structured summary based on positive and negative opinion about features of the product (Kansal and Toshniwal, 2014). The system takes into consideration not only sentence information, but also pieces of information from other sentences or reviews called contextual information. The authors also showed that polarity of words can be different even within one domain.

Kurian and Asokan presented a method with the cross-domain sentiment classification along with the distributional similarity of opinion words (Kurian and Asokan, 2015). This method helps to classify and summarize product reviews and, in contrast with other methods, it does not require labeled data from the target domain or other lexical resources.

Unlike other opinion summarization systems dealing with sentiment polarity, another study formulated opinion summarization as a community leader detection problem (Zhu et al., 2015). Authors proposed a graph-based method to identify informative sentences and evaluated method on product reviews. The study proposed algorithms for leaders detection in the sentence graph.

A system named Gist (Lovinger et al., 2017) intends to deal with a large amount of text and automatically summarizes it into informative and actionable key sentences. Gist tries to summarize original reviews into the short text consisting of a few key sentences that will capture the overall sentiment about the product.

A kind of opinion summarization could be a summarization of travel reviews to give feedback for quality of hotels, restaurants or other services. A clustering based method for summarization of hotel reviews was proposed by Hu et al. (Hu et al., 2017). They also showed additional information as author's reputation or creation date could have a huge impact on relevant summary creation. Raut et al. (Raut and Londhe, 2014) presented machine learning and Senti-WordNet method for mining opinions from hotel reviews and also a method for sentence relevant scoring.

### 3.2 Summarization of Community Answers

Along with the summarization of customer reviews, a very important summarization type considers comments on social networks or answers in question answering (QA) systems as input entries. Investigation in this forms of text entries can lead to easier decision making.

A sub-modular function-based framework was presented by Wang et al. (Wang et al., 2014). This framework can be used for query-focused opinion summarization. Authors evaluated this framework in QA and blog dataset. Statistically learned sentence relevance along with information coverage with respect to diverse topics are encoded as sub-modular functions.

Work of Lloret et al. (Lloret et al., 2015) deals both with the summarization of opinions in social networks and opinions in product reviews. Their method can be characterized with an integration of sentence simplification, but also regeneration of sentence and also internal concept representation

in the summarization task. The method tries to be able to generate abstractive summaries.

There are many topics in this area which can lead to very interesting observations. Guo et al. (Guo et al., 2015) proposed a model for opinion summarization of highly contrastive opinions particularly for controversial issues. They integrated expert opinions with ordinary opinions to create an output of contrastive sentence pairs. The study also presented this method as a unified way for users to better summarize opinions concerning controversial issues.

Another study explores opinion summarization of the spontaneous conversation (Wang and Liu, 2015). Phone conversation corpus was annotated in this study and authors investigated two methods of extractive summarization, graph-based with incorporating topic and sentiment information and supervised method which cast this problem as a classification problem.

A study from Li et al. deals also with opinion summarization in blogging (Li et al., 2016). They proposed a convolutional neural network for opinion summarization based on recent deep-learning research. Maximal marginal relevance is used for extraction of representative opinion sentences.

A very important problem of the volume and volatility of opinionated data published in social media was presented by Tsirakis et al. (Tsirakis et al., 2016). They discussed that most of methods deal only with a small volume of data, where they are quite effective, but usually do not scale up.

## 4  Future Directions

As presented in the previous sections, many challenges are still present in summarization. Standard text summarization usually applied to news articles deals still with the problem of abstractive summarization. Text summarization techniques can be on a different level of abstraction and usually are not fully abstractive (See et al., 2017).

Another big challenge lies in summarization of text in languages other than English. Most of methods were evaluated only on English and interesting could be an evaluation in other ones along with their specifics. Another aspect could be summarization over multiple languages where input text does not need to be in only one language.

Summarization of user-generated content has to deal with a problem of the noisy and ungrammatical documents but also with very diverse and conflicting opinions included within these documents (Murray et al., 2017). This problem is even more protuberant in minor languages where opinion mining and sentiment analysis is not well developed (Krchnavy and Simko, 2017).

In opinion summarization with thousands of input entries a researcher should deal with a change of opinions during the time. When summarizing customer reviews for services like hotels or restaurants, change of quality should be considered. It can lead to a specific time-based summary which considers progress of opinions over the time. This problem is also relevant in summarization of text in social networks, especially with controversial topics reports to the specific mood in society or can be effected by community leaders. Lack of available large datasets for this task is other crucial subject of research in next years, since most of research was evaluated only on small ones.

A significant problem is present in the evaluation phase. Automatic evaluation can be quite controversial as there exist not only one correct summarization. Automatic evaluation measures like ROUGE and its modifications (Lin, 2004) can partially deal with these problems using n-grams, but still do not handle a use of synonyms. Same problems based on multiple formulation of ground truth can cause problems with human evaluation as well. Experiments evaluated with more human participants have to deal with an agreement between users which can be quite low.

In next few years, we expect the opinion summarization to deal with the domain specifics and also with the user satisfaction. The growth of user-generated content in the future can lead to focus on reduction of information overload and also to text summarization itself.

## 5    Research Proposal

As we described earlier, we would like to focus on a specific type of summarization: creation of opinion summaries. Nowadays, travel sites include thousands of reviews from users which visited one of reviewed places. These reviews are very important in decision making of future possible customers but also for owners of services. With tens of new reviews every day it is impossible to read all the reviews and it is often very difficult to choose only the relevant ones. For owners, it is not possible to manually read all the reviews that could be very helpful in service improvement.

Recent advances in neural networks and also in the text summarization showed that employing encoder-decoder architecture can be very useful. The problem of summarization of customer reviews differs from standard single document summarization where the models were applied before. In this task, we should consider multi-modular framework.

The main idea of this proposal lies in getting better user satisfaction with review summary and also in examining of time aspect on opinion summarization. Opinion summarization should process in several phases:

1. aspect detection,

2. clustering opinionated features,

3. sentence generation.

The first step of our proposal lies in the detection of aspects. Before creation of any summary, we need to identify aspects discussed in these reviews. Another mechanism would be needed to distinguish similarity of aspects. A taxonomy of aspects could be a very useful tool to avoid a separation of similar aspects but other approaches utilizing a distributional and vector space should be also examined. We plan to use a bidirectional LSTM neural network with convolutional attention mechanism to identify aspects within text and also to determine polarity of each aspect.

In the second step, we have to cluster opinionated sentences by aspects they talk about. In each cluster, a sentiment and polarity of opinions need to be determined. Whereas in the task of sentiment analysis only overall or average sentiment is typically provided, in the summarization all polarity opinions should be included in the output summary. To reach this goal, all the opinionated sentences and opinions should be identified.

In the final phase, we would like to employ neural network architecture to generate output sentences from collected aspect-oriented information. In this phase, we need to generate sentence to output summary based on clustered aspects and also use the polarity of aspects. We plan to use LSTM network for this stage and generate sentence from extracted aspects and their polarity.

There is also another important point of interest in task of summarization that has not been discussed yet. The time horizon is often a neglected feature which should be considered in opinion summarization of customer reviews, as opinions of customers can develop over the time in a positive, but also a negative way. We plan to include information about created time to process of clustering opinions along with other information about the reviewer, what can lead to better accuracy of summarization as well as resulting user satisfaction with an output summary.

Another significant point to discuss is employing end-to-end deep learning in the task of opinion summarization. The major problem is lack of large dataset which is necessary for such learning. Creation of this kind of dataset is expensive and could take hundreds of hours, if performed manually.

### 5.1 Dataset

To create an appropriate dataset, we plan to gather customer reviews from large travel portals (e.g., *TripAdvisor*, *Booking.com*). All reviews come along with other useful information such as score ranking, which should be included too. However any public information about reviewers could be very useful too as it shows reviewer relevance and also importance.

### 5.2 Experiments

To evaluate the quality of generated summaries a few experiments are required. We will have to create our ground truth or reference summaries to automatically evaluate quality of summary. As we mentioned before, it is not a sufficient way for evaluation and other experiments including human evaluation would be needed. As this type of evaluation is very time consuming and difficult for resources, *a posteriori* evaluation is more feasible way to assess the quality of generated summaries. Very interesting view for opinion summaries is comparison of the sentiment of generated summaries and the sentiment of original input reviews. In human evaluation, we would like to provide users a list of original reviews, generated summary and ask about their satisfaction. We also plan to use some other automatic measures like ROUGE (Lin, 2004) and compare generated summary with summary created by humans. Another important measure is aspect coverage and ratio of included aspect in generated summaries from original reviews.

## 6 Conclusion

In this paper, we described the background for summarization task. More importantly, we described recent contributions and development in this area with many problems the research deals with. We emphasized the main problems and future research directions in process of summarization and also particularly for opinion summarization. We also introduced our future research intentions along with a design of the first experiments and possible model and dataset. We demonstrated that summarization task and especially opinion summarization still have big open issues will be researched in the next few years.

## Acknowledgments

I would like to thank my supervisors Marian Simko and Maria Bielikova. This work has been partially supported by the STU Grant scheme for Support of Young Researchers and grants No. VG 1/0646/15 and No. KEGA 028STU-4/2017.

## References

Giuseppe Carenini, Raymond T. Ng, and Xiaodong Zhou. 2008. Summarizing emails with conversational cohesion and subjectivity. In *Proceedings of ACL-08: HLT*. Association for Computational Linguistics, pages 353–361. http://www.aclweb.org/anthology/P08-1041.

Sumit Chopra, Michael Auli, and Alexander M Rush. 2016. Abstractive Sentence Summarization with Attentive Recurrent Neural Networks. In *Proceedings of the 2016 Conference of the North American Chapter of the Association for Computational Linguistics: Human Language Technologies*. Association for Computational Linguistics, pages 93–98. https://doi.org/10.18653/v1/N16-1012.

Mita K Dalal and Mukesh A Zaveri. 2013. Semisupervised Learning Based Opinion Summarization and Classification for Online Product Reviews. *Applied Computational Intelligence and Soft Computing* 2013:1–8. https://doi.org/10.1155/2013/910706.

Alberto Díaz and Pablo Gervás. 2007. User-model based personalized summarization. *Information Processing & Management* 43(6):1715–1734. https://doi.org/10.1016/j.ipm.2007.01.009.

Rafael Ferreira, Luciano de Souza Cabral, Frederico Freitas, Rafael Dueire Lins, Gabriel de França Silva, Steven J Simske, and Luciano Favaro. 2014. A multi-document summarization system based on statistics and linguistic treatment. *Expert Systems with Applications* 41(13):5780–5787. https://doi.org/10.1016/j.eswa.2014.03.023.

Mahak Gambhir and Vishal Gupta. 2017. Recent automatic text summarization techniques: a survey. *Artificial Intelligence Review* 47(1):1–66. https://doi.org/10.1007/s10462-016-9475-9.

Kavita Ganesan, ChengXiang Zhai, and Jiawei Han. 2010. Opinosis: A graph based approach to abstractive summarization of highly redundant opinions. In *Proceedings of the 23rd International Conference on Computational Linguistics (Coling 2010)*. Association for Computational Linguistics, pages 340–348.

Goran Glavaš and Jan Šnajder. 2014. Event graphs for information retrieval and multi-document summarization. *Expert Systems with Applications* 41(15):6904–6916. https://doi.org/10.1016/j.eswa.2014.04.004.

Jinlong Guo, Yujie Lu, Tatsunori Mori, and Catherine Blake. 2015. Expert-Guided Contrastive Opinion Summarization for Controversial Issues. In *Proceedings of the 24th International Conference on World Wide Web - WWW '15 Companion*. ACM Press, pages 1105–1110. https://doi.org/10.1145/2740908.2743038.

Eduard Hovy and Chin-Yew Lin. 1998. Automated text summarization and the summarist system. In *Proceedings of a Workshop on Held at Baltimore, Maryland: October 13-15, 1998*. Association for Computational Linguistics, TIPSTER '98, pages 197–214. https://doi.org/10.3115/1119089.1119121.

Minqing Hu and Bing Liu. 2004. Mining and summarizing customer reviews. In *Proceedings of the Tenth ACM SIGKDD International Conference on Knowledge Discovery and Data Mining*. ACM, KDD '04, pages 168–177. https://doi.org/10.1145/1014052.1014073.

Ya-Han Hu, Yen-Liang Chen, and Hui-Ling Chou. 2017. Opinion mining from online hotel reviews – A text summarization approach. *Information Processing & Management* 53(2):436–449. https://doi.org/10.1016/j.ipm.2016.12.002.

Hitesh Kansal and Durga Toshniwal. 2014. Aspect based Summarization of Context Dependent Opinion Words. *Procedia Computer Science* 35:166–175. https://doi.org/10.1016/J.PROCS.2014.08.096.

Chris Kedzie, Kathleen McKeown, and Fernando Diaz. 2015. Predicting salient updates for disaster summarization. In *Proceedings of the 53rd Annual Meeting of the Association for Computational Linguistics and the 7th International Joint Conference on Natural Language Processing (Volume 1: Long Papers)*. Association for Computational Linguistics, pages 1608–1617. https://doi.org/10.3115/v1/P15-1155.

R. Krchnavy and M. Simko. 2017. Sentiment analysis of social network posts in slovak language. In *2017 12th International Workshop on Semantic and Social Media Adaptation and Personalization (SMAP)*. pages 20–25. https://doi.org/10.1109/SMAP.2017.8022661.

Neethu Kurian and Shimmi Asokan. 2015. Summarizing User Opinions: A Method for Labeled-data Scarce Product Domains. *Procedia Computer Science* 46:93–100. https://doi.org/10.1016/j.procs.2015.01.062.

Piji Li, Wai Lam, Lidong Bing, and Zihao Wang. 2017. Deep recurrent generative decoder for abstractive text summarization. In *Proceedings of the 2017 Conference on Empirical Methods in Natural Language Processing*. Association for Computational Linguistics, pages 2091–2100. http://aclweb.org/anthology/D17-1222.

Qiudan Li, Zhipeng Jin, Can Wang, and Daniel Dajun Zeng. 2016. Knowle dge-Base d Systems Mining opinion summarizations using convolutional neural networks in Chinese microblogging systems. *Knowledge-Based Systems* 107:289–300. https://doi.org/10.1016/j.knosys.2016.06.017.

Chin-Yew Lin. 2004. ROUGE: A Package for Automatic Evaluation of Summaries 8. http://anthology.aclweb.org/W/W04/W04-1013.pdf.

Fei Liu, Jeffrey Flanigan, Sam Thomson, Norman Sadeh, and Noah A. Smith. 2015. Toward Abstractive Summarization Using Semantic Representations. In *Proceedings of the 2015 Conference of the North American Chapter of the Association for Computational Linguistics: Human Language Technologies*. Association for Computational Linguistics, pages 1077–1086. https://doi.org/10.3115/v1/N15-1114.

Elena Lloret, Ester Boldrini, Tatiana Vodolazova, Patricio Martínez-Barco, Rafael Muñoz, and Manuel Palomar. 2015. A novel concept-level approach for ultra-concise opinion summarization. *Expert Systems with Applications* 42(20):7148–7156. https://doi.org/10.1016/j.eswa.2015.05.026.

Justin Lovinger, Iren Valova, and Chad Clough. 2017. Gist: general integrated summarization of text and reviews. *Soft Computing* https://doi.org/10.1007/s00500-017-2882-2.

H. P. Luhn. 1958. The Automatic Creation of Literature Abstracts. *IBM Journal of Research and Development* 2(2):159–165. https://doi.org/10.1147/rd.22.0159.

Inderjeet Mani. 2001. *Automatic Summarization*, volume 3 of *Natural Language Processing*. John Benjamins Publishing Company. https://doi.org/10.1075/nlp.3.

Robert Moro and Maria Bielikova. 2012. Personalized Text Summarization Based on Important Terms Identification. In *2012 23rd International Workshop on Database and Expert Systems Applications*. IEEE, pages 131–135. https://doi.org/10.1109/DEXA.2012.47.

Gabriel Murray, Enamul Hoque, and Giuseppe Carenini. 2017. Chapter 11 - opinion summarization and visualization. In Federico Alberto Pozzi, Elisabetta Fersini, Enza Messina, and Bing Liu, editors, *Sentiment Analysis in Social Networks*, Morgan Kaufmann, pages 171 – 187. https://doi.org/10.1016/B978-0-12-804412-4.00011-5.

Ramesh Nallapati, Feifei Zhai, and Bowen Zhou. 2017. Summarunner: A recurrent neural network based sequence model for extractive summarization of documents. In *Proceedings of the Thirty-First AAAI Conference on Artificial Intelligence (AAAI-17)*. pages 3075–3081.

Ramesh Nallapati, Bowen Zhou, Cicero dos Santos, Caglar Gulcehre, and Bing Xiang. 2016. Abstractive Text Summarization using Sequence-to-sequence RNNs and Beyond. In *Proceedings of The 20th SIGNLL Conference on Computational Natural Language Learning*. Association for Computational Linguistics, pages 280–290. https://doi.org/10.18653/v1/K16-1028.

Ani Nenkova and Kathleen McKeown. 2011. Automatic Summarization. *Foundations and Trends® in Information Retrieval* 5(2):103–233. https://doi.org/10.1561/1500000015.

Romain Paulus, Caiming Xiong, and Richard Socher. 2017. A Deep Reinforced Model for Abstractive Summarization. *CoRR* abs/1705.04304. http://arxiv.org/abs/1705.04304.

Vijay B Raut and DD Londhe. 2014. Opinion mining and summarization of hotel reviews. In *Computational Intelligence and Communication Networks (CICN), 2014 International Conference on*. IEEE, pages 556–559.

Alexander M Rush, Sumit Chopra, and Jason Weston. 2015. A Neural Attention Model for Abstractive Sentence Summarization. In *Proceedings of the 2015 Conference on Empirical Methods in Natural Language Processing*. Association for Computational Linguistics, pages 379–389. https://doi.org/10.18653/v1/D15-1044.

Abigail See, Peter J. Liu, and Christopher D. Manning. 2017. Get To The Point: Summarization with Pointer-Generator Networks. In *Proceedings of the 55th Annual Meeting of the Association for Computational Linguistics (Volume 1: Long Papers)*. Association for Computational Linguistics, pages 1073–1083. https://doi.org/10.18653/v1/P17-1099.

Ryosuke Tadano, Kazutaka Shimada, and Tsutomu Endo. 2010. Multi-aspects review summarization based on identification of important opinions and their similarity. In *Proceedings of the 24th Pacific Asia Conference on Language, Information and Computation*. http://www.aclweb.org/anthology/Y10-1079.

Jiwei Tan, Xiaojun Wan, and Jianguo Xiao. 2017. Abstractive Document Summarization with a Graph-Based Attentional Neural Model. In *Proceedings of the 55th Annual Meeting of the Association for Computational Linguistics (Volume 1: Long Papers)*. Association for Computational Linguistics, pages 1171–1181. https://doi.org/10.18653/v1/P17-1108.

Nikos Tsirakis, Vasilis Poulopoulos, Panagiotis Tsantilas, and Iraklis Varlamis. 2016. Large scale opinion mining for social, news and blog data. *The Journal of Systems and Software* 127:237–248. https://doi.org/10.1016/j.jss.2016.06.012.

Dong Wang and Yang Liu. 2015. Opinion summarization on spontaneous conversations. *Computer Speech & Language* 34:61–82. https://doi.org/10.1016/j.csl.2015.04.004.

Lu Wang, Hema Raghavan, Claire Cardie, and Vittorio Castelli. 2014. Query-focused opinion summarization for user-generated content. In *Proceedings of COLING 2014, the 25th International Conference on Computational Linguistics: Technical Papers*. pages 1660–1669.

Michihiro Yasunaga, Rui Zhang, Kshitijh Meelu, Ayush Pareek, Krishnan Srinivasan, and Dragomir Radev. 2017. Graph-based Neural Multi-Document Summarization. In *Proceedings of the 21st Conference on Computational Natural Language Learning (CoNLL 2017)*. Association for Computational Linguistics, pages 452–462. https://doi.org/10.18653/v1/K17-1045.

Mahmood Yousefi-Azar and Len Hamey. 2017. Text summarization using unsupervised deep learning. *Expert Systems with Applications* 68:93–105. https://doi.org/10.1016/j.eswa.2016.10.017.

Xiaojun Yuan, Ning Sa, Grace Begany, and Huahai Yang. 2015. What users prefer and why: A user study on effective presentation styles of opinion summarization. In *Human-Computer Interaction – INTERACT 2015*. Springer International Publishing, pages 249–264.

Jiaming Zhan, Han Tong Loh, and Ying Liu. 2009. Gather customer concerns from online product reviews – A text summarization approach. *Expert Systems with Applications* 36(2, Part 1):2107–2115. https://doi.org/10.1016/j.eswa.2007.12.039.

Linhong Zhu, Sheng Gao, Sinno Jialin Pan, Haizhou Li, Dingxiong Deng, and Cyrus Shahabi. 2015. The Pareto Principle Is Everywhere: Finding Informative Sentences for Opinion Summarization Through Leader Detection. In *Lecture Notes in Social Networks*, pages 165–187. https://doi.org/10.1007/978-3-319-14379-8_9.

# Sampling Informative Training Data for RNN Language Models

**Jared Fernandez** and **Doug Downey**
Department of Electrical Engineering and Computer Science
Northwestern University
Evanston, IL 60208
`jared.fern@u.northwestern.edu, ddowney@eecs.northwestern.edu`

## Abstract

We propose an unsupervised importance sampling approach to selecting training data for recurrent neural network (RNN) language models. To increase the information content of the training set, our approach preferentially samples high perplexity sentences, as determined by an easily queryable $n$-gram language model. We experimentally evaluate the heldout perplexity of models trained with our various importance sampling distributions. We show that language models trained on data sampled using our proposed approach outperform models trained over randomly sampled subsets of both the Billion Word (Chelba et al., 2014) and Wikitext-103 benchmark corpora (Merity et al., 2016).

## 1 Introduction

The task of statistical language modeling seeks to learn a joint probability distribution over sequences of natural language words. In recent work, recurrent neural network (RNN) language models (Mikolov et al., 2010) have produced state-of-the-art perplexities in sentence-level language modeling, far below those of traditional $n$-gram models (Melis et al., 2017). Models trained on large, diverse benchmark corpora such as the Billion Word Corpus and Wikitext-103 have seen reported perplexities as low as 23.7 and 37.2, respectively (Kuchaiev and Ginsburg, 2017; Dauphin et al., 2017).

However, building models on large corpora is limited by prohibitive computational costs, as the number of training steps scales linearly with the number of tokens in the training corpus. Sentence-level language models for these large corpora can be learned by training on a set of sentences subsampled from the original corpus. We seek to determine whether it is possible to select a set of training sentences that is significantly more informative than a randomly drawn training set. We hypothesize that by training on higher information and more difficult training sentences, RNN language models can learn the language distribution more accurately and produce lower perplexities than models trained on similar-sized randomly sampled training sets.

We propose an unsupervised importance sampling technique for selecting training data for sentence-level RNN language models. We leverage $n$-gram language models' rapid training and query time, which often requires just a single pass over the training data. We determine a preliminary heuristic for each sentence's importance and information content by calculating its average per-word perplexity. Our technique uses an offline $n$-gram model to score sentences and then samples higher perplexity sentences with increased probability. Selected sentences are then used for training with corrective weights to remove the sampling bias. As entropy and perplexity have a monotonic relationship, selecting sentences with higher average $n$-gram perplexity also increases the average entropy and information content.

We experimentally evaluate the effectiveness of multiple importance sampling distributions at selecting training data for RNN language models. We compare the heldout perplexities of models trained with randomly sampled and importance sampled training data on both the One Billion Word and Wikitext-103 corpora. We show that our importance sampling techniques yield lower perplexities than models trained on similarly sized random samples. By using an $n$-gram model to determine the sampling distribution, we limit added computational costs of our importance sampling approach. We also find that applying perplexity-based importance sampling requires maintaining a relatively high weight on low perplexity sentences. We hypothesize that this is because low

9

*Proceedings of ACL 2018, Student Research Workshop*, pages 9–13
Melbourne, Australia, July 15 - 20, 2018. ©2018 Association for Computational Linguistics

perplexity sentences frequently contain common subsequences that are useful in modeling other sentences.

## 2 Related Work

Standard stochastic gradient descent (SGD) iteratively selects random examples from the training set to perform gradient updates. In contrast, weighted SGD has been proven to accelerate the convergence rates of SGD by leveraging importance sampling as a means of variance reduction (Needell et al., 2014; Zhao and Zhang, 2015). Weighted SGD selects examples from an importance sampling distribution and then trains on the selected examples with corrective weights. Weights of each training example $i$ are set to be $\frac{1}{Pr(i)}$, where $Pr(i)$ is the probability of selecting example $i$. The weighting provides an unbiased estimator of overall loss by removing the bias of the importance sampling distribution. In expectation, each example's contribution to the total loss function is the same as if the example had been drawn uniformly at random.

Alain et al. (2015) developed an importance sampling technique for training deep neural networks by sampling examples directly according to their gradient norm. To avoid the high computational costs of gradient computations, Katharopoulos and Fleuret (2018) sample according to losses as approximated by a lightweight RNN model trained along side their larger primary RNN model. Both techniques observed increased convergence rates and reduced errors in image classification tasks. In comparison, we use a fixed offline $n$-gram model to compute our sampling distribution, which can be trained and queried much more efficiently than a neural network model.

In natural language processing, subsampling of large corpora has been used to speed up training for both language modeling and machine translation. For domain specific language modeling, Moore and Lewis (2010) used an $n$-gram model trained on in-domain data to score sentences and then selected the sentences with low perplexities for training. Both Cho et al. (2014) and Koehn and Haddow (2012) used similar perplexity-based sampling to select training data for domain specific machine translation systems. Importance sampling has also been used to increase rate of convergence for a class of neural network lan-

guage models which use a set of binary classifiers to determine sequence likelihood, rather than calculating the probabilities jointly (Xu et al., 2011).

Because these subsampling techniques are used to learn domain specific distributions different from the distribution of the original corpus, they target lower perplexity sentences and have no need for corrective weighting. In contrast, we study how training sets generated using weighted importance sampling can be selected to maximize knowledge of the entire corpus for the standard language modeling task.

## 3 Methodology

First, we train an offline $n$-gram model over sentences randomly sampled from the training corpus. Using the $n$-gram model, we score perplexities for the remaining sentences in the training corpus.

We propose multiple importance sampling and likelihood weighting schemes for selecting training sequences for an RNN language model. Our proposed sampling distributions (discussed in detail below) bias the training set to select higher perplexity sentences in order to increase the training set's information content. We then train an RNN language model on the sampled sentences with weights set to the reciprocal of the sentence's selection probability.

### 3.1 Z-Score Sampling ($Z_{full}$)

This sampling distribution naively selects sentences according to their z-score, as calculated in terms of their $n$-gram perplexities. The selection probability of sequence $s$ is set as:

$$P_{Keep}(s) = k_{pr} \left( \frac{ppl(s) - \mu_{ppl}}{\sigma_{ppl}} + 1 \right),$$

where $ppl(s)$ is the $n$-gram perplexity of sentence $s$, $\mu_{ppl}$ is the average $n$-gram perplexity, $\sigma_{ppl}$ is the standard deviation of $n$-gram perplexities, and $k_{pr}$ is a normalizing constant to ensure a proper probability distribution.

For sentences with z-scores less than $-1.00$ or sequences where $ppl(s)$ was in the $99^{th}$ percentile of $n$-gram perplexities, sequences are assigned $P_{keep}(s) = k_{pr}$. This ensured all sequences had positive selection probability and limited bias towards the selection of high perplexity sequences in the tail of the distribution. Upon examination, sequences with perplexities in the $99^{th}$ percentile were generally esoteric or nonsensical. Selection of these high perplexity sentences provided minimal accuracy gain in exchange for their boosted selection probability.

## 3.2 Limited Z-Score Sampling ($Z_\alpha$)

Training on low perplexity sentences can be helpful in learning to model higher perplexity sentences which share common sub-sequences. However, naive z-score sampling results in the selection of few low perplexity sentences. Additionally, the low perplexity sentences that are selected tend to dominate the training weight space due to their low selection probability.

To smooth the distribution in the weight space, selection probability is only determined using z-scores for sentences where their perplexities are greater than the mean. Thus, the selection probability of sentence $s$ is:

$$P_{Keep}(s) =$$

$$\begin{cases} k_{pr} \left( \alpha \frac{ppl(s) - \mu_{ppl}}{\sigma_{ppl}} + 1 \right), & \text{if } ppl(s) > \mu_{ppl}. \\ k_{pr}, & \text{else.} \end{cases}$$

where $\alpha$ is a constant parameter that determines the weight of the z-score in calculating the sequence's selection probability.

## 3.3 Squared Z-Score Sampling ($Z^2$)

To investigate the effects of sampling from more complex distributions, we also evaluate an importance sampling scheme where sentences are sampled according to their squared z-score.

$$P_{Keep}(s) =$$

$$\begin{cases} k_{pr} \left( \alpha \left( \frac{ppl(s) - \mu_{ppl}}{\sigma_{ppl}} \right)^2 + 1 \right), & \text{if } ppl(s) > \mu_{ppl}. \\ k_{pr}, & \text{else.} \end{cases}$$

## 4 Experiments

We experimentally evaluate the effectiveness of the $Z_{full}$ and $Z^2$ sampling methods, as well as the $Z_\alpha$ method for various values of parameter $\alpha$.

### 4.1 Dataset Details

Sentence-level models were trained and evaluated on samples from Wikitext-103 and the One Billion Word Benchmark corpus. To create a dataset of independent sentences, the Wikitext-103 corpus was parsed to remove headers and to create individual sentences. The training and heldout sets were combined, shuffled, and then split to create new 250k token test and validation sets. The remaining sequences were set as a new training set of approximately 99 million tokens. In Billion Word experiments, training sequences were sampled from a 500 million subset of the released training split. Billion Word models were evaluated on 250k token test and validation sets randomly sampled from the released heldout split.

Models were trained on 500 thousand, 1 million, and 2 million token training sets sampled from each training split. Rare words were replaced with <unk> tokens, resulting in vocabularies of 267K and 250K for the Wikitext and Billion Word corpora, respectively.

### 4.2 Model Details

To calculate the sampling distribution, an $n$-gram model was trained on a heldout set with the same number tokens used to train each RNN model (Hochreiter and Schmidhuber, 1997). For example, the sampling distribution used to build a 1 million token RNN training set was determined using perplexities calculated by an $n$-gram model also trained on 1 million tokens. $N$-gram models were trained as 5-gram models with Kneser-Ney discounting (Kneser and Ney, 1995) using *SRILM* (Stolcke, 2002). For efficient calculation of sentence perplexities, we query our models using *KenLM* (Heafield, 2011).

RNN models were built using a two-layer long short-term memory (LSTM) neural network, with 200-dimensional hidden and embedding layers. Each training set was trained on for 10 epochs using the Adam gradient optimizer (Kingma and Ba, 2014) with a mini-batch size of 12.

## 5 Results

In Tables 1 and 2, we summarize the performances of models trained on samples from Wikitext-103 and the Billion Word Corpus, respectively. We report the Random and $n$-gram baseline perplexities for RNN and $n$-gram language models trained on randomly sampled data. We also report $\mu_{ngram}$ and $\sigma_{ngram}$ for each training set, which are the mean and standard deviation in sentence perplexity as evaluated by the offline $n$-gram model.

In all experiments, RNN language models trained using our sampling approaches yield a decrease in model perplexity as compared to RNN models trained on similar sized randomly sampled sets. As size of the training set increases, the RNNs trained on importance sampling datasets

| Model | Tokens | $\mu_{ngram}$ | $\sigma_{ngram}$ | ppl |
|---|---|---|---|---|
| $n$-gram | 500k | — | — | 492.3 |
| Random | 500k | 449.0 | 346.4 | 749.1 |
| $Z_{0.5}$ | 500k | 497.1 | 398.8 | 643.9 |
| $Z_{1.0}$ | 500k | 544.1 | 440.1 | 645.2 |
| $Z_{2.0}$ | 500k | 615.7 | 481.3 | 593.2 |
| $Z_{4.0}$ | 500k | 729.0 | 523.6 | **571.4** |
| $Z^2$ | 500k | 576.5 | 499.7 | 720.0 |
| $Z_{full}$ | 500k | 627.1 | 451.9 | 663.7 |
| $n$-gram | 1M | — | — | 502.7 |
| Random | 1M | 448.9 | 380.2 | 550.6 |
| $Z_{0.5}$ | 1M | 495.7 | 431.8 | 545.73 |
| $Z_{1.0}$ | 1M | 540.4 | 475.4 | 435.4 |
| $Z_{2.0}$ | 1M | 615.6 | 528.4 | 426.9 |
| $Z_{4.0}$ | 1M | 732.9 | 584.4 | 420.1 |
| $Z^2$ | 1M | 571.5 | 535.7 | 435.7 |
| $Z_{Full}$ | 1M | 608.6 | 489.9 | **416.3** |
| $n$-gram | 2M | — | — | 502.6 |
| Random | 2M | 430.45 | 392.1 | 341.3 |
| $Z_{0.5}$ | 2M | 471.8 | 445.2 | 292.7 |
| $Z_{1.0}$ | 2M | 514.6 | 493.9 | 289.8 |
| $Z_{2.0}$ | 2M | 582.8 | 544.6 | 346.9 |
| $Z_{4.0}$ | 2M | 684.6 | 604.7 | 294.6 |
| $Z^2$ | 2M | 518.4 | 522.9 | **287.9** |
| $Z_{Full}$ | 2M | 568.4 | 506.5 | 312.5 |

Table 1: Perplexities for Wikitext models. All proposed models outperform the random and $n$-gram baselines as number of training tokens increases.

| Model | Tokens | $\mu_{ngram}$ | $\sigma_{ngram}$ | ppl |
|---|---|---|---|---|
| $n$-gram | 1M | — | — | 432.5 |
| Random | 1M | 433.2 | 515.4 | 484.0 |
| $Z_{0.5}$ | 1M | 476.8 | 410.9 | 436.6 |
| $Z_{1.0}$ | 1M | 543.8 | 529.0 | **421.5** |
| $Z_{4.0}$ | 1M | 726.4 | 517.3 | 427.3 |
| $Z_{full}$ | 1M | 635.19 | 458.69 | 495.75 |
| $Z^2$ | 1M | 639.2 | 593.7 | 435.3 |

Table 2: Perplexities for Billion Word models. $Z_\alpha$ and $Z^2$ both outperform the random baseline and are comparable to the $n$-gram baseline.

also yield significantly lower perplexities than the $n$-gram models trained on randomly sampled training sets. As expected, $\mu_{ngram}$ and $\sigma_{ngram}$ increase substantially for training sets generated using our proposed sampling methods.

Overall, the $Z_{4.0}$ sampling method produced the most consistent reductions in average perplexity of 102.9 and 54.2 compared to the Random and $n$-gram baselines, respectively. $Z_{Full}$ and $Z^2$ exhibit higher variance in their heldout perplexity as compared to the $Z_\alpha$ and baseline methods. We expect that this is because these methods select higher perplexity sequences with significantly higher probability than $Z_\alpha$ methods. As a result, low perplexity sentences, which may contain common subsequences helpful in modeling other sentences, are ignored in training.

## 6   Conclusions and Future Work

We introduce a weighted importance sampling scheme for selecting RNN language model training data from large corpora. We demonstrate that models trained with data generated using this approach yield perplexity reductions of up to 24% when compared to models trained over randomly sampled training sets of similar size. This technique leverages higher perplexity training sentences to learn more accurate language models, while limiting added computational cost of importance calculations.

In future work, we will examine the performance of our proposed selection techniques in additional parameter settings, with various values of $\alpha$ and thresholds in the limited z-score methods $Z_\alpha$. We will evaluate the performance of sampling distributions based on perplexities calculated using small, lightweight RNN language models rather than $n$-gram language models. Additionally, we will also be evaluating the performance of sampling distributions calculated based on a sentence's subsequences and unique $n$-gram content. Furthermore, we plan on adapting this importance sampling approach to use online $n$-gram models trained alongside the RNN language models for determining the importance sampling distribution.

## Acknowledgements

This work was supported in part by NSF Grant IIS-1351029. Support for travel provided in part by the ACL Student Travel Grant (NSF Grant IIS-1827830) and the Conference Travel Grant from Northwestern University's Office of the Provost. We thank Dave Demeter, Thanapon Noraset, Yiben Yang, and Zheng Yuan for helpful comments.

## References

Guillaume Alain, Alex Lamb, Chinnadhurai Sankar, Aaron Courville, and Yoshua Bengio. 2015. Variance reduction in sgd by distributed importance sampling. *arXiv preprint arXiv:1511.06481*.

Ciprian Chelba, Tomas Mikolov, Mike Schuster, Qi Ge, Thorsten Brants, Phillipp Koehn, and Tony Robinson. 2014. One billion word benchmark for measuring progress in statistical language modeling. In *Fifteenth Annual Conference of the International Speech Communication Association*.

Kyunghyun Cho, Bart van Merrienboer, Caglar Gulcehre, Dzmitry Bahdanau, Fethi Bougares, Holger Schwenk, and Yoshua Bengio. 2014. Learning phrase representations using rnn encoder–decoder for statistical machine translation. In *Proceedings of the 2014 Conference on Empirical Methods in Natural Language Processing (EMNLP)*, pages 1724–1734.

Yann N Dauphin, Angela Fan, Michael Auli, and David Grangier. 2017. Language modeling with gated convolutional networks. In *International Conference on Machine Learning*, pages 933–941.

Kenneth Heafield. 2011. Kenlm: Faster and smaller language model queries. In *Proceedings of the Sixth Workshop on Statistical Machine Translation*, pages 187–197. Association for Computational Linguistics.

Sepp Hochreiter and Jürgen Schmidhuber. 1997. Long short-term memory. *Neural computation*, 9(8):1735–1780.

Angelos Katharopoulos and François Fleuret. 2018. Not all samples are created equal: Deep learning with importance sampling. *arXiv preprint arXiv:1803.00942*.

Diederik P Kingma and Jimmy Ba. 2014. Adam: A method for stochastic optimization. *arXiv preprint arXiv:1412.6980*.

Reinhard Kneser and Hermann Ney. 1995. Improved backing-off for m-gram language modeling. In *Acoustics, Speech, and Signal Processing, 1995. ICASSP-95., 1995 International Conference on*, volume 1, pages 181–184. IEEE.

Philipp Koehn and Barry Haddow. 2012. Towards effective use of training data in statistical machine translation. In *Proceedings of the Seventh Workshop on Statistical Machine Translation*, pages 317–321. Association for Computational Linguistics.

Oleksii Kuchaiev and Boris Ginsburg. 2017. Factorization tricks for lstm networks. *arXiv preprint arXiv:1703.10722*.

Gábor Melis, Chris Dyer, and Phil Blunsom. 2017. On the state of the art of evaluation in neural language models. *arXiv preprint arXiv:1707.05589*.

Stephen Merity, Caiming Xiong, James Bradbury, and Richard Socher. 2016. Pointer sentinel mixture models. *arXiv preprint arXiv:1609.07843*.

Tomáš Mikolov, Martin Karafiát, Lukáš Burget, Jan Černocký, and Sanjeev Khudanpur. 2010. Recurrent neural network based language model. In *Eleventh Annual Conference of the International Speech Communication Association*.

Robert C Moore and William Lewis. 2010. Intelligent selection of language model training data. In *Proceedings of the ACL 2010 conference short papers*, pages 220–224. Association for Computational Linguistics.

Deanna Needell, Rachel Ward, and Nati Srebro. 2014. Stochastic gradient descent, weighted sampling, and the randomized kaczmarz algorithm. In *Advances in Neural Information Processing Systems*, pages 1017–1025.

Andreas Stolcke. 2002. Srilm-an extensible language modeling toolkit. In *Seventh International Conference on Spoken Language Processing*.

Puyang Xu, Asela Gunawardana, and Sanjeev Khudanpur. 2011. Efficient subsampling for training complex language models. In *Proceedings of the Conference on Empirical Methods in Natural Language Processing*, pages 1128–1136. Association for Computational Linguistics.

Peilin Zhao and Tong Zhang. 2015. Stochastic optimization with importance sampling for regularized loss minimization. In *International Conference on Machine Learning*, pages 1–9.

# Learning-based Composite Metrics for Improved Caption Evaluation

Naeha Sharif, Lyndon White, Mohammed Bennamoun  and  Syed Afaq Ali Shah,

{naeha.sharif, lyndon.white}@research.uwa.edu.au,
and  {mohammed.bennamoun, afaq.shah}@uwa.edu.au

The University of Western Australia.
35 Stirling Highway, Crawley, Western Australia

## Abstract

The evaluation of image caption quality is a challenging task, which requires the assessment of two main aspects in a caption: adequacy and fluency. These quality aspects can be judged using a combination of several linguistic features. However, most of the current image captioning metrics focus only on specific linguistic facets, such as the lexical or semantic, and fail to meet a satisfactory level of correlation with human judgements at the sentence-level. We propose a learning-based framework to incorporate the scores of a set of lexical and semantic metrics as features, to capture the adequacy and fluency of captions at different linguistic levels. Our experimental results demonstrate that composite metrics draw upon the strengths of stand-alone measures to yield improved correlation and accuracy.

## 1 Introduction

Automatic image captioning requires the understanding of the visual aspects of images to generate human-like descriptions (Bernardi et al., 2016). The evaluation of the generated captions is crucial for the development and fine-grained analysis of image captioning systems (Vedantam et al., 2015). Automatic evaluation metrics aim at providing efficient, cost-effective and objective assessments of the caption quality. Since these automatic measures serve as an alternative to the manual evaluation, the major concern is that such measures should correlate well with human assessments. In other words, automatic metrics are expected to mimic the human judgement process by taking into account various aspects that humans consider when they assess the captions.

The evaluation of image captions can be characterized as having two major aspects: adequacy and

fluency. Adequacy is how well the caption reflects the source image, and fluency is how well the caption conforms to the norms and conventions of human language (Toury, 2012). In the case of manual evaluation, both adequacy and fluency tend to shape the human perception of the overall caption quality. Most of the automatic evaluation metrics tend to capture these aspects of quality based on the idea that "the closer the candidate description to the professional human caption, the better it is in quality" (Papineni et al., 2002). The output in such case is a score (the higher the better) reflecting the similarity.

The majority of the commonly used metrics for image captioning such as BLEU (Papineni et al., 2002) and METEOR (Banerjee and Lavie, 2005) are based on the lexical similarity. Lexical measures (n-gram based) work by rewarding the n-gram overlaps between the candidate and the reference captions. Thus, measuring the adequacy by counting the n-gram matches and assessing the fluency by implicitly using the reference n-grams as a language model (Mutton et al., 2007). However, a high number of n-gram matches cannot always be indicative of a high caption quality, nor a low number of n-gram matches can always be reflective of a low caption quality (Giménez and Màrquez, 2010). A recently proposed semantic metric SPICE (Anderson et al., 2016), overcomes this deficiency of lexical measures by measuring the semantic similarity of candidate and reference captions using *Scene Graphs*. However, the major drawback of SPICE is that it ignores the fluency of the output caption.

Integrating assessment scores of different measures is an intuitive and reasonable way to improve the current image captioning evaluation methods. Through this methodology, each metric plays the role of a judge, assessing the quality of captions in terms of lexical, grammatical or semantic accuracy. For this research, we use the scores conferred



*Proceedings of ACL 2018, Student Research Workshop*, pages 14–20
Melbourne, Australia, July 15 - 20, 2018. ©2018 Association for Computational Linguistics

by a set of measures that are commonly used for captioning and combine them through a learning-based framework. In this work:

**1.** We evaluate various combinations of a chosen set of metrics and show that the proposed composite metrics correlate better with human judgements.

**2.** We analyse the accuracy of composite metrics in terms of differentiating between pairs of captions in reference to the ground truth captions.

## 2 Literature Review

The success of any captioning system depends on how well it transforms the visual information to natural language. Therefore, the significance of reliable automatic evaluation metrics is undeniable for the fine-grained analysis and advancement of image captioning systems. While image captioning has drawn inspiration from the Machine Translation (MT) domain for encoder-decoder based captioning networks (Vinyals et al., 2015), (Xu et al., 2015), (Yao et al., 2016), (You et al., 2016), (Lu et al., 2017), it has also benefited from automatic metrics which were initially proposed to evaluate machine translations/text summaries, such as BLEU (Papineni et al., 2002), ME-TEOR (Denkowski and Lavie, 2014) and ROUGE (Lin, 2004).

In the past few years, two metrics CIDEr (Vedantam et al., 2015) and SPICE (Anderson et al., 2016) were developed specifically for image captioning. Compared to the previously used metrics, these two show a better correlation with human judgements. The authors in (Liu et al., 2016) proposed a linear combination of SPICE and CIDEr called *SPIDEr* and showed that optimizing image captioning models for SPIDEr's score can lead to better quality captions. However, SPIDEr was not evaluated for its correlation with human judgements. Recently, (Kusner et al., 2015) proposed the use of a document similarity metric *Word Mover's Distance* (WMD), which uses the word2vec (Mikolov et al., 2013) embedding space to determine the distance between two texts.

The metrics used for caption evaluation can be broadly categorized as lexical and semantic measures. Lexical metrics reward the n-gram matches between candidate captions and human generated reference texts (Giménez and Màrquez, 2010), and can be further categorized as unigram and n-gram based measures. Unigram based methods such as BLEU-1 (Papineni et al., 2002), assess only the lexical correctness of the candidate. However, in the case of METEOR or WMD, where some sort of synonym-matching/stemming is also involved, unigram-overlaps help to evaluate both the lexical and to some degree the semantic aptness of the output caption. N-gram based metrics such as ROUGE and CIDEr primarily assess the lexical correctness of the caption, but also measure some amount of syntactic accuracy by capturing the word order.

The lexical measures have received criticism based on the argument that the n-gram overlap is neither an adequate nor a necessary indicative measure of the caption quality (Anderson et al., 2016). To overcome this limitation, semantic metrics such as SPICE, capture the sentence meaning to evaluate the candidate captions. Their performance however is highly dependent on a successful semantic parsing. Purely syntactic measures, which capture the grammatical correctness, exist, and have been used in MT (Mutton et al., 2007), but not in the captioning domain.

While fluency (well-formedness) of a candidate caption can be attributed to the syntactic and lexical correctness (Fomicheva et al., 2016), adequacy (informativeness) depends on the lexical and semantic correctness (Rios et al., 2011). We hypothesize that by combining scores from different metrics, which have different strengths in measuring adequacy and fluency, a composite metric that is of overall higher quality is created (Sec. 5).

Machine learning offers a systematic approach to integrate the scores of stand-alone metrics. In the MT evaluation, various successful learning paradigms have been proposed (Bojar et al., 2016), (Bojar et al., 2017) and the existing learning-based metrics can be categorized as *binary functions*–"which classify the candidate translation as good or bad" (Kulesza and Shieber, 2004), (Guzmán et al., 2015) or *continuous functions*–"which score the quality of translation on an absolute scale" (Song and Cohn, 2011), (Albrecht and Hwa, 2008). Our research is conceptually similar to the work in (Kulesza and Shieber, 2004), which induces a *"human-likeness"* criteria. However, our approach differs in terms of the learning algorithm as well as the features used. Moreover, the focus of this work is to assess various combinations of metrics (that capture the caption quality at

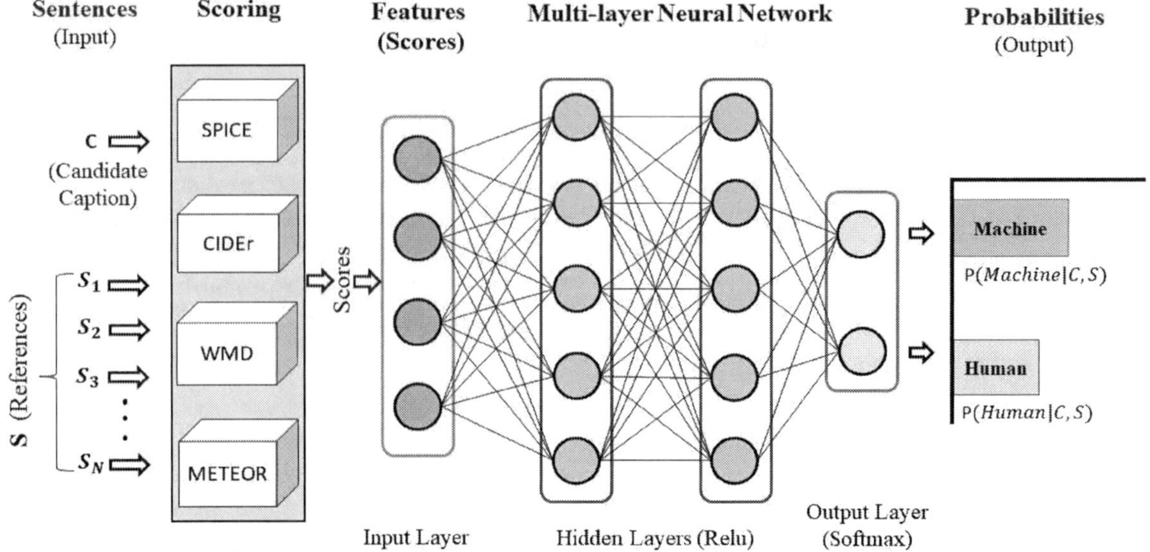


Figure 1: Overall framework of the proposed Composite Metrics

## 3 Proposed Approach

In our approach, we use scores conferred by a set of existing metrics as an input to a multi-layer feed-forward neural network. We adopt a training criteria based on a simple question: *is the caption machine or human generated?* Our trained classifier sets a boundary between good and bad quality captions, thus classifying them as human or machine produced. Furthermore, we obtain a continuous output score by using the class-probability, which can be considered as some "measure of believability" that the candidate caption is human generated. Framing our learning problem as a classification task allows us to create binary training data using the human generated captions and machine generated captions as positive and negative training examples respectively.

Our proposed framework shown in Figure 1 first extracts a set of numeric features using the candidate "C" and the reference sentences "S". The extracted feature vector is then fed as an input to our multi-layer neural network. Each entity of the feature vector corresponds to the score generated by one of the four measures: METEOR, CIDEr, WMD[1] and SPICE respectively. We chose these measures because they show a relatively better correlation with human judgements compared to the other commonly used ones for captioning (Kilickaya et al., 2016). Our composite metrics are named $Eval_{MS}$, $Eval_{CS}$, $Eval_{MCS}$, $Eval_{WCS}$, $Eval_{MWS}$ and $Eval_{MWCS}$. The subscript letters in each name corresponds to the first letter of each individual metric. For example, $Eval_{MS}$ corresponds to the combination of METEOR and SPICE. Figure 2 shows the linguistic aspects captured by the stand-alone[2] and the composite metrics. SPICE is based on sentence meanings, thus it evaluates the semantics. CIDEr covers the syntactic and lexical aspects, whereas Meteor and WMD assess the lexical and semantic components. The learning-based metrics mostly fall in the region formed by the overlap of all three major linguistics facets, leading to better a evaluation.

We train our metrics to maximise the classification accuracy on the training dataset. Since we are primarily interested in maximizing the correlation with human judgements, we perform early stopping based on Kendalls $\tau$ (rank correlation) with the validation set.

## 4 Experimental Setup

To train our composite metrics, we source data from Flicker30k dataset (Plummer et al., 2015) and three image captioning models namely: (1) show and tell (Vinyals et al., 2015), (2) show, attend and tell (soft-attention) (Xu et al., 2015), and (3) adaptive attention (Lu et al., 2017). Flicker30k

---

[1]We convert the WMD distance score to similarity by using a negative exponential, to use it as a feature.

[2]The stand-alone metrics marked with an * in the Figure 2 are used as features for this work.

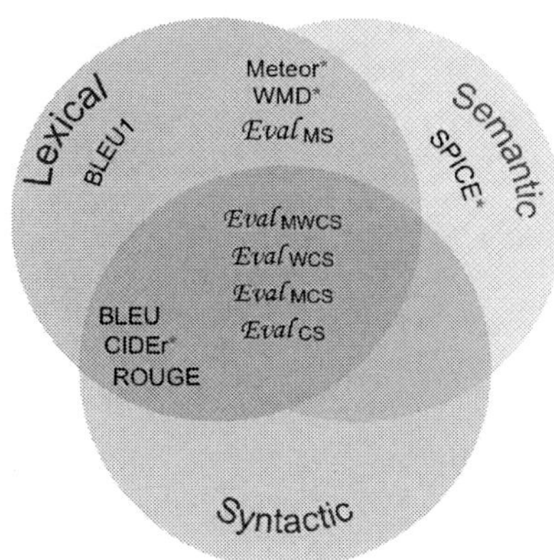



Figure 2: Various automatic measures (stand-alone and combined) and their respective linguistic levels. See Sec. 3 for more details.

dataset consists of 31,783 photos acquired from Flicker[3], each paired with 5 captions obtained through the Amazon Mechanical Turk (AMT) (Turk, 2012). For each image in Flicker30k, we randomly select three of the human generated captions as positive training examples, and three machine generated (one from each image captioning model) captions as negative training examples. We combined the Microsoft COCO (Chen et al., 2015) training and validation set (containing 123,287 images in total, each paired with 5 or more captions), to train the image captioning models using their official codes. These image captioning models achieved state-of-the-art performance when they were published.

In order to obtain reference captions for each training example, we again use the human written descriptions of Flicker30k. For each negative training example (machine-generated caption), we randomly choose 4 out of 5 human written captions originally associated with each image. Whereas, for each positive training example (human-generated caption), we use the 5 human written captions associated with each image, selecting one of these as a human candidate caption (positive example) and the remaining 4 as references. In Figure 3, a possible pairing scenario is shown for further clarification.

For our validation set, we source data from Flicker8k (Young et al., 2014). This dataset contains 5,822 captions assessed by three expert judges on a scale of 1 (the caption is unrelated to the image) to 4 (the caption describes the im-

[3]https://www.flickr.com/

Table 1: Kendall's correlation co-efficient of automatic evaluation metrics and proposed composite metrics against human quality judgements. All correlations are significant at p<0.001

| Individual Metrics | Kendall $\tau$ | Composite Metrics | Kendall $\tau$ |
|---|---|---|---|
| BLEU | 0.202 | $Eval_{MS}$ | **0.386** |
| ROUGE-L | 0.216 | $Eval_{CS}$ | 0.384 |
| METEOR | 0.352 | $Eval_{MCS}$ | **0.386** |
| CIDEr | 0.356 | $Eval_{WCS}$ | 0.379 |
| SPICE | 0.366 | $Eval_{MWS}$ | 0.367 |
| WMD | 0.336 | $Eval_{MWCS}$ | 0.378 |

age without any errors). From our training set, we remove the captions of images which overlap with the captions in the validation and test sets (discussed in Sec. 5), leaving us with a total of 132,984 non-overlapping captions for the training of the composite metrics.

## 5 Results and Discussion

### 5.1 Correlation

The most desirable characteristic of an automatic evaluation metric is its strong correlation with human scores (Zhang and Vogel, 2010). A stronger correlation with human judgements indicates that a metric captures the information that humans use to assess a candidate caption. To evaluate the sentence-level correlation of our composite metrics with human judgements, we source data from a dataset collected by the authors in (Aditya et al., 2017). We use 6993 manually evaluated human and machine generated captions from this set, which were scored by AMT workers for correctness on the scale of 1 (low relevance to image) to 5 (high relevance to image). Each caption in the dataset is accompanied by a single judgement. In Table 1, we report the Kendalls $\tau$ correlation coefficient for the proposed composite metrics and other commonly used caption evaluation metrics.

It can be observed from Table 1 that composite metrics outperform stand-alone metrics in terms of sentence-level correlation. The combination of Meteor and SPICE ($Eval_{MS}$) and METEOR, CIDEr and SPICE ($Eval_{MCS}$) showed the most promising results. The success of these composite metrics can be attributed to the individual strengths of Meteor, CIDEr and SPICE. METEOR is a strong lexical measure based on unigram matching, which uses additional linguistic knowledge for word matching, such as the morphological variation in words via stemming and

Figure 3: Shows an example of a candidate and reference pairing that is used in the training set. (a) Image, (b) human and machine generated captions for the image, and (c) candidate and reference pairings for the image.

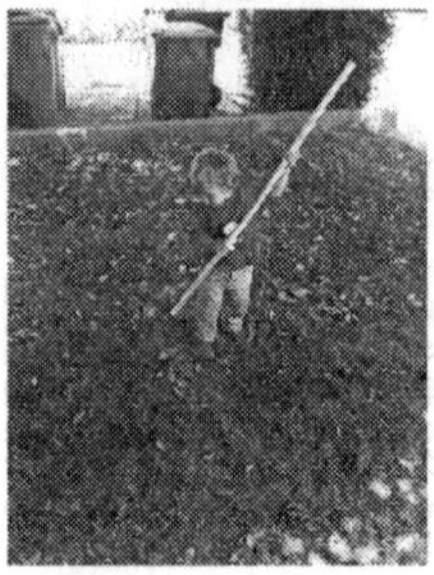

dictionary based look-up for synonyms and para-phrases (Banerjee and Lavie, 2005). CIDEr uses higher order n-grams to account for fluency and down-weighs the commonly occurring (less informative) n-grams by performing Term Frequency Inverse Document Frequency (TF-IDF) weighting for each n-gram in the dataset (Vedantam et al., 2015). SPICE on the other hand is a strong indicator of the semantic correctness of a caption. Together these metrics assess the lexical, semantic and syntactic information. The composite metrics which included WMD in the combination achieved a lower performance, compared to the ones in which WMD was not included. One possible reason is that WMD heavily penalizes shorter candidate captions when the number of words between the output and the reference captions are not equal (Kusner et al., 2015). This penalty might not be consistently useful as it is possible for a shorter candidate caption to be both fluent and adequate. Therefore, WMD is a better suited metric for measuring document distance.

## 5.2 Accuracy

We follow the framework introduced in (Vedantam et al., 2015) to analyse the ability of a metric to discriminate between pairs of captions with reference to the ground truth caption. A metric is considered accurate if it assigns a higher score to the caption preferred by humans. For this experiment, we use PASCAL-50s (Vedantam et al., 2015), which contains human judgements for 4000 triplets of descriptions (one reference caption with two candidate captions). Based on the pairing, the triplets are grouped into four categories (comprising of 1000 triplets each) i.e.,

Table 2: Comparative accuracy results (in percentage) on four kinds of pairs tested on PASCAL-50s

| Metrics | HC | HI | HM | MM | AVG |
|---|---|---|---|---|---|
| BLEU | 53.7 | 93.2 | 85.6 | 61.0 | 73.4 |
| ROUGE-L | 56.5 | 95.3 | 93.4 | 58.5 | 75.9 |
| METEOR | 61.1 | 97.6 | **94.6** | 62.0 | 78.8 |
| CIDEr | 57.8 | 98.0 | 88.8 | 68.2 | 78.2 |
| SPICE | 58.0 | 96.7 | 88.4 | 71.6 | 78.7 |
| WMD | 56.2 | 98.4 | 91.7 | 71.5 | 79.5 |
| $Eval_{MS}$ | **62.8** | 97.9 | 93.5 | 69.6 | **80.9** |
| $Eval_{CS}$ | 59.5 | 98.3 | 90.7 | 71.3 | 79.9 |
| $Eval_{MCS}$ | 60.2 | 98.3 | 91.8 | **71.8** | 80.5 |
| $Eval_{WCS}$ | 58.2 | **98.7** | 91.7 | 70.6 | 79.8 |
| $Eval_{MWS}$ | 56.9 | 98.4 | 91.3 | 71.2 | 79.4 |
| $Eval_{MWCS}$ | 59.0 | 98.5 | 90.7 | 70.2 | 79.6 |

Human-Human Correct (HC), Human-Human Incorrect (HI), Human-Machine (HM), Machine-Machine (MM). We follow the original approach of (Vedantam et al., 2015) and use 5 reference captions per candidate to assess the accuracy of the metrics and report them in Table 2. Table 2 shows that on average composite measures produce better accuracy compared to the individual metrics. Amongst the four categories, HC is the hardest, in which all metrics show the worst performance. Differentiating between two good quality (human generated) correct captions is challenging as it involves a fine-grained analysis of the two candidates. $Eval_{MS}$ achieves the highest accuracy in HC category which shows that as captioning systems continue to improve, this combination of lexical and semantic metrics will continue to perform well. Moreover, human generated captions are usually fluent. Therefore, a combination of strong indicators of adequacy such as SPICE and METEOR is the most suitable for this task. $Eval_{MCS}$ shows the highest accuracy in differentiating between machine captions, which is another important category as one of the main goals of automatic evaluation is to distinguish between two machine algorithms. Amongst the composite metrics, $Eval_{MS}$ is again the best in distinguishing human captions (good quality) from machine captions (bad quality) which was our basic training criteria.

## 6 Conclusion and Future Works

In this paper we propose a learning-based approach to combine various metrics to improve caption evaluation. Our experimental results show that metrics operating along different linguistic dimensions can be successfully combined through a learning-based framework, and they outperform the existing metrics for caption evaluation in term of correlation and accuracy, with $Eval_{MS}$ and $Eval_{MCS}$ giving the best overall performance.

Our study reveals that the proposed approach is promising and has a lot of potential to be used for evaluation in the captioning domain. In the future, we plan to integrate features (components) of metrics instead of their scores for a better performance. We also intend to use syntactic measures, which to the best of our knowledge have not yet been used for caption evaluation (except in an indirect way by the n-gram measures which capture the word order) and study how they can improve the correlation at the sentence level. Majority of the metrics for captioning focus more on adequacy as compared to fluency. This aspect also needs further attention and a combination of metrics/features that can specifically assess the fluency of captions needs to be devised.

### Acknowledgements

The authors are grateful to Nvidia for providing Titan-Xp GPU, which was used for the experiments. This research is supported by Australian Research Council, ARC DP150100294.

## References

Somak Aditya, Yezhou Yang, Chitta Baral, Yiannis Aloimonos, and Cornelia Fermüller. 2017. Image understanding using vision and reasoning through scene description graph. *Computer Vision and Image Understanding*.

Joshua S Albrecht and Rebecca Hwa. 2008. Regression for machine translation evaluation at the sentence level. *Machine Translation*, 22(1-2):1.

Peter Anderson, Basura Fernando, Mark Johnson, and Stephen Gould. 2016. Spice: Semantic propositional image caption evaluation. In *European Conference on Computer Vision*, pages 382–398. Springer.

Satanjeev Banerjee and Alon Lavie. 2005. Meteor: An automatic metric for mt evaluation with improved correlation with human judgments. In *Proceedings of the acl workshop on intrinsic and extrinsic evaluation measures for machine translation and/or summarization*, pages 65–72.

Raffaella Bernardi, Ruket Cakici, Desmond Elliott, Aykut Erdem, Erkut Erdem, Nazli Ikizler-Cinbis, Frank Keller, Adrian Muscat, Barbara Plank, et al. 2016. Automatic description generation from images: A survey of models, datasets, and evaluation measures. *J. Artif. Intell. Res.(JAIR)*, 55:409–442.

Ondřej Bojar, Yvette Graham, Amir Kamran, and Miloš Stanojević. 2016. Results of the wmt16 metrics shared task. In *Proceedings of the First Conference on Machine Translation: Volume 2, Shared Task Papers*, volume 2, pages 199–231.

Ondřej Bojar, Jindřich Helcl, Tom Kocmi, Jindřich Libovický, and Tomáš Musil. 2017. Results of the wmt17 neural mt training task. In *Proceedings of the Second Conference on Machine Translation*, pages 525–533.

Xinlei Chen, Hao Fang, Tsung-Yi Lin, Ramakrishna Vedantam, Saurabh Gupta, Piotr Dollár, and C Lawrence Zitnick. 2015. Microsoft coco captions: Data collection and evaluation server. *arXiv preprint arXiv:1504.00325*.

Michael Denkowski and Alon Lavie. 2014. Meteor universal: Language specific translation evaluation for any target language. In *Proceedings of the ninth workshop on statistical machine translation*, pages 376–380.

Marina Fomicheva, Núria Bel, Lucia Specia, Iria da Cunha, and Anton Malinovskiy. 2016. Cobaltf: a fluent metric for mt evaluation. In *Proceedings of the First Conference on Machine Translation: Volume 2, Shared Task Papers*, volume 2, pages 483–490.

Jesús Giménez and Lluís Màrquez. 2010. Linguistic measures for automatic machine translation evaluation. *Machine Translation*, 24(3-4):209–240.

Francisco Guzmán, Shafiq Joty, Lluís Màrquez, and Preslav Nakov. 2015. Pairwise neural machine translation evaluation. In *Proceedings of the 53rd Annual Meeting of the Association for Computational Linguistics and the 7th International Joint Conference on Natural Language Processing (Volume 1: Long Papers)*, volume 1, pages 805–814.

Mert Kilickaya, Aykut Erdem, Nazli Ikizler-Cinbis, and Erkut Erdem. 2016. Re-evaluating automatic metrics for image captioning. *arXiv preprint arXiv:1612.07600*.

Alex Kulesza and Stuart M Shieber. 2004. A learning approach to improving sentence-level mt evaluation. In *Proceedings of the 10th International Conference on Theoretical and Methodological Issues in Machine Translation*, pages 75–84.

Matt Kusner, Yu Sun, Nicholas Kolkin, and Kilian Weinberger. 2015. From word embeddings to document distances. In *International Conference on Machine Learning*, pages 957–966.

Chin-Yew Lin. 2004. Rouge: A package for automatic evaluation of summaries. *Text Summarization Branches Out*.

Siqi Liu, Zhenhai Zhu, Ning Ye, Sergio Guadarrama, and Kevin Murphy. 2016. Improved image captioning via policy gradient optimization of spider. *arXiv preprint arXiv:1612.00370*.

Jiasen Lu, Caiming Xiong, Devi Parikh, and Richard Socher. 2017. Knowing when to look: Adaptive attention via a visual sentinel for image captioning. In *Proceedings of the IEEE Conference on Computer Vision and Pattern Recognition (CVPR)*, volume 6.

Tomas Mikolov, Ilya Sutskever, Kai Chen, Greg S Corrado, and Jeff Dean. 2013. Distributed representations of words and phrases and their compositionality. In *Advances in neural information processing systems*, pages 3111–3119.

Andrew Mutton, Mark Dras, Stephen Wan, and Robert Dale. 2007. Gleu: Automatic evaluation of sentence-level fluency. In *Proceedings of the 45th Annual Meeting of the Association of Computational Linguistics*, pages 344–351.

Kishore Papineni, Salim Roukos, Todd Ward, and Wei-Jing Zhu. 2002. Bleu: a method for automatic evaluation of machine translation. In *Proceedings of the 40th annual meeting on association for computational linguistics*, pages 311–318. Association for Computational Linguistics.

Bryan A Plummer, Liwei Wang, Chris M Cervantes, Juan C Caicedo, Julia Hockenmaier, and Svetlana Lazebnik. 2015. Flickr30k entities: Collecting region-to-phrase correspondences for richer image-to-sentence models. In *Computer Vision (ICCV), 2015 IEEE International Conference on*, pages 2641–2649. IEEE.

Miguel Rios, Wilker Aziz, and Lucia Specia. 2011. Tine: A metric to assess mt adequacy. In *Proceedings of the Sixth Workshop on Statistical Machine Translation*, pages 116–122. Association for Computational Linguistics.

Xingyi Song and Trevor Cohn. 2011. Regression and ranking based optimisation for sentence level machine translation evaluation. In *Proceedings of the Sixth Workshop on Statistical Machine Translation*, pages 123–129. Association for Computational Linguistics.

Gideon Toury. 2012. *Descriptive Translation Studies and beyond: revised edition*, volume 100. John Benjamins Publishing.

Amazon Mechanical Turk. 2012. Amazon mechanical turk. *Retrieved August*, 17:2012.

Ramakrishna Vedantam, C Lawrence Zitnick, and Devi Parikh. 2015. Cider: Consensus-based image description evaluation. In *Proceedings of the IEEE conference on computer vision and pattern recognition*, pages 4566–4575.

Oriol Vinyals, Alexander Toshev, Samy Bengio, and Dumitru Erhan. 2015. Show and tell: A neural image caption generator. In *Computer Vision and Pattern Recognition (CVPR), 2015 IEEE Conference on*, pages 3156–3164. IEEE.

Kelvin Xu, Jimmy Ba, Ryan Kiros, Kyunghyun Cho, Aaron Courville, Ruslan Salakhudinov, Rich Zemel, and Yoshua Bengio. 2015. Show, attend and tell: Neural image caption generation with visual attention. In *International Conference on Machine Learning*, pages 2048–2057.

Ting Yao, Yingwei Pan, Yehao Li, Zhaofan Qiu, and Tao Mei. 2016. Boosting image captioning with attributes. *OpenReview*, 2(5):8.

Quanzeng You, Hailin Jin, Zhaowen Wang, Chen Fang, and Jiebo Luo. 2016. Image captioning with semantic attention. In *Proceedings of the IEEE Conference on Computer Vision and Pattern Recognition*, pages 4651–4659.

Peter Young, Alice Lai, Micah Hodosh, and Julia Hockenmaier. 2014. From image descriptions to visual denotations: New similarity metrics for semantic inference over event descriptions. *Transactions of the Association for Computational Linguistics*, 2:67–78.

Ying Zhang and Stephan Vogel. 2010. Significance tests of automatic machine translation evaluation metrics. *Machine Translation*, 24(1):51–65.

# Recursive Neural Network Based Preordering for English-to-Japanese Machine Translation


**Yuki Kawara**[†]  **Chenhui Chu**[‡]  **Yuki Arase**[†]

[†]Graduate School of Information Science and Technology, Osaka University
[‡]Institute for Datability Science, Osaka University
{kawara.yuki,arase}@ist.osaka-u.ac.jp,chu@ids.osaka-u.ac.jp



## Abstract

The word order between source and target languages significantly influences the translation quality in machine translation. Preordering can effectively address this problem. Previous preordering methods require a manual feature design, making language dependent design costly. In this paper, we propose a preordering method with a recursive neural network that learns features from raw inputs. Experiments show that the proposed method achieves comparable gain in translation quality to the state-of-the-art method but without a manual feature design.


## 1 Introduction

The word order between source and target languages significantly influences the translation quality in statistical machine translation (SMT) (Tillmann, 2004; Hayashi et al., 2013; Nakagawa, 2015). Models that adjust orders of translated phrases in decoding have been proposed to solve this problem (Tillmann, 2004; Koehn et al., 2005; Nagata et al., 2006). However, such reordering models do not perform well for long-distance reordering. In addition, their computational costs are expensive. To address these problems, preordering (Xia and McCord, 2004; Wang et al., 2007; Xu et al., 2009; Isozaki et al., 2010b; Gojun and Fraser, 2012; Nakagawa, 2015) and post-ordering (Goto et al., 2012, 2013; Hayashi et al., 2013) models have been proposed. Preordering reorders source sentences before translation, while post-ordering reorders sentences translated without considering the word order after translation. In particular, preordering effectively improves the translation quality because it solves long-distance reordering and

computational complexity issues (Jehl et al., 2014; Nakagawa, 2015).

Rule-based preordering methods either manually create reordering rules (Wang et al., 2007; Xu et al., 2009; Isozaki et al., 2010b; Gojun and Fraser, 2012) or extract reordering rules from a corpus (Xia and McCord, 2004; Genzel, 2010). On the other hand, studies in (Neubig et al., 2012; Lerner and Petrov, 2013; Hoshino et al., 2015; Nakagawa, 2015) apply machine learning to the preordering problem. Hoshino et al. (2015) proposed a method that learns whether child nodes should be swapped at each node of a syntax tree. Neubig et al. (2012) and Nakagawa (2015) proposed methods that construct a binary tree and reordering simultaneously from a source sentence. These methods require a manual feature design for every language pair, which makes language dependent design costly. To overcome this challenge, methods based on feed forward neural networks that do not require a manual feature design have been proposed (de Gispert et al., 2015; Botha et al., 2017). However, these methods decide whether to reorder child nodes without considering the sub-trees, which contains important information for reordering.

As a preordering method that is free of manual feature design and makes use of information in sub-trees, we propose a preordering method with a recursive neural network (RvNN). RvNN calculates reordering in a bottom-up manner (from the leaf nodes to the root) on a source syntax tree. Thus, preordering is performed considering the entire sub-trees. Specifically, RvNN learns whether to reorder nodes of a syntax tree[1] with a vector representation of sub-trees and syntactic categories. We evaluate the proposed

---

[1]In this paper, we used binary syntax trees.




*Proceedings of ACL 2018, Student Research Workshop*, pages 21–27
Melbourne, Australia, July 15 - 20, 2018. ©2018 Association for Computational Linguistics

method for English-to-Japanese translations using both phrase-based SMT (PBSMT) and neural MT (NMT). The results confirm that the proposed method achieves comparable translation quality to the state-of-the-art preordering method (Nakagawa, 2015) that requires a manual feature design.

## 2 Preordering with a Recursive Neural Network

We explain our design of the RvNN to conduct preordering after describing how to obtain gold-standard labels for preordering.

### 2.1 Gold-Standard Labels for Preordering

We created training data for preordering by labeling whether each node of the source-side syntax tree has reordered child nodes against a target-side sentence. The label is determined based on Kendall's $\tau$ (Kendall, 1938) as in (Nakagawa, 2015), which is calculated by Equation (1).

$$\tau = \frac{4 \sum_{i=1}^{|\mathbf{y}|-1} \sum_{j=i+1}^{|\mathbf{y}|} \delta(\mathbf{y}_i < \mathbf{y}_j)}{|\mathbf{y}|(|\mathbf{y}|-1)} - 1, \quad (1)$$

$$\delta(x) = \begin{cases} 1 & (x \text{ is true}), \\ 0 & (\text{otherwise}), \end{cases}$$

where $\mathbf{y}$ is a vector of target word indexes that are aligned with source words. The value of Kendall's $\tau$ is in $[-1, 1]$. When it is 1, it means the sequence of $\mathbf{y}$ is in a complete ascending order, *i.e.*, target sentence has the same word order with the source in terms of word alignment. At each node, if Kendall's $\tau$ increases by reordering child nodes, an "Inverted" label is assigned; otherwise, a "Straight" label, which means the child nodes do not need to be reordered, is assigned. When a source word of a child node does not have an alignment, a "Straight" label is assigned.

### 2.2 Preordering Model

RvNN is constructed given a binary syntax tree. It predicts the label determined in Section 2.1 at each node. RvNN decides whether to reorder the child nodes by considering the sub-tree. The vector of the sub-tree is calculated in a bottom-up manner from the leaf nodes. Figure 1 shows an example of preordering of an English sentence "My parents live in London." At the VP node corresponding to "live in London," the vector of the node is calculated by Equation (2), considering its child nodes

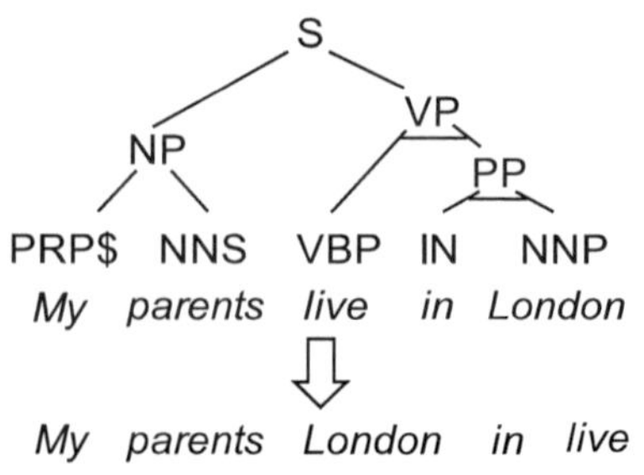


Figure 1: Preordering an English sentence "My parents live in London" with RvNN (Nodes with a horizontal line mean "Inverted").

correspond to "live" and "in London."

$$\mathbf{p} = f([\mathbf{p_l}; \mathbf{p_r}]W + \mathbf{b}), \quad (2)$$
$$\mathbf{s} = \mathbf{p}W_s + \mathbf{b}_s, \quad (3)$$

where $f$ is a rectifier, $W \in \mathbb{R}^{2\lambda \times \lambda}$ is a weight matrix, $\mathbf{p_l}$ and $\mathbf{p_r}$ are vector representations of the left and right child nodes, respectively. $[\cdot; \cdot]$ denotes the concatenation of two vectors. $W_s \in \mathbb{R}^{\lambda \times 2}$ is a weight matrix for the output layer, and $\mathbf{b}, \mathbf{b}_s \in \mathbb{R}^{\lambda}$ are the biases. $\mathbf{s} \in \mathbb{R}^2$ calculated by Equation (3) is a weight vector for each label, which is fed into a softmax function to calculate the probabilities of the "Straight" and "Inverted" labels.

At a leaf node, a word embedding calculated by Equations (4) and (5) is fed into Equation (2).

$$\mathbf{e} = \mathbf{x}W_E, \quad (4)$$
$$\mathbf{p_e} = f(\mathbf{e}W_l + \mathbf{b}_l), \quad (5)$$

where $\mathbf{x} \in \mathbb{R}^N$ is a one-hot vector of an input word with a vocabulary size of $N$, $W_E \in \mathbb{R}^{N \times \lambda}$ is an embedding matrix, and $\mathbf{b}_l \in \mathbb{R}^{\lambda}$ is the bias. The loss function is the cross entropy defined by Equation (6).

$$L(\theta) = -\frac{1}{K} \sum_{k=1}^{K} \sum_{n \in \mathcal{T}} l_k^n \log p(l_k^n; \theta), \quad (6)$$

where $\theta$ is the parameters of the model, $n$ is the node of a syntax tree $\mathcal{T}$, $K$ is a mini batch size, and $l_k^n$ is the label of the $n$-th node in the $k$-th syntax tree in the mini batch.

With the model using POS tags and syntactic categories, we use Equation (7) instead of Equation (2).

$$\mathbf{p} = f([\mathbf{p_l}; \mathbf{p_r}; \mathbf{e}_t]W_t + \mathbf{b}_t), \quad (7)$$

where $\mathbf{e}_t$ represents a vector of POS tags or syntactic categories, $W_t \in \mathbb{R}^{3\lambda \times \lambda}$ is a weight matrix, and $\mathbf{b}_t \in \mathbb{R}^{\lambda}$ is the bias. $\mathbf{e}_t$ is calculated in the same manner as Equations (4) and (5), but the input is a one-hot vector of the POS tags or syntactic categories at each node. $\lambda$ is tuned on a development set, whose effects are investigated in Section 3.2.

## 3 Experiments

### 3.1 Settings

We conducted English-to-Japanese translation experiments using the ASPEC corpus (Nakazawa et al., 2016). This corpus provides 3M sentence pairs as training data, $1,790$ sentence pairs as development data, and $1,812$ sentence pairs as test data. We used Stanford CoreNLP[2] for tokenization and POS tagging, Enju[3] for parsing of English, and MeCab[4] for tokenization of Japanese. For word alignment, we used MGIZA.[5] Source-to-target and target-to-source word alignments were calculated using IBM model 1 and hidden Markov model, and they were combined with the intersection heuristic following (Nakagawa, 2015).

We implemented our RvNN preordering model with Chainer.[6] The ASPEC corpus was created using the sentence alignment method proposed in (Utiyama and Isahara, 2007) and was sorted based on the alignment confidence scores. In this paper, we used 100k sentences sampled from the top 500k sentences as training data for preordering. The vocabulary size $N$ was set to 50k. We used Adam (Kingma and Ba, 2015) with a weight decay and gradient clipping for optimization. The mini batch size $K$ was set to 500.

We compared our model with the state-of-the-art preordering method proposed in (Nakagawa, 2015), which is hereafter referred to as *BTG*. We used its publicly available implementation,[7] and trained it on the same 100k sentences as our model.

We used the 1.8M source and target sentences as training data for MT. We excluded part of the sentence pairs whose lengths were longer than

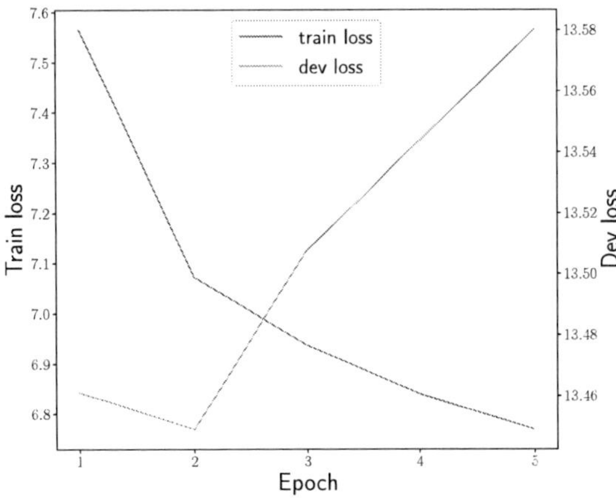



Figure 2: Learning curve of our preordering model.

| Node dimensions | 100 | 200 | 500 |
|---|---|---|---|
| w/o preordering | | 22.73 | |
| w/o tags and categories | 24.63 | 24.95 | 25.02 |
| w/ tags and categories | 25.22 | 25.41 | 25.38 |

Table 1: BLEU scores with preordering by our model and without preordering under different $\lambda$ settings (trained on a 500k subset of the training data).

50 words or the source to target length ratio exceeded 9. For SMT, we used Moses.[8] We trained the 5-gram language model on the target side of the training corpus with KenLM.[9] Tuning was performed by minimum error rate training (Och, 2003). We repeated tuning and testing of each model 3 times and reported the average of scores. For NMT, we used the attention-based encoder-decoder model of (Luong et al., 2015) with 2-layer LSTM implemented in OpenNMT.[10] The sizes of the vocabulary, word embedding, and hidden layer were set to 50k, 500, and 500, respectively. The batch size was set to 64, and the number of epochs was set to 13. The translation quality was evaluated using BLEU (Papineni et al., 2002) and RIBES (Isozaki et al., 2010a) using the bootstrap resampling method (Koehn, 2004) for the significance test.

### 3.2 Results

Figure 2 shows the learning curve of our preordering model with $\lambda = 200$.[11] Both the training and

---

[2]http://stanfordnlp.github.io/CoreNLP/

[3]http://www.nactem.ac.uk/enju/

[4]http://taku910.github.io/mecab/

[5]http://github.com/moses-smt/giza-pp

[6]http://chainer.org/

[7]http://github.com/google/topdown-btg-preordering

[8]http://www.statmt.org/moses/

[9]http://github.com/kpu/kenlm

[10]http://opennmt.net/

[11]The learning curve behaves similarly for different $\lambda$ values.

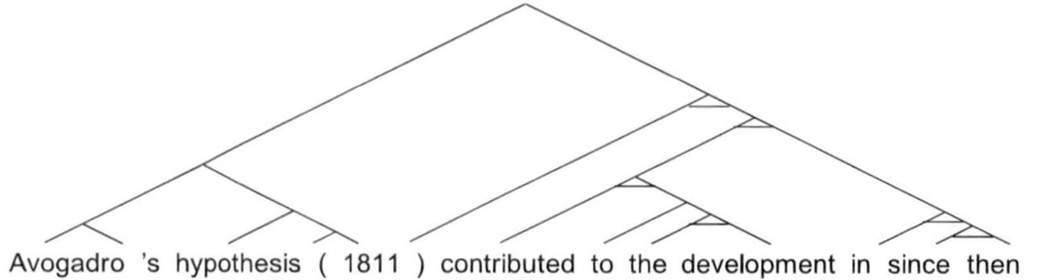


Figure 4: Example of a syntax tree with a parse-error (the phrase "(1811)" was divided in two phrases by mistake). Our preordering result was affected by such parse-errors. (Nodes with a horizontal line means "Inverted".)

|  | PBSMT | | NMT | |
|---|---|---|---|---|
|  | BLEU | RIBES | BLEU | RIBES |
| w/o preordering | 22.88 | 64.07 | **32.68** | **81.68** |
| w/ BTG | **29.51** | **77.20** | 28.91 | 79.58 |
| w/ RvNN | **29.16** | **76.39** | 29.01 | 79.63 |

Table 2: BLEU and RIBES scores on the test set. (All models are trained on the entire training corpus of 1.8M sentence pairs.) Numbers in **bold** indicate the best systems and the systems that are statistically insignificant at $p < 0.05$ from the best systems.

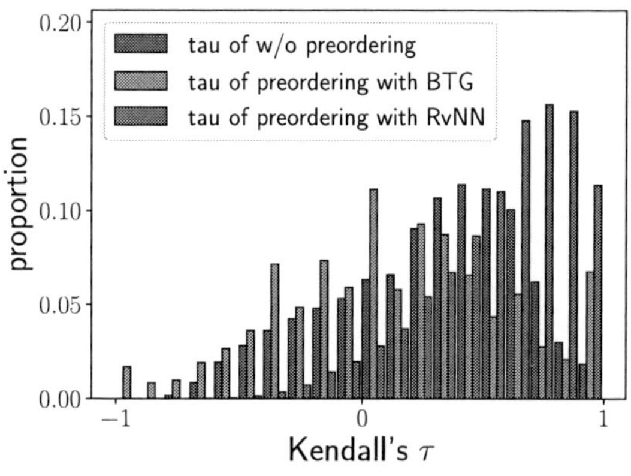


Figure 3: Distribution of Kendall's $\tau$ in the training data without preordering, preordering by BTG, and preordering by our RvNN.

the development losses decreased until 2 epochs. However, the development loss started to increase after 3 epochs. Therefore, the number of epochs was set up to 5, and we chose the model with the lowest development loss. The source sentences in the translation evaluation were preordered with this model.

Next, we investigated the effect of $\lambda$. Table 1 shows the BLEU scores with different $\lambda$ values, as well as the BLEU score without preorder-

ing. In this experiment, PBSMT was trained with a 500k subset of training data, and the distortion limit was set to 6. Our RvNNs consistently outperformed the plain PBSMT without preordering. The BLEU score improved as $\lambda$ increased when only word embedding was considered. In addition, RvNNs involving POS tags and syntactic categories achieved even higher BLEU scores. This result shows the effectiveness of POS tags and syntactic categories in reordering. For these models, setting $\lambda$ larger than 200 did not contribute to the translation quality. Based on these, we further evaluated the RvNN with POS tags and syntactic categories where $\lambda = 200$.

Table 2 shows BLEU and RIBES scores of the test set on PBSMT and NMT trained on the entire training data of 1.8M sentence pairs. The distortion limit of SMT systems trained using preordered sentences by RvNN and BTG was set to 0, while that without preordering was set to 6. Compared to the plain PBSMT without preordering, both BLEU and RIBES increased significantly with preordering by RvNN and BTG. These scores were comparable (statistically insignificant at $p < 0.05$) between RvNN and BTG,[12] indicating that the proposed method achieves a translation quality comparable to BTG. In contrast to the case of PBSMT, NMT without preordering achieved a significantly higher BLEU score than NMT models with preordering by RvNN and BTG. This is the same phenomenon in the Chinese-to-Japanese translation experiment reported in (Sudoh and Nagata, 2016). We assume that one reason is the isolation between preordering and NMT models, where both models are trained using independent optimization functions. In the future, we will investigate this problem and consider a model that unifies

---

[12]The $p$-value for BLEU and RIBES were 0.068 and 0.226, respectively.

| | Preordered examples |
|---|---|
| Source sentence | because of the embedding heterostructure, current leakage around the threshold was minimal. |
| BTG | of the embedding heterostructure because, the threshold around current leakage minimal was. |
| RvNN | embedding heterostructure the of because, around threshold the current leakage minimal was. |
| | Translation examples by PBSMT |
| Reference | 埋込みヘテロ構造のため、しきい値近くでの漏れ電流は非常に小さかった。 |
| | (embedding heterostructure of because, threshold around leakage very minimal.) |
| w/o preordering | 埋込みヘテロ構造のため、漏れ電流のしきい値付近では最低であった。 |
| | (embedding heterostructure of because, leakage threshold around minimal.) |
| BTG | の埋込みヘテロ構造のため、このしきい値付近での漏れ電流の最小であった。 |
| | (of embedding heterostructure of because, the threshold around leakage minimal.) |
| RvNN | 埋込みヘテロ構造のため、周辺のしきい値の電流漏れは認められなかった。 |
| | (embedding heterostructure of because, around threshold leakage recognized not.) |

Table 3: Example where preordering improves translation. (Literal translations are given in the parenthesis under the Japanese sentences.)

| | Preordered examples |
|---|---|
| Source sentence | avogadro's hypothesis (1811) contributed to the development in since then. |
| BTG | avogadro's hypothesis (1811) the then since in development to contributed . |
| RvNN | avogadro's hypothesis (1811 then since in to development the contributed). |
| | Translation examples by PBSMT |
| Reference | Avogadro の仮説 (1811) は，以後の発展に貢献した。 |
| | (Avogadro's hypothesis (1811), since then development to contributed.) |
| w/o preordering | Avogadro の仮説 (1811) の開発に貢献し以後である。 |
| | (Avogadro's hypothesis (1811) development to contributed since then.) |
| BTG | Avogadro の仮説 (1811) 以後の発展に貢献した。 |
| | (Avogadro's hypothesis (1811) since then development to contributed.) |
| RvNN | Avogadro の仮説 (1811 以降のこれらの開発に貢献した。 |
| | (Avogadro's hypothesis (1811 since then these development to contributed.) |

Table 4: Example of a parse-error disturbed preordering in our method. (Literal translations are given in the parenthesis under the Japanese sentences.)

preordering and translation in a single model.

Figure 3 shows the distribution of Kendall's $\tau$ in the original training data as well as the distributions after preordering by RvNN and BTG. The ratio of high Kendall's $\tau$ largely increased in the case of RvNN, suggesting that the proposed method learns preordering properly. Furthermore, the ratio of high Kendall's $\tau$ by RvNN is more than that of BTG, implying that preordering by RvNN is better than that by BTG.

We also manually investigated the preordering and translation results. We found that our model improved both. Table 3 shows a successful preordering and translation example on PBSMT. The word order is notably different between source and reference sentences. After preordering, the word order between the source and reference sentences became the same. Because RvNN depends on parsing, sentences with a parse-error tended to fail in preordering. For example, the phrase "(1811)" in Figure 4 was divided in two phrases by mistake. Consequently, preordering failed. Table 4 shows preordering and translation examples for the sentence in Figure 4. Compared to the translation

without preordering, the translation quality after preordering was improved to deliver correct meaning.

## 4   Conclusion

In this paper, we proposed a preordering method without a manual feature design for MT. The experiments confirmed that the proposed method achieved a translation quality comparable to the state-of-the-art preordering method that requires a manual feature design. As a future work, we plan to develop a model that jointly parses and preorders a source sentence. In addition, we plan to integrate preordering into the NMT model.

## Acknowledgement

This work was supported by NTT communication science laboratories and Grant-in-Aid for Research Activity Start-up #17H06822, JSPS.

## References

Jan A. Botha, Emily Pitler, Ji Ma, Anton Bakalov, Alex Salcianu, David Weiss, Ryan McDonald, and

Slav Petrov. 2017. Natural language processing with small feed-forward networks. In *Proceedings of the Conference on Empirical Methods in Natural Language Processing (EMNLP)*, pages 2879–2885, Copenhagen, Denmark.

Dmitriy Genzel. 2010. Automatically learning source-side reordering rules for large scale machine translation. In *Proceedings of the International Conference on Computational Linguistics (COLING)*, pages 376–384, Beijing, China.

Adrià de Gispert, Gonzalo Iglesias, and Bill Byrne. 2015. Fast and accurate preordering for SMT using neural networks. In *Proceedings of the Conference of the North American Chapter of the Association for Computational Linguistics: Human Language Technologies (NAACL-HLT)*, pages 1012–1017, Denver, Colorado.

Anita Gojun and Alexander Fraser. 2012. Determining the placement of German verbs in English–to–German SMT. In *Proceedings of the Conference of the European Chapter of the Association for Computational Linguistics (EACL)*, pages 726–735, Avignon, France.

Isao Goto, Masao Utiyama, and Eiichiro Sumita. 2012. Post-ordering by parsing for Japanese-English statistical machine translation. In *Proceedings of the Annual Meeting of the Association for Computational Linguistics (ACL)*, pages 311–316, Jeju Island, Korea.

Isao Goto, Masao Utiyama, and Eiichiro Sumita. 2013. Post-ordering by parsing with ITG for Japanese-English statistical machine translation. *ACM Transactions on Asian Language Information Processing*, 12(4):17:1–17:22.

Katsuhiko Hayashi, Katsuhito Sudoh, Hajime Tsukada, Jun Suzuki, and Masaaki Nagata. 2013. Shift-reduce word reordering for machine translation. In *Proceedings of the Conference on Empirical Methods in Natural Language Processing (EMNLP)*, pages 1382–1386, Seattle, Washington, USA.

Sho Hoshino, Yusuke Miyao, Katsuhito Sudoh, Katsuhiko Hayashi, and Masaaki Nagata. 2015. Discriminative preordering meets Kendall's $\tau$ maximization. In *Proceedings of the Annual Meeting of the Association for Computational Linguistics and International Joint Conference on Natural Language Processing (ACL-IJCNLP)*, pages 139–144, Beijing, China.

Hideki Isozaki, Tsutomu Hirao, Kevin Duh, Katsuhito Sudoh, and Hajime Tsukada. 2010a. Automatic evaluation of translation quality for distant language pairs. In *Proceedings of the Conference on Empirical Methods in Natural Language Processing (EMNLP)*, pages 944–952, Cambridge, USA.

Hideki Isozaki, Katsuhito Sudoh, Hajime Tsukada, and Kevin Duh. 2010b. Head finalization: A simple reordering rule for SOV languages. In *Proceedings of the Workshop on Statistical Machine Translation and MetricsMATR*, pages 244–251, Uppsala, Sweden.

Laura Jehl, Adrià de Gispert, Mark Hopkins, and Bill Byrne. 2014. Source-side preordering for translation using logistic regression and depth-first branch-and-bound search. In *Proceedings of the Conference of the European Chapter of the Association for Computational Linguistics (EACL)*, pages 239–248, Gothenburg, Sweden.

M. G. Kendall. 1938. A new measure of rank correlation. *Biometrika*, 30(1/2):81–93.

Diederik P. Kingma and Jimmy Ba. 2015. Adam: A method for stochastic optimization. In *Proceedings of the International Conference for Learning Representations (ICLR)*, San Diego, USA.

Philipp Koehn. 2004. Statistical significance tests for machine translation evaluation. In *Proceedings of the Conference on Empirical Methods in Natural Language Processing (EMNLP)*, pages 388–395, Barcelona, Spain.

Philipp Koehn, Amittai Axelrod, Alexandra Birch-Mayne, Chris Callison-Burch, Miles Osborne, and David Talbot. 2005. Edinburgh system description for the 2005 IWSLT speech translation evaluation. In *Proceedings of the International Workshop on Spoken Language Translation (IWSLT)*, pages 68–75, Pittsburgh, USA.

Uri Lerner and Slav Petrov. 2013. Source-side classifier preordering for machine translation. In *Proceedings of the Conference on Empirical Methods in Natural Language Processing (EMNLP)*, pages 513–523, Seattle, USA.

Thang Luong, Hieu Pham, and Christopher D. Manning. 2015. Effective approaches to attention-based neural machine translation. In *Proceedings of the Conference on Empirical Methods in Natural Language Processing (EMNLP)*, pages 1412–1421, Lisbon, Portugal.

Masaaki Nagata, Kuniko Saito, Kazuhide Yamamoto, and Kazuteru Ohashi. 2006. A clustered global phrase reordering model for statistical machine translation. In *Proceedings of the International Conference on Computational Linguistics and Annual Meeting of the Association for Computational Linguistics (COLING-ACL)*, pages 713–720, Sydney, Australia.

Tetsuji Nakagawa. 2015. Efficient top-down BTG parsing for machine translation preordering. In *Proceedings of the Annual Meeting of the Association for Computational Linguistics and International Joint Conference on Natural Language Processing (ACL-IJCNLP)*, pages 208–218, Beijing, China.

Toshiaki Nakazawa, Manabu Yaguchi, Kiyotaka Uchimoto, Masao Utiyama, Eiichiro Sumita, Sadao Kurohashi, and Hitoshi Isahara. 2016. ASPEC: Asian scientific paper excerpt corpus. In *Proceedings of the International Conference on Language Resources and Evaluation (LREC)*, pages 2204–2208, Portorož, Slovenia.

Graham Neubig, Taro Watanabe, and Shinsuke Mori. 2012. Inducing a discriminative parser to optimize machine translation reordering. In *Proceedings of the Conference on Empirical Methods in Natural Language Processing and Computational Natural Language Learning (EMNLP-CoNLL)*, pages 843–853, Jeju Island, Korea.

Franz Josef Och. 2003. Minimum error rate training in statistical machine translation. In *Proceedings of the Annual Meeting of the Association for Computational Linguistics (ACL)*, pages 160–167, Sapporo, Japan.

Kishore Papineni, Salim Roukos, Todd Ward, and Wei-Jing Zhu. 2002. BLEU: a method for automatic evaluation of machine translation. In *Proceedings of the Annual Meeting of the Association for Computational Linguistics (ACL)*, pages 311–318, Philadelphia, USA.

Katsuhito Sudoh and Masaaki Nagata. 2016. Chinese-to-Japanese patent machine translation based on syntactic pre-ordering for WAT 2016. In *Proceedings of the Workshop on Asian Translation (WAT)*, pages 211–215, Osaka, Japan.

Christoph Tillmann. 2004. A unigram orientation model for statistical machine translation. In *Proceedings of the Human Language Technology Conference of the North American Chapter of the Association for Computational Linguistics (HLT-NAACL)*, pages 101–104, Boston, Massachusetts, USA.

Masao Utiyama and Hitoshi Isahara. 2007. A Japanese-English patent parallel corpus. In *Proceedings of the Machine Translation Summit XI*, pages 475–482, Copenhagen, Denmark.

Chao Wang, Michael Collins, and Philipp Koehn. 2007. Chinese syntactic reordering for statistical machine translation. In *Proceedings of the Conference on Empirical Methods in Natural Language Processing and Computational Natural Language Learning (EMNLP-CoNLL)*, pages 737–745, Prague, Czech Republic.

Fei Xia and Michael McCord. 2004. Improving a statistical MT system with automatically learned rewrite patterns. In *Proceedings of the International Conference on Computational Linguistics (COLING)*, pages 508–514, Geneva, Switzerland.

Peng Xu, Jaeho Kang, Michael Ringgaard, and Franz Och. 2009. Using a dependency parser to improve SMT for subject-object-verb languages. In *Proceedings of the Human Language Technologies: Annual Conference of the North American Chapter of the Association for Computational Linguistics (HLT-NAACL)*, pages 245–253, Boulder, USA.

# Pushing the Limits of Radiology with Joint Modeling of Visual and Textual Information


**Sonit Singh**[1,2]
Department of Computing, Macquarie University[1]
DATA61, CSIRO[2]
Sydney, Australia
`sonit.singh@hdr.mq.edu.au`



## Abstract

Recently, there has been increasing interest in the intersection of computer vision and natural language processing. Researchers have studied several interesting tasks, including generating text descriptions from images and videos and language embedding of images. More recent work has further extended the scope of this area to combine videos and language, learning to solve non-visual tasks using visual cues, visual question answering, and visual dialog. Despite a large body of research on the intersection of vision-language technology, its adaption to the medical domain is not fully explored. To address this research gap, we aim to develop machine learning models that can reason jointly on medical images and clinical text for advanced search, retrieval, annotation and description of medical images.


## 1 Introduction

Integrating information from various modalities is deeply rooted in human lives. Humans combine vision, language, speech and touch to acquire knowledge about the world and comprehend the world (Hall and McKevitt, 1995). *Vision* and *Language* are the most common ways of expressing our knowledge about the world. Both *Computer Vision* (CV) and *Natural Language Processing* (NLP) demonstrated successful results on various general purpose tasks such as image classification, object detection, semantic segmentation, and machine translation. Although research at the intersection of CV and NLP is gaining pace, its applications to healthcare are still under-explored. The success of Artificial Intelligence (AI) tech-

nologies in general purpose tasks is mainly attributed to publicly available large-scale datasets, enhanced compute power due to rise of Graphics Processing Units (GPUs), and due to advancements in Machine Learning (ML) algorithms and its various architectures. One of the biggest hurdles in deploying ML (especially Deep Learning) models in healthcare is a lack of annotated data. Although it is easy to get annotated data for general purpose tasks by crowdsourcing, it is almost impossible for medical data because of limited expertise, privacy and ethical issues. On the positive side, a lot of medical data in the form of medical images and accompanying text reports is stored in hospitals' Picture Archival and Communication Systems (PACS). For instance, Beth Israel Deaconnes Medical Center (Harvard) generates approximately 20 terabytes of image data and one terabyte of text data per year (Mastanduno, 2017). Also, the drive toward structured reporting in radiology definitely enhance NLP accuracy (Cai et al., 2016). *Interpreting* medical images and *summarising* them in natural text is a challenging, complex and tedious task. Various research studies show that the general rate of missed radiological findings can be as much as 30% (Berlin, 2001; Berlin and Hendrix, 1998). These errors are mainly due to limited expertise, increasing patient volumes, the subjectivity of human perception, fatigue, and inability to locate critical and subtle findings (Sohani, 2013). Based on a recent estimate one billion radiology examinations are performed worldwide annually. This equates to about 40 million radiologist errors per annum (Brady, 2017). In order to reduce these errors, there is a need to develop automated clinical decision support systems (CDSS) (Eickhoff et al., 2017) that can interpret medical images and generate written reports to augment radiologist's work.

Our research aims to develop machine learning




*Proceedings of ACL 2018, Student Research Workshop*, pages 28–36
Melbourne, Australia, July 15 - 20, 2018. ©2018 Association for Computational Linguistics

models that reason jointly on medical images and clinical text for advanced search, retrieval, annotation and description of medical images. Specifically, we aim to automatically generate description of medical images, to develop medical visual question answering system and to develop medical dialog agents that interact with patients to answer their queries based on their medical data.

## 2 Background

Deep Neural Networks (DNNs) are a special class of machine learning algorithms that learn in multiple levels, corresponding to different levels of abstraction. In this section, we provide an overview of two of the most common DNNs namely Convolutional Neural Networks (CNNs) and Recurrent Neural Networks (RNNs). Also, we provide a profile of architectures and various successful applications in CV and NLP.

### 2.1 Convolutional Neural Networks

In the past, problems such as image classification and object detection were approached using a traditional CV pipeline where hand-crafted features were first extracted, followed by learning algorithms (Srinivas et al., 2016). The performance of these systems highly depends upon the quality of the extracted features and the ability of the learning algorithms (Fu and Rui, 2017). As CV progressed, extracting these complex features became a tedious task, giving rise to algorithms that can learn directly from the raw data without the need for hand-crafted feature engineering. The major breakthrough happened in 2012 when object classification on ImageNet (Russakovsky et al., 2015) improved vastly from top-5 error of 25% in 2011 to 16% in 2012. This was the result of shift from hand-engineered features to learned deep features (Felsberg, 2017). AlexNet was the first deep learning model that won the ILSVRC championship in 2012 by drastically reducing the top-5 error rate on the ImageNet Challege compared to the previous shallow networks. Since AlexNet, a series of CNN models have been proposed that advanced state-of-the-art such as VGG-16 (Simonyan and Zisserman, 2014), GoogleNet (Szegedy et al., 2015), and Residual Networks (ResNet) (He et al., 2016). All these models differ in terms of various structural decompositions which led them to have better learning ability and high predictive performance.

### 2.2 Recurrent Neural Networks

Recurrent Neural Networks (RNNs) are special networks that process sequential or temporal data including language, speech, and handwriting. Learning sequential data requires memory of previous states and a feedback mechanism. RNNs form an internal state of the network where connections between units form a cycle, which allows it to exhibit dynamic temporal behavior (Lee et al., 2017). Simple RNNs suffer from the vanishing or exploding gradients problem when trained with gradient based techniques. To overcome these challenges, Long Short Term Memory (LSTM) (Hochreiter and Schmidhuber, 1997) and Gated Recurrent Unit (GRU) (Cho et al., 2014) were introduced which are able to learn very deep RNNs and can successfully remember sequences having duration of varying lengths.

### 2.3 Joint Image and Language Modeling

Due to the success of deep learning techniques in individual domains of AI including vision, speech and language, researchers are aiming at problems at the intersection of vision, language, knowledge representation and common-sense reasoning. An ultimate goal of CV is to have comprehensive visual understanding that involves not only naming the classes of objects present in a scene, but also describe their attributes and recognize relationship between objects (Krishna et al., 2017). Much progress has been made towards this goal, including object classification (Krizhevsky et al., 2012), object detection and localisation (Girshick et al., 2014), and object and instance segmentation (He et al., 2017a). On the other hand, the overall goal of NLP is to understand, draw inferences from, summarise, translate and generate accurate natural text and language. State-of-the-art results on various NLP tasks, including Part-of-Speech tagging (Collobert et al., 2011), Parsing (Dyer et al., 2015; Vinyals et al., 2015), Named Entity Recognition (Collobert et al., 2011), Semantic Role Labeling (Zhou and Xu, 2015; He et al., 2017b), and machine translation (Sutskever et al., 2014; Wu et al., 2016) are pushing towards that goal. Early work combining vision with language includes image annotation, where the task is to assign labels to an image. However, image annotation only associates isolated words with the image content and ignores the relationships between objects and their relation to the world. To generate a coherent interpretation of a scene and describe it in a natural way, the task of image captioning emerged within the language-vision community, together with large-scale captioning datasets including Flickr30k [1] and MSCOCO [2]. Captioning involves generating a textual description that verbalizes the most salient aspects (objects, attributes, scene properties) of the image by analyzing it. In order to tackle more complex tasks that combine vision and language and to develop high-level reasoning, Visual Question Answering (VQA) (Stanislaw et al., 2015) was proposed which is equivalent to *Visual Turing Test*. In VQA, the goal is to predict the answer correctly after reasoning over the image and a question in natural text (Teney et al., 2017). To further extend this task, Visual Dialog (Das et al., 2017a,b) was proposed that requires an AI agent to hold meaningful dialog with humans in natural language about visual content. Apart from this, research is moving towards linking language to actions in the real world, also known as language grounding (Chen and Mooney, 2011), which finds applications in human-robot interaction, robotic navigation and manipulation. Although there has been language-vision research for these general purpose tasks, its progress has been underutilised in healthcare.

## 3 Related Work

Developing clinical decision support has long been a major research focus in medical image processing. In recent years, deep learning models have outperformed conventional machine learning approaches in tasks such as dermatologist level classification of skin lesions (Esteva et al., 2017), detection of liver lesions (Ben-Cohen et al., 2016), detection of pathological-image findings (Zhang et al., 2017a), automated detection of pneumonia from chest X-rays (Rajpurkar et al., 2017), and segmentation of brain MRI (Milletari et al., 2016). Although there are many publicly available datasets for general purpose tasks (Ferraro et al., 2015), there are few publicly available datasets in the medical domain. Recently, (Wang et al., 2017) introduced a large-scale Chest X-ray dataset named *ChestX-ray8* that is publicly available. The dataset consists of $112,120$ frontal-view chest X-rays images of $30,805$ patients. The labels of

the images are automatically assigned by applying NLP techniques to the paired radiology reports. (Zhang et al., 2017b) proposed MD-Net, that can read pathology bladder cancer images, can generate diagnostic reports, retrieve images by symptom descriptions, and provide justification of the decision process by highlighting image regions using an attention mechanism. Moreover, (Shin et al., 2016) proposed CNN-RNN model that can efficiently detect a disease in medical image, find the context (*e.g.* location and severity of affected organ) and also correlate the salient regions of the image with Medical Subject Headings (MeSH) terms. They work on Open-i (U.S. NLM), a publicly available dataset that consists of 3955 radiology reports from the Indiana Network for Patient Care, and $7,470$ associated chest X-rays from the hospitals' PACS. Evaluation in terms of BLEU score (Papineni et al., 2002) demonstrates that the model is able to locate diseases and able to generate Medical Subject Headings (MeSH) terms with high precision.

In addition, ImageCLEF challenges[3] have been leading advances in the medical field by promoting evaluation of technologies for annotation, indexing and retrieval of textual data and medical images (Ionescu et al., 2017). Motivated by the need for automated image understanding methods in the healthcare domain, ImageCLEF organized its first *concept detection* and *caption prediction* tasks in 2017 (Eickhoff et al., 2017). The ImageCLEFcaption challenge consists of two sub tasks including Concept detection and Caption prediction. The concept detection task consists of identifying the UMLS Concept Unique Identifiers (CUIs). Majority of the submissions consider concept detection as a *multi-label classification* task. As both of these tasks are inter-related, there has been work where first concepts in the medical images are identified and then captions are generated based on the predicted concepts. (Abacha et al., 2017) consider CUIs in the training set as the labels to be assigned. Two methods namely CNN based approach and the Binary Relevance via Decision Trees (BR-DT) were used. In (Hasan et al., 2017), an encoder-decoder based framework is used where image features are extracted using CNN and RNN-based architecture with attention mechanism is used to translate the image features to relevant captions. In (Rahman et al., 2017), a

---

<sup>1</sup>`http://shannon.cs.illinois.edu/DenotationGraph/`
<sup>2</sup>`http://cocodataset.org/`

<sup>3</sup>`http://www.imageclef.org/`

Content Based Image Retrieval (CBIR) based approach is used where first images in both training and validation sets are indexed by extracting several low-level color, texture and edge-related visual features. The similarity search is then used to find the closest matching image in the train (or validation set) for each each query (test) image for caption prediction. For similarity matching, each feature is concatenated to form a combined feature vector and Euclidean distance is used for k-Nearest Neighbor image similarity.

In the ImageCLEF challenge, submissions varried in their usage of external resources. For instance (Hasan et al., 2017) do semantic preprocessing of captions using MetaMap and UMLS mcta-thesaurus. Pre-training CNN models on PubMed Central images helped in boosting effectiveness compared to training on general purpose ImageNet dataset. Although these challenges provide labeled medical images for modality classification and concept predictions, the datasets are still much smaller (thousands of images) than the ImageNet dataset (Russakovsky et al., 2015) which contains 1.2 million natural images. Moreover, thcrc are issues with ImageCLEFcaption dataset as the UMLS concepts are extracted using probabilistic process which introduces errors. The analysis of dataset showed that some of the images had no concepts attached.

Learning image context from the corresponding clinical text and generating textual reports very similar to radiologists has not yet been achieved. With recent advancements in machine learning (specially deep learning), it is not hard to imagine an opportunity to aid radiologists by developing multimodal clinical decision support systems.

## 4  Proposed Research

We identify research gaps in the intersection of medical imaging, computer vision and natural language processing as listed in in the following research questions. Our work will address some of these gaps.

### How to automatically generate a radiology report for a given medical image?

In medical imaging, the accurate diagnosis or assessment of a disease depends on both image acquisition and image interpretation. While image acquisition has improved substantially due to faster rates and increased resolution of the acquisition devices, image interpretation is still performed by a radiologist, where the radiologist has only a few minutes with an imaging study to describe the findings in the form of radiology report. Such reporting is a time-consuming task and often represents a bottleneck in the clinical diagnosis pipeline (Ionescu et al., 2017). We will develop machine learning models that automatically generate radiology reports by interpreting medical images in order to augment the radiology practice.

### How to develop a question answering system that can reason over medical images?

There has been growing interest in AI to support clinical decision making and in improving clinical work-flow by better patient engagement. Automated systems that can interpret complex medical images and provide findings in natural language text can significantly enhance the productivity of hospitals, reduce burden on radiologists and provide a "second opinion", leading to reduced errors in radiology practice. VQA (Stanislaw et al., 2015) has been successful on generic images, but it has not been explored in the medical domain. We will develop machine learning models that combine NLP and CV techniques to answer clinically relevant questions based on medical images. Subsequently, clinical visual dialog systems could be developed based on the models for medical VQA. The dialog agent will respond to patient's queries in an interactive manner based on medical images, clinical text reports and past history of the patient.

### How to annotate medical images from the accompanied radiology reports in a weakly supervised manner?

A large volume of medical imaging data and text is accumulated in hosptitals' PACS. To harness this data for advancing healthcare is challenging. Manual annotation of medical data is almost impossible due to the complex nature of medical images, requirement of domain expertise, privacy, ethics and healthcare data regulations. The processing of clinical text is challenging due to combinations of ad-hoc formatting, eliding words which can be inferred from context, and liberal use of parenthetical expressions, jargon and acronyms to increase the information density. We will explore NLP techniques to annotate medical images from the accompanying radiology reports.

**How to highlight the relevant area in a medical image based on the features extracted from radiology reports?**

Although machine learning, especially deep learning, models have been successful in various domains, they are often treated as black boxes. While this might not be a problem in other more deterministic domains such as image annotation (where the end user can objectively validate the tags assigned to the images), in health care, not only the quantitative algorithmic performance is important, but also the reason why the algorithms works is relevant. In fact, model interpretability is crucial for convincing medical professionals of the validity of actions recommended by predictive systems. We will develop models using CV, NLP and attention mechanisms which highlight the relevant area in a medical image based on the feature extracted from the radiology reports.

**How to train machine learning models when data is small or classes are imbalanced?**

Obtaining datasets in the medical imaging domain that are as comprehensively annotated as ImageNet remains a challenge. When sufficient data is not available, transfer learning or fine tuning are the ways to proceed. In transfer learning, CNN models pre-trained from natural image dataset or from a different medical domain are used for a new medical task at hand. On the other hand, in fine-tuning, when a medium sized dataset does exist for the task at hand, one suggested scheme is to use a pre-trained CNN as initialisation of the network, following which further supervised training is conducted, of selected network layers, using the new data for the task at hand. In this task, we will explore the effectiveness of transfer learning and fine-tuning in the medical domain.

**How to incorporate the temporal nature of diseases in machine learning models?**

Diseases evolve and change over time in a non-deterministic manner. The existing deep learning models assume static vector-based inputs, which do not take time factor into consideration. In order to understand the temporal nature of healthcare data, we need to develop deep learning models whose parameters gets incrementally updated with time. Considering that the time factor is important in all kinds of healthcare problems, training a time-sensitive machine learning model is critical for a better understanding of the patient condition and providing timely clinical decision support. We will work towards exploring ways of how to incorporate temporal information in the machine learning models to have temporal reasoning. This will help in understanding the progressive nature of diseases and to alert medical staff about the changing conditions of patients at right time.

**How to increase the number of features to improve performance and robustness of CDSS?**

Due to rise of Electronic Health Records (or EHR), hospitals store data in various forms including patient's medical history, demographics, progress notes, medications, vital signs, immunizations, laboratory data, genetics and genomics data, and radiology reports. Combining two or more modalities allows integration of the strengths of individual modalities. We will work towards combining various data sources in healthcare so that better decisions can be made, in turn resulting in achieving the overall goal of precision medicine.

**How to develop bi-directional models for medical indexing and retrieval?**

With the widespread use of EHR and PACS technology in hospitals, the size of medical data is growing rapidly, which in turn demands effective and efficient retrieval systems. Clinical and radiology practices heavily rely on processing stored medical data providing aid in decision making and increasing productivity. Existing medical retrieval systems have limitations in terms of the *semantic gap* (between the low level visual information captured by imaging devices and the high level semantics perceived by humans) (Qayyum et al., 2017). We will develop bi-directional multimodal machine learning models that perform retrieval based on both textual and visual content. The proposed approach can retrieve medical images either based on the textual query as an input or by providing sample query images. In addition, the developed model can also align images and text in large medical data collections.

## 5 Expermental Framework

### 5.1 Datasets

The proposed research work has approval from Macquarie University Human Research Ethics Committee to use medical data from Macquarie University Hospital. We will also use datasets that are publicly available such as ChestX-Ray8, Open-i [4], and ImageCLEF [5] challenge datasets. These datasets comprise of medical images and their accompanied text in the form of disease labels or caption, mined from open source biomedical literature and image collections.

## 5.2 Evaluation Metrics

For medical captioning task, we will use standard image captioning metrics such as BLEU (Papineni et al., 2002), ROUGE (Lin, 2004), METEOR (Banerjee and Lavie, 2005), CIDEr (Vedantam et al., 2015), and SPICE (Anderson et al., 2016). For VQA in the medical domain, we will use *accuracy* for multiple-choice questions, but to measure how much a predicted answer differs from ground truth based on differences in their semantic meaning, *Wu-Palmer Similarity* (Wu and Palmer, 1994) will be used. For the Visual-Dialog task in the medical domain, an algorithm has to return candidate answers for a given medical image, dialog history, question, and a list of candidate answers. We will use two standard retrieval metrics namely, *recall@k* and *mean reciprocal rank* (MRR) (Das et al., 2017a). In the task of medical retrieval system, the evaluation task is to measure how effectively an algorithm is able to produce search results to satisfy the user's query in the form of sample image or complex textual query. For this task, standard information retrieval metrics such as Precision, Recall, and F-score will be used.

## 5.3 Baseline Methods

There are three main approaches to generate image captions: (1) Using templates that rely on detectors and map the output to linguistic structures; (2) Using language models that yield more expressive captions overcoming the limitations of template based approach; and, (3) Caption retrieval and recombination that involves retrieving captions based on training data instead of generating new captions. We will work on CNN-RNN framework and caption retrieval approaches. The model proposed by Hasan et al. (2017) was ranked first in the caption prediction task in the ImageCLEF challenge, which was based on deep learning approach using language models. Apart from this, deep learning methods have demon-

strated successful results in general purpose image captioning, therefore the first baseline method is to incorporate an encoder-decoder based architecture. Specifically, initial image features will be extracted using a CNN model, namely VGG-19, which is pre-trained on the ImageNet dataset and is fine-tuned on the given ImageCLEF training dataset to extract the image features from a lower convolution layer such that the decoder can focus on the salient aspects of the image via an attention mechanism. Second, text features will be extracted and pre-processed. Two reserved words namely *start* and *end* are appended to indicate the start and end of the captions. While training, the output of the last hidden layer of the CNN model (Encoder) is given to the first time step of the LSTM (decoder). We set $x1 = $ start and the desired label, $y1 = $ first word of the caption. Similarly, we set the all the remaining words and finally the last target label $y^T = $ end token. The model will be trained with an adaptive learning rate optimization algorithm, and dropout as a regularization mechanism. The model hyper-parameters are tuned based on the BLEU score on the validation set. Once the model is trained, captions are generated on the test images by predicting one word at every time step based on the context vector, the previous hidden state, and the previously generated words.

## 6 Conclusion

We argue the need for language and vision research in the medical domain by showing its successful applications on general purpose tasks. We identify various research directions in the medical imaging applications that have not been fully explored, and can be solved by combining vision and language processing. This research aims to develop machine learning models that jointly reason over medical images and accompanying clinical text in radiology. The proposed research is fruitful in advancing healthcare by building various clinical decision support systems to augment radiologist's work.

**Acknowledgements** I would like to thank my supervisors, Dr. Sarvnaz Karimi, Dr. Kevin Ho-Shon and Dr. Len Hamey, for their feedback that greatly improved the paper. This research is supported by Macquarie University Research Training Program scholarship. Also thankful to Google for providing travel grant to attend the conference.

---

[4] https://openi.nlm.nih.gov/
[5] http://www.imageclef.org/

## References

Asma Ben Abacha, Alba G. Seco de Herrera, Soumya Gayen, Dina Demner-Fushman, and Sameer Antani. 2017. NLM at ImageCLEF 2017 Caption Task. In *CLEF2017 Working Notes*, CEUR Workshop Proceedings, Dublin, Ireland.

Peter Anderson, Basura Fernando, Mark Johnson, and Stephen Gould. 2016. SPICE: Semantic Propositional Image Caption Evaluation. In *European Conference on Computer Vision*, Amsterdam, The Netherlands.

Satanjeev Banerjee and Alon Lavie. 2005. METEOR: An automatic metric for MT evaluation with improved correlation with human judgments. In *Proceedings of the ACL Workshop on Intrinsic and Extrinsic Evaluation Measures for Machine Translation and/or Summarization*, pages 65–72, Ann Arbor, Michigan, United States.

Avi Ben-Cohen, Idit Diamant, Eyal Klang, Michal Amitai, and Hayit Greenspan. 2016. Fully convolutional network for liver segmentation and lesions detection. In *Deep Learning and Data Labeling for Medical Applications*, pages 77–85, Cham. Springer International Publishing.

Leonard Berlin. 2001. Defending the "missed" radiographic diagnosis. *American Journal of Roentgenology*, 176(2):863–867.

Leonard Berlin and Ronald W. Hendrix. 1998. Perceptual errors and negligence. *American Journal of Roentgenology*, 170(4):863–867.

Adrian P. Brady. 2017. Error and discrepancy in radiology: inevitable or avoidable? *Insights into Imaging*, 8(1):171–182.

Tianrun Cai, Andreas A. Giannopoulos, Sheng Yu, Tatiana Kelil, Beth Ripley, Kanako K. Kumamaru, Frank J. Rybicki, and Dimitrios Mitsouras. 2016. Natural language processing technologies in radiology research and clinical applications. *RadioGraphics*, 36(1):176–191. PMID: 26761536.

David L. Chen and Raymond J. Mooney. 2011. Learning to interpret natural language navigation instructions from observations. In *Proceedings of the 25th AAAI Conference on Artificial Intelligence*, pages 859–865, San Francisco, California.

Kyunghyun Cho, Bart van Merrienboer, Caglar Gulcehre, Dzmitry Bahdanau, Fethi Bougares, Holger Schwenk, and Yoshua Bengio. 2014. Learning phrase representations using RNN encoder–decoder for statistical machine translation. In *Proceedings of the 2014 Conference on Empirical Methods in Natural Language Processing (EMNLP)*, pages 1724–1734, Doha, Qatar.

Ronan Collobert, Jason Weston, Léon Bottou, Michael Karlen, Koray Kavukcuoglu, and Pavel Kuksa. 2011. Natural language processing (almost) from scratch. *Journal of Machine Learning Research*, 12:2493–2537.

Abhishek Das, Satwik Kottur, Khushi Gupta, Avi Singh, Deshraj Yadav, José M.F. Moura, Devi Parikh, and Dhruv Batra. 2017a. Visual Dialog. In *Proceedings of the IEEE Conference on Computer Vision and Pattern Recognition*, pages 1080–1089, Hawaii, United States.

Abhishek Das, Satwik Kottur, José M.F. Moura, Stefan Lee, and Dhruv Batra. 2017b. Learning cooperative visual dialog agents with deep reinforcement learning. In *Proceedings of the IEEE International Conference on Computer Vision*, pages 2970–2979, Venice, Italy.

Chris Dyer, Miguel Ballesteros, Wang Ling, Austin Matthews, and Noah A. Smith. 2015. Transition-based dependency parsing with stack Long Short-Term Memory. In *Proceedings of the 53rd Annual Meeting of the Association for Computational Linguistics and the 7th International Joint Conference on Natural Language Processing (Volume 1: Long Papers)*, pages 334–343, Beijing, China.

Carsten Eickhoff, Immanuel Schwall, Alba Garcia Seco de Herrera, and Henning Müller. 2017. Overview of ImageCLEFcaption 2017 - Image Caption Prediction and Concept Detection for Biomedical Images. In *Working Notes of CLEF 2017 - Conference and Labs of the Evaluation Forum, Dublin, Ireland, September 11-14, 2017*.

Andre Esteva, Brett Kuprel, Roberto A. Novoa, Justin Ko, Susan M. Swetter, Helen M. Blau, and Sebastian Thrun. 2017. Dermatologist-level classification of skin cancer with deep neural networks. *Nature*, 542:115–118.

Michael Felsberg. 2017. Five years after the deep learning revolution in computer vision: State of the art methods for online image and video analysis. *Linkoping: Linkoping University Press*, pages 1–13.

Francis Ferraro, Nasrin Mostafazadeh, Ting-Hao Huang, Lucy Vanderwende, Jacob Devlin, Michel Galley, and Margaret Mitchell. 2015. A survey of current datasets for vision and language research. In *Proceedings of the 2015 Conference on Empirical Methods in Natural Language Processing*, pages 207–213, Lisbon, Portugal.

Jianlong Fu and Yong Rui. 2017. Advances in deep learning approaches for image tagging. *APSIPA Transactions on Signal and Information Processing*, 6:e11.

Ross Girshick, Jeff Donahue, Trevor Darrell, and Jitendra Malik. 2014. Rich feature hierarchies for accurate object detection and semantic segmentation. In *Proceedings of the 2014 IEEE Conference on Computer Vision and Pattern Recognition*, pages 580–587, Washington, DC, United States.

Peter Hall and Paul McKevitt. 1995. Integrating vision processing and natural language processing with a clinical application. In *Proceedings 1995 2nd New Zealand International Two-Stream Conference on Artificial Neural Networks and Expert Systems*, pages 373–376, Dunedin, New Zealand.

Sadid A. Hasan, Yuan Ling, Joey Liu, Rithesh Sreenivasan, Shreya Anand, Tilak Raj Arora, Vivek Datla, Kathy Lee, Ashequl Qadir, Christine Swisher, and Oladimeji Farri. 2017. PRNA at ImageCLEF 2017 Caption Prediction and Concept Detection tasks. In *CLEF2017 Working Notes*, CEUR Workshop Proceedings, Dublin, Ireland.

Kaiming He, Georgia Gkioxari, Piotr Dollr, and Ross Girshick. 2017a. Mask R-CNN. In *2017 IEEE International Conference on Computer Vision*, pages 2980–2988, Venice, Italy.

Kaiming He, Xiangyu Zhang, Shaoqing Ren, and Jian Sun. 2016. Deep residual learning for image recognition. In *2016 IEEE Conference on Computer Vision and Pattern Recognition*, pages 770–778, Nevada, United States.

Luheng He, Kenton Lee, Mike Lewis, and Luke Zettlemoyer. 2017b. Deep semantic role labeling: What works and what's next. In *Proceedings of the 55th Annual Meeting of the Association for Computational Linguistics (Volume 1: Long Papers)*, pages 473–483, Vancouver, Canada.

Sepp Hochreiter and Jürgen Schmidhuber. 1997. Long Short-Term Memory. *Neural Computation*, 9(8):1735–1780.

Bogdan Ionescu, Henning Müller, Mauricio Villegas, Helbert Arenas, Giulia Boato, Duc-Tien Dang-Nguyen, Yashin Dicente Cid, Carsten Eickhoff, Alba G. Seco de Herrera, Cathal Gurrin, Bayzidul Islam, Vassili Kovalev, Vitali Liauchuk, Josiane Mothe, Luca Piras, Michael Riegler, and Immanuel Schwall. 2017. Overview of ImageCLEF 2017: Information extraction from images. In *Experimental IR Meets Multilinguality, Multimodality, and Interaction*, pages 315–337, Cham. Springer International Publishing.

Ranjay Krishna, Yuke Zhu, Oliver Groth, Justin Johnson, Kenji Hata, Joshua Kravitz, Stephanie Chen, Yannis Kalantidis, Li-Jia Li, David A. Shamma, Michael S. Bernstein, and Li Fei-Fei. 2017. Visual genome: Connecting language and vision using crowdsourced dense image annotations. *International Journal of Computer Vision*, 123(1):32–73.

Alex Krizhevsky, Ilya Sutskever, and Geoffrey E. Hinton. 2012. ImageNet classification with deep convolutional neural networks. In *Proceedings of the 25th International Conference on Neural Information Processing Systems - Volume 1*, NIPS'12, pages 1097–1105, USA.

JG Lee, S Jun, YW Cho, H Lee, GB Kim, JB Seo, and N Kim. 2017. Deep learning in medical imaging: General overview. *Korean Journal of Radiology*, 18(4):570–584.

Chin-Yew Lin. 2004. ROUGE: A package for automatic evaluation of summaries. In *42nd Annual Meeting of the Association for Computational Linguistics*, volume Text Summarization Branches Out, pages 1–8, Barcelona, Spain.

Mike Mastanduno. 2017. Survey of deep learning in radiology. [Online; posted 19-January-2017].

Fausto Milletari, Nassir Navab, and Seyed-Ahmad Ahmadi. 2016. V-Net: Fully convolutional neural networks for volumetric medical image segmentation. *CoRR*, abs/1606.04797.

Kishore Papineni, Salim Roukos, Todd Ward, and Wei-Jing Zhu. 2002. BLEU: a method for automatic evaluation of machine translation. In *Proceedings of the 40th Annual Meeting of the Association for Computational Linguistics*, Philadelphia, Pennsylvania, United States.

Adnan Qayyum, Syed Muhammad Anwar, Muhammad Awais, and Muhammad Majid. 2017. Medical image retrieval using deep convolutional neural network. *Neurocomputing*, 266:8 – 20.

Mahmudur Rahman, Terrance Lagree, and Martina Taylor. 2017. A cross-modal concept detection and caption prediction approach in ImageCLEFcaption track of ImageCLEF 2017. In *CLEF2017 Working Notes*, CEUR Workshop Proceedings, Dublin, Ireland.

Pranav Rajpurkar, Jeremy Irvin, Kaylie Zhu, Brandon Yang, Hershel Mehta, Tony Duan, Daisy Ding, Aarti Bagul, Curtis Langlotz, Katie Shpanskaya, Matthew P. Lungren, and Andrew Y. Ng. 2017. CheXNet: Radiologist-level pneumonia detection on chest X-rays with deep learning. *CoRR*, abs/1711.05225.

Olga Russakovsky, Jia Deng, Hao Su, Jonathan Krause, Sanjeev Satheesh, Sean Ma, Zhiheng Huang, Andrej Karpathy, Aditya Khosla, Michael Bernstein, Alexander C. Berg, and Li Fei-Fei. 2015. ImageNet Large Scale Visual Recognition Challenge. *International Journal of Computer Vision*, 115(3):211–252.

Hoo-Chang Shin, Kirk Roberts, Le Lu, Dina Demner-Fushman, Jianhua Yao, and Ronald M. Summers. 2016. Learning to read chest X-rays: Recurrent neural cascade model for automated image annotation. In *2016 IEEE Conference on Computer Vision and Pattern Recognition*, pages 2497–2506.

Karen Simonyan and Andrew Zisserman. 2014. Very deep convolutional networks for large-scale image recognition. *CoRR*, abs/1409.1556.

C. A Sohani. 2013. A difficult challenge for radiology. *The Indian Journal of Radiology and Imaging*, 23(1):110–112.

Suraj Srinivas, Ravi Kiran Sarvadevabhatla, Konda Reddy Mopuri, Nikita Prabhu, Srinivas S. S. Kruthiventi, and R. Venkatesh Babu. 2016. A taxonomy of deep convolutional neural nets for computer vision. *Frontiers in Robotics and AI*, 2:36.

Antol Stanislaw, Agrawal Aishwarya, Lu Jiasen, Mitchell Margaret, Batra Dhruv, Zitnick C. Lawrence, and Parikh Devi. 2015. VQA: Visual Question Answering. In *International Conference on Computer Vision*, pages 2425–2433, Santiago, Chile.

Ilya Sutskever, Oriol Vinyals, and Quoc V. Le. 2014. Sequence to sequence learning with neural networks. In *Proceedings of the 27th International Conference on Neural Information Processing Systems - Volume 2*, NIPS'14, pages 3104–3112, Cambridge, MA, United States.

Christian Szegedy, Wei Liu, Yangqing Jia, Pierre Sermanet, Scott Reed, Dragomir Anguelov, Dumitru Erhan, Vincent Vanhoucke, and Andrew Rabinovich. 2015. Going deeper with convolutions. In *2015 IEEE Conference on Computer Vision and Pattern Recognition*, pages 1–9, Boston, Massachusetts, United States.

Damien Teney, Qi Wu, and Anton van den Hengel. 2017. Visual Question Answering: A tutorial. *IEEE Signal Processing Magazine*, 34(6):63–75.

NIH U.S. NLM. Open-i: An open access biomedical search engine. `https://openi.nlm.nih.gov/`.

Ramakrishna Vedantam, C. Lawrence Zitnick, and Devi Parikh. 2015. CIDEr: Consensus-based image description evaluation. In *2015 IEEE Conference on Computer Vision and Pattern Recognition*, pages 4566–4575, Boston, Massachusetts, United States.

Oriol Vinyals, Lukasz Kaiser, Terry Koo, Slav Petrov, Ilya Sutskever, and Geoffrey Hinton. 2015. Grammar as a foreign language. In *Proceedings of the 28th International Conference on Neural Information Processing Systems - Volume 2*, NIPS'15, pages 2773–2781, Cambridge, MA, United States.

Xiaosong Wang, Yifan Peng, Le Lu, Zhiyong Lu, Mohammadhadi Bagheri, and Ronald M. Summers. 2017. ChestX-Ray8: Hospital-scale chest X-Ray database and benchmarks on weakly-supervised classification and localization of common thorax diseases. In *2017 IEEE Conference on Computer Vision and Pattern Recognition*, pages 3462–3471, Hawaii, United States.

Yonghui Wu, Mike Schuster, Zhifeng Chen, Quoc V. Le, Mohammad Norouzi, Wolfgang Macherey, Maxim Krikun, Yuan Cao, Qin Gao, Klaus Macherey, Jeff Klingner, Apurva Shah, Melvin Johnson, Xiaobing Liu, Lukasz Kaiser, Stephan Gouws, Yoshikiyo Kato, Taku Kudo, Hideto Kazawa, Keith Stevens, George Kurian, Nishant Patil, Wei Wang, Cliff Young, Jason Smith, Jason Riesa, Alex Rudnick, Oriol Vinyals, Greg Corrado, Macduff Hughes, and Jeffrey Dean. 2016. Google's neural machine translation system: Bridging the gap between human and machine translation. *CoRR*, abs/1609.08144.

Zhibiao Wu and Martha Palmer. 1994. Verb semantics and lexical selection. In *32nd Annual Meeting of the Association for Computational Linguistics*, pages 133–138, Las Cruces, New Mexico.

Zizhao Zhang, Pingjun Chen, Manish Sapkota, and Lin Yang. 2017a. TandemNet: Distilling knowledge from medical images using diagnostic reports as optional semantic references. In *Medical Image Computing and Computer-Assisted Intervention MICCAI 2017*, pages 320–328, Quebec City, Quebec, Canada.

Zizhao Zhang, Yuanpu Xie, Fuyong Xing, Mason McGough, and Lin Yang. 2017b. MDNet: A semantically and visually interpretable medical image diagnosis network. In *2017 IEEE Conference on Computer Vision and Pattern Recognition*, pages 3549–3557, Hawaii, United States.

Jie Zhou and Wei Xu. 2015. End-to-end learning of semantic role labeling using recurrent neural networks. In *Proceedings of the 53rd Annual Meeting of the Association for Computational Linguistics and the 7th International Joint Conference on Natural Language Processing (Volume 1: Long Papers)*, pages 1127–1137, Beijing, China.

# Recognizing Complex Entity Mentions: A Review and Future Directions

**Xiang Dai**

CSIRO Data61 and School of IT, University of Sydney
Sydney, Australia
`dai.dai@csiro.au`



## Abstract

Standard named entity recognizers can effectively recognize entity mentions that consist of contiguous tokens and do not overlap with each other. However, in practice, there are many domains, such as the biomedical domain, in which there are nested, overlapping, and discontinuous entity mentions. These complex mentions cannot be directly recognized by conventional sequence tagging models because they may break the assumptions based on which sequence tagging techniques are built. We review the existing methods which are revised to tackle complex entity mentions and categorize them as token-level and sentence-level approaches. We then identify the research gap, and discuss some directions that we are exploring.


## 1 Introduction

Named entity recognition (NER), the task of identifying and classifying named entities (NE) within text, has received substantial attention. This is largely due to its crucial role in conducting several downstream tasks, such as entity linking (Limsopatham and Collier, 2016; Pan et al., 2017), relation extraction (Zeng et al., 2014), question answering (Mollá et al., 2007) and knowledge base construction (Zhang, 2015).

Traditionally, the NER problem can be defined as: given a sequence of tokens, output a list of tuples $< I_s, I_e, t >$, each of which is a NE mention in text. Here, $I_s$ and $I_e$ are the starting and ending index of the NE mention, respectively, and $t$ is the type of the entity from a pre-defined category scheme. There are two assumptions associated with this perspective:

1. An NE mention consists of contiguous tokens, where all the tokens indexed between $I_s$ and $I_e$ are part of the mention; and,

2. These linear spans do not overlap with each other. In other words, no token in the text can belong to more than one NE mention.

Based on these two assumptions, the most common approach to NER is to use sequence tagging techniques with a BIO or BIOLU label set. Each token is assigned with a tag which is usually composed of a position indicator and an entity type. The position indicator is used to represent the token's role in a NE mention. In the BIOLU schema, B stands for the beginning of a mention, I for the intermediate of a mention, O for outside a mention, L for the last token of a mention, and U for a mention having only one token (Ratinov and Roth, 2009).

Sequential tagging models, such as linear-chain CRFs and BiLSTM-CRF, have achieved start-of-the-art effectiveness in many NER data sets (Lample et al., 2016; Ma and Hovy, 2016; Chiu and Nichols, 2016), since most training data sets are also annotated based on these two assumptions.

However, in practice, there are many domains, such as the biomedical domain, which involve nested, overlapping, discontinuous NE mentions that break the two assumptions mentioned above. We categorize these mentions as *complex entity mentions*, and note that standard tagging techniques cannot be applied directly to recognize these mentions (Muis and Lu, 2016; Dai et al., 2017). In the following paragraphs, we explain these complex entity mentions in details.

**Nested NE mentions** One NE mention is completely contained by the other. We call both of the mentions involved as nested entity mentions. Figure 1a is an example taken from the GENIA cor-




*Proceedings of ACL 2018, Student Research Workshop*, pages 37–44
Melbourne, Australia, July 15 - 20, 2018. ©2018 Association for Computational Linguistics

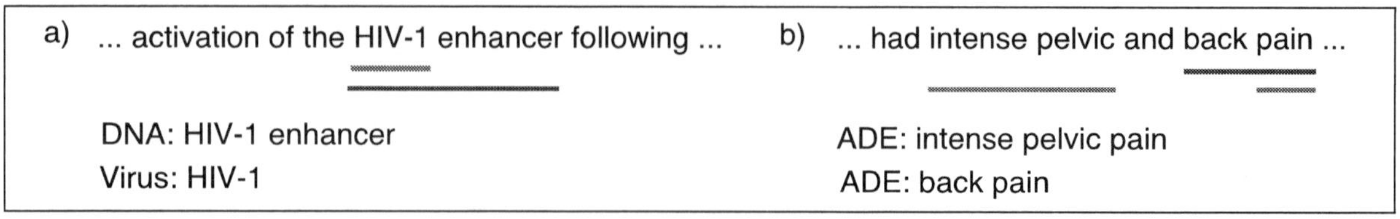

a) ... activation of the HIV-1 enhancer following ...   b) ... had intense pelvic and back pain ...

DNA: HIV-1 enhancer                                    ADE: intense pelvic pain
Virus: HIV-1                                           ADE: back pain

Figure 1: Examples involving overlapping, discontinuous and nested NE mentions. In (a), '*HIV-1 enhancer*' and '*HIV-1*' are nested NE mentions. In (b), '*intense pelvic pain*' and '*back pain*' overlap, meanwhile, '*intense pelvic pain*' is a discontinuous mention.

pus (Kim et al., 2003). Here, '*HIV-1 enhancer*' is a DNA mention, and it contains another mention '*HIV-1*', which is a virus.

**Multi-type NE mentions** An extreme case of nested NE mentions is one on which an NE mention has multiple entity types. For example, in the EPPI corpus (Alex et al., 2007), proteins can also be annotated as drug/compound, indicating that the protein is used as a drug to affect the function of a cell. Such a mention should be classified as both protein and drug/compound. In this case, we consider this mention as two mentions of different types, and these two mentions contain each other.

**Overlapping NE mentions** Two NE mentions overlap, but no one is completely contained by the other. Figure 1b is an example taken from the CADEC corpus (Karimi et al., 2015), which is annotated for adverse drug events (ADE) and relevant concepts. In this example, two ADEs: '*intense pelvic pain*' and '*back pain*', share a common token '*pain*', and neither is contained by the other.

**Discontinuous NE mentions** The mention consists of discontiguous tokens. In other words, the mention contains at least one gap. In Figure 1b, '*intense pelvic pain*' is a discontinuous NE mention since it is interrupted by '*and back*'.

These complex NE mentions can hold very useful information for downstream tasks. Sometimes, the nested and overlapping structure itself are already good indicators of the relationship between different entities involved. For example, an ORG mention '*University of Sydney*' contains a LOC mention '*Sydney*'. This structure has implied the location of the organization, and recognition of these mentions can potentially speed up the construction of a knowledge base. In addition, such entities often have fixed representations

in different languages. Therefore, recognizing NE mentions, especially these discontinuous NE mentions, can improve the performance of a machine translation system (Klementiev and Roth, 2006). Furthermore, we notice that similar complex structures also exist in other NLP tasks, such as multi-word expressions recognition (Baldwin and Kim, 2010). The ideas proposed for a NER task can thus be applied to tackle similar difficulties in other tasks.

Below, we briefly review existing methods to recognize complex mentions and discuss their strengths and limitations. We also discuss the research directions we are exploring to address the research gaps.

## 2 Token-level Approach

Sequence tagging techniques take the representation of each token as input and output a label for each token. These local decisions are chained together to perform joint inference. Figure 2 is an illustration of a linear-chain CRF model where the tag of one token depends on both the features of that token in context and the tag of the previous token. The tag sequence predicted by the tagger is finally decoded into NE mentions using explicit rules. Here, the intermediate outputs for each token are usually BIO tags in standard NER tasks. However, since the BIO tags cannot effectively represent complex NE mentions, a natural direction is to expand the BIO tag set so that different kinds of complex entity mentions can be captured. We categorize the methods based on conventional sequence tagging as token-level approach.

Metke-Jimenez and Karimi (2015) introduced a BIO variant schema to represent discontinuous and overlapping NE mentions. Concretely, in addition to the BIO tags, four new position indicators, BD, ID, BH, and IH are proposed to denote **B**eginning of **D**iscontinuous body, **I**nside

38

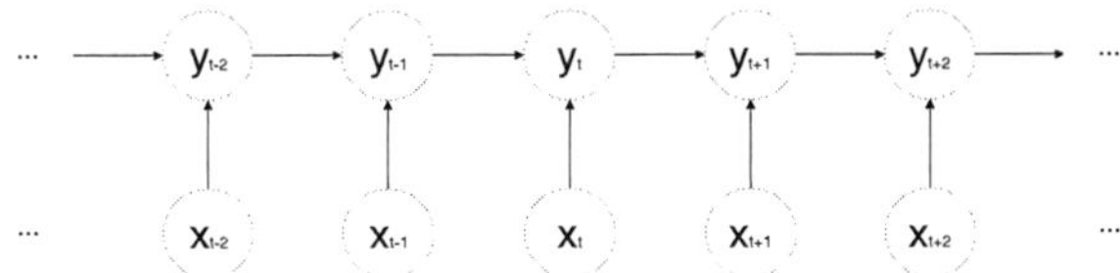

Figure 2: In a linear-chain CRF model, the output for each token depends on the features of that token in context and the output for the previous token.

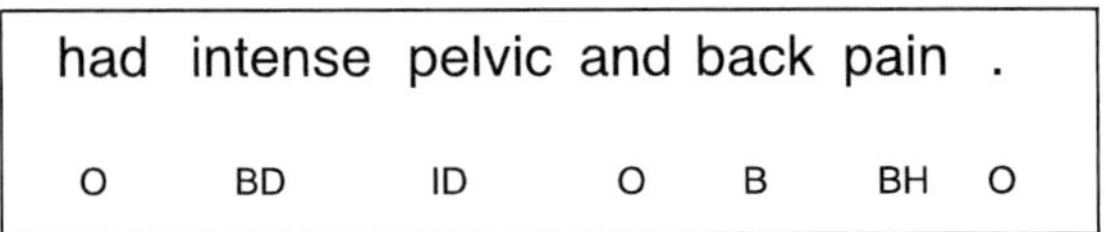


Figure 3: An encoding example of two NE mentions: 'intense pelvic pain' and 'back pain'. Here, we keep only the position indicator and remove the entity type, since this schema can only represent overlapping mentions of the same entity type.

of **D**iscontinuous body, **B**eginning of **H**ead, and **I**nside of **H**ead. Here, the word sequences which are shared by multiple mentions are called head, and the remaining parts of the discontinuous mention are called body. Figure 3 is an encoding example using this schema. 'pain' is the beginning of the head that is shared by two mentions, and therefore tagged as *BH*. 'intense pelvic' is the body of a discontinuous mention, while 'back' is the beginning of a continuous mention. We note that, even in this simple example, it is still impossible to represent several discontinuous mentions unambiguously. For example, this encoding can also be decoded as having three mentions: 'intense pelvic pain', 'back pain' and 'pain'. Muis and Lu (2016) introduced the notion of *model ambiguity* and theoretically demonstrated that the models based on BIO variants usually have high ambiguity level, and therefore low precision in practice. Another limitation of this schema is that it supports only overlapping mentions of the same entity type.

Schneider et al. (2014) also proposed several BIO schema variants to encode multiword expressions with gaps and nested structure. They include two strict restrictions which are motivated linguistically in their work:

1. An expression can be completely contained within another expression, but no overlapping is allowed; and,

2. A contained expression cannot contain other expressions. In other words, the nested structure has maximum two levels.

We note that these strict restrictions cannot be applied directly on our NER tasks.

Alex et al. (2007) proposed three approaches based on a maximum entropy model (Curran and Clark, 2003) to deal with nested NE mentions:

**Layering** The tagger first identifies the innermost (or outermost) mentions, then the following taggers are used to identify increasingly next level mentions. Finally, the output of the taggers on different layers is combined by taking the union.

**Joined labeling** Each word is assigned a tag by concatenating the tags of all levels of nesting. Then a tagger is trained on the data containing the joined labels. During inference, the joined labels are decoded into their original BIO format for each entity type.

**Cascade** Separate models are trained for each entity type or by grouping several entity types without nested structures. Similar to the layering approach, the latter models can utilize the outputs from previous models as input features. Despite the difficulty of ordering and grouping entity models and the fact that this approach cannot deal with nested mentions of the same entity type, the cascade approach still achieves the best results among these three approaches.

Byrne (2007) and Xu et al. (2017) used a similar approach to deal with nested NE mentions. They concatenated adjacent tokens (up to a certain length) into potential mention spans. Then these spans, together with their left and right contexts, are fed into a classifier (a maximum entropy tagger in (Byrne, 2007) and a feedforward neural network in (Xu et al., 2017)). The classifier is trained to first predict whether the span is a valid NE mention, and then its entity type if it is a NE mention.

## 3 Sentence-level Approach

Instead of predicting whether a specific token or several tokens belong to a NE mention and its role in the mention, some methods predict directly a combination of NE mentions within a sentence. We categorize these methods as sentence-level approach.

Bill and Hilary Clinton traveled to Canada .

| P | O | O | P | O | O | O | O |
|---|---|---|---|---|---|---|---|
| O | O | P | P | O | O | O | O |
| O | O | O | O | O | O | L | O |

Figure 4: An example of sentence with three NE mentions. P(ER) and L(OC) refer to the entity types.

McDonald et al. (2005) proposed a new perspective of NER as structured multi-label classification. Instead of starting index and ending index, they represent each NE mention using the set of token positions that belong to the mention. Figure 4 is an example of this representation, with each token tagged using an I/O schema. This representation is very flexible as it allows NE mentions consisting of discontiguous tokens and does not require mentions to exclude each other. Using this representation, the NER problem is converted into the multi-label classification problem of finding up to $k$ correct labels among all possible labels, where $k$ is a hyper-parameter of the model. Labels can be decoded to all possible NE mentions in the sentence. They do not come from a pre-defined category but depend on the sentence being processed. McDonald et al. (2005) used large-margin online learning algorithms to train the model, so that the scores of correct labels (NE mentions) are higher than those of all other possible incorrect mentions. Another advantage of this method is that the outputs of the model are unambiguous for all kinds of complex entity mentions and easy to be decoded, although the method suffers from a $O(n^3T)$ inference algorithm, where $n$ is the length of the sentence and $T$ is the number of entity types.

Finkel and Manning (2009) used a discriminative constituency parser to recognize nested NE mentions. They represent each sentence as a constituency tree, where each mention corresponds to a phrase in the tree. In addition, each node needs to be annotated with its parent and grandparent labels, so that the CRF-CFG parser can learn how NE mentions nest. Ringland (2016) also explored a joint model using the Berkeley parser (Petrov et al., 2006), and showed that it performed well even without specialized NER features. However, one disadvantage of their models, as in (McDonald et al., 2005), is that their time complexity is cubic in the number of tokens in the sentence. Furthermore, the high quality parse training data, which

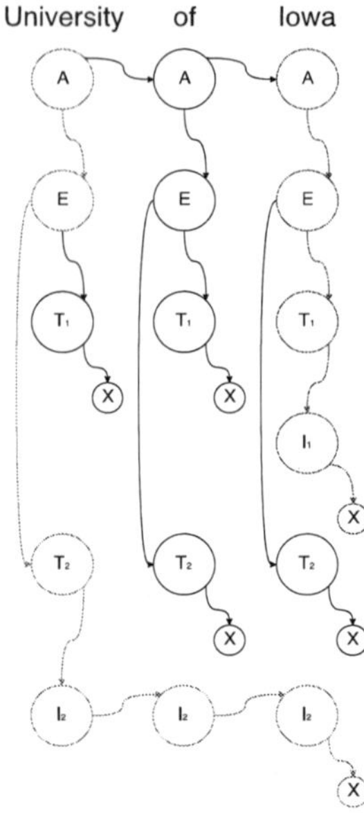



Figure 5: An example sub-hypergraph with two nested NE mentions: '*University of Iowa*' (ORG) and '*Iowa*' (LOC). Here, one mention corresponds to a path consisting of (AETI+X) nodes. Note that this hypergraph cannot be used to represent discontinuous mentions, but, in (Muis and Lu, 2016), they expand the hypergraph representation to capture discontinuous mentions through two new node types: B for within the mention, and O for part of the gap.

is not always available, plays a crucial role in the success of the joint model (Li et al., 2017).

Lu and Roth (2015), extended by Muis and Lu (2016), proposed a novel hypergraph to compactly represent exponentially many possible nested mentions in one sentence, and one sub-hypergraph of the complete hypergraph can therefore be used to represent a combination of mentions in the sentence. Figure 5 is an example of such a sub-hypergraph, which represents two nested NE mentions.

The training objectives of these models are to maximize the log-likelihood of training instances consisting of the sentence and mention-encoded hypergraph. During inference, the model will first predict a sub-hypergraph among all possible sub-hypergraph of the complete hypergraph, and predicted mentions can be decoded from the output sub-hypergraph.

This hypergraph representation still suffers from some degree of ambiguity during decoding stage. For example, when one mention is contained by another mention with the same entity type and their boundaries are all different, the hypergraph can be decoded in different ways. This ambiguity comes from the fact that, if one node has multiple parent nodes and multiple child nodes, there is no mechanism to decide which of the parent node is paired with which child node.

## 4 Research Plan

We note that the drawbacks of existing methods can be broadly categorized into: (1) lack of expressivity; and (2) computational complexity. Most of token-level approaches were proposed for some specific scenarios or data sets, therefore usually with strict restrictions. For example, the BIO variant schema in (Schneider et al., 2014) was designed for nested structure with maximum depth of two. Therefore, it is difficult to be applied on GENIA corpus (Kim et al., 2003), which contains nested entities up to four layers of embedding. In addition, these token-level methods are usually devised to deal with only either nested or discontinuous mentions, and seldom can be used to tackle all kinds of complex entity mentions simultaneously.

In contrast, sentence-level approaches are overall more flexible and less ambiguous, however with higher computational cost. For example, both Finkel and Manning (2009) and McDonald et al. (2005) methods suffer from a high time complexity which is cubic in the number of tokens in the sentence. Our aim is to propose a model that recognizes all kinds of complex entity mentions, with low ambiguity level and low computational complexity. Some specific directions include:

- The representation in (McDonald et al., 2005), introduced in Section 3, is most flexible and straightforward among all schemes designed for representing complex entity mentions. It can be used to represent all nested, overlapping and discontinuous entity mentions with unbounded length and depth. We are exploring recent advances in *multi-label classification* methods (Xu et al., 2016; Shi et al., 2017) to reduce the computational complexity of this approach.

- Sequence-to-sequence models (Sutskever et al., 2014; Cho et al., 2014) had achieved great success in machine translation and text generation tasks, especially after enhanced by attention mechanisms (Luong et al., 2015). We are exploring extending the encoder-decoder architecture to recognize complex entity mentions. During inference stage, instead of one tag sequence capturing all mentions in the sentence, the decoder can produce multiple sequences, each of which corresponds to one possible mention combination, analogous to several possible target sentences in machine translation tasks.

- Supervised learning NER methods are affected by the quantity and quality of the available annotated corpora. However, since annotating mentions with complex structure requires more human efforts than annotating only the outermost or longest continuous spans, training data for complex entity mention recognition is rare. Furthermore, the medical domain is where complex mentions widely exist, such as disorder mentions and adverse drug events. The cost of producing gold standard corpus in such a domain is very high, due to the expertise required and the limited access to some medical text, such as electronic health records.

  *Active learning* aims to reduce the cost of constructing a labeled dataset by allowing a human-in-the-loop (Settles and Craven, 2008; Stanovsky et al., 2017). The model selects one or several most informative instances and presents these instances to the annotators. Since only these most informative instances need to be manually annotated by human experts, it can reduce the need for human effort and therefore the cost of constructing large labeled dataset. We are exploring this method to relieve the pain of lacking training data.

- Finally, we are going to utilize recent advances in NER domain to improve the effectiveness of complex entity mentions recognizers, such as character-level embedding (Kuru et al., 2016) and joint models (Luo et al., 2015).

Besides employing active learning to create specific data set with nested, overlapping, discontinuous entity mentions, we notice that there are some off-the-shelf corpora in biomedical domain that we can use to evaluate our proposed methods, although, to our knowledge, none of these data sets contains all three kinds of complex mentions, e.g., GENIA (Kim et al., 2003) only contains nested entity mentions, and CADEC (Karimi et al., 2015) and SemEval2014 (Pradhan et al., 2014) contain overlapping and discontinuous mentions. In addition, ACE [1] and NNE (Ringland, 2016) are newswire corpora with nested entity mentions.

On these data sets, we will use standard evaluation metrics for NER tasks, namely micro-average precision, recall and f1-score, to evaluate the effectiveness of proposed methods in recognizing both complex and simple mentions. However, due to the complexity of complex NE mentions, we will include different boundary matching relaxation, such as partial match and approximate match (Tsai et al., 2006), to measure the proposed methods in identifying these complex mentions.

## 5 Summary

We reviewed the existing methods of recognizing nested, overlapping and discontinuous entity mentions, categorizing them as token-level and sentence-level approaches, and discussed their strengths and limitations. We also identified the research gap and introduce some directions we are exploring.

**Acknowledgments** The author thanks Sarvnaz Karimi, Ben Hachey, Cecile Paris and Data61's Language and Social Computing team for their support and helpful discussions. The author also thanks three anonymous reviewers for their insightful comments.

## References

Beatrice Alex, Barry Haddow, and Claire Grover. 2007. Recognising nested named entities in biomedical text. In *ACL Workshop on Biological, Translational, and Clinical Language Processing*, pages 65–72, Prague, Czech Republic.

Timothy Baldwin and Su Nam Kim. 2010. Multiword expressions. In *Handbook of Natural Language Processing*, pages 267–292.

Kate Byrne. 2007. Nested named entity recognition in historical archive text. In *International Conference on Semantic Computing*, pages 589–596, Irvine, California.

Jason Chiu and Eric Nichols. 2016. Named entity recognition with bidirectional lstm-cnns. *Transactions of the Association for Computational Linguistics*, 4:357–370.

Kyunghyun Cho, Bart van Merrienboer, Caglar Gulcehre, Dzmitry Bahdanau, Fethi Bougares, Holger Schwenk, and Yoshua Bengio. 2014. Learning phrase representations using rnn encoder–decoder for statistical machine translation. In *Conference on Empirical Methods in Natural Language Processing*, pages 1724–1734, Doha, Qatar.

James Curran and Stephen Clark. 2003. Language independent ner using a maximum entropy tagger. In *Conference on Natural Language Learning*, pages 164–167.

Xiang Dai, Sarvnaz Karimi, and Cecile Paris. 2017. Medication and adverse event extraction from noisy text. In *Australasian Language Technology Workshop*, pages 79–87, Brisbane, Australia.

Jenny Rose Finkel and Christopher D. Manning. 2009. Nested named entity recognition. In *Conference on Empirical Methods in Natural Language Processing*, pages 141–150, Suntec, Singapore.

Sarvnaz Karimi, Alejandro Metke-Jimenez, Madonna Kemp, and Chen Wang. 2015. CADEC: A corpus of adverse drug event annotations. *Journal of Biomedical Informatics*, 55:73–81.

J-D Kim, Tomoko Ohta, Yuka Tateisi, and Junichi Tsujii. 2003. Genia corpusa semantically annotated corpus for bio-textmining. *Bioinformatics*, 19(suppl_1):i180i182.

Alexandre Klementiev and Dan Roth. 2006. Weakly supervised named entity transliteration and discovery from multilingual comparable corpora. In *International Conference on Computational Linguistics and Annual Meeting of the Association for Computational Linguistics*, pages 817–824, Sydney, Australia.

Onur Kuru, Ozan Arkan Can, and Deniz Yuret. 2016. Charner: Character-level named entity recognition. In *International Conference on Computational Linguistics*, pages 911–921, Osaka, Japan.

Guillaume Lample, Miguel Ballesteros, Sandeep Subramanian, Kazuya Kawakami, and Chris Dyer. 2016. Neural architectures for named entity recognition. In *Annual Conference of the North American Chapter of the Association for Computational Linguistics: Human Language Technologies*, pages 260–270, San Diego, California.

Peng-Hsuan Li, Ruo-Ping Dong, Yu-Siang Wang, Ju-Chieh Chou, and Wei-Yun Ma. 2017. Leveraging linguistic structures for named entity recognition with bidirectional recursive neural networks. In *Conference on Empirical Methods in Natural Language Processing*, pages 2654–2659, Copenhagen, Denmark.

---

[1] https://www.ldc.upenn.edu/collaborations/past-projects/ace

Nut Limsopatham and Nigel Collier. 2016. Normalising medical concepts in social media texts by learning semantic representation. In *Annual Meeting of the Association for Computational Linguistics*, pages 1014–1023, Berlin, Germany.

Wei Lu and Dan Roth. 2015. Joint mention extraction and classification with mention hypergraphs. In *Conference on Empirical Methods in Natural Language Processing*, pages 857–867, Lisbon, Portugal.

Gang Luo, Xiaojiang Huang, Chin-Yew Lin, and Zaiqing Nie. 2015. Joint entity recognition and disambiguation. In *Conference on Empirical Methods in Natural Language Processing*, pages 879–888, Lisbon, Portugal.

Minh-Thang Luong, Hieu Pham, and Christopher D Manning. 2015. Effective approaches to attention-based neural machine translation. In *Conference on Empirical Methods in Natural Language Processing*, pages 1412–1421, Lisbon, Portugal.

Xuezhe Ma and Eduard Hovy. 2016. End-to-end sequence labeling via bi-directional lstm-cnns-crf. In *Annual Meeting of the Association for Computational Linguistics*, pages 1064–1074, Berlin, Germany.

Ryan McDonald, Koby Crammer, and Fernando Pereira. 2005. Flexible text segmentation with structured multilabel classification. In *Human Language Technology Conference and Conference on Empirical Methods in Natural Language Processing*, pages 987–994, Vancouver, Canada.

Alejandro Metke-Jimenez and Sarvnaz Karimi. 2015. Concept extraction to identify adverse drug reactions in medical forums: A comparison of algorithms. *CoRR abs/1504.06936*.

Diego Mollá, Menno Zaanen, and Steve Cassidy. 2007. Named entity recognition in question answering of speech data. In *Australasian Language Technology Workshop*, pages 57–65, Melbourne, Australia.

Aldrian Obaja Muis and Wei Lu. 2016. Learning to recognize discontiguous entities. In *Conference on Empirical Methods in Natural Language Processing*, pages 75–84, Austin, Texas.

Xiaoman Pan, Boliang Zhang, Jonathan May, Joel Nothman, Kevin Knight, and Heng Ji. 2017. Cross-lingual name tagging and linking for 282 languages. In *Annual Meeting of the Association for Computational Linguistics*, pages 1946–1958, Vancouver, Canada.

Slav Petrov, Leon Barrett, Romain Thibaux, and Dan Klein. 2006. Learning accurate, compact, and interpretable tree annotation. In *International Conference on Computational Linguistics and Annual Meeting of the Association for Computational Linguistics*, pages 433–440, Sydney, Australia.

Sameer Pradhan, Noémie Elhadad, Wendy Chapman, Suresh Manandhar, and Guergana Savova. 2014. Semeval-2014 task 7: Analysis of clinical text. In *International Workshop on Semantic Evaluation*, pages 54–62, Dublin, Ireland.

Lev Ratinov and Dan Roth. 2009. Design challenges and misconceptions in named entity recognition. In *Conference on Natural Language Learning*, pages 147–155, Boulder, Colorado.

Nicky Ringland. 2016. *Structured Named Entities*. Ph.D. thesis, University of Sydney.

Nathan Schneider, Emily Danchik, Chris Dyer, and Noah A Smith. 2014. Discriminative lexical semantic segmentation with gaps: Running the mwe gamut. *Transactions of the Association for Computational Linguistics*, 2:193–206.

Burr Settles and Mark Craven. 2008. An analysis of active learning strategies for sequence labeling tasks. In *Conference on Empirical Methods in Natural Language Processing*, pages 1070–1079, Honolulu, Hawaii.

Haoran Shi, Pengtao Xie, Zhiting Hu, Ming Zhang, and Eric P. Xing. 2017. Towards automated icd coding using deep learning. *CoRR abs/1711.04075*.

Gabriel Stanovsky, Daniel Gruhl, and Pablo N Mendes. 2017. Recognizing mentions of adverse drug reaction in social media using knowledge-infused recurrent models. In *Conference of the European Chapter of the Association for Computational Linguistics*, pages 142–151, Valencia, Spain.

Ilya Sutskever, Oriol Vinyals, and Quoc V Le. 2014. Sequence to sequence learning with neural networks. In *Conference on Neural Information Processing Systems*, pages 3104–3112, Montreal, Canada.

Richard Tzong-Han Tsai, Shih-Hung Wu, Wen-Chi Chou, Yu-Chun Lin, Ding He, Jieh Hsiang, Ting-Yi Sung, and Wen-Lian Hsu. 2006. Various criteria in the evaluation of biomedical named entity recognition. *BMC Bioinformatics*, 7(1):92.

Chang Xu, Dacheng Tao, and Chao Xu. 2016. Robust extreme multi-label learning. In *Conference on Knowledge Discovery and Data Mining*, pages 1275–1284, San Francisco, California.

Mingbin Xu, Hui Jiang, and Sedtawut Watcharawittayakul. 2017. A local detection approach for named entity recognition and mention detection. In *Annual Meeting of the Association for Computational Linguistics*, pages 1237–1247, Vancouver, Canada.

Daojian Zeng, Kang Liu, Siwei Lai, Guangyou Zhou, and Jun Zhao. 2014. Relation classification via convolutional deep neural network. In *International Conference on Computational Linguistics*, pages 2335–2344, Dublin, Ireland.

Ce Zhang. 2015. *DeepDive: A Data Management System for Automatic Knowledge Base Construction.* Ph.D. thesis, University of Wisconsin Madison.

# Automatic Detection of Cross-Disciplinary Knowledge Associations

**Menasha Thilakaratne, Katrina Falkner, Thushari Atapattu**
School of Computer Science
University of Adelaide
Adelaide, Australia
`{firstname.lastname}@adelaide.edu.au`

## Abstract

Detecting interesting, cross-disciplinary knowledge associations hidden in scientific publications can greatly assist scientists to formulate and validate scientifically sensible novel research hypotheses. This will also introduce new areas of research that can be successfully linked with their research discipline. Currently, this process is mostly performed manually by exploring the scientific publications, requiring a substantial amount of time and effort. Due to the exponential growth of scientific literature, it has become almost impossible for a scientist to keep track of all research advances. As a result, scientists tend to deal with fragments of the literature according to their specialisation. Consequently, important and hidden associations among these fragmented knowledge that can be linked to produce significant scientific discoveries remain unnoticed. This doctoral work aims to develop a novel knowledge discovery approach that suggests most promising research pathways by analysing the existing scientific literature.

## 1 Problem Statement

Formulation of scientifically sensible novel research hypotheses requires a comprehensive analysis of the existing literature. However, the voluminous nature of literature (Cheadle et al., 2016) makes the hypothesis generation process extremely difficult and time-consuming even in the narrow specialisation of a scientist. In this regard, *Literature-Based Discovery (LBD)* research is highly beneficial as it aims to detect non-trivial implicit associations by analysing a massive number of documents that have the potential to generate novel research hypotheses (Ganiz et al., 2005). Moreover, LBD outcomes encourage the progress of cross-disciplinary research by suggesting promising cross domain research pathways, which are typically unnoticed during manual analysis (Sebastian et al., 2017b).

Independent of the domain, LBD is highly valuable to accelerate knowledge acquisition and research development process. However, the existing LBD approaches are mostly limited to *medical domain* that attempt to find associations among *genes*, *proteins*, *drugs*, and *diseases*. The main reason for this can be the highly specific and descriptive nature of medical literature that is suitable for LBD research (Ittipanuvat et al., 2014). The application of LBD process in domains such as *Computer Science (CS)* is challenging due to the rapidly evolving nature of terms in the content of research publications. The medical related LBD approaches are strongly coupled with the medical domain knowledge by utilising resources such as Unified Medical Language System (UMLS), MetaMap, and Medical Subject Headings (MeSH) descriptors (Sebastian et al., 2017a). This makes the applicability of these approaches to other domains challenging.

LBD research outside of medical domain is still in an immature state. There are only a few LBD studies performed outside of medical domain (e.g., *Water Purification* (Kostoff et al., 2008), *Technology & Social Issues* (Ittipanuvat et al., 2014), *Humanities* (Cory, 1997)). To date, a work by Gordon and Lindsay (2002) is the only available CS-related LBD research. Hence, in this doctoral research, we attempt to contribute to LBD discipline outside of medical domain by automating cross-disciplinary knowledge discovery process. As a proof of concept, the proposed solution will be applied to different CS-related concepts.



*Proceedings of ACL 2018, Student Research Workshop*, pages 45–51
Melbourne, Australia, July 15 - 20, 2018. ©2018 Association for Computational Linguistics

# 2 LBD Discovery Models

Most of the LBD literature are based on the fundamental premise introduced by Swanson namely, *ABC Model* (Swanson, 1986). It employs a simple syllogism to identify the potential knowledge associations. i.e. given two concepts A and C in two disjoint scientific literature, if A is associated with concept B, and the same concept B is associated with C, the model deduces that A is associated with C. Swanson demonstrated how these combined knowledge pairs contribute to reach solutions by manually making several medical discoveries (e.g., *Raynaud's disease* ↔ *Fish Oil* (Swanson, 1986) and *Migraine* ↔ *Magnesium* (Swanson, 1988)). These medical discoveries are the basis of the LBD discipline.

The ABC model has two variants named as *open* and *closed* discovery models (Figure 1) (Henry and McInnes, 2017). Open discovery starts with an initial user-defined concept (e.g., *Learning Analytics (LA)*) where the LBD process automatically analyses the literature related to the initial concept to detect the potential interesting and implicit associations. This model is generally used when there is a single problem (A-concept) with limited knowledge on what concepts can be involved (B and C concepts). This model greatly assists in *hypothesis generation* process. On the contrary, closed discovery process requires two user-defined concepts (e.g., *LA* and *Deep Learning*) as the input to output potential hidden associations (B-concepts) between these specified two concepts A and C. This model is generally used for *hypotheses testing and validation*. However, the derived associations of the model can also be considered to generate more granular hypotheses. The granularity of the user-defined concepts of the two discovery models can vary depending on the researcher's interest (Ganiz et al., 2005).

# 3 Related Work

Even though the early work in LBD was performed manually, over the time, different computational techniques were adopted to automate the LBD process. Most of the existing LBD research are semi-automated and requires a human expert to make decisions during the LBD process (Sebastian et al., 2017a).

Much of the early computational approaches utilise lexical statistics (Swanson and Smalheiser, 1997) such as term frequency-inverse document

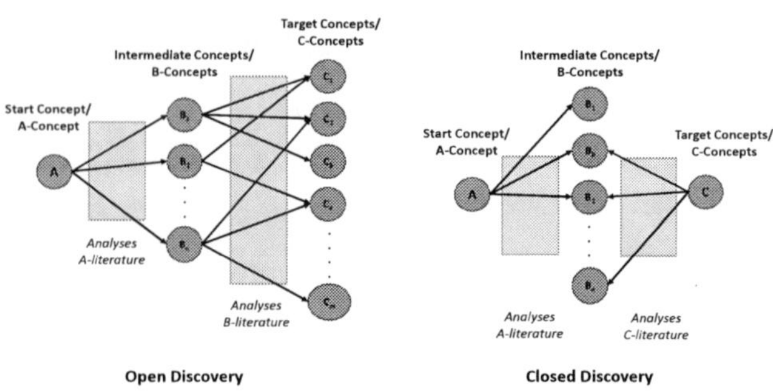


Figure 1: Open and closed discovery models.

frequency, token frequencies, which can be considered as the most primitive LBD approach. Later, Distributional Semantics approaches (Gordon and Dumais, 1998) such as Latent Semantic Indexing, Reflective Random Indexing were introduced. Subsequently, knowledge-based approaches (Weeber et al., 2001) were adopted in the LBD process that heavily rely on the existence of external structured knowledge-based resources to acquire domain-specific knowledge.

Relations-based approaches (Hristovski et al., 2006) make use of user-defined explicit predicates to convey the meaning of the associations. However, these approaches are restricted to problems where semantic types and predicates are known in advance. Another category is Graph-based approaches (Cameron et al., 2015) that generate a number of bridging terms to define the associations. Bibliometrics-based approaches (Kostoff, 2014) utilise bibliographic link structures in the LBD process to identify potential knowledge associations. Several attempts have been taken in LBD literature to employ link prediction techniques (Sebastian et al., 2015). i.e. attributes of the concepts and observed links are used to predict the existence of new links between the concepts.

As discussed earlier, majority of the LBD research are in medical domain and dependent on medical domain knowledge. As a result, it is not feasible to apply these approaches to other domains. To date, there are only a handful of LBD research studies performed outside of the medical domain. This points out the importance of contributing to non-medical LBD research which is still in an early stage.

# 4 Goals and Research Questions

Development of an automatic LBD system can significantly improve the typical research process

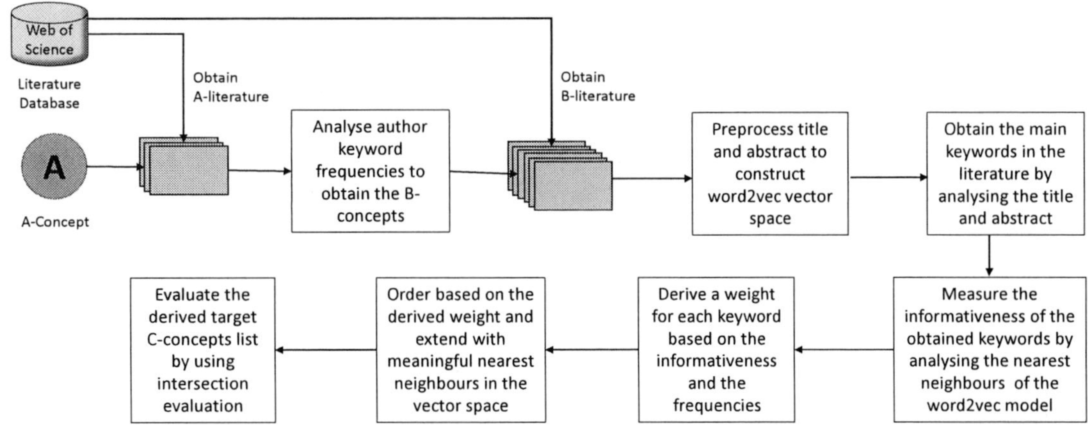


Figure 2: High-level overview of the proposed open discovery model.

followed by the scientists. With such system, scientists can generate scientifically sensible research hypotheses in a shorter time by considering the suggestions provided by the system. Moreover, the cross-domain knowledge discovery process of LBD facilitates the development of cross disciplinary research. Thus, in this study we are aiming to develop a novel knowledge discovery approach by utilising both the variants of LBD process namely, *open* and *closed* discovery.

Our main intention is to uplift the LBD process in non-medical domains. The ultimate goals of this doctoral research are; 1) Fully automate the LBD process: Most of the existing LBD approaches are semi-automatic and require human decisions to direct the knowledge discovery process at various stages. Thus, automating the entire LBD process will be highly beneficial for the users of the LBD model. 2) Provide a generic LBD solution that is independent of domain specific knowledge: Most of the existing LBD approaches rely on domain-specific knowledge to identify the knowledge associations. As a result, the applicability of these approaches to other domains are limited. Therefore, it is important to generate a LBD model that is suitable for any domain, without incorporating any domain specific knowledge.

While focusing on technical literature, in particular, CS domain, the research questions of this study are; 1) How to leverage NLP and Machine Learning techniques to enhance the understanding of content in the literature to accurately detect research areas with different levels of granularity? 2) How bibliometrics analysis can be integrated to enhance identification of implicit knowledge associations? 3) What are the scoring schemes that can be used to rank the identified associations? 4) How to improve the existing evaluation approaches to accurately validate the LBD outcomes? This doctoral work plans to answer these research questions to fulfill the aforementioned goals.

## 5 Current Work and Future Directions

We have conducted a comprehensive literature analysis and have defined our research questions based on the gaps identified in the literature. Currently, we are carrying out preliminary studies to identify potential techniques that would be useful to enhance the predictability of the open discovery LBD model. Figure 2 depicts the high-level overview of our methodology that addresses research questions 1 and 3. The proposed LBD approach is based on Swanson's ABC discovery model. In this approach we are attempting to identify the importance of *neural word embeddings* (Mikolov et al., 2013b) to accurately capture the context of the main keywords of the abstracts. As for the literature database, we are using *Web of Science Core Collection (WoS)*[1] to obtain the meta data of the literature such as title, abstract, and author keywords.

As shown in Figure 2, initially the frequencies of the author keywords were analysed to obtain the B-literature. The retrieved title and abstract in B-literature were cleaned using several carefully picked preprocessing techniques. In summary, the potential abbreviations in the text are identified by using multiple regex patterns. Afterwards, variable length n-grams in the text were

---

[1] https://clarivate.com/products/web-of-science/

identified by using a formula based on collocation patterns described in Mikolov et al. (2013a). We also removed numbers, punctuation marks and terms constituent of single letters before analysing the texts.

After the preprocessing phase, we identified the sentence in the abstract that describes the intention/purpose of the study by using multiple intention-based word patterns. We further processed the identified purpose sentence along with the title by removing stop words. The intention of using the purpose sentence and title is that they typically include the most important concepts that best describe the study.

For each post-processed n-grams ($w_i$) of the purpose sentence and title, we calculated a semantic importance (*informativeness*) score based on *word2vec* (Mikolov et al., 2013b) word embedding method. In other words, we measured the informativeness of $w_i$ based on the validity and semantic richness of $N$ neighbouring terms derived using *cosine similarity*. To measure the validity and semantic richness of $N$ neighbouring terms, we imposed the following three criterions for the three categories of the neighbouring terms; unigrams, abbreviations and n-grams respectively. 1) valid technical unigram 2) valid detected abbreviation 3) valid n-gram by eliminating partial n-grams with different Part of Speech (POS) tag patterns. If the neighbouring term ($n_i$) fulfills the relevant criteria based on its category, it will be considered as a *valid, quality neighbouring term* ($n_i \in \mathcal{N}$ & $\mathcal{N} \subset N$). We excluded $w_i$ if its informativeness is less than or equal to 50%. i.e. the excluded terms have majority of neighbours that does not fulfill the valid, quality neighbouring criterions.

$$informativeness(w_i) = \frac{1}{N} \sum_{i=1}^{N} [n_i \in \mathcal{N}]$$

The frequency of $w_i$ denotes the importance of the term within B-literature. Therefore, we multiplied informativeness($w_i$) by the number of occurrences $w_i$ appeared in the title and purpose sentences to obtain the final weighted score. This score was used to rank the derived $w_i$ terms which represent the important concepts in B-literature (i.e. *seed concepts*). Each seed concept was extended by linking valid quality neighbouring terms (using the same criteria used to measure the validity and semantic richness of the neighbouring terms) in *word2vec* vector space.

We performed the same steps of the experiment with *fastText* (Bojanowski et al., 2016) word embedding method. An important observation is that with respect to *word2vec*, we obtained a broad topic coverage in the same field showing what areas are connected with the seed concept whereas with *fastText*, we obtained topics in a narrow range.

We used *Learning Analytics (LA)* as the A-concept to evaluate our approach. The reason for choosing LA is that it is a relatively novel but rapidly growing area connected to many disciplines like education, psychology, machine learning etc. We utilised *intersection evaluation* of Gordon and Lindsay's work (2002) to evaluate the C-concepts obtained for LA. As for the evaluation literature database, we used WoS and Scopus[2] to obtain the intersection frequencies. We categorised the derived C-concepts as *existing, emerging* and *novel* based on the intersection frequencies. In total we obtained 564 knowledge associations [3].

Unlike Gordon and Lindsay's work (2002), the knowledge discovery process of our approach is fully automated and does not require any human intervention to make decisions during the process. Therefore, verifying the validity of the obtained concepts is important to ensure that the associated intersections are meaningful. We performed an expert-based concept validation by utilising *legitimate concept criteria* discussed in Hurtado et al. (2016). From the evaluation performed by two LA researchers with CS background, we obtained an average accuracy of 97.87%, 98.21%, 95.68% for existing, emerging, and novel associations respectively. The experts' agreement for the valid terms is 93.6%. Through our experiment, we could successfully identify many interesting C-concepts that have the potential to generate scientifically sensible novel research hypothesis. For example, our *existing* C-concepts included well-established research areas in LA such as *machine learning*, *data mining*, and *e-learning* whereas the *emerging* C-concepts included infrequently used potential research areas in LA such as *computer vision*, *linked open data*, and *cognitive science*. We could also obtain many interesting *novel* C-concepts such as *word embedding techniques, deep learning architectures such as LSTM, BLSTM, CNN*, that can be utilised in future

---

[2] https://www.scopus.com/
[3] https://bit.ly/2rApl7C

Table 1: Methodology comparison

| | (Gordon and Lindsay, 2002) | Our Approach |
|---|---|---|
| Process | Requires human intervention | Fully automatic |
| Concepts | Bi-grams only | Uni-grams, abbreviations and variable length n-grams |
| Techniques | Lexical Statistics | Lexical Statistics & Distributional Semantics |
| Output | List of bi-grams | Detailed contextualised semantics groupings |

LA research. Therefore, the suggestions provided through our approach will greatly influence to uplift the process of research in LA. In comparison with the only existing CS-related LBD approach (Gordon and Lindsay, 2002), our approach utilises an improved methodology (Table 1).

To the best of our knowledge, this is the first non-medical LBD study that utilises neural word embeddings to detect the target C-concepts. Our initial results demonstrate the importance of exploiting neural word embeddings to effectively identify potential cross-disciplinary knowledge associations buried in literature. We would like to further enhance our existing approach by considering the below-mentioned future directions that are categorised based on our four research questions (RQ) described in Section 4.

**RQ 1 (Content Analysis):** A subtle analysis of literature is needed to accurately capture the hidden knowledge associations. In our current experiment, we are considering concepts at keywords-level by identifying seed concepts. As an improvement, we would like to have an organised topic structure with different levels of granularity. In order to achieve that, we are intending to utilise semantic web technologies and pre-existing topical categories (e.g., Dewey Decimal Classification) to enhance the understanding of the content. Moreover, the identified topic structure will also be useful to provide a clearly structured, logical output to the user than merely listing the identified associations. Due to the lack of LBD research that

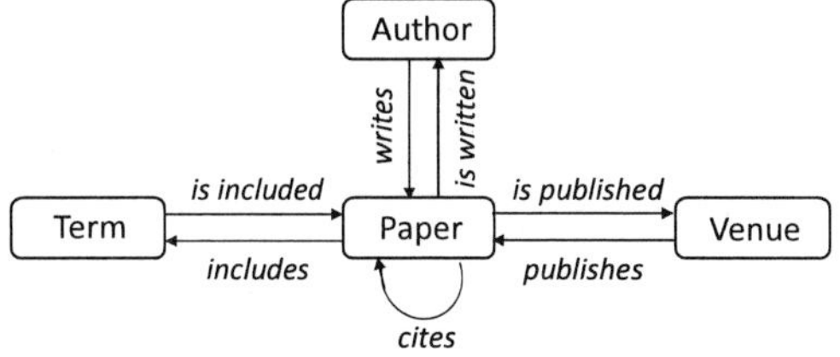


Figure 3: Entity & relation types (Shakibian and Charkari, 2017).

analyse the effects of topic modeling (Sebastian et al., 2017b), it is also important to study how topical information propagate among research publications to detect interesting, implicit knowledge associations. Another interesting future direction would be to utilise deep language understanding techniques to infer ontologies from the scientific literature automatically which can be utilised to identify more granular knowledge associations.

**RQ 2 (Bibliometrics Analysis):** In our current experiment, we are utilising the popular ABC model to discover the knowledge associations. However, the inference steps introduced through ABC model is simple and not foolproof. Therefore, in our future research studies, we are intending to analyse more complex inference steps to identify complex knowledge associations that cannot be identified through ABC model. To achieve that, we are aiming to integrate a graph-based approach by analysing the relationships among the four entity types (i.e. *author*, *term*, *paper*, *venue*) illustrated in Figure 3. In other words, we are intending to utilise different bibliographics-based link structures such as co-author relationships, direct citation links, co-word analysis, bibliographics coupling, and co-citation links to uncover complex knowledge associations. For example, when authors from disjoint research fields collaborate for a research, it implies a potential association between the two knowledge areas. This simple co-author relationship can be further expanded to more complex associations by analysing shared authors in the citations of the source and target literature, analysing authors in source literature that are cited by the target literature etc. Same as for the *author* entity, this procedure can be followed for the remaining entities (i.e. *paper*, *term*, *venue*) of the network schema in Figure 3 to derive more complex and implicit associations. With regards to *term* entity, the identified associations can be further expanded by leveraging topic modeling and topical categories. We are intending to automatically generate all the aforementioned associations (up to four degree meta path associations) for the four entity types by traversing through the network schema in Figure 3. From the derived associations we would like to identify the most effective association links by comparing the output results. The identified effective association links will provide an improved understanding of an implicit association than the simple ABC model.

**RQ 3 (Associations Ranking):** The generated target concepts list should be ordered in a way where the most significant knowledge association should be listed in the top. Therefore, it is important to identify the factors that can be utilised to rank the derived associations. In our current approach, we are incorporating semantic importance and frequency to rank the associations. In frequently evolving domains like CS, it is also important to consider the temporal factors to accurately identify the new research advancements. Therefore, we would like to propose different temporal-related weighting mechanisms to rank the target C-concepts. To accomplish this, we need to analyse the concepts in chronologically ordered time slices. For example, when deriving the temporal weight of a concept, factors such as the significance of the concept in its corresponding time interval, and changes of the concept's trend over the time using a sliding-window mechanism need to be considered. Moreover, we can also utilise pre-existing algorithms that analyse the evolution of topics (e.g., Dynamic Topic Model (Wang and McCallum, 2006), Topics over Time Model (Blei and Lafferty, 2006)) in this regard.

**RQ 4 (Evaluation):** Evaluating the validity of the identified knowledge associations outside of medical domain is very challenging due to the unavailability of gold standard datasets. Medical LBD literature mostly attempted to replicate Swanson's manually detected medical discoveries (e.g., Raynaud's Disease $\leftrightarrow$ Fish Oil) to evaluate their results (Sebastian et al., 2017a). However, when dealing with other domains, the possible evaluation approaches that can be utilised are intersection evaluation (Gordon and Lindsay, 2002), time-sliced evaluation (Yetisgen-Yildiz and Pratt, 2009) and expert based evaluation (Gordon and Lindsay, 2002) that have number of inherent limitations in accurately validating the results. Therefore, we would like to improve the existing LBD evaluation approaches to accurately evaluate our results. In our current evaluation, we are using intersection evaluation along with expert-based concept validation. In our future experiments, we would like to quantitatively evaluate the knowledge associations by utilising information retrieval metrics such as *precision* and *recall* (to evaluate the complete set of target C-concepts) and *11-point average interpolated precision curves, precision at k*, and *mean average precision* (to evaluate the rankings of the target C-concepts). To quantitatively evaluate the overall quality of the results a ground truth is required. For this purpose, we are intending to create a time-sliced dataset described in the work of Yetisgen-Yildiz and Pratt (2009). In other words, the literature is divided into two sets namely, pre-cut-off set (includes literature before a cut-off date) and post-cut-off set (includes literature after the cut-off date). Afterwards, the LBD methodology is applied to pre-cut-off set to obtain the implicit knowledge associations. Later, the existence of these identified associations (that do not exist explicitly in pre-cut-off set) is checked in the post-cut-off set. A major limitation of this approach is that a knowledge association considered as a false positive can become a true positive once a new research is published. This limitation can be overcome upto some extent by incorporating human experts to further evaluate validity of the false positives. Another interesting avenue for evaluation would be *user performance evaluation* by incorporating users with diversified range of expertise such as users with limited prior knowledge and experts in the field (Qi and Ohsawa, 2016). Through this approach, we can evaluate the extent to which the proposed LBD approach assist different levels of users to generate hypotheses by utilising the suggested knowledge associations.

Thus, this doctoral work can be expanded in numerous ways since LBD outside of medical domain is still in an early stage. Our next phase is to address the above discussed four focus points. Moreover, in our future work, we are also aiming to test our proposed LBD methodology on the better studied medical domain as well as on other domains such as humanities and social sciences.

# References


David M. Blei and John D. Lafferty. 2006. Dynamic topic models. In *Proceedings of the 23rd interna-*

*tional conference on Machine learning - ICML '06*, pages 113–120.

Piotr Bojanowski, Edouard Grave, Armand Joulin, and Tomas Mikolov. 2016. Enriching word vectors with subword information. *arXiv preprint arXiv:1607.04606*.

Delroy Cameron, Ramakanth Kavuluru, Thomas C. Rindflesch, Amit P. Sheth, Krishnaprasad Thirunarayan, and Olivier Bodenreider. 2015. Context-driven automatic subgraph creation for literature-based discovery. *Journal of Biomedical Informatics*, 54:141–157.

Chris Cheadle, Hongbao Cao, Andrey Kalinin, and Jaqui Hodgkinson. 2016. Advanced literature analysis in a Big Data world. *Annals of the New York Academy of Sciences*, 1387(1):25–33.

Kenneth A. Cory. 1997. Discovering hidden analogies in an online humanities database. *Computers and the Humanities*, 31:1–12.

Mc Ganiz, Wm Pottenger, and Cd Janneck. 2005. Recent advances in literature based discovery. Technical report.

M. Gordon and R. K. Lindsay. 2002. Literature-based discovery on the world wide web. *ACM Transactions on Internet Technology*, 2:261–275.

Michael D Gordon and Susan Dumais. 1998. Using latent semantic indexing for literature based discovery. *J. Am. Soc. Inf. Sci. Technol.*, 49(8):674–685.

Sam Henry and Bridget T. McInnes. 2017. Literature Based Discovery: Models, methods, and trends.

Dimitar Hristovski, Carol Friedman, Thomas C Rindflesch, and Borut Peterlin. 2006. Exploiting semantic relations for literature-based discovery. *AMIA ... Annual Symposium proceedings / AMIA Symposium. AMIA Symposium*, pages 349–353.

Jose L. Hurtado, Ankur Agarwal, and Xingquan Zhu. 2016. Topic discovery and future trend forecasting for texts. *Journal of Big Data*, 3(1).

V. Ittipanuvat, K. Fujita, I. Sakata, and Y. Kajikawa. 2014. Finding linkage between technology and social issue: a literature based discovery approach. *Journal of Engineering and Technology Management*, pages 160–184.

Ronald N. Kostoff. 2014. Literature-related discovery: Common factors for Parkinson's Disease and Crohn's Disease. *Scientometrics*, 100(3):623–657.

Ronald N. Kostoff, Jeffrey L. Solka, Robert L. Rushenberg, and Jeffrey A. Wyatt. 2008. Literature-related discovery (LRD): Water purification. *Technological Forecasting and Social Change*, 75(2):256–275.

Tomas Mikolov, Kai Chen, Greg Corrado, and Jeffrey Dean. 2013a. Distributed representations of words and hrases and their compositionality. In *NIPS*, pages 1–9.

Tomas Mikolov, Kai Chen, Greg Corrado, and Jeffrey Dean. 2013b. Efficient estimation of word representations in vector space. *arXiv preprint arXiv:1301.3781*, pages 1–12.

Ji Qi and Yukio Ohsawa. 2016. Matrix-like visualization based on topic modeling for discovering connections between disjoint disciplines. *Intelligent Decision Technologies*, 10(3):273–283.

Yakub Sebastian, Eu Gene Siew, and Sylvester O. Orimaye. 2017a. Emerging approaches in literature-based discovery: techniques and performance review.

Yakub Sebastian, Eu Gene Siew, and Sylvester Olubolu Orimaye. 2015. Predicting future links between disjoint research areas using heterogeneous bibliographic information network. In *Lecture Notes in Computer Science (including subseries Lecture Notes in Artificial Intelligence and Lecture Notes in Bioinformatics)*, volume 9078, pages 610–621.

Yakub Sebastian, Eu Gene Siew, and Sylvester Olubolu Orimaye. 2017b. Learning the heterogeneous bibliographic information network for literature-based discovery. *Knowledge-Based Systems*, 115:66–79.

Hadi Shakibian and Nasrollah Moghadam Charkari. 2017. Mutual information model for link prediction in heterogeneous complex networks. *Scientific Reports*, 7.

D. R. Swanson. 1988. Migraine and magnesium: eleven neglected connections. *Perspectives in Biology and Medicine*, 31:526–557.

Don R. Swanson. 1986. Fish Oil, Raynaud's Syndrome, and Undiscovered Public Knowledge. *Perspectives in Biology and Medicine*, 30(1):1–18.

Don R. Swanson and Neil R. Smalheiser. 1997. An interactive system for finding complementary literatures: A stimulus to scientific discovery. *Artificial Intelligence*, 91(2):183–203.

Xuerui Wang and Andrew McCallum. 2006. Topics over time: A non-Markov continuous-time model of topical trends. In *Proceedings of the 12th ACM SIGKDD International Conference on Knowledge Discovery and Data Mining*, pages 424–433.

Marc Weeber, Henny Klein, Lolkje T.W. De Jong-Van Den Berg, and Rein Vos. 2001. Using concepts in literature-based discovery: Simulating Swanson's Raynaud-fish oil and migraine-magnesium discoveries. *Journal of the American Society for Information Science and Technology*, 52(7):548–557.

Meliha Yetisgen-Yildiz and Wanda Pratt. 2009. A new evaluation methodology for literature-based discovery systems. *Journal of Biomedical Informatics*, 42(4):633–643.

# Language Identification and Named Entity Recognition in Hinglish Code Mixed Tweets


**Kushagra Singh**
IIIT Delhi

**Indira Sen**
IIIT Delhi

**Ponnurangam Kumaraguru**
IIIT Delhi

`{kushagra14056,indira15021,pk}@iiitd.ac.in`



## Abstract

While growing code-mixed content on Online Social Networks (OSNs) provides a fertile ground for studying various aspects of code-mixing, the lack of automated text analysis tools render such studies challenging. To meet this challenge, a family of tools for analyzing code-mixed data such as language identifiers, parts-of-speech (POS) taggers, chunkers have been developed. Named Entity Recognition (NER) is an important text analysis task which is not only informative by itself, but is also needed for downstream NLP tasks such as semantic role labeling. In this work, we present an exploration of automatic NER of code-mixed data. We compare our method with existing off-the-shelf NER tools for social media content, and find that our systems outperforms the best baseline by 33.18 % ($F_1$ score).


## 1 Introduction

Code-switching or code-mixing occurs when "lexical items and grammatical features from two languages appear in one sentence" (Muysken, 2000). [1] It is frequently seen in multilingual communities and is of interest to linguists due to its complex relationship with societal factors (Sridhar and Sridhar, 1980).

With the rise of Web 2.0, the volume of text on online social networks (OSN) such as Twitter, Facebook, Reddit has grown. It is estimated that around 240 Million Indian users, alone, are active on Twitter [2]. A significant fraction of these users are bilingual, or even trilingual, and their tweets can be monolingual in English or their vernacular, or code-mixed. Past research has looked at multiple dimensions of this behaviour such as its relationship to emotion expression (Rudra et al., 2016) and identity. Code-mixing or multilingualism of tweets poses a significant problem to both the OSNs' underlying text mining algorithms as well as researchers trying to study online discourse, since most existing tools for analyzing OSN text content caters to monolingual data. For example, Twitter's abuse detection systems fail to flag code-mixed tweets as offensive. [3] Recent efforts to build tools for code-mixed content include language identifiers (Solorio and Liu, 2008), parts-of-speech(POS) taggers (Vyas et al., 2014), and chunking (Sharma et al., 2016). A natural extension of these set of automated natural language processing (NLP) tools is a Named Entity Recognizer (NER) for code-mixed social media data, which we present in this paper. Additionally, as language tags are an essential feature for NLP tasks, including NER, we also present a neural network based language identifier.

Our main contributions are:

1. Building a token-level language identification system for Hindi-English (Hi-En) code mixed tweets, described in detail in Section 3.

2. Building an NER for En-Hi code-mixed tweets, which we explain in Section 4. We also show, in Section 5, that our NER performs better than existing baselines.

## 2 Related Work

In this section we briefly describe the approaches for automatic language identification and extrac-

---

[1] Many researchers use code-mixing and code-switching interchangeably, which we follow in this work

[2] https://www.statista.com/statistics/381832/twitter-users-india/

[3] http://timesofindia.indiatimes.com/india/to-avoid-social-media-police-indian-trolls-go-vernacular/articleshow/60139671.cms




*Proceedings of ACL 2018, Student Research Workshop*, pages 52–58
Melbourne, Australia, July 15 - 20, 2018. ©2018 Association for Computational Linguistics

tion of named entities.

Language Identification for code-mixed content has been previously explored in Barman et al. (2014). Particularly close to our work is the use of deep-learning approaches for detecting token-level language tags for code-mixed content (Jaech et al., 2016).

We particularly focus on efforts to building NERs for social media content and, NERs for Indian languages and code-mixed corpora. Social Media text, including and especially tweets, have subtle variations from written and spoken text. These include slacker grammatical structure, spelling variations, ad-hoc abbreviations and more. See Ritter et al. (2011) for detailed differences between tweets and traditional textual sources. Monolingual NER for tweets include (Ritter et al., 2011; Li et al., 2012). We build on these approaches to account for code-mixing and use the former as a baseline to test our method against.

## 3 Language Identification using Transliteration

We build a token level language identification model (LIDF) for code-mixed tweets using monolingual corpora available for both the languages, supplemented by a small set of annotated code-mixed tweets. We hypothesize that words or character sequences of different languages encode different structures. Therefore, we aim to capture this character structure for both languages. Subsequently, given a token, we try to see which language fits better. Our LIDF algorithm comprises of multiple steps, described in Figure 1. Each of the steps have been explained in detail below.

### 3.1 Roman-Devanagari transliteration

We restrict ourselves to instances of En-Hi code-mixing where the Hindi component is written in Roman script. [4] Therefore, any model trained on Hindi corpora (which will be in Devanagari) is not directly usable. To make use of such a corpus, we first transliterate words written in Roman to Devanagari script.

We train a model $T$, that takes a token written in Roman characters and generates its Devanagari equivalent (given token *school*, $T$ generates स्कूल). We follow an approach used by (Rosca

---

[4]This is followed in previous studies since the quantity of code-mixed content with non-Roman Hindi is negligible.

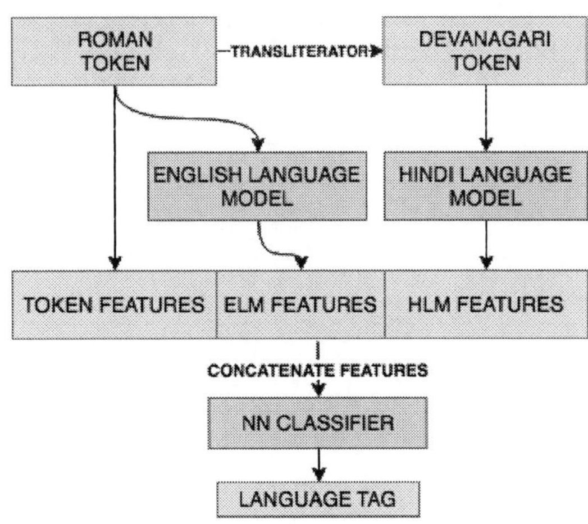



Figure 1: Different steps of our language identification pipeline. We extract features using language models trained on monolingual corpora, and train a classifier based on these features.

and Breuel, 2016) for English-Arabic transliteration and, and train an Attention Sequence to Sequence (Seq2Seq) model (Bahdanau et al., 2014). Given an input sequence of Roman characters, $T$ generates a sequence of Devanagari characters.

We train $T$ using Roman-Devanagari transliteration pairs mined by (Gupta et al., 2012) and (Khapra et al., 2014). After combining the two sets and removing duplicates, we were left with 41,383 unique pairs.

We explore multiple Seq2Seq models, experimenting with different RNN cells, encoder and decoder depths, output activation functions and the number of RNN cells in each layer. We evaluate their performance using the character error rate metric, comparing with LITCM (Bhat et al., 2015) as a baseline. We report the performance of our top five models in Table 1, all of which perform better than the baseline.

Our best model comprises of a 2 layer bidirectional RNN encoder and a 2 layer RNN decoder, each layer comprising of 128 GRU units with ReLU activation. We use the Adagrad optimizer to train $T$, adding a dropout of 0.5 after each layer and use the early stopping technique to prevent over fitting. Larger and deeper networks perform relatively poorer since they start overfitting quickly.

We observe that Hindi words which have multiple spellings when written in Roman script are all transliterated to the same Hindi token. Therefore, $T$ could also be used for normalization and

| Model | Depth | # Units | Cell | CER |
|---|---|---|---|---|
| LITCM | – | – | – | 18.88 |
| Seq2Seq | 3 | 256 | LSTM | 17.23 |
| Seq2Seq | 2 | 64 | GRU | 17.09 |
| Seq2Seq | 3 | 128 | GRU | 16.99 |
| Seq2Seq | 2 | 128 | LSTM | 16.67 |
| **Seq2Seq** | **2** | **128** | **GRU** | **16.54** |

Table 1: Performance of different transliteration models. Reported CER is in percentage and was calculated after a 5-fold cross validation. Depth was kept the same for both encoding and decoding layers.

we hope to investigate this in more detail in future.

## 3.2 Extracting features using monolingual corpora

For both languages, we learn the structure of the language at a character level. We do this by training a model which for a token of length $n$, learns to predict the last character given the first $n - 1$ characters as input. More formally, for each token $\{c_1, c_2, ..., c_n\}$, the model learns to predict $c_n$ given the input sequence $\{c_1, c_2, ..., c_{n-1}\}$. We model this as a sequence classification problem using LSTM RNNs (Hochreiter and Schmidhuber, 1997). We use ELM to refer to the English language model, and HLM to refer to the Hindi language model.

The same architecture is used for both ELM and HLM, as shown in Figure 1. Both comprise of two RNN layers with 128 LSTM cells each, using ReLU activation. The output of the second RNN layer at the last time step is connected to a fully connected (FC) layer with softmax activation. The size of this FC layer is equal to the character vocabulary $V$ of the language. We take a softmax over the FC layer to predict $c_n$. The normalized outputs from the FC layer can be thought of as a probability distribution over $V$, the $i^{th}$ normalized output being equal to $P(V_i | c_1, c_2, ..., c_{n-1})$, where $V_i$ is the $i^{th}$ character in the vocabulary. We refer to the normalized outputs from the FC layer of ELM and HLM as $P_{ELM}$ and $P_{HLM}$ respectively, and use them as features for our language detection classifier.

For training ELM, we use the News Crawl dataset provided as a part of the WMT 2014 trans-

lation task.[5] As a preprocessing step, we remove all non-alphabetic characters (such as numbers and punctuations), and convert all uppercase alphabets to lowercase. After preprocessing, we were left with a total of 98,565,179 tokens, 189,267 of which were unique. For HLM, we use the IIT Bombay Hindi corpus (Kunchukuttan et al., 2017). We follow the same preprocessing steps, except for converting to lowercase (since there is no concept of case in Hindi). This yielded 59,494,325 tokens, of which 161,020 were unique.

The input sequence is encoded into a sequence of one hot vectors before feeding it to the network. We use categorical cross-entropy as the loss function, optimizing the model using gradient descent (Adagrad). 20% of the unique tokens are held out and used to validate the performance of our model. Once again, we use the early stopping technique and add a dropout of 0.5 after each layer to avoid over-fitting.

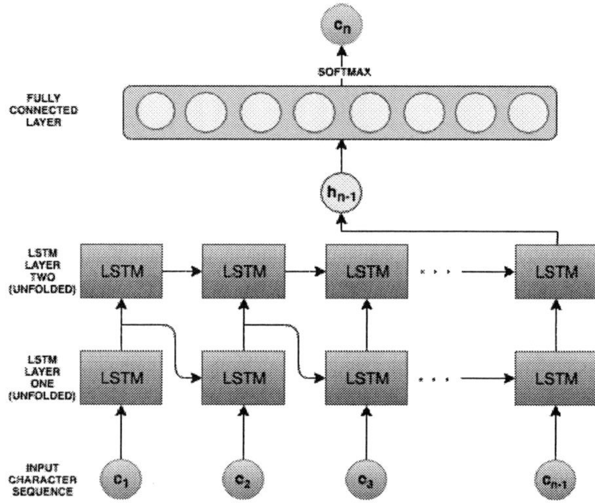


Figure 2: Architecture for ELM and HLM. The figure shows one cell in each LSTM layer unrolled over time.

## 3.3 Predicting language tag using $P_{ELM}$ and $P_{HLM}$

Given a word $\{c_1, c_2, ..., c_n\}$ we first transliterate it to Devanagari using $T$, generating $\{c'_1, c'_2, ..., c'_k\}$. Then by passing $\{c_1, c_2, ..., c_{n-1}\}$ and $\{c'_1, c'_2, ..., c'_{k-1}\}$ through ELM and HLM respectively, we obtain $P_{ELM}$ and $P_{HLM}$. Our hypothesis is that we can differentiate $P_{ELM}$ of a Hindi word from the $P_{ELM}$ of an English word,

---

[5]http://statmt.org/wmt14/translation-task.html

since the character sequence structure of a Hindi word is different from that of English words (which are used to train ELM). Similarly, we can differentiate $P_{HLM}$ of an English word from the $P_{HLM}$ of a Hindi word.

We use a set of tweets curated by Sakshi Gupta and Radhika (2016) which are annotated for language at a token level (each token is either English, Hindi or Rest) to train a three class classifier using (i) $P_{ELM}$ (ii) $P_{HLM}$, (iii) ratio of non-alphabetic characters in $W$, (iv) ratio of capitalization in $W$ and (v) Binary feature indicating whether $W$ is title-case as features. The last three features help identify the *Rest* tokens. Our 3-class classifier is a fully connected neural network with 2 hidden layers using ReLU activation. On 5-fold cross validation, our model achieves an average $F_1$ score of 0.934 and an average accuracy of 0.961 across the three classes. This is a slight improvement over the model proposed by Sharma et al. (2016), which had an accuracy of 0.938 on the same dataset (as reported by reported by Sakshi Gupta and Radhika (2016)).

## 4   Named Entity Recognition

Named entity recognition typically comprises of two components, (i) entity segmentation and (ii) entity classification. Both these components can either be modeled separately as done by Ritter et al. (2011), or they can be combined and tackled together like the model proposed by Finkel et al. (2005). We adopt the latter approach, modeling both components together as a sequence labeling task. Our hypothesis is that named entities can be identified using features extracted from words surrounding it. We explore models using Conditional Random Fields and LSTM RNNs using handcrafted features described below.

### 4.1   Features

Our hand-crafted features are described below.

- ***Token based features*** : The current token $T$, $T$ after stripping all characters which are not in the Roman alphabet ($T_{clean}$), and converting all characters in $T_{clean}$ to lowercase ($T_{norm}$) generates three different features. We create $T_{wordhsape}$ by replacing all uppercase letters in $T$ with $X$, all lowercase letters with $x$, all numerals with $o$ and leave all other characters as they are. For example,

**Adam123** becomes **Xxxxooo**. We also use token length $T_L$ as as feature.

- ***Affixes*** : Prefixes and suffixes of length 1 to 5 extracted from $T$, padded with whitespace if needed. These help in identifying phrases that are not entities. For example, an English token ending in ***ing*** is highly unlikely to be a named entity.

- ***Character based features*** : Binary features indicating (i) whether $T$ is title case, (ii) whether $T$ has an uppercase letter, (iii) whether $T$ has all uppercase characters, (iv) whether $T$ has a non-alphanumeric character and (v) whether $T$ is a hashtag. We also calculate the fraction of characters in $T$ which are ASCII

- ***Language based features*** : The language which $T$ belongs to, as predicted by the model proposed in section 3. For the LSTM model, we also use $P_{ELM}$ and $P_{HLM}$ generated for $T$.

- ***Syntactic features*** : POS tag for $T$ as predicted by the model trained by Owoputi et al. (2013), POS tag and chunk tag for $T$ and as predicted by the shallow parser trained by Sharma et al. (2016)

- ***Tweet capitalization features*** : From the tweet that $T$ belongs to, we extract (i) fraction of characters that are uppercase, (ii) fraction of characters that are lowercase, (iii) fraction of tokens that are title case.[6]

### 4.2   Proposed Models

Our LSTM model (Figure 3) comprises of two bidirectional RNN layers using LSTM cells and ReLU activation. The input at the time step $t$ is $F_t$, i.e. the feature vector for the token at position $t$ in the tweet. $F_t$ is generated by concatenating the extracted features for the token at position $t$. $T$, $T_{clean}$, $T_{norm}$, $T_{wordhsape}$ and affixes are passed through embedding layers which are randomly initialized and learnt during the training phase. All real-valued features are encoded into one-hot vectors of length 10, using percentile binning.

The output ($h_t$) of the second RNN layer at each time step is passed to a separate fully connected

---

[6]Using the output of the T_cap classifier trained by Ritter et al reduces accuracy.

| Type | Lample | Ritter | LSTM | CRF | N |
|------|--------|--------|------|------|------|
| PER | 38.73 | 38.45 | 65.47 | **72.23** | 1644 |
| LOC | 38.35 | 46.84 | 67.53 | **72.50** | 744 |
| ORG | 16.99 | 13.54 | 50.94 | **70.35** | 375 |
| **All** | 33.77 | 36.88 | 64.64 | **72.06** | 2763 |

Table 2: Performance ($F_1$ scores) of different models on segmentation and classification. N is the total number of entities in the entire dataset. Reported numbers are in percentages. Results of CRF and LSTM are on 5-fold cross validation.

layer $FC_t$. We take a softmax over the output of $FC_t$ to predict the label ($L_t$) for the token at position $t$. While training, we use the Adagrad optimizer and add a dropout of 0.5 after each layer.

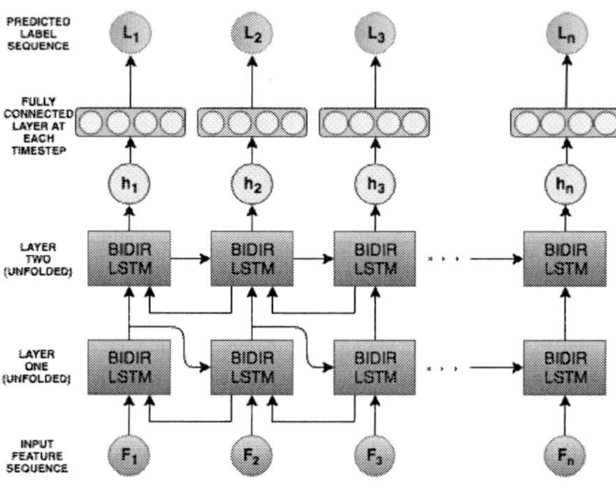


Figure 3: LSTM NER architecture. The figure shows one cell in each LSTM layer unrolled over time

Our CRF model is the standard generalized CRF proposed by Lafferty et al. (2001), which allows a flow of information across the sequence in both directions. We add $L_1$ and $L_2$ regularization to prevent over-fitting, and do an extensive grid search to come up with optimum values for these constants.

## 5 Experiments and Results

### 5.1 Data collection and annotation

We randomly sampled 50,000 tweets from the code mixed tweet dataset collected by (Patro et al., 2017). On this set, we ran our language detection algorithm and filtered tweets which had at least five $Hi$ tokens. The filtered data also had tweets containing Roman tokens belonging to languages other than English and Hindi (like transliterated Telugu), such tweets were removed during the annotation process.

The final dataset comprised of 2079 tweets (35,374 tokens). 13,860 (39.18 %) of the tokens were $En$, 11,391 (32.2 %) $Hi$ and 10,123 (28.61 %) $Rest$. Each tweet was annotated at a token level for three classical named entity types *Person*, *Location* and *Organisation*, using the IOB format. The annotation process was carried out by three linguists proficient in both English and Hindi. The final label was decided based on majority vote and any instance (around 2%) where all three annotators disagreed was resolved through discussion. In all, the annotators identified 2763 entity phrases (3751 tokens) which included 1,644 *Person* entities, 744 *Location* entities and 375 *Organisation* entities.

### 5.2 Baselines and Results

We compare our proposed models (LSTM and CRF) with two baseline systems, (i) a state of the art English NER model proposed by Lample et al. (2016) and (ii) a state of the art NER model for tweets proposed by Ritter et al. (2011). Named Entities do not have belong to one particular language though the same NE might have different forms in different languages, such as Cologne in English, is Kln in German. For the purpose of this study, we do not assign NEs any language tags and leave the detection and mapping of multiple NE forms as future work.

The results are summarized in Table 2 (segmentation) and Table 3 (segmentation and classification). All metrics are calculated on a phrase level, no partial credit is awarded. An incorrectly identified boundary is penalized as both, a false positive and a false negative. For computing Table 2, we generalize entity tags (B-PER, B-LOC, B-ORG become B-ENT, I-PER, I-LOC, I-ORG become I-ENT). As expected, both these systems fare poorly on our data at both entity segmentation and entity classification. We believe this is due to the high number of out of vocabulary tokens (belonging to Hindi) in the data.

## 6 Discussion

In this paper, we present a Named Entity Recognition tool specifically targeting Hindi-English code-mixed content. To build our NER model, we

| Model | Precision | Recall | $F_1$ score |
| --- | --- | --- | --- |
| Lample | 36.55 | 46.59 | 40.97 |
| Ritter | 64.64 | 34.24 | 44.77 |
| LSTM | 74.45 | 64.87 | 69.33 |
| **CRF** | **84.95** | **69.91** | **76.70** |

Table 3: Performance of different models at entity segmentation. All numbers are in percentages.

also present a unique semi-supervised language identifier which exploits the character-level differences in languages. We validate the performance of our NER against off-the-shelf NER for Twitter and observe that our model outperforms them.

In future, we plan to explore building other downstream NLP tools such as Semantic Role Labeling or Entity-specific Sentiment Analyzers which make use of NER for code-mixed data.

## References


Dzmitry Bahdanau, Kyunghyun Cho, and Yoshua Bengio. 2014. Neural machine translation by jointly learning to align and translate. *CoRR* abs/1409.0473. http://arxiv.org/abs/1409.0473.

Utsab Barman, Amitava Das, Joachim Wagner, and Jennifer Foster. 2014. Code mixing: A challenge for language identification in the language of social media. In *Proceedings of the first workshop on computational approaches to code switching*. pages 13–23.

Irshad Ahmad Bhat, Vandan Mujadia, Aniruddha Tammewar, Riyaz Ahmad Bhat, and Manish Shrivastava. 2015. Iiit-h system submission for fire2014 shared task on transliterated search. In *Proceedings of the Forum for Information Retrieval Evaluation*. ACM, New York, NY, USA, FIRE '14, pages 48–53. https://doi.org/10.1145/2824864.2824872.

Jenny Rose Finkel, Trond Grenager, and Christopher Manning. 2005. Incorporating non-local information into information extraction systems by gibbs sampling. In *Proceedings of the 43rd Annual Meeting on Association for Computational Linguistics*. Association for Computational Linguistics, Stroudsburg, PA, USA, ACL '05, pages 363–370. https://doi.org/10.3115/1219840.1219885.

Kanika Gupta, Monojit Choudhury, and Kalika Bali. 2012. Mining hindi-english transliteration pairs from online hindi lyrics. In *Proceedings of the Tenth International Conference on Language Resources and Evaluation (LREC 2012)*. pages 2459–2465.

Sepp Hochreiter and Jürgen Schmidhuber. 1997. Long short-term memory. *Neural Comput.* 9(8):1735–1780. https://doi.org/10.1162/neco.1997.9.8.1735.

Aaron Jaech, George Mulcaire, Mari Ostendorf, and Noah A Smith. 2016. A neural model for language identification in code-switched tweets. In *Proceedings of The Second Workshop on Computational Approaches to Code Switching*. pages 60–64.

Mitesh M. Khapra, Ananthakrishnan Ramanathan, Anoop Kunchukuttan, Karthik Visweswariah, and Pushpak Bhattacharyya. 2014. When transliteration met crowdsourcing : An empirical study of transliteration via crowdsourcing using efficient, non-redundant and fair quality control. In Nicoletta Calzolari (Conference Chair), Khalid Choukri, Thierry Declerck, Hrafn Loftsson, Bente Maegaard, Joseph Mariani, Asuncion Moreno, Jan Odijk, and Stelios Piperidis, editors, *Proceedings of the Ninth International Conference on Language Resources and Evaluation (LREC'14)*. European Language Resources Association (ELRA), Reykjavik, Iceland.

Anoop Kunchukuttan, Pratik Mehta, and Pushpak Bhattacharyya. 2017. The IIT bombay english-hindi parallel corpus. *CoRR* abs/1710.02855. http://arxiv.org/abs/1710.02855.

John D. Lafferty, Andrew McCallum, and Fernando C. N. Pereira. 2001. Conditional random fields: Probabilistic models for segmenting and labeling sequence data. In *Proceedings of the Eighteenth International Conference on Machine Learning*. Morgan Kaufmann Publishers Inc., San Francisco, CA, USA, ICML '01, pages 282–289. http://dl.acm.org/citation.cfm?id=645530.655813.

Guillaume Lample, Miguel Ballesteros, Sandeep Subramanian, Kazuya Kawakami, and Chris Dyer. 2016. Neural architectures for named entity recognition. *CoRR* abs/1603.01360. http://arxiv.org/abs/1603.01360.

Chenliang Li, Jianshu Weng, Qi He, Yuxia Yao, Anwitaman Datta, Aixin Sun, and Bu-Sung Lee. 2012. Twiner: named entity recognition in targeted twitter stream. In *Proceedings of the 35th international ACM SIGIR conference on Research and development in information retrieval*. ACM, pages 721–730.

Pieter Muysken. 2000. *Bilingual speech: A typology of code-mixing*, volume 11. Cambridge University Press.

Olutobi Owoputi, Brendan O'Connor, Chris Dyer, Kevin Gimpel, Nathan Schneider, and Noah A Smith. 2013. Improved part-of-speech tagging for online conversational text with word clusters. Association for Computational Linguistics.

Jasabanta Patro, Bidisha Samanta, Saurabh Singh, Abhipsa Basu, Prithwish Mukherjee, Monojit Choudhury, and Animesh Mukherjee. 2017. All that is english may be hindi: Enhancing language identification through automatic ranking of likeliness of word borrowing in social media. *CoRR* abs/1707.08446. http://arxiv.org/abs/1707.08446.

Alan Ritter, Sam Clark, Oren Etzioni, et al. 2011. Named entity recognition in tweets: an experimental study. In *Proceedings of the Conference on Empirical Methods in Natural Language Processing*. Association for Computational Linguistics, pages 1524–1534.

Mihaela Rosca and Thomas Breuel. 2016. Sequence-to-sequence neural network models for transliteration. *CoRR* abs/1610.09565. http://arxiv.org/abs/1610.09565.

Koustav Rudra, Shruti Rijhwani, Rafiya Begum, Kalika Bali, Monojit Choudhury, and Niloy Ganguly. 2016. Understanding language preference for expression of opinion and sentiment: What do hindi-english speakers do on twitter? In *EMNLP*. pages 1131–1141.

Piyush Bansal Sakshi Gupta and Mamidi Radhika. 2016. Resource creation for hindi-english code mixed social media text .

Arnav Sharma, Sakshi Gupta, Raveesh Motlani, Piyush Bansal, Manish Shrivastava, Radhika Mamidi, and Dipti M Sharma. 2016. Shallow parsing pipeline for hindi-english code-mixed social media text. In *Proceedings of NAACL-HLT*. pages 1340–1345.

Thamar Solorio and Yang Liu. 2008. Learning to predict code-switching points. In *Proceedings of the Conference on Empirical Methods in Natural Language Processing*. Association for Computational Linguistics, pages 973–981.

Shikaripur N Sridhar and Kamal K Sridhar. 1980. The syntax and psycholinguistics of bilingual code mixing. *Canadian Journal of Psychology/Revue canadienne de psychologie* 34(4):407.

Yogarshi Vyas, Spandana Gella, Jatin Sharma, Kalika Bali, and Monojit Choudhury. 2014. Pos tagging of english-hindi code-mixed social media content. In *EMNLP*. volume 14, pages 974–979.

# German and French Neural Supertagging Experiments for LTAG Parsing


**Tatiana Bladier**     **Andreas van Cranenburgh**     **Younes Samih**     **Laura Kallmeyer**
Heinrich Heine University of Düsseldorf
Universitätsstraße 1, 40225 Düsseldorf, Germany
`{bladier,cranenburgh,samih,kallmeyer}@phil.hhu.de`



## Abstract

We present ongoing work on data-driven parsing of German and French with Lexicalized Tree Adjoining Grammars. We use a supertagging approach combined with deep learning. We show the challenges of extracting LTAG supertags from the French Treebank, introduce the use of *left-* and *right-sister-adjunction*, present a neural architecture for the supertagger, and report experiments of n-best supertagging for French and German.


## 1 Introduction

Lexicalized Tree Adjoining Grammar (LTAG; Joshi and Schabes, 1997) is a linguistically motivated grammar formalism. Productions in an LTAG support an extended domain of locality (EDL). This allows them to express linguistic generalizations that are not captured by typical statistical parsers based on context-free grammars or dependency parsing. Each derivation step is triggered by a lexical element and a principled distinction is made between its arguments and modifiers, which is reflected in richer derivations. This has applications in the context of other tasks which can make use of linguistically rich analyses, such as frame semantic parsing or semantic role labeling (Sarkar, 2007). On the other hand, the increased expressiveness of LTAG makes efficient parsing and statistical estimations more challenging.

Previous work (Bangalore and Joshi, 1999; Sarkar, 2007) has shown that the task of parsing with LTAGs can be facilitated through the intermediate step of *supertagging*—a task of assigning possible *supertags* (i.e. elementary trees) for each word in a given sentence (Chen, 2010). Supertagging has been referred to as "almost pars-

ing" (Bangalore and Joshi, 1999), since supertagging performs a large part of the task of syntactic disambiguation and increases the parsing efficiency by lexicalizing syntactic decisions before moving on to the more expensive polynomial parsing algorithm (Sarkar, 2007).

Recently, several papers proposed neural architectures for supertagging with Combinatory Categorial Grammar (CCG; Lewis et al., 2016; Vaswani et al., 2016) and LTAG (Kasai et al., 2017). Supertagging with LTAG is more challenging than with CCG due to a higher number of supertags (counting on average 4000 distinct supertags for LTAGs). Also, almost half of the LTAG supertags occur only once. Nevertheless, the reported neural supertagging approach for LTAG (Kasai et al., 2017) reaches an accuracy of 88-90 % for English (compared to over 95 % for CCG). In this paper we apply a similar recurrent neural architecture to supertagging with LTAGs based on Samih (2017) and Kasai et al. (2017) to German and French data and compare against previously reported results. For the German data, we compare our results to the LTAG supertaggers reported in Bäcker and Harbusch (2002) and Westburg (2016). To our knowledge, no results for French supertagging based on LTAG or CCG have been reported so far.

## 2 Neural Supertagging with LTAGs

### 2.1 Lexicalized Tree Adjoining Grammar

A *Tree Adjoining Grammar* (TAG; Joshi and Schabes, 1997) is a linguistically and psychologically motivated tree rewriting formalism (Sarkar, 2007). A TAG consists of a finite set of *elementary trees*, which can be combined to form larger trees via the operations of *substitution* (replacing a leaf node marked with $\downarrow$ with an initial tree) or *adjunction* (replacing an internal node with an auxiliary tree).




*Proceedings of ACL 2018, Student Research Workshop*, pages 59–66
Melbourne, Australia, July 15 - 20, 2018. ©2018 Association for Computational Linguistics

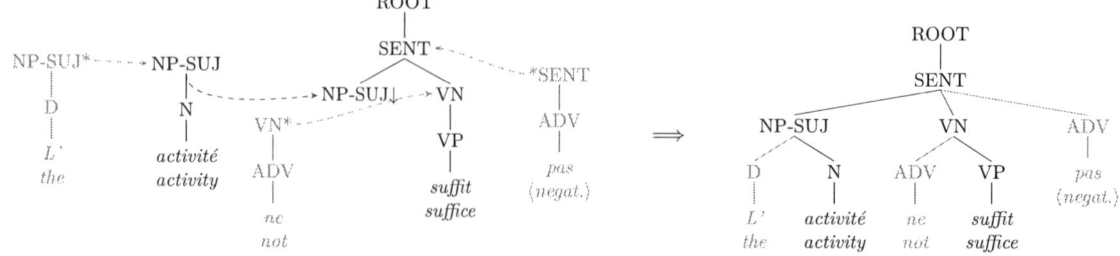

Figure 1: Supertagging with French LTAG for *L'activité ne suffit pas* ("The activity does not suffice")

An auxiliary tree has a *foot node* (marked with ∗) with the same label as the root node. When adjoining an *auxiliary tree* to some node $n$, the daughter nodes of $n$ become daughters of the foot node. A sample TAG derivation is shown in Figure 2, in which the elementary trees for *Mary* and *pizza* are substituted to the subject and object slots of the *likes* tree and the auxiliary tree for *absolutely* is adjoined at the VP-node.

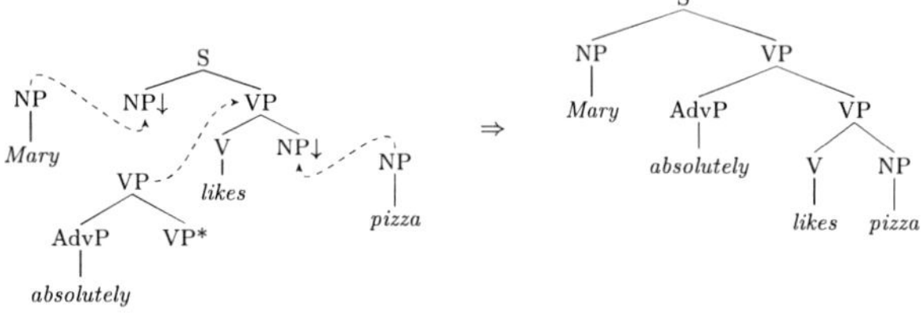

Figure 2: Elementary trees and a derived tree in LTAG

In a lexicalized version of TAG (LTAG) every tree is associated with a lexical item and represents the span over which this item can specify its syntactic or semantic constraints (for example, subject-verb number agreement or semantic roles) capturing also long-distance dependencies between the sentence tokens (Kipper et al., 2000).

## 2.2 RNN-based TAG supertagging

A supertagger is a partial parsing model which is used to assign a sequence of LTAG elementary trees to the sequence of words in a sentence (Sarkar, 2007). Supertagging can thus be seen as preparation for further syntactic parsing which improves the efficiency of the TAG parser through reducing syntactic lexical ambiguity and sentence complexity. Figure 1 provides an example of supertagging with an LTAG for French.

Several techniques were proposed for supertagging over the years, among which are HMM-based (Bäcker and Harbusch, 2002), n-gram-based (Chen et al., 2002), and Lightweight Dependency Analysis models (Srinivas, 2000). Recent ad-

vances show the applicability of recurrent neural networks (RNNs) for supertagging (Lewis et al., 2016; Vaswani et al., 2016; Kasai et al., 2017).

RNN-based supertagging with LTAGs can be seen as a standard sequence labeling task, albeit with a large set of labels (i.e., several thousand classes as supertags). Our deep learning pipeline is shown in Figure 3. A similar architecture showed good results for POS tagging across many languages (Plank et al., 2016).

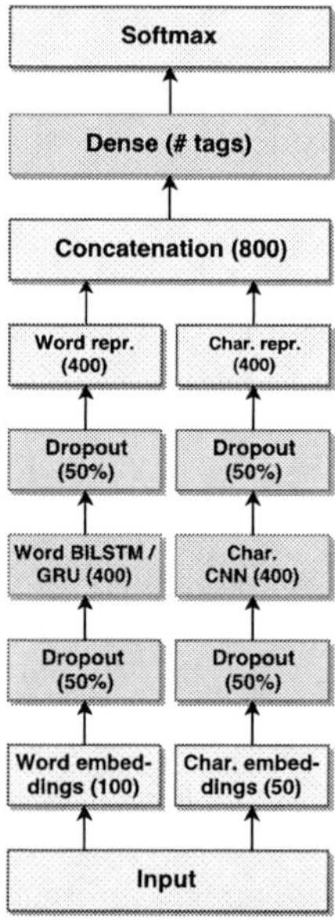

Figure 3: Supertagging architecture based on Samih (2017); dimensions shown in parentheses.

We use two kinds of embeddings: pre-trained word embeddings from the Sketch Engine collection of language models (Jakubíček et al., 2013; Bojanowski et al., 2016), and character embeddings based on the training set data. The pre-trained word embeddings encode distributional information from large corpora. The advantage of the character embeddings is that they can additionally encode subtoken information such as morphological features and help in dealing with unseen words, without doing any feature engineering on

| Parameters | French | German, reduced set | German, full set | English |
|---|---|---|---|---|
| | (this work) | (Kaeshammer, 2012) | (Kaeshammer, 2012) | (Kasai et al., 2017) |
| Supertags | 5145 | 2516 | 3426 | 4727 |
| Supertags occur. once | 2693 | 1123 | 1562 | 2165 |
| POS tags | 13 | 53 | 53 | 36 |
| Sentences | 21550 | 28879 | 50000 | 44168 |
| Avg. sentence length | 31.34 | 17.51 | 17.71 | appr. 20 |
| Accuracy | **78.54** | 85.91 | **88.51** | **89.32** |

Table 1: Supertagging experiments

morphological features.

The embeddings go through a recurrent layer to capture the influence of tokens in the preceding and subsequent context for each token. For the recurrent layer we use either bidirectional Long Short Term Memory (LSTM) or Gated Recurrent Units (GRU). We use a Convolutional Neural Network (CNN) layer for character embeddings, since it was proved to be one of the best options for extracting morphological information from word tokens (Ma and Hovy, 2016). The results for the word and character models are concatenated and fed through a softmax layer that gives a probability distribution for possible supertags. Dropout layers are added to counter overfitting. We replaced words without an entry in the word embeddings with a randomly instantiated vector of the same dimension (100). Table 2 provides an overview of the hyper-parameters we used for the supertagger architecture.

| Layer | Hyper-parameters | Value |
|---|---|---|
| Characters CNN | numb. of filters | 40 |
| | state size | 400 |
| Bi-GRU | state size | 400 |
| | initial state | 0.0 |
| Words embedding | vector dim. | 100 |
| | window size | 5 |
| Char. embedding | dimension | 50 |
| | batch size | 128 |
| Dropout | dropout rate | 0.5 |

Table 2: Hyper-parameters of the supertagger.

## 3 LTAG induction from the French Treebank

Inducing a grammar from a treebank entails identifying a set of productions that could have produced its parse trees. In the case of LTAG this means decomposing the trees into a sequence of elementary trees, one for each word in the sentence.

In order to extract a TAG from the French Treebank (FTB; Abeillé et al., 2003), we applied the heuristic procedure described by Xia (1999). The main idea of this approach is to consider the trees in the treebank as derived trees from an LTAG. Elementary trees are extracted in top-down fashion using percolation tables to identify grammatically obligatory elements (i.e., complements), grammatically optional elements (i.e., modifiers), as well as a head child for each constituent. All sub-trees corresponding to modifiers and complements are extracted in a further step forming auxiliary trees and initial trees, respectively, while the head child and its lexical anchor are kept in the tree. When extracted in this way, elementary trees contain the corresponding lexical anchor and the branches represent a particular syntactic context of a construction with slots for its complements.

### 3.1 LTAG induction: pre-processing steps

Before induction of different LTAGs for French, we carried out pre-processing steps described in Candito et al. (2010) and Crabbé and Candito (2008) including extension of the original POS tag set in FTB from 13 to 26 POS tags and undoing multi-word expressions (MWEs) with regular syntactic patterns (e.g. *(MWN (A ancien) (N élève))* → *(NP (AP (A ancien)) (N élève)))*. About 14 % of the word tokens (79,466 out of the total of 557,095 tokens) in FTB belong to flat MWEs. After rewriting compounds with regular syntactic patterns, the number of MWEs is reduced to approximately 5 %.

We also restructured some trees in order to bring the complements on a higher level in the tree. In particular, we shifted the initial prepositional phrase of the VPinf constituents to a higher level and raised the subordinating conjunction (*C-S*) of the final clause constituents (*Ssub*) (see Figure 4).

After the preprocessing we extracted the following LTAGs from FTB for our supertagging experiments: including 13 or 26 POS tags, with and without compounds, including and excluding

| Gold supertag | Predicted supertag | Example |
|---|---|---|
| (PP (APPR < >)(NP↓ )) | (PP* (APPR < >)(NP↓ )) | **zu** einem Eigenheim zu verhelfen |
| (NP (DP↓ )(NN < >)) | (NP (NN < >)) | das heutige und künftige **Kreditvolumen** |
| (S (S* )($, < >)(S↓ )) | ($,* < >) | |
| (S (NP↓ )(VVFIN < >)(NP↓ )(PTKVZ↓ )) | (S (NP↓ )(VVFIN < >)(NP↓ )) | der Umsatzminus **geht** auf 125 Millionen [...] zurück |

Table 3: Most common error classes for German TAG supertagging with TiGer treebank

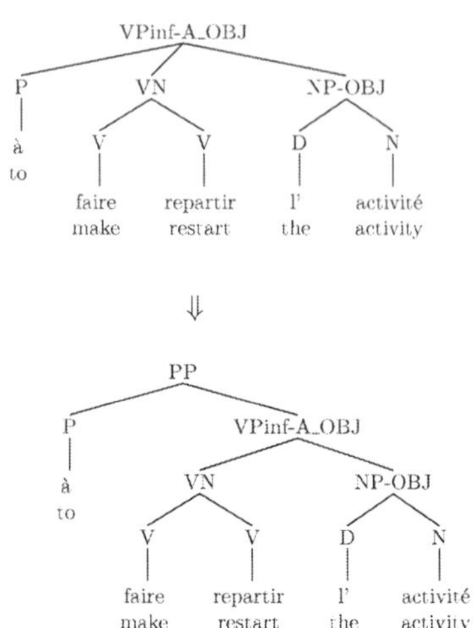

Figure 4: FTB preprocessing: complement raising

punctuation marks. Table 1 provides some statistics on the extracted LTAG which led to the most accurate supertagging results (13 POS tags, without compounds, including punctuation marks).

## 3.2 Left- and right-sister-adjunction

Extraction of an LTAG from FTB is challenging due to the flat structure of the trees, which allows any combination of arguments and modifiers. In order to preserve the original flat structures in the FTB as far as possible and to facilitate the extraction of the elementary trees we decided against the traditional notion of adjunction in TAG which relies on nested structures and apply *sister-adjunction*; i.e., the root of a sister-adjoining tree can be attached as a daughter of any node of another tree with the same node label.

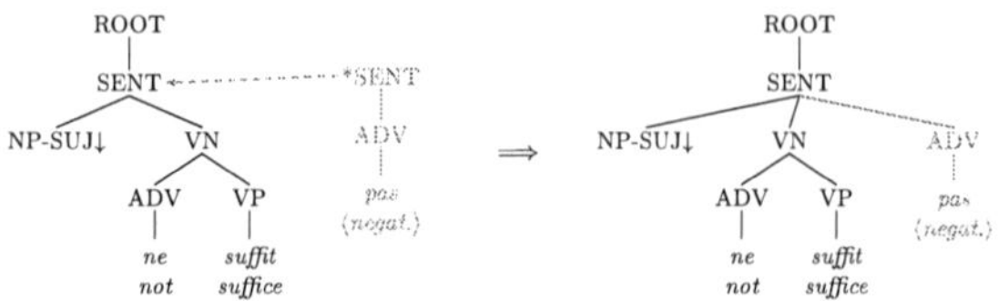

Figure 5: Left-sister-adjunction

Since a modifier can appear on the right or on

the left side relative to the position of the constituent head, we distinguish between *right-* and *left-sister-adjoining trees* (marked with * on the left or the right side of the root label as shown in Figure 5).

A left-sister-adjoining tree $\gamma$ can only be adjoined to a node $\eta$ in the tree $\tau$ if the root label of $\gamma$ is the same as the label of $\eta$ and the anchor of the elementary tree $\tau$ comes in the sentence before the anchor of $\gamma$. The children of $\gamma$ are inserted on the right side of the children in $\eta$ and become the children of $\eta$. A *right-sister-adjunction* is defined in a similar way.

The resulting LTAGs with sister-adjunction are basically LTIGs (*Lexicalized Tree Insertion Grammar*; Schabes and Waters, 1995) in the way that the auxiliary trees do not allow wrapping adjunction or adjunction on the root node but permit multiple simultaneous adjunction on a single node of initial trees. However, since LTIG is a special variant of LTAG, we refer to the extracted grammar as LTAG in the remainder of the paper.

## 4 Experiments and error analysis

### 4.1 Experimental setups for German and French

In order to compare the performance of our supertagger with previous work of Kasai et al. (2017) and LTAG-based supertaggers for German (Bäcker and Harbusch, 2002; Westburg, 2016), we experimented with the supertags extracted by Kaeshammer (2012) from the German TiGer treebank (Brants et al., 2004). The set of supertags for German has the following train, test, and dev. split: 39,925, 5035, and 5040 sentences. We ran a supertagging experiment with this number of sentences, since it is compatible with the experimental setup described in Kasai et al. (2017). Since the number of sentences in FTB is smaller than in TiGer, we created a sample of the train set of the TiGer treebank with a comparable number of sentences in the train set (18,809). For the supertagging experiments with the French LTAG, we divided FTB in the standard train, development and test sets (19,080, 1235, and 1235 sentences), making our test and dev. sets comparable to the dev. and test set reported in Candito et al. (2009).

Tables 3 and 5 show the most frequent erroneous supertags for German and French. The symbol < > in the supertags signifies the spot for the lexical anchor, while * marks the foot node of auxiliary trees and ↓ represents a substitution site.

## 4.2 German TAG supertagging with TiGer

Generally, results for supertagging with German LTAGs appear to be slightly lower than for English. Westburg (2016) reports an accuracy of 82.92 % for German TAG with a supertagger based on perceptron training algorithm, while Bäcker and Harbusch (2002) reached 78.3 % with a HMM-based TAG supertagger.

Supertagging for German is more challenging than for English due to a higher number of word order variations and the resulting sparseness of the data (Bäcker and Harbusch, 2002). However, our experiments show that the proposed neural supertagging architecture reaches the best performance among the previously described supertaggers for German (88.51 %) and gets comparable results to the supertagging model for English described in Kasai et al. (2017) (see Tables 1 and 4).

| System | Accuracy |
|---|---|
| Bäcker and Harbusch (2002) (HMM-based) | 78.3 |
| Westburg (2016) | 82.92 |
| This work, full training set (Bi-LSTM) | 87.67 |
| This work, full training set (GRU) | **88.51** |
| This work, reduced training set (Bi-LSTM) | 85.26 |
| This work, reduced training set (GRU) | **85.91** |

Table 4: Supertagging experiments with German TiGer treebank.

The biggest class of errors for German supertagging contains wrong predictions concerning the type of the elementary tree (e.g. the supertagger predicts an auxiliary tree instead of an initial tree or vice versa). The main reason for this kind of error is the particularity of German which allows dependent elements in a sentence being divided by a big number of other tokens. For example, a determiner and the determined word or the separable verb prefix and the verb stem can be separated by a dozen other tokens, as in the sentence *Der Umsatzminus* **geht** *auf 125 Millionen [..]* **zurück** (Engl. "The sales drop goes down to 125 millions"), the verb *geht* and its prefix *zurück* are separated by 11 tokens (see Table 3).

Since the window size of tokens presented to the supertagger is limited, the connection between the tokens can be overlooked by the supertagger. However, increasing the window size leads to greater noise in the data. We experimented with window sizes of 5, 9, and 13 for German and got the best results with a window size of 5 (two words before and after the token).

Another source of mistakes for German is the intersentential punctuation in large complex sentences containing several subordinated clauses. This error can also be explained by the window size of tokens presented to the supertagger—the supertagger does not capture the complex structure of the sentence and classifies the punctuation mark as a one-child auxiliary tree (see Table 3).

Another big class of errors comes from PPs which can be either optional (modifiers) or obligatory elements. For example, the supertagger did not recognize that the verb *verhelfen* (Engl. "to help") requires a prepositional phrase as an argument (e.g. *zu einem Eigenheim zu verhelfen*; Engl. "to help someone to buy a property") and erroneously classified this complement as a modifier PP.

## 4.3 French TAG supertagging with FTB

Supertagging with French LTAGs appears to be more challenging compared to German or English. There are several general reasons for the performance drop of the supertagger, one of which is a higher average sentence length in FTB (31.34 tokens per sentence, compared to 17.51 in TiGer). Sentences in FTB more frequently have a complex syntactic structure including explicative elements separated with brackets or commas.

The large number of supertags lead to higher data sparsity and make the sequence labeling problem more difficult for the supertagger. One explanation for the larger number of supertags, besides the longer and more complex sentence structures in FTB, is the large number of flat multiword expressions in FTB. Our experiments show that rewriting MWEs with regular compounds improves the supertagging performance.

A large number of supertagging errors for French occur due to different sites of attachment of the intersentential punctuation marks in FTB. The punctuation marks in FTB are attached to the corresponding constituents and not consistently to the

| Gold supertag | Predicted supertag | Example |
|---|---|---|
| (NP* (PP (P <>) (NP↓ ))) | (PP (P <>) (NP↓ )) | 32 % **par** an |
| (NP* (PONCT < >)) | (SENT* (PONCT <>)) | **-LRB-** 66,7 % **-RRB-** |
| (NP* (N < >)) | (N < >) | Mme Dominique **Alduy** |
| (ROOT (SENT (NP↓ ) (VN (V < >)))) | (VN (V < >)) | le droit est officiellement **transgressé** |

Table 5: Most common error classes for LTAG supertagging with French Treebank

| System | Accuracy |
|---|---|
| This work (GRU), 13 POS, undone comp. | **78.54** |
| This work (GRU), 13 POS, no punct. marks | 74.44 |
| This work (GRU), 13 POS, with compounds | 76.78 |
| This work (GRU), 26 POS, with compounds | 74.84 |
| This work (Bi-LSTM), 13 POS, undone comp. | 77.67 |

Table 6: Supertagging experiments with French Treebank (FTB).

root node of the whole sentence. However, since punctuation marks also help to identify possible constituents, omitting them does not improve supertagging.

Similar to supertagging with German LTAGs, PP attachments are also a major source of errors with French LTAGs. In addition to difficulties with classifying PPs as modifiers or complements (as with German data), the supertagger for French more frequently encounters problems with identifying the correct site for attaching the PPs to a node in the syntactic tree. The reason for these errors could be that FTB—in comparison to TiGer—does not offer additional function marks to distinguish PPs as modifiers from prepositional complements of the support verbs.

### 4.4 N-best supertagging experiments

The softmax layer of the supertagging model we described in section 2.2 provides a distribution of probabilities of the supertags when classifying words in a sentence, and we used this distribution to enable our supertagger to predict n-best supertags.

| n-best | Accuracy German (full set) | Accuracy German (red. set) | Accuracy French |
|---|---|---|---|
| 1-best | 88.51 | 85.91 | 78.54 |
| 2-best | 94.37 | 93.04 | 87.34 |
| 3-best | 96.08 | 95.00 | 90.85 |
| 5-best | 97.45 | 96.66 | 94.38 |
| 7-best | 98.03 | 97.40 | 96.00 |
| 10-best | 98.52 | 97.97 | 97.08 |

Table 7: N-best supertagging experiments.

We experimented with different numbers of n-best supertags for every word, counting the number of accurately predicted supertags each time when at least one of the n-best supertags was predicted correctly. The experiments show a quick growth in accuracy prediction up to 5-best supertags, while for ranks $n > 5$ the improvement of accuracy is not as big (see Table 7).

## 5 Conclusion and Future Work

We proposed a neural architecture for supertagging with TAG for German and French and carried out experiments to measure the performance of the supertagging model for these languages. We induced several different LTAGs from FTB in order to compare the supertagging performance. The results with German LTAG show that the neural supertagging model achieves comparable results to the state-of-the art TAG supertagging model described in Kasai et al. (2017) for English, even though German is more difficult for supertagging due to the free word order and the data sparseness. Supertagging for French appears to be more difficult due to the larger average length of sentences and a big number of multiword expressions.

In future work we plan to increase performance of the supertagger for French by dividing the supertagging algorithm in two steps: factorization of the extracted supertags in tree families and deciding afterwards on the correct supertag within the predicted tree family. We plan to use the improved supertagger for graph-based parsing. In particular, we aim at adapting the A*-based PARTAGE parser for LTAGs developed by Waszczuk (2017) for parsing with extracted supertags. We also intend to add deep syntactic features and information on semantic roles to the supertags in order to test whether the proposed supertagging architecture can be used for semantic role labeling.

### Acknowledgements

This work was carried out as a part of the research project TREEGRASP (http://treegrasp.phil.hhu.de) funded by a Consolidator Grant of the European Research Council (ERC). We thank three anonymous reviewers for their careful reading, valuable suggestions and constructive comments.

# References

Anne Abeillé, Lionel Clément, and François Toussenel. 2003. Building a treebank for french. In *Treebanks*, pages 165–187. Springer.

Jens Bäcker and Karin Harbusch. 2002. Hidden markov model-based supertagging in a user-initiative dialogue system. In *Proceedings of TAG+ 6*, pages 269–278.

Srinivas Bangalore and Aravind K Joshi. 1999. Supertagging: An approach to almost parsing. *Computational linguistics*, 25(2):237–265.

Piotr Bojanowski, Edouard Grave, Armand Joulin, and Tomas Mikolov. 2016. Enriching word vectors with subword information. *arXiv preprint arXiv:1607.04606*.

Sabine Brants, Stefanie Dipper, Peter Eisenberg, Silvia Hansen-Schirra, Esther König, Wolfgang Lezius, Christian Rohrer, George Smith, and Hans Uszkoreit. 2004. Tiger: Linguistic interpretation of a german corpus. *Research on language and computation*, 2(4):597–620.

Marie Candito, Benoît Crabbé, and Pascal Denis. 2010. Statistical french dependency parsing: treebank conversion and first results. In *Seventh International Conference on Language Resources and Evaluation-LREC 2010*, pages 1840–1847. European Language Resources Association (ELRA).

Marie Candito, Benoît Crabbé, and Djamé Seddah. 2009. On statistical parsing of french with supervised and semi-supervised strategies. In *Proceedings of the EACL 2009 Workshop on Computational Linguistic Aspects of Grammatical Inference*, CLAGI '09, pages 49–57, Stroudsburg, PA, USA. Association for Computational Linguistics.

John Chen. 2010. Semantic labeling and parsing via tree-adjoining grammars. *Supertagging: Using Complex Lexical Descriptions in Natural Language Processing*, pages 431–448.

John Chen, Srinivas Bangalore, Michael Collins, and Owen Rambow. 2002. Reranking an n-gram supertagger. In *Proceedings of the Sixth International Workshop on Tree Adjoining Grammar and Related Frameworks (TAG+ 6)*, pages 259–268.

Benoit Crabbé and Marie Candito. 2008. Expériences d'analyse syntaxique statistique du français. In *15ème conférence sur le Traitement Automatique des Langues Naturelles-TALN'08*, pages pp–44.

Miloš Jakubíček, Adam Kilgarriff, Vojtěch Kovář, Pavel Rychlỳ, and Vít Suchomel. 2013. The tenten corpus family. In *7th International Corpus Linguistics Conference CL*, pages 125–127.

Aravind K Joshi and Yves Schabes. 1997. Tree-adjoining grammars. In *Handbook of formal languages*, pages 69–123. Springer.

Miriam Kaeshammer. 2012. *A German treebank and lexicon for tree-adjoining grammars*. Ph.D. thesis, MasterâĂŹs thesis, Universitat des Saarlandes, Saarlandes, Germany.

Jungo Kasai, Bob Frank, Tom McCoy, Owen Rambow, and Alexis Nasr. 2017. Tag parsing with neural networks and vector representations of supertags. In *Proceedings of the 2017 Conference on Empirical Methods in Natural Language Processing*, pages 1712–1722.

Karin Kipper, Hoa Trang Dang, William Schuler, and Martha Palmer. 2000. Building a class-based verb lexicon using tags. In *Proceedings of the Fifth International Workshop on Tree Adjoining Grammar and Related Frameworks (TAG+ 5)*, pages 147–154.

Mike Lewis, Kenton Lee, and Luke Zettlemoyer. 2016. LSTM CCG parsing. In *Proceedings of the 2016 Conference of the North American Chapter of the Association for Computational Linguistics: Human Language Technologies*, pages 221–231.

Xuezhe Ma and Eduard Hovy. 2016. End-to-end sequence labeling via bi-directional lstm-cnns-crf. *arXiv preprint arXiv:1603.01354*.

Barbara Plank, Anders Søgaard, and Yoav Goldberg. 2016. Multilingual part-of-speech tagging with bidirectional long short-term memory models and auxiliary loss. In *Proceedings of the 54th Annual Meeting of the Association for Computational Linguistics (Volume 2: Short Papers)*, pages 412–418, Berlin, Germany. Association for Computational Linguistics.

Younes Samih. 2017. *Dialectal Arabic processing Using Deep Learning*. Ph.D. thesis, Düsseldorf, Germany.

Anoop Sarkar. 2007. Combining supertagging and lexicalized tree-adjoining grammar parsing. *Complexity of Lexical Descriptions and its Relevance to Natural Language Processing: A Supertagging Approach*, page 113.

Yves Schabes and Richard C Waters. 1995. Tree insertion grammar: a cubic-time, parsable formalism that lexicalizes context-free grammar without changing the trees produced. *Computational Linguistics*, 21(4).

Bangalore Srinivas. 2000. A lightweight dependency analyzer for partial parsing. *Natural Language Engineering*, 6(2):113–138.

Ashish Vaswani, Yonatan Bisk, Kenji Sagae, and Ryan Musa. 2016. Supertagging with LSTMs. In *Proceedings of the 2016 Conference of the North American Chapter of the Association for Computational Linguistics: Human Language Technologies*, pages 232–237.

Jakub Waszczuk. 2017. *Leveraging MWEs in practical TAG parsing: towards the best of the two world*. Ph.D. thesis.

Anika Westburg. 2016. Supertagging for german - an implementation based on tree adjoining grammars. Master's thesis, Heinrich Heine University of Düsseldorf.

Fei Xia. 1999. Extracting tree adjoining grammars from bracketed corpora. In *Proceedings of the 5th Natural Language Processing Pacific Rim Symposium (NLPRS-99)*, pages 398–403.

# SuperNMT: Neural Machine Translation with Semantic Supersenses and Syntactic Supertags


**Eva Vanmassenhove**
Adapt Centre
Dublin City University
Ireland
eva.vanmassenhove@adaptcentre.ie

**Andy Way**
Adapt Centre
Dublin City University
Ireland
andy.way@adaptcentre.ie



## Abstract

In this paper we incorporate semantic supersensetags and syntactic supertag features into EN–FR and EN–DE factored NMT systems. In experiments on various test sets, we observe that such features (and particularly when combined) help the NMT model training to converge faster and improve the model quality according to the BLEU scores.


## 1 Introduction

Neural Machine Translation (NMT) models have recently become the state-of-the art in the field of Machine Translation (Bahdanau et al., 2014; Cho et al., 2014; Kalchbrenner et al., 2014; Sutskever et al., 2014). Compared to Statistical Machine Translation (SMT), the previous state-of-the-art, NMT performs particularly well when it comes to word-reorderings and translations involving morphologically rich languages (Bentivogli et al., 2016). Although NMT seems to partially 'learn' or generalize some patterns related to syntax from the raw, sentence-aligned parallel data, more complex phenomena (e.g. prepositional-phrase attachment) remain problematic (Bentivogli et al., 2016). More recent work showed that explicitly (Sennrich and Haddow, 2016; Nadejde et al., 2017; Bastings et al., 2017; Aharoni and Goldberg, 2017) or implicitly (Eriguchi et al., 2017) modeling extra syntactic information into an NMT system on the source (and/or target) side could lead to improvements in translation quality.

When integrating linguistic information into an MT system, following the central role assigned to syntax by many linguists, the focus has been mainly on the integration of syntactic features. Although there has been some work on semantic features for SMT (Banchs and Costa-Jussà, 2011), so far, no work has been done on enriching NMT systems with more general semantic features at the word-level. This might be explained by the fact that NMT models already have means of learning semantic similarities through word-embeddings, where words are represented in a common vector space (Mikolov et al., 2013). However, making some level of semantics more explicitly available at the word level can provide the translation system with a higher level of abstraction beneficial to learn more complex constructions. Furthermore, a combination of both syntactic and semantic features would provide the NMT system with a way of learning semantico-syntactic patterns.

To apply semantic abstractions at the word-level that enable a characterisation beyond that what can be superficially derived, coarse-grained semantic classes can be used. Inspired by Named Entity Recognition which provides such abstractions for a limited set of words, supersense-tagging uses an inventory of more general semantic classes for domain-independent settings (Schneider and Smith, 2015). We investigate the effect of integrating supersense features (26 for nouns, 15 for verbs) into an NMT system. To obtain these features, we used the *AMALGrAM 2.0* tool (Schneider et al., 2014; Schneider and Smith, 2015) which analyses the input sentence for Multi-Word Expressions as well as noun and verb supersenses. The features are integrated using the framework of Sennrich et al. (2016), replicating the tags for every subword unit obtained by byte-pair encoding (BPE). We further experiment with a combination of semantic supersenses and syntactic supertag features (CCG syntactic categories (Steedman, 2000) using EasySRL (Lewis et al., 2015)) and less complex features such as POS-tags, assuming that supersense-tags have the potential to be useful especially in combination with syntactic information.




*Proceedings of ACL 2018, Student Research Workshop*, pages 67–73
Melbourne, Australia, July 15 - 20, 2018. ©2018 Association for Computational Linguistics

The remainder of this paper is structured as follows: First, in Section 2, the related work is discussed. Next, Section 3 presents the semantic and syntactic features used. The experimental set-up is described in Section 4 followed by the results in Section 5. Finally, We conclude and present some of the ideas for future work in Section 6.

## 2   Related Work

In SMT, various linguistic features such as stems (Toutanova et al., 2008) lemmas (Mareček et al., 2011; Fraser et al., 2012), POS-tags (Avramidis and Koehn, 2008), dependency labels (Avramidis and Koehn, 2008) and supertags (Hassan et al., 2007; Haque et al., 2009) are integrated using pre- or post-processing techniques often involving factored phrase-based models (Koehn and Hoang, 2007). Compared to factored NMT models, factored SMT models have some disadvantages: (a) adding factors increases the sparsity of the models, (b) the $n$-grams limit the size of context that is taken into account, and (c) features are assumed to be independent of each other. However, adding syntactic features to SMT systems led to improvements with respect to word order and morphological agreement (Williams and Koehn, 2012; Sennrich, 2015).

One of the main strengths of NMT is its strong ability to generalize. The integration of linguistic features can be handled in a flexible way without creating sparsity issues or limiting context information (within the same sentence). Furthermore, the encoder and attention layers can be shared between features. By representing the encoder input as a combination of features (Alexandrescu and Kirchhoff, 2006), Sennrich and Haddow (2016) generalized the embedding layer in such a way that an arbitrary number of linguistic features can be explicitly integrated. They then investigated whether features such as lemmas, subword tags, morphological features, POS tags and dependency labels could be useful for NMT systems or whether their inclusion is redundant.

Similarly, on the syntax level, Shi et al. (2016) show that although NMT systems are able to partially learn syntactic information, more complex patterns remain problematic. Furthermore, sometimes information is present in the encoding vectors but is lost during the decoding phase (Vanmassenhove et al., 2017). Sennrich and Haddow (2016) show that the inclusion of linguistic features leads to improvements over the NMT baseline for EN–DE (0.6 BLEU), DE–EN (1.5 BLEU) and EN–RO (1.0 BLEU). When evaluating the gains from the features individually, it results that the gain from different features is not fully cumulative. Nadejde et al. (2017) extend their work by including CCG supertags as explicit features in a factored NMT systems. Moreover, they experiment with serializing and multitasking and show that tightly coupling the words with their syntactic features leads to improvements in translation quality (measured by BLEU) while a multitask approach (where the NMT predicts CCG supertags and words independently) does not perform better than the baseline system. A similar observation was made by Li et al (2017), who incorporate the linearized parse trees of the source sentences into ZH–EN NMT systems. They propose three different sorts of encoders: (a) a parallel RNN, (b) a hierarchical RNN, and (c) a mixed RNN. Like Nadejde et al. (2017), Li et al (2017) observe that the mixed RNN (the simplest RNN encoder), where words and label annotation vectors are simply stitched together in the input sequences, yields the best performance with a significant improvement (1.4 BLEU). Similarly, Eriguchi et al. (2016) integrated syntactic information in the form of linearized parse trees by using an encoder that computes vector representations for each phrase in the source tree. They focus on source-side syntactic information based on Head-Driven Phrase Structure Grammar (Sag et al., 1999) where target words are aligned not only with the corresponding source words but with the entire source phrase. Wu et al. (2017) focus on incorporating source-side long distance dependencies by enriching each source state with global dependency structure.

To the best of our knowledge, there has not been any work on explicitly integrating semantic information in NMT. Similarly to syntactic features, we hypothesize that semantic features in the form of semantic 'classes' can be beneficial for NMT providing it with an extra ability to generalize and thus better learn more complex semantico-syntactic patters.

## 3   Semantics and Syntax in NMT

### 3.1   Supersense Tags

The novelty of our work is the integration of explicit semantic features *supersenses* into an NMT system. Supersenses are a term which refers to the top-level hypernyms in the WordNet (Miller, 1995) taxonomy, sometimes also referred to as *semantic fields* (Schneider and Smith, 2015). The supersenses cover all nouns and verbs with a total of 41 supersense categories, 26 for nouns and 15 for verbs. To obtain the supersense tags we used the *AMALGrAM (A Machine Analyzer of Lexical Groupings and Meanings) 2.0* tool [1] which in addition to the noun and verb supersenses analyzes English input sentences for MWEs. An example of a sentence annotated with the AMALGrAM tool is given in (1):[2]

**(1)**
   (a)  "He seemed to have little faith in our democratic structures, suggesting that various articles could be misused by governments."
   (b)  "He **seemed|cognition** to have|stative little **faith|COGNITION** in our democratic structures|ARTIFACT , suggesting|communication that various articles|COMMUNICATION could be|'a misused|social by governments|GROUP ."

As can be noted in (1), some supersenses, such as *cognition* exist for both nouns and verbs. However, the supersense tags for verbs are always lowercased while the ones for nouns are capitalized. This way, the supersenses also provide syntactic information useful for disambiguation as in (2), where the word *work* is correctly tagged as a noun (with its capitalized supersense tag *ACT*) in the first part of the sentence and as a verb (with the lowercased supersense tag *social*). Furthermore, there is a separate tag to distinguish auxiliary verbs from main verbs.

**(2)**
   (a)  "In the course of my work on the opinion, I in fact became aware of quite a number of problems and difficulties for EU citizens who live and work in Switzerland"
   (b)  "In the course|EVENT of my work|ACT on the opinion|COGNITION , I **in_fact** became|stative aware of quite **a_number_of** problems|COGNITION and difficulties|COGNITION for **EU_citizens|GROUP** who live|social and work|social in Switzerland|LOCATION ."

Since MWEs and supersenses naturally complement each other, Schneider and Smith (2015) integrated the MWE identification task (Schneider et al., 2014) with the supersense tagging task of Ciaramita and Altun (2006). In Example (2), the

MWEs *in fact*, *a number of* and *EU citizens* are retrieved by the tagger.

We add this semantico-syntactic information in the source as an extra feature in the embedding layer following the approach of Sennrich and Haddow (2016), who extended the model of Bahdanau et al. (2014). A separate embedding is learned for every source-side feature provided (the word itself, POS-tag, supersense tag etc.). These embedding vectors are then concatenated into one embedding vector and used in the model instead of the simple word embedding one (Sennrich and Haddow, 2016).

To reduce the number of out-of-vocabulary (OOV) words, we follow the approach of Sennrich et al. (2016) using a variant of BPE for word segmentation capable of encoding open vocabularies with a compact symbol vocabulary of variable-length subword units. For each word that is split into subword units, we copy the features of the word in question to its subword units. In (3), we give an example with the word 'stormtroopers' that is tagged with the supersense tag 'GROUP'. It is split into 5 subword units so the supersense tag feature is copied to all its five subword units. Furthermore, we add a *none* tag to all words that did not receive a supersense tag.

**(3)**
   Input:    "the stormtroopers"
   SST:     "the stormtroopers|GROUP"
   BPE:     "the stor@@ m@@ tro@@ op@@ ers"
   Output:  "the|**none** stor@@|**GROUP** ... op@@|**GROUP** ers|**GROUP**"

For the MWEs we decided to copy the supersense tag to all the words of the MWE (if provided by the tagger), as in (4). If the MWE did not receive a particular tag, we added the tag *mwe* to all its components, as in example (5)

**(4)**
   Input:    "EU citizens"
   SST:     "EU_ citizens|GROUP"
   Output:  "EU|GROUP citizens|GROUP"

**(5)**
   Input:    "a number of"
   SST:     "a_ number _ of"
   Output:  "a|**mwe** number|**mwe** of|**mwe** "

### 3.2 Supertags and POS-tags

We hypothesize that more general semantic information can be particularly useful for NMT in combination with more detailed syntactic information. To support our hypothesis we also experimented

---


[2] All the examples are extracted from our data used later on to train the NMT systems

with syntactic features (separately and in combination with the semantic ones): POS tags and CCG supertags.

The POS tags are generated by the Stanford POS-tagger (Toutanova et al., 2003); for the supertags we used the EasySRL tool (Lewis et al., 2015) which annotates words with CCG tags. CCG tags provide global syntactic information on the lexical level. This kind of information can help resolve ambiguity in terms of prepositional attachment, among others. An example of a CCG-tagged sentence is given in (6):

**(6)**

It|NP is|(S[dcl]\NP)/NP a|NP/N modern|N/N form|N/PP of|PP/NP colonialism|N .|.

## 4 Experimental Set-Up

### 4.1 Data sets

Our NMT systems are trained on 1M parallel sentences of the Europarl corpus for EN–FR and EN–DE (Koehn, 2005). We test the systems on 5K sentences (different from the training data) extracted from Europarl and the newstest2013. Two different test sets are used in order to show how additional semantic and syntactic features can help the NMT system translate different types of test sets and thus evaluate the general effect of our improvement.

### 4.2 Description of the NMT system

We used the `nematus` toolkit (Sennrich et al., 2017) to train encoder-decoder NMT models with the following parameters: *vocabulary size:* 35000, *maximum sentence length:* 60, *vector dimension:* 1024, *word embedding layer:* 700, *learning optimizer:* `adadelta`. We keep the embedding layer fixed to 700 for all models in order to ensure that the improvements are not simply due to an increase of the parameters in the embedding layer. In order to by-pass the OOV problem and reduce the number of dictionary entries we use word-segmentation with BPE (Sennrich, 2015). We ran the BPE algorithm with 89, 500 operations. We trained all our BPE-ed NMT systems with CCG tag features, supersensetags (SST), POS tags and the combination of syntactic features (POS or CCG) with the semantic ones (SST). All systems are trained for 150,000 iterations and evaluated after every 10,000 iterations.

## 5 Results

### 5.1 English–French

For both test sets, the NMT system with supersenses (SST) converges faster than the baseline (BPE) NMT system. As we hypothesized, the benefits of the features added, was more clear on the newstest2013 than on the Europarl test set. Figure 1 compares the BPE-ed baseline system (BPE) with the supertag-supersensetag system (CCG–SST) automatically evaluated on the newstest2013 (in terms of BLEU (Papineni et al., 2002)) over all 150,000 iterations. From the graph, it can also be observed that the system has a more robust, consistent learning curve.

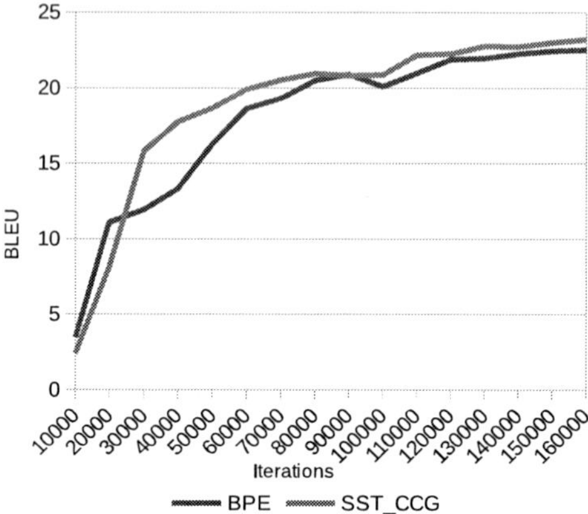



Figure 1: Baseline (BPE) vs Combined (SST–CCG) NMT Systems for EN–FR, evaluated on the newstest2013.

To see in more detail how our semantically enriched SST system compares to an NMT system with syntactic CCG supertags and how a system that integrates both semantic features and syntactic features (SST–CCG) performs, a more detailed graph is provided in Figure 2 where we zoom in on later stages of the learning process. Although Sennrich and Haddow (2016) observe that features are not necessarily cumulative (possibly since the information from the syntactic features partially overlapped), the system enriched with both semantic and syntactic features outperforms the two separate systems as well as the baseline system. The best CCG-SST model (23.21 BLEU) outperforms the best BPE-ed baseline model (22.54 BLEU) with 0.67 BLEU (see Table 1). Moreover, the benefit of syntactic and semantic features seems to be more than cumulative at some points, confirming the idea that providing both information sources can help the NMT system learn semantico-syntactic patterns. This supports our hypothesis that semantic and syntactic features are particularly useful when combined.

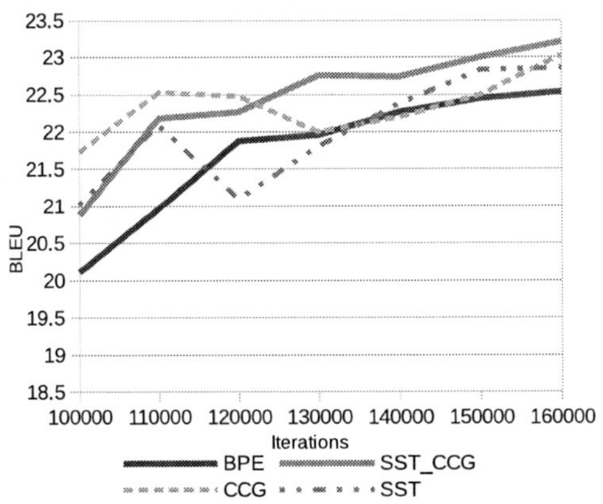

Figure 2: Baseline (BPE) vs Syntactic (CCG) vs Semantic (SST) and Combined (SST–CCG) NMT Systems for EN–FR, evaluated on the newstest2013.

| BLEU | BPE | CCG | SST | SST–CCG |
|---|---|---|---|---|
| Best Model | 22.54 | 23.03 | 22.86 | 23.21 |

Table 1: Best BLEU scores for Baseline (BPE), Syntactic (CCG), Semantic (SST) and Combined (SST–CCG) NMT systems for EN-FR evaluated on the newstest2013

## 5.2 English–German

The results for the EN–DE system are very similar to the EN–FR system: the model converges faster and we observe the same trends with respect to the BLEU scores of the different systems. Figure 3 compares the BPE-ed baseline system (BPE) with the NMT system enriched with SST and CCG tags (SST–CCG). In the last iterations, see Figure 4, we see how the two systems enriched with super-sense tags and CCG tags lead to small improvements over the baseline. However, their combination (SST–CCG) leads to a more robust NMT system with a higher BLEU (see Table 2).

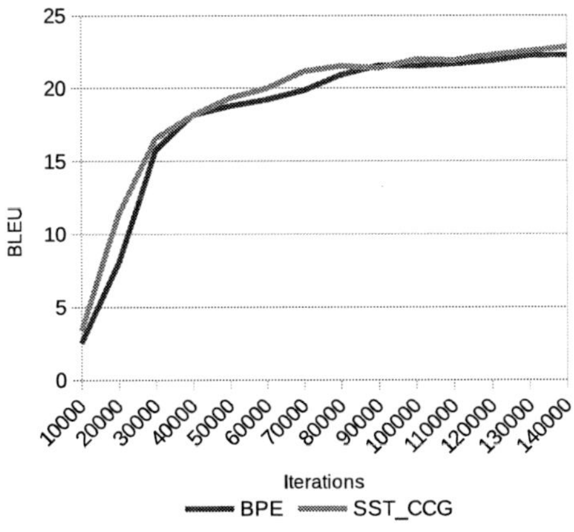

Figure 3: Baseline (BPE) vs Combined (CCG–SST) NMT Systems for English–German, evaluated on the Europarl test set.

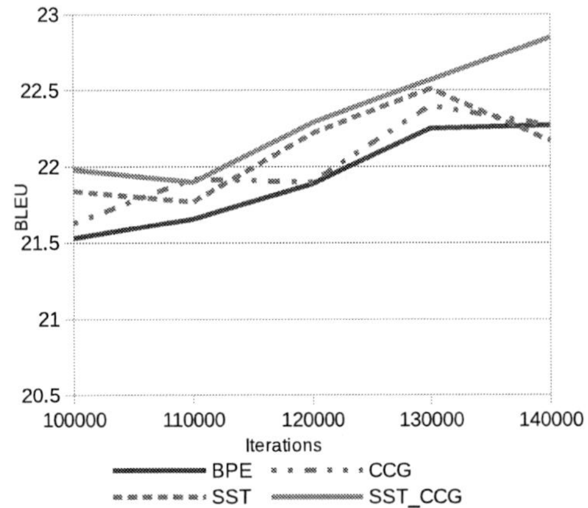

Figure 4: Baseline (BPE) vs Syntactic (CCG) vs Semantic (SST) and Combined (CCG–SST) NMT Systems for EN–DE, evaluated on the Europarl test set.

| BLEU | BPE | CCG | SST | SST–CCG |
|---|---|---|---|---|
| Best Model | 22.32 | 22.47 | 22.51 | **22.85** |

Table 2: Best BLEU scores for Baseline (BPE), Syntactic (CCG), Semantic (SST) and Combined (SST–CCG) NMT systems for EN-DE evaluated on the Europarl test set.

## 6 Conclusions and Future Work

In this work we experimented with EN–FR and EN–DE data augmented with semantic and syntactic features. For both language pairs we observe that adding extra semantic and/or syntactic features leads to faster convergence. Furthermore, the benefit of the additional features is more clear on a dissimilar test set which is in accordance with our original hypothesis stating that semantic and syntactic features (and their combination) can be beneficial for generalization. In the future, we would like to perform manual evaluations on the outputs of our systems to see whether they correlate with the BLEU scores. In the next step, we will let the models converge, create the ensemble models for the different systems and compute whether the increase in BLEU score is significant. Furthermore, we would like to experiment with larger datasets to verify whether the positive effect of the linguistic features remains.

## 7 Acknowledgements

I would like to thank Natalie Schluter for her insightful comments and feedback and Roam Analytics for sponsoring the ACL SRW travel grant. This work has been supported by the Dublin City University Faculty of Engineering & Computing under the Daniel O'Hare Research Scholarship scheme and by the ADAPT Centre for Digital Content Technology which is funded under the SFI Research Centres Programme (Grant 13/RC/2106) and is co-funded under the European Regional Development Fund.

# References

Roee Aharoni and Yoav Goldberg. 2017. Towards string-to-tree neural machine translation. In *Proceedings of the Association for Computational Linguistics, ACL*, Vancouver, Canada.

Andrei Alexandrescu and Katrin Kirchhoff. 2006. Factored Neural Language Models. In *Proceedings of the Human Language Technology Conference of the NAACL, Companion Volume: Short Papers*, pages 1–4, New York, USA.

Eleftherios Avramidis and Philipp Koehn. 2008. Enriching Morphologically Poor Languages for Statistical Machine Translation. In *Proceedings of The Association for Computer Linguistics (ACL-08)*, pages 763–770, Ohio, USA.

Dzmitry Bahdanau, Kyunghyun Cho, and Yoshua Bengio. 2014. Neural Machine Translation by Jointly Learning to Align and Translate. Banff, Canada.

Rafael E Banchs and Marta R Costa-Jussà. 2011. A Semantic Feature for Statistical Machine Translation. In *Proceedings of the Fifth Workshop on Syntax, Semantics and Structure in Statistical Translation*, pages 126–134, Portland, Oregon, USA.

Joost Bastings, Ivan Titov, Wilker Aziz, Diego Marcheggiani, and Khalil Sima'an. 2017. Graph Convolutional Encoders for Syntax-Aware Neural Machine Translation. In *Conference on Empirical Methods in Natural Language Processing (EMNLP)*, Copenhagen, Denmark.

Luisa Bentivogli, Arianna Bisazza, Mauro Cettolo, and Marcello Federico. 2016. Neural versus Phrase-Based Machine Translation Quality: a Case Study. In *Proceedings of the 2016 Conference on Empirical Methods in Natural Language Processing, EMNLP*, pages 257–267, Austin, Texas, USA.

Kyunghyun Cho, Bart van Merriënboer, Çalar Gülçehre, Dzmitry Bahdanau, Fethi Bougares, Holger Schwenk, and Yoshua Bengio. 2014. Learning Phrase Representations using RNN Encoder–Decoder for Statistical Machine Translation. In *Proceedings of EMNLP 2014*, pages 1724–1734, Doha, Qatar.

Massimiliano Ciaramita and Yasemin Altun. 2006. Broad-Coverage Sense Disambiguation and Information Extraction with a Supersense Sequence Tagger. In *Proceedings of the 2006 Conference on Empirical Methods in Natural Language Processing*, pages 594–602, Sydney, Australia.

Akiko Eriguchi, Kazuma Hashimoto, and Yoshimasa Tsuruoka. 2016. Tree-to-Sequence Attentional Neural Machine Translation. In *Proceedings of the 54th Annual Meeting of the Association for Computational Linguistics (ACL)*, pages 823–833, Berlin, Germany.

Akiko Eriguchi, Yoshimasa Tsuruoka, and Kyunghyun Cho. 2017. Learning to parse and translate improves neural machine translation. In *Proceedings of the Association for Computational Linguistics, ACL*, Vancouver, Canada.

Alexander Fraser, Marion Weller, Aoife Cahill, and Fabienne Cap. 2012. Modeling Inflection and Word-Formation in SMT. In *Proceedings of the 13th Conference of the European Chapter of the Association for Computational Linguistics (ACL)*, pages 664–674, Jeju Island, Republic of Korea.

Rejwanul Haque, Sudip Kumar Naskar, Yanjun Ma, and Andy Way. 2009. Using supertags as source language context in smt. In *European Association for Machine Translation*, Barcelona, Spain.

Hany Hassan, Khalil Sima'an, and Andy Way. 2007. Supertagged phrase-based statistical machine translation. In *Proceedings of the 45th Annual Meeting of the Association of Computational Linguistics*, pages 288–295, Prague, Czech Republic.

Zhaopeng Tu Muhua Zhu Min Zhang Guodong Zhou Junhui Li, Deyi Xiong. 2017. Modeling Source Syntax for Neural Machine Translation. In *Proceedings of the Association for Computational Linguistics, ACL*, page 688697, Vancouver, Canada.

Nal Kalchbrenner, Edward Grefenstette, and Phil Blunsom. 2014. A Convolutional Neural Network for Modelling Sentences. In *Proceedings of the 52nd Annual Meeting of the Association for Computational Linguistics, ACL, Volume 1: Long Papers*, pages 655–665, Baltimore, MD, USA.

Philipp Koehn. 2005. Europarl: A parallel corpus for statistical machine translation. In *MT summit*, volume 5, pages 79–86, Phuket, Thailand.

Philipp Koehn and Hieu Hoang. 2007. Factored translation models. In *Proceedings of Conference on Empirical Methods in Natural Language Processing Conference on Computational Natural Language Learning Joint Meeting following ACL (EMNLP-CONLL*, pages 868–876, Prague, Czech Republic.

Mike Lewis, Luheng He, and Luke Zettlemoyer. 2015. Joint A* CCG Parsing and Semantic Role Labelling. In *Proceedings of the 2015 Conference on Empirical Methods in Natural Language Processing, EMNLP*, pages 1444–1454, Lisbon, Portugal.

David Mareček, Rudolf Rosa, Petra Galuščáková, and Ondřej Bojar. 2011. Two-step Translation with Grammatical Post-Processing. In *Proceedings of the Sixth Workshop on Statistical Machine Translation*, pages 426–432, Edinburgh, UK.

Tomas Mikolov, Wen-tau Yih, and Geoffrey Zweig. 2013. Linguistic Regularities in Continuous Space Word Representations. In *hlt-Naacl*, volume 13, pages 746–751, Atlanta, USA.

George A Miller. 1995. Wordnet: a lexical database for english. *Communications of the ACM*, 38(11):39–41.

Maria Nadejde, Siva Reddy, Rico Sennrich, Tomasz Dwojak, Marcin Junczys-Dowmunt, Philipp Koehn, and Alexandra Birch. 2017. Predicting Target Language CCG Supertags Improves Neural Machine Translation. In *Proceedings of the Second Conference on Machine Translation*, pages 68–79, Copenhagen, Denmark.

Kishore Papineni, Salim Roukos, Todd Ward, and Wei-Jing Zhu. 2002. Bleu: a method for automatic evaluation of machine translation. In *Proceedings of the 40th annual meeting on association for computational linguistics*, pages 311–318.

Ivan A Sag, Thomas Wasow, Emily M Bender, and Ivan A Sag. 1999. *Syntactic theory: A formal introduction*, volume 92. Center for the Study of Language and Information Stanford, CA.

Nathan Schneider, Emily Danchik, Chris Dyer, and Noah A. Smith. 2014. Discriminative Lexical Semantic Segmentation with Gaps: Running the MWE Gamut. volume 2, pages 193–206, Baltimore, Maryland, USA.

Nathan Schneider and Noah A. Smith. 2015. A Corpus and Model Integrating Multiword Expressions and Supersenses. In *NAACL HLT 2015, The 2015 Conference of the North American Chapter of the Association for Computational Linguistics: Human Language Technologies,*, pages 1537–1547, Denver, Colorado, USA.

Rico Sennrich. 2015. Modelling and Optimizing on Syntactic N-grams for Statistical Machine Translation. *Transactions of the Association for Computational Linguistics*, 3:169–182.

Rico Sennrich, Orhan Firat, Kyunghyun Cho, Alexandra Birch, Barry Haddow, Julian Hitschler, Marcin Junczys-Dowmunt, Samuel L"aubli, Antonio Valerio Miceli Barone, Jozef Mokry, and Maria Nadejde. 2017. Nematus: a Toolkit for Neural Machine Translation. In *Proceedings of the Software Demonstrations of the 15th Conference of the European Chapter of the Association for Computational Linguistics*, pages 65–68, Valencia, Spain.

Rico Sennrich and Barry Haddow. 2016. Linguistic Input Features Improve Neural Machine Translation. In *Proceedings of the First Conference on Machine Translation, WMT, ACL*, pages 83–91, Berlin, Germany.

Rico Sennrich, Barry Haddow, and Alexandra Birch. 2016. Neural Machine Translation of Rare Words with Subword Units. In *Proceedings of the 54th Annual Meeting of the Association for Computational Linguistics, ACL Volume 1: Long Papers*, Berlin, Germany.

Xing Shi, Inkit Padhi, and Kevin Knight. 2016. Does String-Based Neural MT Learn Source Syntax? In *Proceedings of Empirical Methods on Natural Language Processing (EMNLP 2016)*, Austin, Texas, USA.

Mark Steedman. 2000. *The Syntactic Process*, volume 24. Cambridge: MIT Press.

Ilya Sutskever, Oriol Vinyals, and Quoc V. Le. 2014. Sequence to Sequence Learning with Neural Networks. In *Advances in Neural Information Processing Systems 27: Annual Conference on Neural Information Processing Systems*, pages 3104–3112, Montreal, Quebec, Canada.

Kristina Toutanova, Dan Klein, Christopher D Manning, and Yoram Singer. 2003. Feature-rich Part-of-Speech Tagging with a Cyclic Dependency Network. In *Proceedings of the 2003 Conference of the North American Chapter of the Association for Computational Linguistics on Human Language Technology-Volume 1*, pages 173–180.

Kristina Toutanova, Hisami Suzuki, and Achim Ruopp. 2008. Applying Morphology Generation Models to Machine Translation. In *ACL*, pages 514–522.

Eva Vanmassenhove, Jinhua Du, and Andy Way. 2017. Investigating 'aspect' in nmt and smt: Translating the english simple past and present perfect. *Computational Linguistics in the Netherlands Journal*, 7:109–128.

Philip Williams and Philipp Koehn. 2012. Ghkm Rule Extraction and Scope-3 Parsing in Moses. In *Proceedings of the Seventh Workshop on Statistical Machine Translation*, pages 388–394.

Shuangzhi Wu, Ming Zhou, and Dongdong Zhang. 2017. Improved Neural Machine Translation with Source Syntax. In *Proceedings of the Twenty-Sixth International Joint Conference on Artificial Intelligence (IJCAI 2017).*, pages 4179–4185, Melbourne, Australia.

# Unsupervised Semantic Abstractive Summarization


**Shibhansh Dohare**
CSE Department
IIT Kanpur
`sdohare'`

**Vivek Gupta**
Microsoft Research
Bangalore
`t-vigu"`

**Harish Karnick**
CSE Department
IIT Kanpur
`hk'`



## Abstract

Automatic abstractive summary generation remains a significant open problem
for natural language processing. In this
work, we develop a novel pipeline for Semantic Abstractive Summarization (SAS).
SAS, as introduced by Liu et al. (2015)
first generates an AMR graph of an input
story, through which it extracts a summary
graph and finally, creates summary sentences from this summary graph. Compared to earlier approaches, we develop
a more comprehensive method to generate the story AMR graph using state-of-
the-art co-reference resolution and *Meta
Nodes*. Which we then use in a novel
unsupervised algorithm based on how humans summarize a piece of text to extract the summary sub-graph. Our algorithm outperforms the state of the art SAS
method by 1.7% F1 score in node prediction.


## 1 Introduction

Summarization of large texts is still an open problem in natural language processing. Automatic
summarization is often used in summarizing large
texts like stories, journal papers, news articles and
even larger texts like books and court judgments.

Existing methods for summarization can be
broadly categorized into two categories *Extractive* and *Abstractive*. Most of the work done
on summarization in the past has been Extractive
Dang and Owczarzak (2008). Extractive methods directly pick up words and sentences from the
text to generate a summary. Vanderwende et al.
(2004) transformed the input to nodes, then used

the Pagerank algorithm to score nodes, and finally
grow the nodes from high-value to low-value using some heuristics. Some of the approaches combine this with sentence compression so that more
sentences can be packed in the summary. McDonald (2007), Martins and Smith (2009), Almeida
and Martins (2013), and Gillick and Favre (2009)
among others used ILPs and approximations for
encoding compression and extraction. However,
human level summary generation require rephras-
ing sentences and combining information from
different parts of the text. Thus, these methods
are inherently limited in the sense that they can
never generate human level summaries for large
and complicated documents.

On the other hand, most Abstractive methods
take advantages of the recent developments in
deep learning. Specifically, the recent success of
the sequence to sequence Sutskever et al. (2014)
learning models, where recurrent networks read
the text; encodes it and then generate target text
produce promising results. Rush et al. (2015),
Chopra et al. (2016), Nallapati et al. (2016),
See et al. (2017) used standard encoder-decoder
models along with their variants to generate summaries. Takase et al. (2016) incorporated the
AMR information in the standard encoder-decoder
models to improve results. These approaches have
produced promising results and have been recently
shown to be competitive with the extractive methods, but they are still far from reaching human
level quality in summary generation. One of the
significant problems with these methods is that
there is no guarantee that they can handle sub-
tleties of language like the presence of a word that
negates the meaning of the full text, hard to capture co-references, etc.

Banarescu et al. (2013) introduced AMR as a
base for work on statistical natural language understanding and generation. AMR tries to cap-

---


'@cse.iitk.ac.in, "@microsoft.com, Shibhansh is the
corresponding author





*Proceedings of ACL 2018, Student Research Workshop*, pages 74–83
Melbourne, Australia, July 15 - 20, 2018. ©2018 Association for Computational Linguistics

ture *"who is doing what to whom"* in a sentence. An AMR represents the meaning of a sentence using rooted, acyclic, labeled, directed graphs. Figure 2 shows the AMR graph of the sentence *"I looked carefully all around me"* generated by the JAMR parser Flanigan et al. (2014). The nodes in the AMR are labeled with *concepts*, in Figure 2 *'around'* represents one such concept. Edges contain the information regarding the *semantic relation* between the concepts. In Figure 2 *direction* is the relation between the concepts *look-01* and *around*. AMR relies on Propbank for semantic relations (edge labels). Concepts can also be of the form *run-01* where the index *01* represents the first sense of the word *run*. Further details about the AMR can be found in the AMR guidelines Banarescu et al. (2015). Liu et al. (2015) started the work on summarization using AMR, which we call Semantic Abstractive Summarization (SAS).

Liu et al. (2015) introduced the fundamental idea behind SAS. In SAS the final summary is produced by extracting a summary subgraph from the story graph and generating the summary from this extracted graph (See Figure 1). But the work was limited to obtaining the summary graph due to the absence of AMR to text generators at that time. They used various graphical features like distance from the root, the number of outgoing edges, etc. and sentence number as features for nodes. The procedure then learned weights over these features with the constraint that the nodes must form a connected graph.

In this work, we propose an alternative method to use AMRs for abstractive summarization. Our approach is inspired by the way humans summarize any piece of text. User studies Chin et al. (2009); Kang et al. (2011) have shown that humans summarize by first writing down the key phrases and then try to figure out the relationships among them and then organize the data accordingly. Falke and Gurevych (2017) used similar ideas to propose the task of concept map based summarization. We design our algorithm along the same lines. The first step is to find the most important entities/events in the text. The second step is to identify the key relations among the most important entities/events, and finally, in the last step, we capture information around the selected relation. AMRs provide a natural way to achieve this process, as all the events/entities can be represented by a node Rao et al. (2017) or a group

of nodes, while any relation can be captured by a path in the AMR graph. We also develop a more comprehensive method to generate the story AMR from the sentence AMRs based on event/entity co-reference resolution and *Meta Nodes*. Our algorithm outperforms the previous state of the art methods for SAS by 1.7% F1 score on Node prediction.

Our major contributions in this work are :

- We propose a novel unsupervised algorithm for the key step of summary graph extraction, which provides a stronger baseline for future work on SAS.

- We propose a novel method to generate the story AMR based on a more comprehensive co-reference resolution and *Meta Nodes*.

The rest of the paper is organized as follows. Section 2 and 3 contain description of the datasets and the algorithm used for summary generation respectively. Section 4 contains the results of experiments using our approach.

## 2  Datasets

We use the proxy report section of the AMR Bank Knight et al. (2014), as it is the only section that is relevant for the task because it contains the gold-standard (human-generated) AMR graphs for news articles and their summaries. In the training set, the stories and summaries contain 17.5 sentences and 1.5 sentences on average respectively. The training and test sets include 298 and 33 summary document pairs respectively.

## 3  Pipeline for Summary Generation

The pipeline consists of three major steps. The first step is to convert the document into an AMR (step-1). The next step is to extract a summary AMR from the document AMR constructed in the previous step (step-2). The final step generates text from the extracted sub-graph (step-3). In the following subsections, we expand on each step.

### 3.1  Step 1: Story to AMR: Document graph generation

*Document AMR* refers to the AMR representing the meaning of the whole document. The AMR

---

Code for the complete pipeline for the end to end summarization is available at `https://github.com/shibhansh/Unsupervised-SAS`

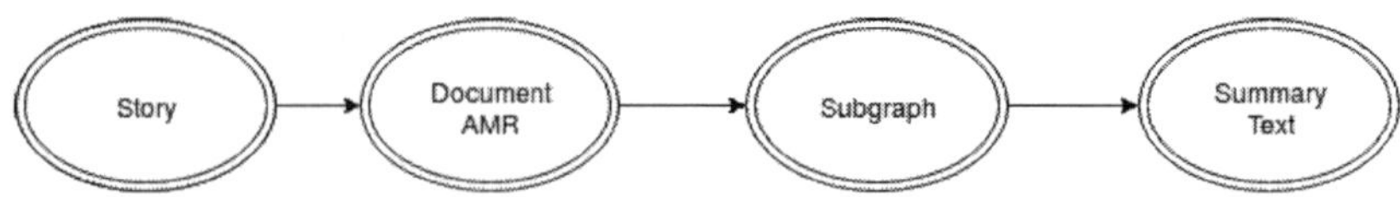

Figure 1: The pipeline proposed by (Liu et al., 2015) had the following step - AMR Parsing, Naive node merging, Subgraph selection and Text generation

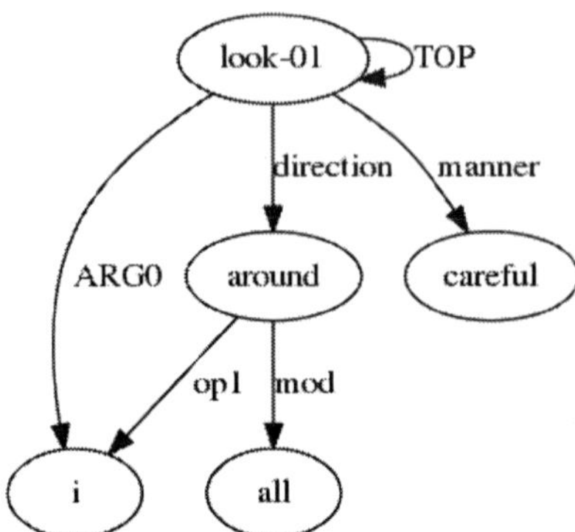


Figure 2: The graphical representation of the AMR graph of the sentence : *"I looked carefully all around me"* using AMRICA  Saphra and Lopez (2015)

formalism guarantees that no two nodes refer to the same event/entity. Liu et al. (2015) extends this principle to multiple sentences by merging nodes referring to the same named entity (or date) across sentences. However, they adopted a naive approach to for co-reference resolution using a simple name and date matching 3.1. The co-reference resolution can be greatly improved if we take advantage of the huge literature on text co-reference resolution. We solve *node co-reference resolution* using *text co-reference resolution* followed by mapping the text to a node using *Alignments*.

*Node Co-reference Resolution* is a crucial step, as a wrongly generated document AMR can produce a factually wrong summary. To mitigate wrong mergers, we implement multiple sanity checks to avoid wrong mergers. Text co-reference resolution techniques can be broadly categorized into three major categories - neural, statistical and rule-based. We used the state-of-the-art end-to-end neural co-reference resolution system Lee et al. (2017). Future work can use an ensemble of co-reference resolvers to improve robustness. A list of major sanity checks that we employed

- Don't merge nodes which have an outgoing edge with label *:name* if the value of

*:name* argument is different, and neither of the names is the initials of the other

- Don't merge if, cycle emerges in the graph after the merger

- Don't merge if, the nodes to be merged have common outgoing edge labels, and the nodes that are connected with these edges are different

For mapping text to the node, we use *alignments*. *Alignments* provide a mapping from a word in the text to the corresponding node in the AMR. Most co-reference systems provide co-references between noun phrases instead of individual words. But for *node co-reference resolution* we are required to merge individual nodes rather than a group of nodes. However, Lee et al. (2017) system also outputs attention weight for every word of a noun phrase which signifies the importance of each word in the noun phrase. We merge the nodes corresponding to the word that has the maximum attention weight among the words in the noun phrase.

Merging nodes that refer to the same event/entity suggests that the merged node is more important in the graph than the original nodes as there are more incoming and outgoing edges in the graph now. Co-reference resolution captures explicit reference of an event/entity, which implies that the nodes should be merged as they are same and thus it helps increase the importance of the node. But, there are many cases where words are not referring to the same entity or event but they refer to the same abstract concept, or there might be cases where the words are talking about the same event without explicitly referring to it. In such cases, these words should reinforce the importance of each other, but simple co-reference resolution does not capture this, and hence co-reference resolution is not enough. We need something new in the graph that captures when two nodes are reinforcing the importance of each other without actually merging the two nodes. In table 1 we present two examples where words reinforce the importance of each other without referring to the exact same thing.

These examples inspire us to introduce a new set of nodes which we call *Meta nodes*. In this work, we use *Meta nodes* to increase the importance of only common nouns. Common nouns like drugs, opium, etc. can occur a lot of times in the text which suggests that they are relevant for the text, but they are not identified by co-reference systems as their different occurrences do not refer to exactly the same thing. To capture the important *common nouns* which are otherwise not captured in the co-reference resolution, we add a new *Meta node* in the graph for each such set of *common nouns*. In Example 2 of Fig. 1, we introduce a *Meta Node* for the common noun *Opium*, which is present twice in the story. Each *Meta node* is connected to all the occurrences of the corresponding common noun. The nodes connected with a meta node signifies that the nodes at some level might refer to the same thing. *Meta nodes* are used as representative for the group during ranking but they are not extracted in the final summary graph, and hence they are not used during the final step of summary generation.

The cases that we examined in Table 1 are cases where the words don't have a perfect identity but rather a near identity. This points out that co-reference resolution is not a simple yes/no question but rather a complicated one. This problem of the complexity of co-reference resolution has been explored theoretically in the literature Recasens et al. (2011); Versley (2008) and our work will benefit directly from more work on the complexity of co-reference resolution. In our current work, we don't implement any procedure to detect reinforcements of the sort given in Example 2 of Table 1. Future works may include event co-reference resolution and word similarity using word embeddings to identify such reinforcements.

## 3.2 Step 2: Summary Graph Extraction

Summary graph extraction is a key step in SAS. In this step, we extract the summary sentence AMR graphs from the document AMR produced in Step-1. We take our cue from the way humans summarize a text by first identifying the most important entities/events in the text then finding the most important relationships among these events/entities and finally include information surrounding the

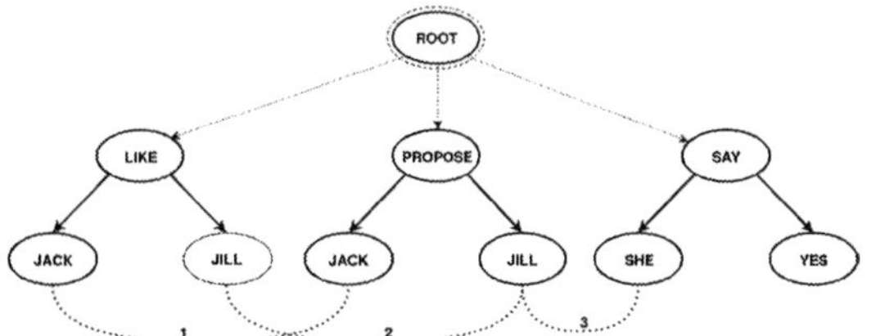


Figure 3: An example of node merging in a very basic AMR, The mergers *1* and *2* were also present in the methods proposed by Liu et al. (2015) but not the merger *3*. Here, dash line represent node to be merged.

selected relationship(s).

**Step-A: Finding Important Nodes -** For finding important events/entities, we use *term frequency-inverse document frequency* (Tf − IDF) to determine the importance of any node. We first find the top $n$ nodes in the graph using *term frequency*. This $n$ depends upon the size of the summary required. Similar to earlier approaches we use *Alignments* to find text corresponding to the nodes. Finally, we use Tf-IDF values of the text corresponding to the nodes to rank the selected $n$ nodes. The proxy report section of the AMR Bank is quite small with only 298 training stories. We use the CNN-Dailymail Hermann et al. (2015) corpus containing around 300,000 news articles to evaluate the Document Frequencies (DF). We calculate Tf − Idf as -

$$\text{Tf} - \text{Idf} = \text{Tf} \times \log_{10}(300,000/(\text{DF}+1))$$

As explained in section 3.1, *Meta Nodes* are used as a representative for a set of nodes during importance evaluation. Hence, during importance evaluation we do not consider nodes that are connected with any *Meta Node*. To evaluate the importance of a *Meta Node*, we take the number of nodes connected with a *Meta Node* as the *term frequency* for the *Meta Node*.

**Step-B: Finding Key Relation-** The next step is to find the important relationship between a pair of selected nodes. We use a heuristic in this step. The idea is that the key relationship between the nodes will generally be present in the sentence where they occur together for the first time. If there is no such sentence, then there is probably no important direct relationship between the two nodes, and we ignore the pair. AMRs contain semantic information at the top of the AMR graph.

Table 1: In Example 1, the words **illegal** and **ban** reinforce each others importance but they are not captured by co-reference resolution. We add a *Meta Node* connected to the nodes corresponding to the words **illegal** and **ban**. During importance evaluation, the occurrences of this *Meta Node* will be these occurrences of **illegal** and **ban** and *term frequency* for this *Meta Node* will be 2. Similarly, in the second example both the occurrences of the word **opium** are connected to a new *Meta Node*

| |
|---|
| 1. On 011006 The Citizen newspaper stated that it is **illegal** for South Africans to be involved in mercenary activity or to render foreign military assistance inside or outside of South Africa. The Citizen newspaper stated that the South African Foreign Ministry announced on 011005 that the South African government imposed the mercenary activity **ban** following reports that 1000 Muslims with military training have enlisted to leave South Africa for Afghanistan to fight for the Taliban against the United States. |
| 2. Head of the U.N. drug office Antonio Maria Costa said that Afghanistan has produced so much **opium** in recent years that the Taliban are cutting back poppy cultivation and stockpiling raw opium in an effort to support prices and preserve a major source of financing for the insurgency. Costa said this to reporters last week as the U.N. Drug Office Office prepared to release its latest survey of Afghanistan's **opium** crop. |

Table 2: Results on the Proxy report section of the AMR bank. First-half contains the Recall, Precision, and F-1 for the nodes in the generated summary AMR. The second half contains the scores for the final summary generated using state-of-the-art text generator evaluated using the ROUGE metric

| Method | Subgraph extraction | | | Full pipeline | | |
|---|---|---|---|---|---|---|
| | Recall | Precision | $F_1$ | R-1 | R-2 | R-L |
| Liu et al. (2015) | 63.5 | 54.7 | 58.7 | - | - | - |
| Unsupervised SAS (Naive co-reference) | **67.9** | 57.2 | 60.3 | - | - | - |
| Unsupervised SAS (Lee et al. (2017) co-reference) | 67.0 | **58.0** | **60.4** | 39.5 | 16.5 | 29.0 |
| Unsupervised SAS (Human co-reference) | 67.7 | 60.4 | 62.4 | 40.9 | 16.7 | 29.5 |

Thus, in the selected sentence we find a path between the two nodes closest to the root. If one of the selected nodes happens to be a *Meta Node*, the occurrences of the *Meta Node* include all the occurrences of all the nodes that the *Meta Node* represents (Fig. 1).

**Step-C: Capture Surrounding Information -** The final step in subgraph extraction is to expand around the selected path to capture the surrounding information. We use OpenIE Banko (2009) at this step. The output of the OpenIE system are tuples of the form $(arg; relation; arg)$. The relevant tuples for us are the set of tuples that contain the selected path. As, these tuples contain all the auxiliary information about the relationship that they are describing, selecting a tuple will solve the problem of graph expansion. To capture the maximum amount of auxiliary information we choose the largest tuple among the set of relevant tuples. This ends the process of summary graph extraction. Algorithm 1 provides an overview of the entire algorithm.

### 3.3 Step 3: Summary Generation

To generate sentences from the extracted AMR graphs we use state of the art AMR to text generator Konstas et al. (2017).

## 4 Experiments

In table 2 we report results on the test set of the proxy report section of the AMR bank. The table contains results using the human annotated AMRs. We outperform the state-of-the-art in SAS by 1.7% F1 scores in node prediction. Similar to previous methods we use the target summary size to control the length of the output summary.

To evaluate the effectiveness of the method till the summary graph extraction step, we compare the generated summary graph with the gold-standard target summary graph. We report Recall, Precision, and F1 for graph nodes. Finally, to evaluate the effectiveness of the pipeline, we evaluate the performance using ROUGE Lin (2004), and we report ROUGE-1, ROUGE-2, and ROUGE-L.

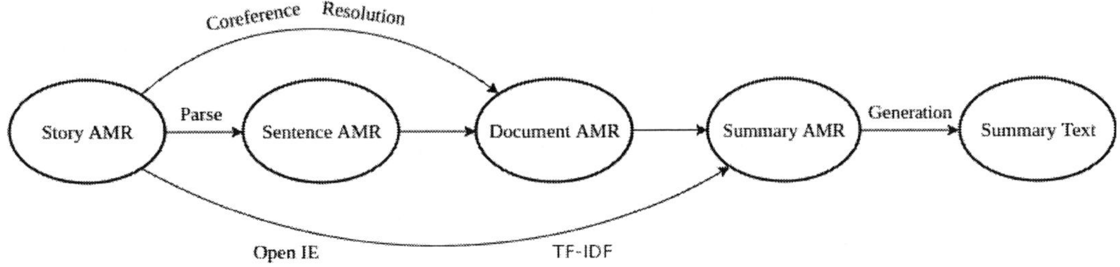


Figure 4: The updated pipeline proposed by us has the following step - AMR Parsing, Co-reference resolution, Open Information Extraction,TF-IDF calculation, Subgraph selection and Text generation

---

**Algorithm 1** Overview of Algorithm

---

**Input.** Input original text data
Node co-reference resolution and Meta node formation
Node ranking using Tf-idf
Rank nodes
Rank node pairs, using node weights
**for** Sorted node pairs **do**
   Select the first co-occurrence sentence
   **if** no such sentence **then**
     Continue
   **end if**
   Find the path closest to root in the sentence
   Find relevant tuples using OpenIE
   Choose the largest tuple containing the path
   **if** no such tuple **then**
     Output the selected sentence AMR
   **end if**
   **if** summary size $>$ required size **then**
     Break
   **end if**
**end for**
AMR to text conversion

---

As clear from table 2 there is not much difference between the scores when we use naive node resolution and date merging and when we use state-of-art co-reference resolution. To check the impact of co-reference resolution, we also did manual co-reference resolution on the test set which resulted in a further 2% increase in the scores to 62.4%. We suspect that a significant reason for lower performance with state of the art co-reference resolution might be the inability of the system to handle cataphoric references. These references are particularly crucial in news articles where the first occurrence of an entity/event is generally essential.

## 5 Conclusion and Future Work

In this work, we present a new method to do Semantic Abstractive Summarization (Figure 4). We outperform the previous state-of-the-art methods for SAS by 1.7% and by 3.7% using human co-reference resolution. In the process, we complete the SAS pipeline for the first time showing that SAS can be used to construct high-quality summaries. We also extend the method to construct a document AMR graph from the sentence AMRs using *Meta nodes* which can further be used in some future formalism for Document Meaning Representation.

The work will benefit directly from improvements in each step of the pipeline. Specifically, the advances in co-reference resolution for the near-identity cases might significantly improve the summary quality. We are currently experimenting with bigger text summarization datasets like DUC 2004 and DUC 2006. The hypothesis we used to find the key relations is the main hurdle in extending the work to multi-document summarization as all other steps can be directly applied in multi-document summarization. Using different methods that might be based on supervision to find the key relation is an interest direction for future work.

## Acknowledgments


We would like to thank the anonymous ACL reviewers for their insightful comments. We also thank Susmit Wagle and Prerna Bharti of IIT Kanpur for helpful discussions. Vivek Gupta acknowledges support from Microsoft Research Travel Award. We would also like to thank Roam Analytics for sponsoring Shibhansh's ACL SRW travel grant. The opinions stated in this paper are of authors alone.

## References

Miguel Almeida and Andre Martins. 2013. Fast and robust compressive summarization with dual decomposition and multi-task learning. In *Proceedings of the 51st Annual Meeting of the Association for Computational Linguistics (Volume 1: Long Papers)*, pages 196–206. Association for Computational Linguistics.

Laura Banarescu, Claire Bonial, Shu Cai, Madalina Georgescu, Kira Griffitt, Ulf Hermjakob, Kevin Knight, Philipp Koehn, Martha Palmer, and Nathan Schneider. 2015. Amr-guidelines.

Laura Banarescu, Claire Bonial, Shu Cai, Madalina Georgescu, Kira Griffitt, Ulf Hermjakob, Kevin Knight, Martha Palmer, Philipp Koehn, and Nathan Schneider. 2013. Abstract meaning representation for sembanking. Proceedings of Linguistic Annotation Workshop.

Michele Banko. 2009. *Open Information Extraction for the Web*. Ph.D. thesis, Seattle, WA, USA. AAI3370456.

George Chin, Olga A. Kuchar, and Katherine E. Wolf. 2009. Exploring the analytical processes of intelligence analysts. In *InProceedings of the SIGCHI Conference on Human Factors in Computing Systems*, page 1120. Association for Computational Linguistics.

Sumit Chopra, Michael Auli, and Alexander M. Rush. 2016. Abstractive sentence summarization with attentive recurrent neural networks. In *Proceedings of the 2016 Conference of the North American Chapter of the Association for Computational Linguistics: Human Language Technologies*, pages 93–98, San Diego, California. Association for Computational Linguistics.

Hoa Trang Dang and Karolina Owczarzak. 2008. Overview of the tac 2008 update summarization task. In Proceedings of Text Analysis Conference (TAC).

Tobias Falke and Iryna Gurevych. 2017. Bringing structure into summaries: Crowdsourcing a benchmark corpus of concept maps. In *Proceedings of the 2017 Conference on Empirical Methods in Natural Language Processing*, pages 2951–2961. Association for Computational Linguistics.

Jeffrey Flanigan, Sam Thomson, Jaime Carbonell, Chris Dyer, and Noah A. Smith. 2014. A discriminative graph-based parser for the abstract meaning representation. In *Proceedings of the 52nd Annual Meeting of the Association for Computational Linguistics (Volume 1: Long Papers)*, pages 1426–1436. Association for Computational Linguistics.

Dan Gillick and Benoit Favre. 2009. A scalable global model for summarization. In Proceedings of the NAACL Workshop on Integer Linear Programming for Natural Langauge Processing.

Karl Moritz Hermann, Tomas Kocisky, Edward Grefenstette, Lasse Espeholt, Will Kay, Mustafa Suleyman, and Phil Blunsom. 2015. Teaching machines to read and comprehend.

Youn-ah Kang, Carsten Gorg, and John Stasko. 2011. How can visual analytics assist investigative analysis? design implications from an evaluation. *IEEE Transactions on Visualization and Computer Graphics*, 17(5):570–583.

Kevin Knight, Laura Baranescu, Claire Bonial, Madalina Georgescu, Kira Griffitt, Ulf Hermjakob, Daniel Marcu, Martha Palmer, and Nathan Schneider. 2014. Deft phase 2 amr annotation r1 ldc2015e86. philadelphia: Linguistic data consortium. Abstract meaning representation (AMR) annotation release 1.0 LDC2014T12. Web Download. Philadelphia: Linguistic Data Consortium.

Ioannis Konstas, Srinivasan Iyer, Mark Yatskar, Yejin Choi, and Luke Zettlemoyer. 2017. Neural amr: Sequence-to-sequence models for parsing and generation. In Proceedings of the 52nd Annual Meeting of the Association for Computational Linguistics. Association for Computational Linguistics.

Kenton Lee, Luheng He, Mike Lewis, and Luke Zettlemoyer. 2017. End-to-end neural coreference resolution. *CoRR*, abs/1707.07045.

C. Lin. 2004. Rouge: A package for automatic evaluation of summaries. Text Summarization Branches Out, Post-Conference Workshop of ACL 2004. Barcelona, Spain.

Fei Liu, Flanigan Jeffrey, Thomson Sam, Sadeh Norman, and Smith Noah A. 2015. Toward abstractive summarization using semantic representations. In Proceedings of the 2015 Conference of the North American Chapter of the Association for Computational Linguistics. Association for Computational Linguistics, Denver, Colorado, pages 10771086.

Andre F. T. Martins and Noah A. Smith. 2009. Summarization with a joint model for sentence extraction and compression. In Proceedings of the ACL Workshop on Integer Linear Programming for Natural Language Processing.

Ryan McDonald. 2007. A study of global inference algorithms in multi-document summarization. In *Proceedings of the 29th European Conference on IR Research*, ECIR'07, pages 557–564, Berlin, Heidelberg. Springer-Verlag.

Ramesh Nallapati, Bowen Zhou, Cicero dos Santos, Caglar Gulcehre, and Bing Xiang. 2016. Abstractive text summarization using sequence-to-sequence rnns and beyond. In *Proceedings of The 20th SIGNLL Conference on Computational Natural Language Learning*, pages 280–290, Berlin, Germany. Association for Computational Linguistics.

Sudha Rao, Daniel Marcu, Kevin Knight, and Hal Daumé III. 2017. Biomedical event extraction using abstract meaning representation. In *BioNLP 2017*, pages 126–135, Vancouver, Canada,. Association for Computational Linguistics.

Marta Recasens, Eduard Hovy, and M. Antnia Mart. 2011. Identity, non-identity, and near-identity: Addressing the complexity of coreference. *Lingua*, 121(6):1138 – 1152.

Alexander M. Rush, Sumit Chopra, and Jason Weston. 2015. A neural attention model for sentence summarization.

Naomi Saphra and Adam Lopez. 2015. Amrica: an amr inspector for cross-language alignments. In *Proceedings of the 2015 Conference of the North American Chapter of the Association for Computational Linguistics: Demonstrations*, pages 36–40, Denver, Colorado. Association for Computational Linguistics.

Abigail See, Peter J. Liu, and Christopher D. Manning. 2017. Get to the point: Summarization with pointer-generator networks.

Ilya Sutskever, Oriol Vinyals, and Quoc V Le. 2014. Sequence to sequence learning with neural networks. In *Advances in Neural Information Processing Systems 27*, pages 3104–3112. Curran Associates, Inc.

Sho Takase, Jun Suzuki, Naoaki Okazaki, Tsutomu Hirao, and Masaaki Nagata. 2016. Neural headline generation on abstract meaning representation. In *Proceedings of the 2016 Conference on Empirical Methods in Natural Language Processing*, pages 1054–1059, Austin, Texas. Association for Computational Linguistics.

Lucy Vanderwende, Michele Banko, and Arul Menezes. 2004. Event-centric summary generation. In Proceedings of DUC.

Yannick Versley. 2008. Vagueness and referential ambiguity in a large-scale annotated corpus. *Research on Language and Computation*, 6(3):333–353.

## A  Example to generate document AMR from sentence AMR

In this appendix, we give an example showing how to generate Document AMR from the sentence AMRs. Consider a short multi-sentence story -

*A Kathmandu police officer reports –. 1 soldier of the Royal Nepal Army was seriously injured on 29 August 2002 when a bomb disposal team attempted to defuse the bomb left at an electricity pole in okubahal near Sundhara in Lalitpur district in Kathmandu. Anti-government insurgents are believed to have planted the bomb. The injured soldier has been admitted to the army hospital in Kathmandu.*

Figure 5 shows the sentence AMRs of the four sentences of the short story. The nodes that refer to the similar entity have to be merged; the dashed lines connect the nodes to be merged. Figure 6 shows, the generated document AMR from the merger. Fig 6 also shows how large the AMRs of even short stories can become after merging.

If the summarization process were to follow, we would've started by finding the key nodes in the document graph based on $TF - IDF$. The Term frequency is the number of incoming edges in the AMR. It is clear from the document AMR that the important nodes based on Term frequency are *Soldier, Bomb,* and *Kathmandu*. Then we use $TF - IDF$ to rank among these key nodes, it turns out that the key nodes that the final ranking in decreasing order of importance is *Kathmandu, Soldier* and *Bomb*. The next step is to find the key relation, which according to our hypothesis lies in the sentence where they first co-occur, i.e., the second sentence. The exact relation is the highest path. As clear from Figure 5 the path will include the nodes corresponding to the words *Kathmandu, Soldier, Injured*. And finally in the last step we use the OpenIE system to capture important information surrounding this path.

81

Figure 5: The AMRs of the 4 sentence of the short story. Dashed lines represent the nodes to be merged.

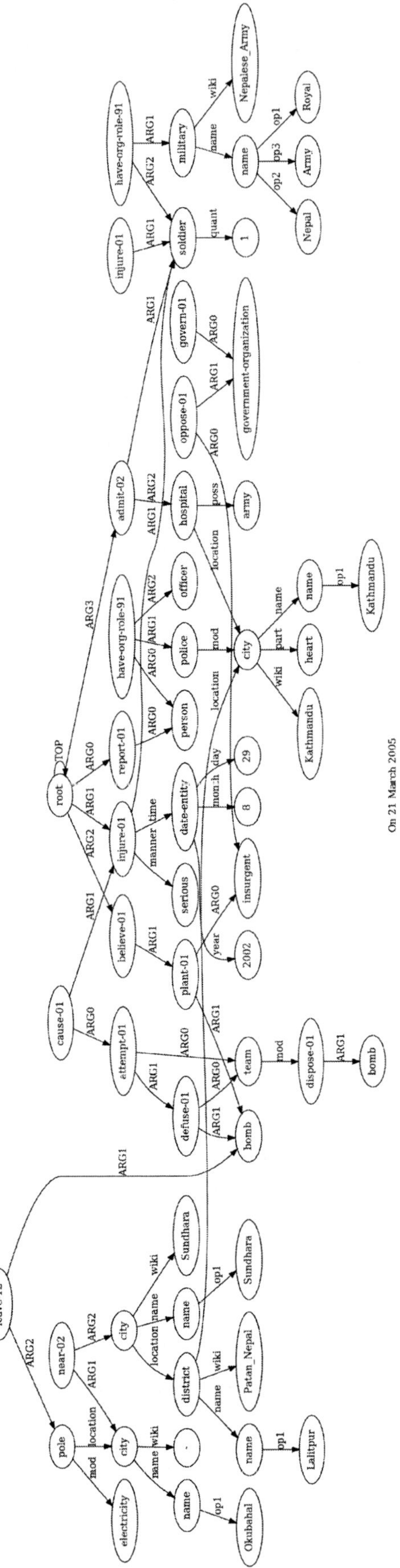

Figure 6: The document AMR generated by merging the four sentence AMRs of the story.

# Biomedical Document Retrieval for Clinical Decision Support System


**Jainisha Sankhavara**
IRLP lab,
Dhirubhai Ambani Institute of Information and Communication Technology
Gandhinagar, Gujarat, India
jainishasankhavara@gmail.com



## Abstract

The availability of huge amount of biomedical literature have opened up new possibilities to apply Information Retrieval and NLP for mining documents from them. In this work, we are focusing on biomedical document retrieval from literature for clinical decision support systems. We compare statistical and NLP based approaches of query reformulation for biomedical document retrieval. Also, we have modeled the biomedical document retrieval as a learning to rank problem. We report initial results for statistical and NLP based query reformulation approaches and learning to rank approach with future direction of research.


## 1 Introduction and Motivation

Medical and Healthcare related searches are having major focus of internet search now a days. The recent statistics shows that 61% of adults look online for health information (Jones, 2009). This demands proper search and retrieval systems for health related biomedical queries. Biomedical Information Retrieval (BIR) seeks special attention due to the characteristics of biomedical terminologies. Major challenges in biomedical domain are in handling complex, ambiguous, inconsistent medical terms and their ad-hoc abbreviations. Many medical terms are very complex. The average length of biomedical entities is much higher than general entities which makes entity identification task difficult for biomedical domain. Entity identification and normalization helps to better solve the problems of retrieval and ranking of documents for medical search systems, biomedical text summarization, biomedical text data visualization, etc.

As we are focusing here on biomedical document retrieval and ranking system, biomedical literature should be in consideration. Biomedical literature is an important source of study in medical science. Thousands of articles are being added into biomedical literature each year. This large set of biomedical text articles can be used as a collection for Clinical Decision Support System where the related biomedical articles are extracted and suggested to medical practitioners to best care their patients. For this purpose, dataset from Clinical Decision Support (CDS) track is used which contains millions of full text biomedical articles from PMC (PubMed Central)[1]. The statistics of CDS 2014, 2015 and 2016 datasets are given in the table 1. CDS[2] track focuses on retrieval of biomedical articles which are related to patient's medical case reports. These medical case reports which are being used as queries are case narratives of patients medical condition. They describes patients' medical condition i.e. medical history, symptoms, tests performed, treatments etc. For a given query/case report, the main problem is to find relevant documents from the available collection and rank them.

## 2 Background

'Information Retrieval: A Health and Biomedical Perspective' (Hersh, 2008) provides basic theory, implementation and evaluation of IR systems in health and biomedicine. The tasks of named entity recognition and relation and event extraction, summarization, question answering, and literature based discovery are outlined in Biomedical text mining: a survey of recent progress (Simpson and Demner-Fushman, 2012).

Automatic processing of biomedical text also

---

[1] http://www.ncbi.nlm.nih.gov/pmc/
[2] http://www.trec-cds.org/




*Proceedings of ACL 2018, Student Research Workshop*, pages 84–90
Melbourne, Australia, July 15 - 20, 2018. ©2018 Association for Computational Linguistics

| Dataset | CDS 2014 | CDS 2015 | CDS 2016 |
| --- | --- | --- | --- |
| #Documents | 733,138 | 733,138 | 1,255,259 |
| Collection size | 47.2 GB | 47.2 GB | 87.8 GB |
| #Total terms | 1,600,536,286 | 1,600,536,286 | 2,954,366,841 |
| #Uniq. terms | 3,689,317 | 3,689,317 | 4,564,612 |
| #Topics | 30 | 30 | 30 |
| #Rel. docs/Topic | 112 | 150 | 182 |
| Query forms | Description, Summary | Description, Summary | Note, Description, Summary |
| Avg. length of Description (in words) | 75.8 | 80.4 | 119.9 |
| Avg. length of Summary (in words) | 24.6 | 20.4 | 33.3 |
| Avg. length of Note (in words) | - | - | 239.4 |
| Avg. Doc length (in words) | 2183 | 2183 | 2353 |

Table 1: CDS DATA statistics

suffers from lexical ambiguity (homonymy and polysemy) and synonymy. Automatic query expansion (AQE) (Maron and Kuhns, 1960; Carpineto and Romano, 2012) which has a long history in information retrieval can be useful to deal with such problems. For instance, medical queries were expanded with other related terms from RxNorm, a drug dictionary, to improve the representation of a query for relevance estimation (Demner-Fushman et al., 2011). The emergence of medical domain specific knowledge like UMLS can contribute to the retrieval system to gain more understanding of the biomedical documents and queries. The Unified Medical Language System (UMLS) (Bodenreider, 2004) is a metathesaurus for medical domain. It is maintained by National Library of Medicine (NLM) and it is the most comprehensive resource, unifying over 100 dictionaries, terminologies, and ontologies. Various approaches of information retrieval with the UMLS Metathesaurus have been reported: some with decline in results (Hersh et al., 2000) and some with gain in results (Aronson and Rindflesch, 1997). The next section of this paper includes statistical approaches as well as NLP based approaches.

## 3 Query Reformulation for Biomedical Document Retrieval

Here, we present statistical and NLP based query reformulation approaches for biomedical document retrieval. Statistical approaches include feedback based query expansion and feedback document discovery based query expansion. An NLP based approach that is UMLS concept based query reformulation is also discussed here.

### 3.1 Automatic Query Expansion With Pseudo Relevance Feedback & Relevance Feedback

Query Expansion (QE) is the process of reformulating a query to improve retrieval performance and efficiency of IR systems. QE is proved to be efficient in case of document retrieval (Carpineto and Romano, 2012). It helps to overcome vocabulary mismatch issues by expanding the user query with additional relevant terms and by re-weighting all terms. Query Expansion which uses the top retrieved relevant documents is known as Relevance Feedback. It requires human judgment to identify relevant documents from top retrieved documents. While pseudo Relevance Feedback technique assumes the top retrieved documents to be relevant and uses as feedback documents. It does not require human input at all. The Query expansion based approaches for biomedical domain gives better results as compared to retrieval without query expansion (Sankhavara et al., 2014).

Table 2 and table 3 shows the results of standard retrieval (without expansion), Pseudo-Relevance Feedback (PRF) based Query Expansion and Relevance Feedback (RF) based Query Expansion with BM25 and In_expC2 retrieval models (Amati et al., 2003) on CDS 2014, 2015 and 2016 datasets. The retrieval model BM25 is a ranking function based on probabilistic retrieval framework while In_expC2 is also a probabilistic but based on Divergence From Randomness (DFR). These models are available in Terrier IR Plateform[3] (Ounis et al., 2005) which is developed at School of Computing Science, University of Glas-

---

[3] http://terrier.org

85

| MAP | CDS 2014 | CDS 2015 | CDS 2016 |
|---|---|---|---|
| BM25 | 0.1071 | 0.1147 | 0.062 |
| BM25+PRF$_{10}$ | 0.1542 (+44%) | 0.1805 (+57.4%) | 0.0769 (+24%) |
| BM25+RF$_{10}$ | 0.205 (+91.4%) | 0.1941 (+69.2%) | 0.0984 (+58.7%) |
| BM25+RF$_{50}$ | 0.2768 (+158.5%) | 0.2283 (+99%) | 0.1456 (+134.8%) |
| In_expC2 | 0.1096 | 0.1201 | 0.0632 |
| In_expC2+PRF$_{10}$ | 0.1623 (+48.1%) | 0.1725 (+43.6%) | 0.0754 (+19.3%) |
| In_expC2+RF$_{10}$ | 0.2117 (+93.2%) | 0.1895 (+57.8%) | 0.0992 (+57%) |
| In_expC2+RF$_{50}$ | 0.2587 (+136%) | 0.2191 (+82.4%) | 0.1275 (+101.7%) |

Table 2: Results (MAP) of Query Expansion with PRF and RF

| infNDCG | CDS 2014 | CDS 2015 | CDS 2016 |
|---|---|---|---|
| BM25 | 0.1836 | 0.2115 | 0.171 |
| BM25+PRF$_{10}$ | 0.2522 (+37.4%) | 0.283 (+33.8%) | 0.2047 (+19.7%) |
| BM25+RF$_{10}$ | 0.3355 (+82.7%) | 0.3028 (+43.2%) | 0.2428 (+42%) |
| BM25+RF$_{50}$ | 0.4186 (+128%) | 0.3478 (+64.4%) | 0.3094 (+80.9%) |
| In_expC2 | 0.2002 | 0.2132 | 0.1785 |
| In_expC2+PRF$_{10}$ | 0.2724 (+36.1%) | 0.2734 (+28.2%) | 0.2018 (+13.1%) |
| In_expC2+RF$_{10}$ | 0.3426 (+71.1%) | 0.3015 (+41.4%) | 0.245 (+37.3%) |
| In_expC2+RF$_{50}$ | 0.4019 (+100.7%) | 0.339 (+59%) | 0.3219 (+80.3%) |

Table 3: Results (infNDCG) of Query Expansion with PRF and RF

gow. Here, we have used terrier plateform for the experiments. Summary part of the query is used for retrieval with top 10 and 50 top documents for feedback in expansion. MAP and infNDCG are used as evaluation metrics (Manning et al., 2008). Higher the value of evaluation measure, better the retrieval result of system. The result improves with PRF and RF based query expansion giving statistically significant results ($p < 0.05$) as compared to no expansion. Here RF is giving 50-60% more improvement than PRF over no expansion. We argue that biomedical retrieval should be done keeping human in the loop. A small human intervention can increase the retrieval accuracy to 60% more.

### 3.2 Feedback Document Discovery for Query Reformulation

Feedback Document Discovery based query expansion as described in (Sankhavara and Majumder, 2017) learns to identify relevant documents for query expansion from top retrieved documents. The main aim is to use small amount of human judgement and learn pseudo judgement for other documents to reformulate the queries. One approach is based on classification. If we have human judgements available for some of the feedback documents, then it will serve as a training data for classification. The documents were represented as a collection of bag-of-words, the TF-IDF scores of the words represent features and human relevance scores provides the classes. Then the relevance is predicted for other top retrieved feedback documents. The second approach is based on and classification+clustering. It first applies classification in similar way as in first approach and then applies clustering on relevance predicted class by the classification method, thus filtering out more non-relevant documents from relevant ones. Since, the convergence of K-means clustering depends on the initial choice of cluster centroids, the initial cluster centroids are chosen as the average of relevant documents vectors and the average of non-relevant documents vectors from training data.

Here we have used that approach with different features. The TF-IDF features are weighted based on type of words. CliNER tool (Boag et al., 2015) has been used to identify medical entities of type 'problem', 'test' and 'treatment' from documents, which was trained on i2b2 2010 dataset (Uzuner et al., 2011). The i2b2 2010 dataset includes discharge summaries from Partners HealthCare, from Beth Israel Deaconess Medical Center and from University of Pittsburgh Medical Center. These discharge summaries are fully de-identified and manually annotated for concept, assertion, and relation information. Here, we have

| | CDS 2014 | | | |
| --- | --- | --- | --- | --- |
| | MAP | | infNDCG | |
| | No feature weighting | Feature weighting using CliNER | No feature weighting | Feature weighting using CliNER |
| Original Queries | 0.1071 | | 0.1836 | |
| Queries+RF$_{50}$ | 0.2768 | | 0.4186 | |
| {Nearest neighbors}$_{50\_200}$ | 0.2761 | 0.2747 | 0.4177 | 0.4140 |
| {Nearest neighbors + k-means}$_{50\_200}$ | 0.2794 | 0.2777 | 0.4220 | 0.4195 |
| {Neural net}$_{50\_200}$ | 0.2790 | 0.2787 | 0.4235 | 0.4240 |
| {Neural net + k-means}$_{50\_200}$ | 0.2790 | 0.2807 | 0.4218 | **0.4269** |

Table 4: Results of Feedback Document Discovery

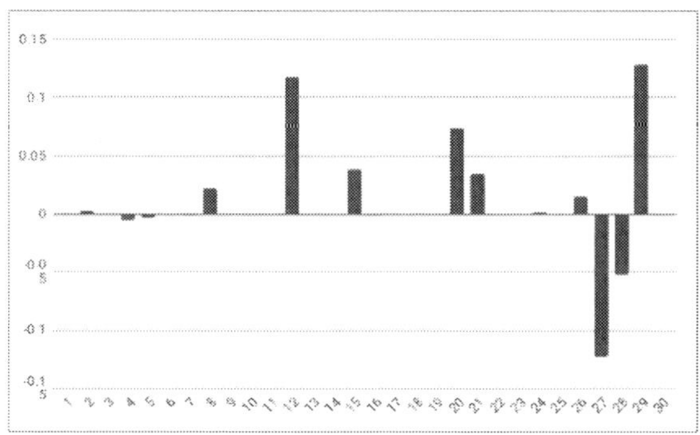

Figure 1: Query wise difference graph of infNDCG for feedback document discovery and relevance feedback

used these discharge summaries along with their concept annotations to train CliNER. This trained model is applied on CDS documents to identify 'problem', 'test' and 'treatment' concept entities. The features related to these entities in CDS documents are weighted thrice, thus giving importance to these entities while learning to identify feedback document. For feedback document discovery with weighted entities, we have used top 50 documents and their corresponding relevance for training, then the relevance was predicted for next top 200 documents and used for expansion of queries. For classification two methods, nearest neighbour classifier and neural net classifier, have been used and k-means is used for clustering with k=2 for relevant and non-relevant documents. In all cases, only relevant identified documents are used for expanding queries. The comparison of results of original queries without expansion, expansion with relevance feedback and expansion with two approaches of feedback document discovery (classification and classification+clustering) for CDS 2014 dataset is given in table 4.

The results clearly indicates improvement over original queries and relevance feedback. Fig 1 shows query wise difference in infNDCG between {Neural net + k-means}$_{50\_200}$ and Queries+RF$_{50}$. Out of 30 queries of CDS 2014, 2 queries degrade performance but 7 queries improve.

## 3.3 UMLS Concepts Based Query Reformulation

Medical domain-specific knowledge can be incorporated to the process of query reformulation in Biomedical IR system. There are knowledge based approaches proposed in the literature (Aronson and Rindflesch, 1997; Demner-Fushman et al., 2011; Hersh, 2008). In the biomedical text retrieval, medical concepts and entities are more informative than other common terms. Moreover, medical ontologies, thesaurus and biomedical entity identifiers are available to identify medical related concepts.

Here we have used the resource UMLS. The following three query reformulation experiments are done using it. First: The UMLS concepts are identified from the query text and used with queries. Second: Along with the UMLS concepts, MeSH (Medical Subject Heading) terms are also identified and used in queries. MeSH is a hierarchically organized vocabulary of UMLS. Third: Medical entities are identified manually and used with queries. One example query with all these reformulations is presented in Appendix A.

Table 5 shows the results of these reformulated queries of CDS 2014. PRF and RF based query expansion is also carried out on each form of the queries. The results shows clear improvement when using UMLS concepts in queries as compared to original queries. One more important observation here to make is that, for no-expansion

| infNDCG | CDS 2014 | | | |
| --- | --- | --- | --- | --- |
| | BM25 | | In_expC2 | |
| | MAP | infNDCF | MAP | infNDCF |
| Original Queries | 0.1071 | 0.1836 | 0.1096 | 0.2002 |
| Original Queries + PRF$_{10}$ | 0.1542 | 0.2522 | 0.1623 | 0.2724 |
| Original Queries + RF$_{10}$ | 0.2050 | 0.3355 | 0.2117 | 0.3426 |
| Original Queries + RF$_{50}$ | 0.2768 | 0.4186 | 0.2587 | 0.4019 |
| Queries + UMLS concepts | 0.1660 | 0.1830 | 0.1597 | 0.1781 |
| Queries + UMLS concepts + PRF$_{10}$ | **0.1607** | **0.2607** | **0.1486** | **0.2431** |
| Queries + UMLS concepts + RF$_{10}$ | **0.2164** | **0.3423** | **0.2138** | **0.3459** |
| Queries + UMLS concepts + RF$_{50}$ | **0.2776** | **0.4232** | **0.2569** | **0.4021** |
| Queries + UMLS concepts + Mesh terms | 0.1039 | 0.1749 | 0.1086 | 0.1792 |
| Queries + UMLS concepts + Mesh terms + PRF$_{10}$ | 0.1460 | 0.2409 | 0.1411 | 0.2376 |
| Queries + UMLS concepts + Mesh terms + RF$_{10}$ | 0.2052 | 0.1992 | 0.3321 | 0.3291 |
| Queries + Manual Entities | 0.1112 | 0.1860 | 0.1140 | 0.2114 |
| Queries + Manual Entities + PRF$_{10}$ | 0.1601 | 0.2634 | 0.1584 | 0.2650 |
| Queries + Manual Entities + RF$_{10}$ | 0.2112 | 0.3394 | 0.2120 | 0.3414 |

Table 5: Results of UMLS based query processing

and PRF, the manual entities fail to improve MAP when compared to UMLS entities but certainly give better results in terms of infNDCG.

## 4 Learning To Rank

Learning to rank (LTR) (Liu et al., 2009) is an application of machine learning in the construction of ranking models for information retrieval systems where retrieval problem is modeled as a ranking problem. LTR framework requires training data of queries and documents matching them together with relevance degree of each match. Training data is used by a learning algorithm to produce a ranking model which computes relevance of documents for actual queries.

The LTR framework is applied on CDS 2014 dataset where the features for query document pairs are computed similarly as the features used for OHSUMED LETOR dataset (Qin et al., 2010). These features are mainly based on TF, IDF and their normalized versions. Since the whole document pool is too large, document pooling has been done and top K documents (by BM25) for each query are used for feature extraction. SVMRank has been used as a machine learning framework.

Table 6 shows the results of LTR when the features are computed on Title+Abstract part of the documents, on Title+Abstract+Content of the documents (i.e. full documents). With these variations of features, the experiments are carried out on original queries, queries with UMLS concepts and queries with manually identified medical con-

| infNDCG | OHSUMED features on T, A and T+A | OHSUMED features on T, A and C |
| --- | --- | --- |
| Original Queries | 0.097 | 0.1769 |
| Queries + UMLS | 0.0833 | 0.1556 |
| Queries + Manual | 0.1049 | 0.1785 |

Table 6: Results of Learning to Rank with different features

| | infNDCG |
| --- | --- |
| Retrieval (BM25) | 0.1836 |
| LTR using human judgements | 0.1769 |
| Pseudo LTR K=1000 | 0.1849 |
| Pseudo LTR K=1500 | **0.1872** |
| Pseudo LTR K=2000 | 0.1859 |
| Pseudo LTR K=2500 | 0.1865 |
| Pseudo LTR K=3000 | 0.1865 |

Table 7: Results Learning To Rank with pseudo judgements

cepts.

All these LTR experiments require human judgement for training. To overcome the need of manual judgement, pseudo judgements were considered where out of k training documents, Top k/2 documents are considered to be relevant and other k/2 documents to be non-relevant.

As shown in table 7, the results of LTR trained using pseudo qrels are better than one with actual human judged qrels but the difference is not statistically significant. The results of LTR are comparable to retrieval using BM25.

## 5 Future Research Directions

Biomedical text processing and information retrieval being a new field of research opens up many research directions. In this article, we have presented a preliminary study of statistical and NLP based biomedical document retrieval techniques for clinical decision support systems. It included query reformulation based information retrieval framework with pseudo relevance feedback, relevance feedback, feedback document discovery and UMLS concept based reformulation for Biomedical domain. Standard IR frameworks PRF and RF works good enough for Clinical Decision Support System. Feedback document discovery based query reformulation which is a statistical approaches can be improvised in future for significant improvement. Another statistical model Learning to Rank is also having future scope for more improvement. The initial framework for NLP based approach UMLS concept based retrieval also shows improvement in the results. Therefore, we plan to combine statistical and NLP based approaches and come up with new better model for biomedical document retrieval for Decision Support Systems. Also, we are planning to do feature weighting using NLP at entity level in feedback document discovery approach.

## References


Gianni Amati, Cornelis Joost, and Van Rijsbergen. 2003. Probabilistic models for information retrieval based on divergence from randomness.

Alan R Aronson and Thomas C Rindflesch. 1997. Query expansion using the umls metathesaurus. In *Proceedings of the AMIA Annual Fall Symposium*, page 485. American Medical Informatics Association.

William Boag, Kevin Wacome, Tristan Naumann, and Anna Rumshisky. 2015. Cliner: A lightweight tool for clinical named entity recognition. *AMIA Joint Summits on Clinical Research Informatics (poster)*.

Olivier Bodenreider. 2004. The unified medical language system (umls): integrating biomedical terminology. *Nucleic acids research*, 32(suppl 1):D267–D270.

Claudio Carpineto and Giovanni Romano. 2012. A survey of automatic query expansion in information retrieval. *ACM Computing Surveys (CSUR)*, 44(1):1.

Dina Demner-Fushman, Swapna Abhyankar, Antonio Jimeno-Yepes, Russell F Loane, Bastien Rance, François-Michel Lang, Nicholas C Ide, Emilia Apostolova, and Alan R Aronson. 2011. A knowledge-based approach to medical records retrieval. In *TREC*.

William Hersh. 2008. *Information retrieval: a health and biomedical perspective*. Springer Science & Business Media.

William Hersh, Susan Price, and Larry Donohoe. 2000. Assessing thesaurus-based query expansion using the umls metathesaurus. In *Proceedings of the AMIA Symposium*, page 344. American Medical Informatics Association.

S Jones. 2009. The social life of health information. *Pew research center, Washington, DC, Pew Internet & American Life Project*.

Tie-Yan Liu et al. 2009. Learning to rank for information retrieval. *Foundations and Trends® in Information Retrieval*, 3(3):225–331.

Christopher D Manning, Prabhakar Raghavan, Hinrich Schütze, et al. 2008. *Introduction to information retrieval*, volume 1. Cambridge university press.

Melvin Earl Maron and John L Kuhns. 1960. On relevance, probabilistic indexing and information retrieval. *Journal of the ACM (JACM)*, 7(3):216–244.

Iadh Ounis, Gianni Amati, Vassilis Plachouras, Ben He, Craig Macdonald, and Douglas Johnson. 2005. Terrier information retrieval platform. In *European Conference on Information Retrieval*, pages 517–519.

Tao Qin, Tie-Yan Liu, Jun Xu, and Hang Li. 2010. Letor: A benchmark collection for research on learning to rank for information retrieval. *Information Retrieval*, 13(4):346–374.

Jainisha Sankhavara and Prasenjit Majumder. 2017. Biomedical information retrieval. In *Working notes of FIRE 2017 - Forum for Information Retrieval Evaluation*, pages 154–157.

Jainisha Sankhavara, Fenny Thakrar, Prasenjit Majumder, and Shamayeeta Sarkar. 2014. Fusing manual and machine feedback in biomedical domain. In *Proceedings of The Twenty-Third Text REtrieval Conference, TREC 2014, Gaithersburg, Maryland, USA, November 19-21, 2014*.

Matthew S Simpson and Dina Demner-Fushman. 2012. Biomedical text mining: a survey of recent progress. In *Mining text data*, pages 465–517. Springer.

Özlem Uzuner, Brett R South, Shuying Shen, and Scott L DuVall. 2011. 2010 i2b2/va challenge on concepts, assertions, and relations in clinical text. *Journal of the American Medical Informatics Association*, 18(5):552–556.

## A   Example Query

```
<topic number="1" type="diagnosis">
<summary>
  58-year-old woman with hypertension and obesity presents with
exercise-related episodic chest pain radiating to the back.
</summary>
<UMLS_entities>
  hypertension obesity exercise related chest pain radiating back nos
</UMLS_entities>
<MeSH_entities>
  Vascular Diseases Overnutrition Overweight Motor Activity Human
Activities Torso Bone and Bones Neurologic Manifestations Sensation
</MeSH_entities>
<manual_entities>
  woman hypertension obesity exercise-related episodic chest pain
radiating back </manual_entities>
</topic>
```

## B   Example Document

https://www.ncbi.nlm.nih.gov/pmc/articles/PMC 3990010/pdf/1745-6215-15-124.pdf

## C   OHSUMED features

Table    Learning Features for the OHSUMED Corpus

| ID | Feature Description |
|---|---|
| 1 | $\sum_{q_i \in q \cap d} c(q_i, d)$ in title |
| 2 | $\sum_{q_i \in q \cap d} \log \left( c(q_i, d) + 1 \right)$ in title |
| 3 | $\sum_{q_i \in q \cap d} \frac{c(q_i, d)}{|d|}$ in title |
| 4 | $\sum_{q_i \in q \cap d} \log \left( \frac{c(q_i, d)}{|d|} + 1 \right)$ in title |
| 5 | $\sum_{q_i \in q} \log \left( \frac{|C|}{df(q_i)} \right)$ in title |
| 6 | $\sum_{q_i \in q} \log \left( \log \left( \frac{|C|}{df(q_i)} \right) \right)$ in title |
| 7 | $\sum_{q_i \in q} \log \left( \frac{|C|}{c(q_i, C)} + 1 \right)$ in title |
| 8 | $\sum_{q_i \in q \cap d} \log \left( \frac{c(q_i, d)}{|d|} \cdot \log \left( \frac{|C|}{df(q_i)} \right) + 1 \right)$ in title |
| 9 | $\sum_{q_i \in q \cap d} c(q_i, d) \cdot \log \left( \frac{|C|}{df(q_i)} \right)$ in title |
| 10 | $\sum_{q_i \in q \cap d} \log \left( \frac{c(q_i, d)}{|d|} \cdot \frac{|C|}{c(q_i, C)} + 1 \right)$ in title |
| 11 | BM25 of title |
| 12 | log(BM25) of title |
| 13 | LMIR.DIR of title |
| 14 | LMIR.JM of title |
| 15 | LMIR.ABS of title |

# A Computational Approach to Feature Extraction for Identification of Suicidal Ideation in Tweets

**Ramit Sawhney**     **Prachi Manchanda**     **Raj Singh**     **Swati Aggarwal**
Netaji Subhas Institute of Technology, New Delhi 110078, India
{ramits, prachim, rajs}.co@nsit.net.in     swati1178@gmail.com

## Abstract

Technological advancements in the World Wide Web and social networks in particular coupled with an increase in social media usage has led to a positive correlation between the exhibition of Suicidal ideation on websites such as Twitter and cases of suicide. This paper proposes a novel supervised approach for detecting suicidal ideation in content on Twitter. A set of features is proposed for training both linear and ensemble classifiers over a dataset of manually annotated tweets. The performance of the proposed methodology is compared against four baselines that utilize varying approaches to validate its utility. The results are finally summarized by reflecting on the effect of the inclusion of the proposed features one by one for suicidal ideation detection.

## 1 Introduction

According to World Health Organization, suicide is the second leading cause of death among 15-29-year-olds across the world. In fact, close to 800,000 people die due of suicide each year. The number of people who attempt suicide is much higher. While an individual suicide is often a solitary act, it can often have a devastating impact on families (Cerel et al., 2008). Many suicide deaths are preventable and it is important to understand the ways in which individuals communicate their depression and thoughts for preventing such deaths. (Sher, 2004) Suicide prevention is mainly hinged on surveillance and monitoring of suicide attempts and self-harm tendencies.

The younger generation has started to turn to the Internet (Chan and Fang, 2007) for seeking help, discussing depression and suicide-related information and offering support. The availability of suicide-related material on the Internet plays an important role in the process of suicide ideation. Due to this increasing availability of content on social media websites (such as Twitter, Facebook and Reddit etc.), and blogs (Yates et al., 2017) there is an urgent need to identify affected individuals and offer help. Suicidal ideation refers to thoughts of killing oneself or planning suicide, while suicidal behavior is often defined to include all possible acts of self-harm with the intention of causing death (Costello et al., 2002). Although Twitter provides a unique opportunity to identify at-risk of individuals (Jashinsky et al., 2014) and a possible avenue for intervention at both the individual and social level, there exist no best practices for suicide prevention using social media.

While there is a developing body of literature on the topic of identifying patterns in the language used on social media that expresses suicidal ideation (De Choudhury et al., 2016), very few attempts have been made to employ feature extraction methods for binary classifiers that separate text related to suicide from text that clearly indicates the author exhibiting suicidal intent. A number of successful models (Yates et al., 2017) have been used for sentence level classification, however, ones that are successful for being able to learn to separate suicidal ideation from depression as well as less worrying content such as reporting of a suicide, memorial, campaigning, and support. etc, require a greater analysis to select more specific features and methods to build an accurate and robust model. The drastic impact that suicide has on surrounding community coupled with the lack of specific feature extraction and classification models for the identification of suicidal ideation on social media, so that action can be taken is the driving motivation for the work presented in this paper.

Suicide prevention by suicide detection (Zung, 1979) is one of the most effective ways to drasti-

91

*Proceedings of ACL 2018, Student Research Workshop*, pages 91–98
Melbourne, Australia, July 15 - 20, 2018. ©2018 Association for Computational Linguistics

cally reduce suicidal rates. The major practical application of this work lies in it's easy adaptability to any social media forum (Robinson et al., 2016), wherein it can be used directly for analyzing text-based content posted by its users and flag it if the content is concerning.

The main contributions of this paper can be summarized as follows:

1. The creation of a labeled dataset for learning the patterns in tweets exhibiting suicidal ideation by manual annotation.

2. Proposed a set of features to be fed into classifiers to improve the performance.

3. Employed four binary classifiers with the proposed set of features and compared them against baselines utilizing varied approaches to validate the proposed methodology.

## 2   Related Work

Media communication can have both positive and negative influence on suicidal ideation. A systematic review of all articles in PsycINFO, MEDLINE, EMBASE, Scopus, and CINAH from 1991 to 2011 for language constructs relating to self-harm or suicide by Daine et al. (2013) concluded that internet may be used as an intervention tool for vulnerable individuals under the age of 25. However, not all language constructs containing the word suicide indicate suicidal intent, specific semantic constructs may be used for predicting whether a sentence implies self-harm tendencies or not.

A suicide note analysis method for automating the identification of suicidal ideation was built using binary support vector machine classifiers by Desmet and Hoste (2013) using fine-grained emotion detection for classifier optimization with lexico-semantic features for optimization. In 2014, Huang et al. (2014) used rule-based methods with hand-crafted unsupervised classification for developing a real-time suicidal ideation detection system deployed over Weibo[1], a microblogging platform. This approach differs from the proposed approach in terms of both features and the reach of the social media platforms. Topic modeling in Chinese microblogs (Huang et al., 2015) for suicide ideation detection has also proven to be

efficient, however for a limited subset with a fairly different set of features.

Studies corresponding to rise in suicidal ideation associated with specific temporal events (Kumar et al., 2015) have also been performed, but do not specifically focus on building a robust system that simply analyzes content coupled with no other factors. Related literature also focuses on building systems that analyze tweets of users who have committed suicide (Coppersmith et al., 2016), that may not specifically hint at suicidal ideation, as opposed to the proposed problem.

## 3   Data

### 3.1   Data Collection

Traditionally, it has been difficult extracting data related to suicidal ideation or mental illnesses due to social stigma but now, an increasing number of people are turning to the Internet to vent their frustration, seek help and discuss mental health issues (Milne et al., 2016), (Sueki et al., 2014). To maintain the privacy of the individuals in the dataset, we do not present direct quotes from any data, nor any identifying information.

Anonymised data was collected from microblogging website Twitter - specifically, content containing self-classified suicidal ideation (i.e. text posts tagged with the word 'suicide) over the period of December 3, 2017 to January 31, 2018. The Twitter REST API[2] was used for collection of tweets containing any of the following English words or phrases that are consistent with the vernacular of suicidal ideation (O'Dea et al., 2015):

*suicidal; suicide; kill myself; my suicide note; my suicide letter; end my life; never wake up; can't go on; not worth living; ready to jump; sleep forever; want to die; be dead; better off without me; better off dead; suicide plan; suicide pact; tired of living; don't want to be here; die alone; go to sleep forever; wanna die; wanna suicide; commit suicide; die now; slit my wrist; cut my wrist; slash my wrist; do not want to be here; want it to be over; want to be dead; nothing to live for; ready to die; not worth living; why should I continue living; take my own life; thoughts of suicide; to take my own life; suicide ideation; depressed; I wish I were dead; kill me now*

The texts were collected without knowing the sentiment. For example, when collecting tweets

---

on hashtag *#suicide*, it is not known initially whether:

- the tweet is posted for suicide awareness and prevention;

- the person is talking about suicidal ideation and/or ways to kill himself;

- the tweet reports a third persons suicide *eg: news report*;

- the tweet uses suicide as a figure of speech *eg: career suicide*

### 3.2 Data Annotation

Then, text posts equaling 5213 in all were collected which were subsequently human annotated. The Human annotators consisted of both university students fairly active on social media, and aware of aspects of cognitive psychology as well as university faculty in the domain of Psychology and Machine Learning. Human annotators were asked to indicate if the text implied suicidal ideation using binary criteria by answering the question *Does this text imply self-harm tendencies or suicidal intent?*. Each post was scrutinized and analyzed by three independent annotators ($H_1$, $H_2$ and $H_3$), due to the subjectivity of text annotation, wherein ambiguous posts were set to the default level, *Suicidal intent absent*. Posts were examined individually and annotated according to the following classification system:

1. **Suicidal intent present**:

    - Text conveys a serious display of suicidal ideation; e.g., *I want to die* or *I want to kill myself* or *I wish my last suicide attempt was successful*;
    - Care was taken to classify only those posts as suicidal where suicide risk is not conditional unless some event is a clear risk factor eg: depression, bullying, substance use;
    - Posts where suicide plan and/or previous attempts are discussed; e.g., *"The fact that I tried to kill myself and it didn't work makes me more depressed."*
    - Tone of text is sombre and not flippant, eg: *This makes me want to kill myself, lol*, *"This day is horrible, I want to kill myself hahaha"* are not included in this category.

| | $H_1$ | $H_2$ | $H_3$ |
|---|---|---|---|
| $H_1$ | – | 0.61 | 0.48 |
| $H_2$ | 0.61 | – | 0.51 |
| $H_3$ | 0.48 | 0.51 | – |

Table 1: Cohen's Kappa for three annotators $H_1$, $H_2$ and $H_3$

2. **Suicidal intent absent:**

    - The default category for all posts.
    - Posts emphasizing on suicide related news or information; e.g., *Two female suicide bombers hit crowded market in Maiduguri.*
    - Posts such as *Suicide squad sounds like a good option*; no reasonable evidence to suggest that the risk of suicide is present; includes posts containing song lyrics, etc, were marked within this category.
    - Posts pertaining to condolence and suicide awareness; e.g., *"5 suicide prevention helplines in India you need to know about"*, *Politician accused of driving his wife to suicide.*

Annotators were instructed to select only one of the above categories and to select the default level in case of ambiguity. In all, 15.76% (822) of all tweets were annotated to be suicidal, which were then used to train and validate the classifiers presented in the following sections. A satisfactory agreement between the annotators (e.g., 0.61 for $H_1$ and $H_2$) can be inferred from Table 1.

## 4 Proposed Methodology

The overall methodology is divided into three phases. The initial phase consists of preprocessing the text within a tweet, the second phase involves feature extraction from preprocessed tweets for the training and testing of binary classifiers for the suicidal ideation identification, and the final phase actually classifies and identifies tweets exhibiting suicidal ideation. The details of these individual phases are presented below.

### 4.1 Preprocessing

Preprocessing is achieved by applying a series of filters, based on Xiang et al. (2012), in the order given below to process the raw tweets.

1. Removal of non-English tweets using Ling-Pipe (Baldwin and Carpenter, 2003) with Hadoop.

2. Identification and elimination of user mentions in tweet bodies having the format of @username, URLs as well as retweets in the format of RT.

3. Removal of all hashtags with length $> 10$ due to a great volume of hashtags being concatenated words, which tends to amplify the vocabulary size inadvertently.

4. Stopword removal.

## 4.2 Feature Extraction

Tweets exhibiting suicidal ideation lack a semi-rigid pre-defined lexico-syntactic pattern. Hence, they warrant the use of hand engineering and analyzing a set of features (Wang et al., 2016) in contrast to sentence and word embeddings in a supervised setting using Deep Learning Models such as Convolutional Neural Networks (Kim, 2014) (CNN). The proposed methodology utilizes the following set of features for classification.

- *Statistical Features.* These encompass the number of tokens, and their length.

- *LIWC Features.* Features extracted using the Linguistic Inquiry and Word Count program (LIWC) (Pennebaker et al., 2001) capture people's social and psychological states by analyzing the text to generate labels. Owing to the immense similarity in the nature of the problem of Suicidal Ideation detection in text and the background of LIWC in social, clinical, and cognitive psychology, LIWC features are an ideal candidate for inclusion as a subset of features for our overall classification problem.

  As an example, the accompanying tweet is associated with negative emotions and cognitive processes with a high authenticity and emotional tone. *I'm holding a gun and deciding if I want to go through with suicide or not. I want to commit suicide really badly... Help?*

- *Part of Speech counts.* POS counts for each label assigned by the Stanford Part-Of-Speech Tagger (Manning et al., 2014) are used as a feature. POS Tags include nouns, adjectives, adverbs, verbs, etc.

- *TF-IDF.* The Term Frequency-Inverse Document Frequency (TF-IDF) is used as a feature to reflect the importance of a particular word within the corpus and is given by:

$$tfidf(t) = freq(t) \times ln\frac{N}{|\{d \in D : t \in d\}|}$$

where, $t$ is the word feature, $N$ is the number of tweets, and $d$ is a document in the document set $D$.

- *Topics Probability.* The probability distribution of each topic over its terms are used as a feature, which is based on the approach that the tweets are represented as random mixtures over latent topics. Latent Dirichlet Allocation (LDA) (Blei et al., 2003) is a generative probabilistic model that is used to describe each such topic as a generative model which generates words of the vocabulary with certain probabilities, and forms the basis of evaluating Topics Probability.

## 4.3 Classification

Suicidal Ideation detection is formulated as a supervised binary classification problem. For every tweet $t_i \in D$, the document set, a binary valued variable $y_i \in \{0, 1\}$ is introduced, where $y_i = 1$ denotes that the tweet $t_i$ exhibits Suicidal Ideation. To learn this, the classifiers must determine whether any sentence in $t_i$ possesses a certain structure or keywords that mark the existence of any possible Suicidal thoughts. The features presented above are the used to train classification models to identify tweets exhibiting Suicidal Ideation. Linear classifiers such as Logistic Regression as well as Ensemble Classifiers including Random Forest (Liaw et al., 2002), Gradient Boosting Decision Tree (Friedman, 2002) and XGBoost (Chen and Guestrin, 2016) are employed for classification.

Both XGBoost and Gradient Boosting Decision Trees aim to boost the performance of a classifier in a stage-wise fashion by iteratively adding a new classifier to the ensemble to allow the optimization of a differentiable loss function. The Random Forest classifier is one of the most popular ensemble machine learning algorithm based on Bootstrap Aggregation (Quinlan et al., 1996) or *bagging*. It modifies the bagging procedure so that the learning algorithm is limited to a random sample of features of which to search, which has shown promise in text classification problems.

## 5   Baselines

Validation of the proposed methodology is done by comparison against Baseline models that act as a useful point for comparison. Comparison in terms of the evaluation metrics presented below are also done with other recent models for Suicidal Ideation classification as follows:

Long Short Term Memory (LSTM) models are more robust to noise in comparison to Recurrent Neural Networks (RNN) (Liu et al., 2016), and better able to capture long-term dependencies in a sequence, due to their ability to learn how to forget past observations. The LSTM model uses $h = 128$ memory units, with a dropout probability of 0.2, and ReLU (Nair and Hinton, 2010) was used for activation. For training, the Adam Optimizer was used to minimize log loss. A batch size of 64 was chosen and trained for a total of 100 epochs. Pre-Trained word2vec word embeddings that were trained on 100 billion words from Google News are employed as features for classification. Support Vector Machines (Desmet and Hoste, 2013) (SVM) have been shown to work well with short informal text (Pak and Paroubek, 2010) and other promising results in the cognitive behavior domain (De Choudhury et al., 2013). The features described in Desmet and Hoste (2013) are used by the SVM for classification. Rule-based approaches focusing on maximizing the information gain aim to reduce the uncertainty of the class a particular tweet belongs to. A J48 decision tree (C4.5) (Quinlan et al., 1996) was used with the features above for classification.
Lastly, a Negation Resolution (Gkotsis et al., 2016) based approach that is relatively recent, that employs parse trees to build a set of basic rules that rely on minimum domain knowledge is used.

## 6   Results and Analysis

### 6.1   Analysis: Comparison with Baselines

Table 2 presents the results for both baselines as well as the classifiers with the proposed methodology in terms of four evaluation metrics: *Accuracy, Precision, Recall and F1 Score*. The first

four rows represent the results of the proposed features with both Linear and Ensemble classifiers as described in the Classification section above. The final four rows represent the baseline results.

The proposed features used in conjunction with the first four models described in the Classification section supersede the baseline models in terms of performance along most metrics. The LSTM model has the highest recall, owing to its ability to capture long term dependencies, however its overall performance in terms of accuracy and F1 score is relatively less. Both SVM and Rule-based classification don't perform as well as the proposed methodology, owing to the lack of features used in these models that are not suitable for learning how to classify tweets with Suicidal Ideation. Both of these methods are more suitable in a general domain, however, the features in the proposed methodology are more specific to the particular problem domain of Suicidal Ideation detection, particularly the *LIWC* features and Topics probability. Lastly, the Negation Resolution method performs poorly on the dataset, due to its inability to adapt to a vast and highly diverse form of suicidal ideation communication and its implicit rigidity. This in comparison to the proposed methodology, is unable to effectively learn and extract the essential features from input text, and thus does not perform as well.
In conclusion, the proposed methodology consisting of feature extraction coupled with ensemble and linear classifiers supersedes the baselines presented from various domains in terms of performance.

### 6.2   Classifiers with proposed features

The first four rows of Table 2 represent the results in terms of the evaluation metrics for different classifiers, both Linear and Ensemble, using the proposed set of features. While the performance of the four classifiers is comparable, Random Forest classifiers perform the best. This is attributed to the ability of Random Forest classifiers that tackle error reduction by reducing variance rather than reducing bias. As has been seen with various text classification problems, Logistic Regression performs fairly well despite its simplicity, and has a greater accuracy and F1 score in comparison with both Boosting Algorithms.

Table 3 shows the variation in performance of the Random Forest classifier with the inclusion of

Table 2: Classification Results in terms of Evaluation metrics.

| Model | Accuracy | Precision | Recall | F1 score |
|---|---|---|---|---|
| Logistic Regression | 0.830 | 0.819 | 0.850 | 0.832 |
| Random Forest | **0.858** | **0.842** | 0.846 | **0.844** |
| Gradient Boosting Decision Tree | 0.805 | 0.802 | 0.820 | 0.807 |
| XGBoost | 0.817 | 0.831 | 0.800 | 0.812 |
| LSTM | 0.789 | 0.745 | **0.874** | 0.796 |
| Support Vector Machine | 0.792 | 0.821 | 0.692 | 0.754 |
| Rule-based Classification | 0.801 | 0.824 | 0.743 | 0.781 |
| Negation Resolution | 0.527 | 0.542 | 0.752 | 0.635 |

Table 3: Variation in performance with the inclusion of features

| Features used | Accuracy | Precision | Recall | F1 score |
|---|---|---|---|---|
| Statistical Features(SF) only | 0.596 | 0.547 | 0.600 | 0.569 |
| SF + TF-IDF | 0.669 | 0.663 | 0.753 | 0.702 |
| SF + TF-IDF + POS counts | 0.789 | 0.821 | 0.705 | 0.721 |
| SF + TF-IDF + POS + Topics Probability | 0.807 | 0.814 | 0.820 | 0.817 |
| All Features | 0.858 | 0.842 | 0.846 | 0.844 |

the various features. The precision reduces by a small amount with the inclusion of Topics probability feature implying that a greater subset of tweets is classified as suicidal due to the LDA unigrams included via Topics probability features, but is finally boosted by the inclusion of the LIWC features. The POS counts also lead to a reduction in the recall, which is compensated with the subsequent inclusion of Topics Probability and LIWC features. The drastic improvements are attributed to the TF-IDF, POS counts and LIWC features in terms of most evaluation metrics. It is observed that the proposed set of features perform the best in conjunction with Random Forest classifiers, and the improvement in performance with the inclusion of each feature validates the need for the extraction of that feature.

### 6.3 Error Analysis

Some categories of errors that occur are:

1. **Seemingly Suicidal tweets:** Human annotators as well as our classifier could not identify whether *"I want to kill myself, lol. :("* was representative of suicidal ideation or a frivolous reference to suicide.

2. **Pragmatic difficulty:** The tweet *"I lost my baby. Signing off.."* was correctly identified by our human annotators as a tweet with suicidal intent present. This tweet contains an element of topic change with no explicit mention of suicidal ideation, but our classifier could not capture it.

3. **Ambiguity:** The tweet *"Is it odd to know I'll commit suicide?"* is a tweet that both human annotators as well as the proposed methodology couldn't classify due to it's ambiguity.

## 7  Conclusion and Future Work

This paper proposes a model to analyze tweets, by developing a set of features to be fed into classifiers for identification of Suicidal Ideation using Machine Learning. When annotated by humans, 15.76% of the total dataset of 5213 tweets was found to be suicidal. Both linear and ensemble classifiers were employed to validate the selection of features proposed for Suicidal Ideation detection. Comparisons with baseline models employing various strategies such as Negation Resolution, LSTMs, Rule-based methods were also performed. The major contribution of this work is the improved performance of the Random forest classifier as compared to other classifiers as well as the baselines. This indicates the promise of the proposed set of features with a bagging based approach with minimal correlation show as compared to other classifiers. In the future, there is scope for larger amounts of data to be scraped from more social media websites as well as investigate the performance withdeep learning models such as CNNs, LSTM-CNNs, etc.

## References

Breck Baldwin and Bob Carpenter. 2003. Lingpipe. *Available from World Wide Web: http://alias-i. com/lingpipe.*

David M Blei, Andrew Y Ng, and Michael I Jordan. 2003. Latent dirichlet allocation. *Journal of machine Learning research*, 3(Jan):993–1022.

Julie Cerel, John R Jordan, and Paul R Duberstein. 2008. The impact of suicide on the family. *Crisis*, 29(1):38–44.

Kara Chan and Wei Fang. 2007. Use of the internet and traditional media among young people. *Young Consumers*, 8(4):244–256.

Tianqi Chen and Carlos Guestrin. 2016. Xgboost: A scalable tree boosting system. In *Proceedings of the 22nd acm sigkdd international conference on knowledge discovery and data mining*, pages 785–794. ACM.

Glen Coppersmith, Kim Ngo, Ryan Leary, and Anthony Wood. 2016. Exploratory analysis of social media prior to a suicide attempt. In *Proceedings of the Third Workshop on Computational Lingusitics and Clinical Psychology*, pages 106–117.

E Jane Costello, Daniel S Pine, Constance Hammen, John S March, Paul M Plotsky, Myrna M Weissman, Joseph Biederman, H Hill Goldsmith, Joan Kaufman, Peter M Lewinsohn, et al. 2002. Development and natural history of mood disorders. *Biological psychiatry*, 52(6):529–542.

Kate Daine, Keith Hawton, Vinod Singaravelu, Anne Stewart, Sue Simkin, and Paul Montgomery. 2013. The power of the web: a systematic review of studies of the influence of the internet on self-harm and suicide in young people. *PloS one*, 8(10):e77555.

Munmun De Choudhury, Michael Gamon, Scott Counts, and Eric Horvitz. 2013. Predicting depression via social media. *ICWSM*, 13:1–10.

Munmun De Choudhury, Emre Kiciman, Mark Dredze, Glen Coppersmith, and Mrinal Kumar. 2016. Discovering shifts to suicidal ideation from mental health content in social media. In *Proceedings of the 2016 CHI conference on human factors in computing systems*, pages 2098–2110. ACM.

Bart Desmet and VéRonique Hoste. 2013. Emotion detection in suicide notes. *Expert Systems with Applications*, 40(16):6351–6358.

Jerome H Friedman. 2002. Stochastic gradient boosting. *Computational Statistics & Data Analysis*, 38(4):367–378.

George Gkotsis, Sumithra Velupillai, Anika Oellrich, Harry Dean, Maria Liakata, and Rina Dutta. 2016. Don't let notes be misunderstood: A negation detection method for assessing risk of suicide in mental health records. In *Proceedings of the Third Workshop on Computational Lingusitics and Clinical Psychology*, pages 95–105.

Xiaolei Huang, Xin Li, Tianli Liu, David Chiu, Tingshao Zhu, and Lei Zhang. 2015. Topic model for identifying suicidal ideation in chinese microblog. In *Proceedings of the 29th Pacific Asia Conference on Language, Information and Computation*, pages 553–562.

Xiaolei Huang, Lei Zhang, David Chiu, Tianli Liu, Xin Li, and Tingshao Zhu. 2014. Detecting suicidal ideation in chinese microblogs with psychological lexicons. In *Ubiquitous Intelligence and Computing, 2014 IEEE 11th Intl Conf on and IEEE 11th Intl Conf on and Autonomic and Trusted Computing, and IEEE 14th Intl Conf on Scalable Computing and Communications and Its Associated Workshops (UTC-ATC-ScalCom)*, pages 844–849. IEEE.

Jared Jashinsky, Scott H Burton, Carl L Hanson, Josh West, Christophe Giraud-Carrier, Michael D Barnes, and Trenton Argyle. 2014. Tracking suicide risk factors through twitter in the us. *Crisis: The Journal of Crisis Intervention and Suicide Prevention*, 35(1):51.

Yoon Kim. 2014. Convolutional neural networks for sentence classification. *arXiv preprint arXiv:1408.5882.*

Mrinal Kumar, Mark Dredze, Glen Coppersmith, and Munmun De Choudhury. 2015. Detecting changes in suicide content manifested in social media following celebrity suicides. In *Proceedings of the 26th ACM Conference on Hypertext & Social Media*, pages 85–94. ACM.

Andy Liaw, Matthew Wiener, et al. 2002. Classification and regression by randomforest. *R news*, 2(3):18–22.

Pengfei Liu, Xipeng Qiu, and Xuanjing Huang. 2016. Recurrent neural network for text classification with multi-task learning. *arXiv preprint arXiv:1605.05101.*

Christopher Manning, Mihai Surdeanu, John Bauer, Jenny Finkel, Steven Bethard, and David McClosky. 2014. The stanford corenlp natural language processing toolkit. In *Proceedings of 52nd annual meeting of the association for computational linguistics: system demonstrations*, pages 55–60.

David N Milne, Glen Pink, Ben Hachey, and Rafael A Calvo. 2016. Clpsych 2016 shared task: Triaging content in online peer-support forums. In *Proceedings of the Third Workshop on Computational Lingusitics and Clinical Psychology*, pages 118–127.

Vinod Nair and Geoffrey E Hinton. 2010. Rectified linear units improve restricted boltzmann machines. In *Proceedings of the 27th international conference on machine learning (ICML-10)*, pages 807–814.

Bridianne O'Dea, Stephen Wan, Philip J Batterham, Alison L Calear, Cecile Paris, and Helen Christensen. 2015. Detecting suicidality on twitter. *Internet Interventions*, 2(2):183–188.

Alexander Pak and Patrick Paroubek. 2010. Twitter as a corpus for sentiment analysis and opinion mining. In *LREc*, volume 10.

James W Pennebaker, Martha E Francis, and Roger J Booth. 2001. Linguistic inquiry and word count: Liwc 2001. *Mahway: Lawrence Erlbaum Associates*, 71(2001):2001.

J Ross Quinlan et al. 1996. Bagging, boosting, and c4. 5. In *AAAI/IAAI, Vol. 1*, pages 725–730.

Jo Robinson, Georgina Cox, Eleanor Bailey, Sarah Hetrick, Maria Rodrigues, Steve Fisher, and Helen Herrman. 2016. Social media and suicide prevention: a systematic review. *Early intervention in psychiatry*, 10(2):103–121.

L Sher. 2004. Preventing suicide. *Qjm*, 97(10):677–680.

Hajime Sueki, Naohiro Yonemoto, Tadashi Takeshima, and Masatoshi Inagaki. 2014. The impact of suicidality-related internet use: A prospective large cohort study with young and middle-aged internet users. *PloS one*, 9(4):e94841.

Yufei Wang, Stephen Wan, and Cécile Paris. 2016. The role of features and context on suicide ideation detection. In *Proceedings of the Australasian Language Technology Association Workshop 2016*, pages 94–102.

Guang Xiang, Bin Fan, Ling Wang, Jason Hong, and Carolyn Rose. 2012. Detecting offensive tweets via topical feature discovery over a large scale twitter corpus. In *Proceedings of the 21st ACM international conference on Information and knowledge management*, pages 1980–1984. ACM.

Andrew Yates, Arman Cohan, and Nazli Goharian. 2017. Depression and self-harm risk assessment in online forums. In *Proceedings of the 2017 Conference on Empirical Methods in Natural Language Processing*, pages 2968–2978.

William WK Zung. 1979. Suicide prevention by suicide detection. *Psychosomatics*, 20(3):153–155.

# BCSAT : A Benchmark Corpus for Sentiment Analysis in Telugu Using Word-level Annotations

**Sreekavitha Parupalli, Vijjini Anvesh Rao and Radhika Mamidi**
Language Technologies Research Center (LTRC)
International Institute of Information Technology, Hyderabad
{sreekavitha.parupalli, vijjinianvesh.rao}@research.iiit.ac.in
radhika.mamidi@iiit.ac.in

## Abstract

The presented work aims at generating a systematically annotated corpus that can support the enhancement of sentiment analysis tasks in Telugu using word-level sentiment annotations. From OntoSenseNet, we extracted 11,000 adjectives, 253 adverbs, 8483 verbs and sentiment annotation is being done by language experts. We discuss the methodology followed for the polarity annotations and validate the developed resource. This work aims at developing a benchmark corpus, as an extension to SentiWordNet, and baseline accuracy for a model where lexeme annotations are applied for sentiment predictions. The fundamental aim of this paper is to validate and study the possibility of utilizing machine learning algorithms, word-level sentiment annotations in the task of automated sentiment identification. Furthermore, accuracy is improved by annotating the bi-grams extracted from the target corpus.

## 1 Introduction

Sentiment analysis deals with the task of determining the polarity of text. To distinguish positive and negative opinions in simple texts such as reviews, blogs, and news articles, sentiment analysis (or opinion mining) is used. Over time, it evolved from focusing on explicit opinion expressions to addressing a type of opinion inference which is a result of opinions expressed towards events having positive or negative effects on entities.

There are three ways in which one can perform sentiment analysis : document-level, sentence-level, entity or word-level. These determine the polarity value considering the whole document, sentence-wise polarity, word-wise in some given text respectively (Naidu et al., 2017). Despite extensive research, the existing solutions and systems have a lot of scope for improvement, to meet the standards of the end users. The main problem arises while cataloging the possibly infinite set of conceptual rules that operate behind the analyzing the hidden polarity of the text (Das and Bandyopadhyay, 2011). In this paper, we perform a word-level sentiment annotation to validate the usage of such techniques for improving sentiment analysis task. Furthermore, we use word embeddings of the word-level sentiment annotated lexicon to predict the sentiment label of a document. We experiment with various machine learning algorithms to analyze the affect of word-level sentiment annotations on (document-level) sentiment analysis.

The paper is organized as follows. In section 2 we discuss the previous works in the field of sentiment analysis, existing resources for Telugu and specific advances that are made in Telugu. Section 3 describes our corpus and annotation scheme. 4 section describes several experiments that are carried out and the accuracies obtained. We also explain the results in detail in 4.3. Section 5 showcases our conclusions and section 6 shows the scope for future work.

## 2 Related Work

- Sentiment Analysis: Several approaches have been proposed to capture the sentiment in the text where each approach addresses the issue at different levels of granularity. Some researchers have proposed methods for document-level sentiment classification (Pang et al., 2002; Turney and Littman, 2003). At the top level of granularity, it is



*Proceedings of ACL 2018, Student Research Workshop*, pages 99–104
Melbourne, Australia, July 15 - 20, 2018. ©2018 Association for Computational Linguistics

often impossible to infer the sentiment expressed about any particular entity, because a document may convey different opinions for different entities. Hence, when we consider the tasks of opinion mining where the sole aim is to capture the sentiment polarities about entities, such as products in product reviews, it has been shown that sentence-level and phrase-level analysis lead to a performance gain (Wilson et al., 2005; Choi and Wiebe, 2014). In the context of Indian languages, (Das et al., 2012) proposes an alternate way to build the resources for multilingual affect analysis where translations into Telugu are done using WordNet.

- `SentiWordNet` : (Das and Bandyopadhyay, 2010) proposes multiple computational techniques like, WordNet based, dictionary based, corpus based and generative approaches to generate Telugu SentiWordNet. (Das and Bandyopadhyay, 2011) proposes a tool Dr Sentiment where it automatically creates the PsychoSentiWordNet which is an extension of SentiWordNet that presently holds human psychological knowledge on a few aspects along with sentiment knowledge.

- `Advances in Telugu`: (Naidu et al., 2017) utilizes Telugu SentiWordNet on the news corpus to perform the task of Sentiment Analysis. (Mukku and Mamidi, 2017) developed a polarity annotated corpus where positive, negative, neutral polarities are assigned to 5410 sentences in the corpus collected from several sources. They developed a gold standard annotated corpus of Telugu sentences aimed at improving sentiment analysis in Telugu. To minimize the dependence of machine learning(ML) approaches for sentiment analysis on abundance of corpus, this paper proposes a novel method to learn representations of resource-poor languages by training them jointly with resource-rich languages using a siamese network (Choudhary et al., 2018a). A novel approach to classify sentences into their corresponding sentiment using contrastive learning is proposed by (Choudhary et al., 2018b) which utilizes the shared parameters of siamese networks.

(Gangula and Mamidi, 2018) and (Mukku and Mamidi, 2017) are the only reported works for Telugu sentiment analysis using sentence-level annotations who developed annotated corpora. Ours is the first of it's kind NLP research which uses sentiment annotation of bi-grams for sentiment analysis (opinion mining).

## 3    Building the Benchmark Corpus

Lexicons play an important role in sentiment analysis. Having annotated lexicon is key to carry out sentiment analysis efficiently. The primary task in sentiment analysis is to identify the polarity of text in any given document. The polarity may be either positive, negative or neutral (Naidu et al., 2017). Sentiment is a property of human intelligence and is not entirely based on the features of a language. Thus, peoples involvement is required to capture the sentiment (Das and Bandyopadhyay, 2011). Having said this, we establish that annotated lexicons are of immense importance in any language for sentiment analysis (a.k.a opinion mining).

For our experiments, we utilize the reviews dataset from Sentiraama [1] corpus. It contains 668 reviews in total for 267 movies, 201 products and 200 books. Product reviews has 101 positive and 100 negative entries; movie reviews has 136 positive and 132 negative reviews; book reviews data has 100 positive and 100 negative entries. Since the obtained corpus is only annotated with document-level sentiment labels, we perform the word-level sentiment annotation manually.

### 3.1    Annotation Procedure

In this paper, sentiment polarities are classified into 4 labels : positive, negative, neutral and ambiguous. Positive and negative labels are given in case of positive and negative sentiments in the word respectively. Ambiguous label is given to words which acquire sentiment based on the words it is used along with or it's position in a sentence. Neutral label is given when the word has no sentiment in it. However, neutral and ambiguous sentiment labels are of no significant use for the task of sentiment analysis. Henceforth, those labels are ignored in our experiments.

Sentiment annotations are performed on two different kinds of data. Table 1 showcases the distribution of sentiment labels at the word-level.

---

[1] `https://ltrc.iiit.ac.in/showfile.php?filename=downloads/sentiraama/`

- `Unigrams`: We obtain 7,663 words from Telugu SentiWordNet [2] resource to calculate the base-line accuracy of any word-level sentiment annotated model. These words are already annotated for sentiment/polarity. However, it doesn't provide extensive coverage of Telugu. Later on, we discover a newly developed large resource of Telugu words by (Parupalli and Singh, 2018), OntoSenseNet, which has a collection of 21,000 words (adjectives+verbs+adverbs). We perform the task of word-level sentiment annotation on the words obtained from this resource and we refer to these annotated words as unigrams throughout this paper. Language experts who performed the annotations are given some guidelines to follow. Experts are implored to look at the word, it's gloss and then decide which one of the four sentiment labels is more apt for a given word. Aforementioned word-level sentiment annotation is an attempt to improve the coverage of SentiWordNet.

- `Bigrams`: Furthermore, sentiment cannot always be captured in a single word.This paper aims to check if bigram annotation is a suitable approach for improving the efficiency of sentiment analysis. To validate the hypothesis, we extract bigrams, which occurred at least more than once, only from the target corpus - Sentiraama dataset developed by (Gangula and Mamidi, 2018). For example, consider the bigram ('DhokA', 'ledu'). The words individually mean 'hurdle (DhokA)', 'no (ledu)'. Thus, in word-level annotation task they would be given a negative label. However, the bigram means there is 'nothing that can stop' which invokes a positive sentiment. Such occurrences are quite common in the text, especially reviews, which lead us to believe that bigram polarity has potential to enhance sentiment analysis, opinion mining. The usage of this developed resource in experiments performed is explained in section 4.

## 3.2 Validation

Annotations are done by 2 native speakers of Telugu. If the annotators aren't able to decide which

label to assign, they are advised to tag it as uncertain. In case of a disagreement, the label given by the annotator with more experience is given priority. Validation of the developed resource is done using Cohen's Kappa (Cohen, 1968). By considering the uncertain cases as borderline cases (where at least one annotator tagged the word as uncertain), Kappa value is seen as 0.91. This shows almost perfect agreement and this proves the consistency in annotation task. This is especially high because when both the annotators are uncertain, we did a re-iteration to finalize the tag. Such re-iterative task is done for about 2,400 words during the development of our resource.

## 4 Experiments and Results

In this section we will analyze and observe how word-level polarity affects overall sentiment of the text through majority polling approach and machine learning based classification approaches.

## 4.1 Majority Polling Approach

A simple intuitive approach to identify the sentiment label of the text is to calculate the sum of positive(+1) and negative(-1) polarity values in it. If the sum is positive, it shows that number of positive words have outnumbered the number of negative words thus resulting in a positive sentiment on the whole. Otherwise, the polarity of the text is negative. Cases where the sum equals to 0 are ignored. Following are the word-level polarities we consider for positive and negative labels:

- `Unigram`: We use the annotated unigram data that is discussed in 3. For each review, we consider the unigram labels to carry the majority polling approach.

- `Bigram`: The extracted bigrams are annotated for positive and negative polarity. Initially, we divide our data into training and testing sets in 7:3 ratio. We only consider the annotated bigrams from the training corpus to predict the sentiment polarity of reviews in the test data.

- `Unigram+Bigram`: In this trial, we combine the unigram and bigram data to perform majority polling. We consider the whole unigram data whereas bigrams extracted from the training set are only considered for predictions.

[2]http://amitavadas.com/sentiwordnet.php

| Resource | Positive | Negative | Neutral | Ambiguous | Total |
|---|---|---|---|---|---|
| SentiWordNet [3] | 2135 | 4076 | 359 | 1093 | 7663 |
| Dictionary (Parupalli and Singh, 2018) | 3080 | 4232 | 3391 | 10199 | 20896 |
| Bigrams | 1978 | 1762 | 8990 | 1996 | 14826 |

Table 1: Distribution of Sentiment Labels in Several Resources

Furthermore, as Telugu is agglutinative in nature (Pingali and Varma, 2006), we experiment with the above mentioned approaches after performing morphological segmentation provided by Indic NLP library [4]. Morphological segmentation is performed on the original reviews data and n-grams (positive and negative labels) to see if we could get more accurate sentiment prediction of the reviews due to increment in the coverage.

## 4.2 Machine Learning Based Classification Approach

In this section, we perform document-level sentiment analysis task with word embedding models, specifically Word2Vec. We utilize a Word2Vec model that is trained on corpus consisting of scrapped data from Telugu websites, with 270 million non-unique tokens on the whole. Furthermore, to obtain vectors for each review, we take word vector of every word in the review and calculate their average to get a single document vector.

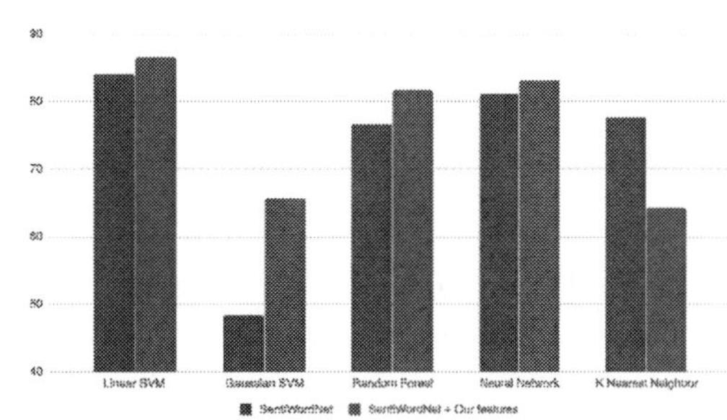


Figure 1: Comparative analysis of percentage accuracies produced by various classifiers

Though traditional vector-based word representations help us accomplish various natural language processing tasks, they often lack information related to sentiment analysis. Thus, we aim to enrich the Word2Vec vectors obtained from corpus by incorporating word-level polarity features. We do this by adding the features we propose in 4.1 to the original averaged Word2Vec vector,

which is expected to increase the accuracy of polarity prediction. The additional features we added are: *positive unigrams* (number of positive polarity unigrams in the review), *negative unigrams* (number of negative polarity unigrams in the review), *positive bigrams* (number of positive polarity bigrams in the review), *negative bigrams* (number of negative polarity bigrams in the review). We partition these document vectors into training and testing sets to develop various classifier models. In this paper, we have implemented 5 classifiers, namely, Linear SVM, Gaussian SVM, Random Forest, Neural Network, K Nearest Neighbor (KNN). Percentage accuracies are illustrated along with the improvement in accuracies after addition of our proposed features in Figure 1 and results are discussed in 4.3.

## 4.3 Results

In this section, we showcase and analyze the results of the two experiments we have done in section 4.

### 4.3.1 Majority Polling Approach :

Results illustrated in Table 2 show that certain word-level features do capture information relevant to document-level sentiment analysis. Our hypothesis in Section 3.1 shows that bigram polarity annotations have potential to enhance sentiment analysis. High accuracy obtained by using only bigrams for majority polling proves our hypothesis. However, there is a trade-off between coverage and accuracy. This can be depicted from the huge increase in the count of unclassified reviews in case of bigram majority poling. We also observe that effect of morphological segmentation on accuracy is hardly positive. This indicates that in case of Telugu, morphological data has relevance to sentiment expressed and morphological segmentation would result in loss of such valuable information for sentiment analysis tasks.

[4]http://anoopkunchukuttan.github.io/indic_nlp_library/

| | SentiWordNet | Our resource | Bigram | Uni+Bigrams |
|---|---|---|---|---|
| Before Segmentation | 61.86 | 62.84 | 78.97 | 55.44 |
| Unclassified reviews | 23/201 | 14/201 | 108/201 | 10/201 |
| After Segmentation | 60.23 | 58.29 | 49.46 | 57.89 |
| Unclassified reviews | 20/201 | 18/201 | 36/201 | 8/201 |

Table 2: Comparison of accuracies obtained through majority polling on different resources.

### 4.3.2 Machine Learning Based Classification Approach:

This approach shows that across all the classifiers, addition of word-level polarity features improves the process of classification. Therefore, classifiers can predict document-level sentiment polarity with better accuracies. Hence, our hypothesis is validated once again. Accuracies doesn't improve significantly over the baseline value but show a small increment always. KNN classifier shows a huge drop in accuracy after inclusion of the new features proposed. This is observed because KNN assumes all features to hold equal importance for classification. Hence, KNN fails to ignore the noisy features which explains the drop. Random forest and neural network classifiers don't show significant learning from the proposed features. Finally, we observe that linear SVM classifier works best to identify the polarity of a text for our features indicating linear separability of the data. This also explains the bad performance of Gaussian SVM. Linear SVM produces an accuracy of 84.08% when SentiWordNet words alone are used as a feature, which can be considered as the baseline accuracy. It gives an accuracy of 83.44% ,84.34% and 86.57% for unigrams, bigrams and unigrams+bigrams respectively as features of Linear SVM classifier.

## 5 Conclusions

In this paper, efforts are made to develop an annotated corpus of 21,000 words to enrich Telugu SentiWordNet. This is a work in progress. We perform annotations of 14,000 bigrams that are extracted from target corpus to validate their importance. This is a first-of-it's-kind approach in Telugu to enhance sentiment analysis. Manual annotations done show perfect agreement which validates the developed resource. Furthermore, we provide a justification to why word-level sentiment annotation of bigrams enhances sentiment analysis though an intuitive majority polling approach, by using several ML classifiers. The results are analyzed for further insights.

## 6 Future Work

We extract bigrams only from the target corpus because we wanted to mainly validate the importance of bigrams in sentiment analysis. However, attempts should be made to enhance the SentiWordNet with, at least, some most occurring bigrams in Telugu. We hope this corpus can serve as a basis for more work to be done in the area of sentiment analysis for Telugu. A continuation to this paper could be handling the enrichment of adjectives and adverbs available in OntoSenseNet for Telugu.

### 6.1 Crowd sourcing

We can develop a crowd sourcing platform where the annotations can be done by several language experts instead of a few. This helps in the annotation of large corpora. We aim to develop a crowd sourcing model for the same in near future. This would be of immense help in annotation of 21,000 unigrams extracted from the dictionary developed by (Parupalli and Singh, 2018).

## 7 Acknowledgements

This work is part of the ongoing MS thesis in Exact Humanities under the guidance of Prof. Radhika Mamidi. I am immensely grateful to Vijaya Lakshmi for helping me with data collection. I would like to thank Nurendra Choudary for reviewing the paper and for his part in the ideation. I would like to extend my gratitude to Abhilash Reddy for annotating the dataset, reviewing the work carefully and constantly pushing us to do better. I want to thank Rama Rohit Reddy for his support and for validating the novelty of this research at several points. I acknowledge the support of Google in the form of an International Travel Grant, which enabled me to attend this conference.

## References

Yoonjung Choi and Janyce Wiebe. 2014. +/-effectwordnet: Sense-level lexicon acquisition for opinion inference. In *Proceedings of the 2014 Conference on Empirical Methods in Natural Language Processing (EMNLP)*, pages 1181–1191.

Nurendra Choudhary, Rajat Singh, Ishita Bindlish, and Manish Shrivastava. 2018a. Emotions are universal: Learning sentiment based representations of resource-poor languages using siamese networks. *arXiv preprint arXiv:1804.00805*.

Nurendra Choudhary, Rajat Singh, Ishita Bindlish, and Manish Shrivastava. 2018b. Sentiment analysis of code-mixed languages leveraging resource rich languages. *arXiv preprint arXiv:1804.00806*.

Jacob Cohen. 1968. Weighted kappa: Nominal scale agreement provision for scaled disagreement or partial credit. *Psychological bulletin*, 70(4):213.

Amitava Das and Sivaji Bandyopadhyay. 2010. Sentiwordnet for indian languages. In *Proceedings of the Eighth Workshop on Asian Language Resouces*, pages 56–63.

Amitava Das and Sivaji Bandyopadhyay. 2011. Dr sentiment knows everything! In *Proceedings of the 49th annual meeting of the association for computational linguistics: human language technologies: systems demonstrations*, pages 50–55. Association for Computational Linguistics.

Dipankar Das, Soujanya Poria, Chandra Mohan Dasari, and Sivaji Bandyopadhyay. 2012. Building resources for multilingual affect analysis–a case study on hindi, bengali and telugu. In *Workshop Programme*, page 54.

Rama Rohit Reddy Gangula and Radhika Mamidi. 2018. Resource creation towards automated sentiment analysis in telugu (a low resource language) and integrating multiple domain sources to enhance sentiment prediction. In *Proceedings of the Eleventh International Conference on Language Resources and Evaluation (LREC 2018)*, Paris, France. European Language Resources Association (ELRA).

Sandeep Sricharan Mukku and Radhika Mamidi. 2017. Actsa: Annotated corpus for telugu sentiment analysis. In *Proceedings of the First Workshop on Building Linguistically Generalizable NLP Systems*, pages 54–58.

Reddy Naidu, Santosh Kumar Bharti, Korra Sathya Babu, and Ramesh Kumar Mohapatra. 2017. Sentiment analysis using telugu sentiwordnet.

Bo Pang, Lillian Lee, and Shivakumar Vaithyanathan. 2002. Thumbs up?: sentiment classification using machine learning techniques. In *Proceedings of the ACL-02 conference on Empirical methods in natural language processing-Volume 10*, pages 79–86. Association for Computational Linguistics.

Sreekavitha Parupalli and Navjyoti Singh. 2018. Enrichment of ontosensenet: Adding a sense-annotated telugu lexicon. *arXiv preprint arXiv:1804.02186*.

Prasad Pingali and Vasudeva Varma. 2006. Hindi and telugu to english cross language information retrieval at clef 2006. In *CLEF (Working Notes)*.

Peter D Turney and Michael L Littman. 2003. Measuring praise and criticism: Inference of semantic orientation from association. *ACM Transactions on Information Systems (TOIS)*, 21(4):315–346.

Theresa Wilson, Janyce Wiebe, and Paul Hoffmann. 2005. Recognizing contextual polarity in phrase-level sentiment analysis. In *Proceedings of the conference on human language technology and empirical methods in natural language processing*, pages 347–354. Association for Computational Linguistics.

# Reinforced Extractive Summarization with Question-Focused Rewards


**Kristjan Arumae    Fei Liu**
Department of Computer Science
University of Central Florida, Orlando, FL 32816, USA
`k.arumae@knights.ucf.edu    feiliu@cs.ucf.edu`



## Abstract

We investigate a new training paradigm for extractive summarization. Traditionally, human abstracts are used to derive gold-standard labels for extraction units. However, the labels are often inaccurate, because human abstracts and source documents cannot be easily aligned at the word level. In this paper we convert human abstracts to a set of Cloze-style comprehension questions. System summaries are encouraged to preserve salient source content useful for answering questions and share common words with the abstracts. We use reinforcement learning to explore the space of possible extractive summaries and introduce a question-focused reward function to promote concise, fluent, and informative summaries. Our experiments show that the proposed method is effective. It surpasses state-of-the-art systems on the standard summarization dataset.


## 1    Introduction

We study extractive summarization in this work where salient word sequences are extracted from the source document and concatenated to form a summary (Nenkova and McKeown, 2011). Existing supervised approaches to extractive summarization frequently use human abstracts to create annotations for extraction units (Gillick and Favre, 2009; Li et al., 2013; Cheng and Lapata, 2016). E.g., a source word is labelled 1 if it appears in the abstract, 0 otherwise. Despite the usefulness, there are two issues with this scheme. First, a vast majority of the source words are tagged 0s, only a small portion are 1s. This is due to the fact that human abstracts are short and concise; they often contain words not present in the source. Second,

| Source Document |
| --- |
| *The first doses of the Ebola vaccine were on a commercial flight to West Africa and were expected to arrive on Friday,* according to a spokesperson from GlaxoSmithKline (GSK) one of the companies that has created the vaccine with the National Institutes of Health. |
| Another vaccine from Merck and NewLink will also be tested. |
| "Shipping the vaccine today is a major achievement and shows that we remain on track with the accelerated development of our candidate Ebola vaccine," Dr. Moncef Slaoui, chairman of global vaccines at GSK said in a company release. (Rest omitted.) |

| Abstract |
| --- |
| The first vials of an Ebola vaccine should land in Liberia Friday |

| Questions |
| --- |
| **Q:** The first vials of an ____ vaccine should land in Liberia Friday |
| **Q:** The first vials of an Ebola vaccine should ____ in Liberia Friday |
| **Q:** The first vials of an Ebola vaccine should land in ____ Friday |

Table 1: Example source document, the top sentence of the abstract, and system-generated Cloze-style questions. Source content related to the abstract is *italicized*.

not all labels are accurate. Source words that are labelled 0 may be paraphrases, generalizations, or otherwise related to words in the abstracts. These source words are often mislabelled. Consequently, leveraging human abstracts to provide supervision for extractive summarization remains a challenge.

Neural abstractive summarization can alleviate this issue by allowing the system to either copy words from the source texts or generate new words from a vocabulary (Rush et al., 2015; Nallapati et al., 2016; See et al., 2017). While the techniques are promising, they face other challenges, such as ensuring the summaries remain faithful to the original. Failing to reproduce factual details has been revealed as one of the main obstacles for neural abstractive summarization (Cao et al., 2018; Song and Liu, 2018). This study thus chooses to focus on neural extractive summarization.

We explore a new training paradigm for extractive summarization. We convert human abstracts to a set of Cloze-style comprehension questions, where the question body is a sentence of the abstract with a blank, and the answer is an entity or a keyword. Table 1 shows an example. Because the

105


*Proceedings of ACL 2018, Student Research Workshop*, pages 105–111
Melbourne, Australia, July 15 - 20, 2018. ©2018 Association for Computational Linguistics

questions cannot be answered by applying general world knowledge, system summaries are encouraged to preserve salient source content that is relevant to the questions ($\approx$ human abstract) such that the summaries can work as a document surrogate to predict correct answers. We use an attention mechanism to locate segments of a summary that are relevant to a given question so that the summary can be used to answer multiple questions.

This study extends the work of (Lei et al., 2016) to use reinforcement learning to explore the space of extractive summaries. While the original work focuses on generating rationales to support supervised classification, the goal of our study is to produce fluent, generic document summaries. The question-answering (QA) task is designed to fulfill this goal and the QA performance is only secondary. Our research contributions can be summarized as follows:

- we investigate an alternative training scheme for extractive summarization where the summaries are encouraged to be semantically close to human abstracts in addition to sharing common words;

- we compare two methods to convert human abstracts to Cloze-style questions and investigate its impact on QA and summarization performance. Our results surpass those of previous systems on a standard summarization dataset.

## 2   Related Work

This study focuses on generic summarization. It is different from the query-based summarization (Daumé III and Marcu, 2006; Dang and Owczarzak, 2008), where systems are trained to select text pieces related to *predefined* queries. In this work we have no predefined queries but the system carefully generates questions from human abstracts and learns to produce generic summaries that are capable of answering all questions.

Cloze questions have been used in reading comprehension (Richardson et al., 2013; Weston et al., 2016; Mostafazadeh et al., 2016; Rajpurkar et al., 2016) to test the system's ability to perform reasoning and language understanding. Hermann et al. (2015) describe an approach to extract (context, question, answer) triples from news articles. Our work draws on this approach to automatically create questions from human abstracts.

Reinforcement learning (RL) has been recently applied to a number of NLP applications, includ-

ing dialog generation (Li et al., 2017), machine translation (MT) (Ranzato et al., 2016; Gu et al., 2018), question answering (Choi et al., 2017), and summarization and sentence simplification (Zhang and Lapata, 2017; Paulus et al., 2017; Chen and Bansal, 2018; Narayan et al., 2018). This study leverages RL to explore the space of possible extractive summaries. The summaries are encouraged to preserve salient source content useful for answering questions as well as sharing common words with the abstracts.

## 3   Our Approach

Given a source document $X$, our system generates a summary $Y = (y_1, y_2, \cdots, y_{|Y|})$ by identifying consecutive sequences of words: $y_t$ is 1 if the $t$-th source word is included in the summary, 0 otherwise. In this section we investigate a question-oriented reward $\mathcal{R}(Y)$ that encourages summaries to contain sufficient content useful for answering key questions about the document (§3.1); we then use reinforcement learning to explore the space of possible extractive summaries (§3.2).

### 3.1   Question-Focused Reward

We reward a summary if it can be used as a document surrogate to answer important questions. Let $\{(Q_k, e_k^*)\}_{k=1}^{K}$ be a set of question-answer pairs for a source document, where $e_k^*$ is the ground-truth answer corresponding to an entity or a keyword. We encode the question $Q_k$ into a vector: $\mathbf{q}_k = \text{Bi-LSTM}(Q_k) \in \mathbb{R}^d$ using a bidirectional LSTM, where the last outputs of the forward and backward passes are concatenated to form a question vector. We use the same Bi-LSTM to encode the summary $Y$ to a sequence of vectors: $(\mathbf{h}_1^S, \mathbf{h}_2^S, \cdots, \mathbf{h}_{|S|}^S) = \text{Bi-LSTM}(Y)$, where $|S|$ is the number of words in the summary; $\mathbf{h}_t^S \in \mathbb{R}^d$ is the concatenation of forward and backward hidden states at time step $t$. Figure 1 provides an illustration of the system framework.

An attention mechanism is used to locate parts of the summary that are relevant to $Q_k$. We define $\alpha_{k,i} \propto \exp(\mathbf{q}_k \mathbf{W}^a \mathbf{h}_i^S)$ to represent the importance of the $i$-th summary word ($\mathbf{h}_i^S$) to answering the $k$-th question ($\mathbf{q}_k$), characterized by a bilinear term (Chen et al., 2016a). A context vector $\mathbf{c}_k$ is constructed as a weighted sum of all summary words relevant to the $k$-th question, and it is used to predict the answer. We define the QA reward $\mathcal{R}_a(Y)$ as the log-likelihood of correctly predict-

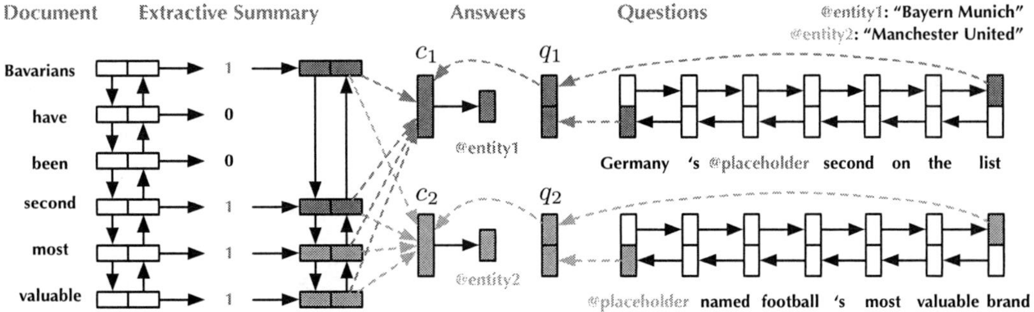


Figure 1: System framework. The model uses an extractive summary as a document surrogate to answer important questions about the document. The questions are automatically derived from the human abstract.

ing all answers. $\{\mathbf{W}^a, \mathbf{W}^c\}$ are learnable model parameters.

$$\alpha_{k,i} = \frac{\exp(\mathbf{q}_k \mathbf{W}^a \mathbf{h}_i^S)}{\sum_{i=1}^{|S|} \exp(\mathbf{q}_k \mathbf{W}^a \mathbf{h}_i^S)} \quad (1)$$

$$\mathbf{c}_k = \sum_{i=1}^{|S|} \alpha_{k,i} \mathbf{h}_i^S \quad (2)$$

$$P(e_k|Y, Q_k) = \text{softmax}(\mathbf{W}^c \mathbf{c}_k) \quad (3)$$

$$\mathcal{R}_a(Y) = \frac{1}{K} \sum_{k=1}^{K} \log P(e_k^*|Y, Q_k) \quad (4)$$

In the following we describe approaches to obtain a set of question-answer pairs $\{(Q_k, e_k^*)\}_{k=1}^{K}$ from a human abstract. In fact, this formulation has the potential to make use of multiple human abstracts (subject to availability) in a unified framework; in that case, the QA pairs will be extracted from all abstracts. According to Eq. (4), the system is optimized to generate summaries that preserve salient source content sufficient to answer *all questions* ($\approx$ human abstract).

We expect to harvest one question-answer pair from each sentence of the abstract. More are possible, but the QA pairs will contain duplicate content. There are a few other noteworthy issues. If we do not collect any QA pairs from a sentence of the abstract, its content will be left out of the system summary. It is thus crucial for the system to extract at least one QA pair from *any* sentence in an automatic manner. Further, the questions must not be answered by simply applying general world knowledge. We expect the adequacy of the summary to have a direct influence on whether or not the questions will be correctly answered. Motivated by these considerations, we perform the following steps. We split a human abstract to a set of sentences, identify an answer token from each

sentence, then convert the sentence to a question by replacing the token with a placeholder, yielding a Cloze question. We explore two approaches to extract answer tokens:

- *Entities.* We extract four types of named entities {PER, LOC, ORG, MISC} from sentences and treat them as possible answer tokens.

- *Keywords.* This approach identifies the ROOT word of a sentence dependency parse tree and treats it as a keyword-based answer token. Not all sentences contain entities, but every sentence has a root word; it is often the main verb of the sentence.

We obtain $K$ question-answer pairs from each human abstract, one pair per sentence. If there are less than $K$ sentences in the abstract, the QA pairs of the top sentences will be duplicated, with the assumption that the top sentences are more important than others. If multiple entities reside in a sentence, we randomly pick one as the answer token; otherwise if there are no entities, we use the root word instead.

To ensure that the extractive summaries are concise, fluent, and close to the original wording, we add additional components to the reward function: (i) we define $\mathcal{R}_s(Y) = |\frac{1}{|Y|} \sum_{t=1}^{|Y|} y_t - \delta|$ to restrict the summary size. We require the percentage of selected source words to be close to a predefined threshold $\delta$. This constraint works well at restricting length, with the average summary size adhering to this percentage; (ii) we further introduce $\mathcal{R}_f(Y) = \sum_{t=2}^{|Y|} |y_t - y_{t-1}|$ to encourage the summaries to be fluent. This component is adopted from (Lei et al., 2016), where few 0/1 switches between $y_{t-1}$ and $y_t$ indicates the system is selecting consecutive word sequences; (iii) we encourage system and reference summaries to share common bigrams. This practice has shown success in earlier studies (Gillick and Favre, 2009). $\mathcal{R}_b(Y)$ is defined as the percentage of reference bigrams successfully covered by the system summary. These three components together ensure the well-formedness of extractive summaries. The final reward function $\mathcal{R}(Y)$ is a linear interpolation of all the components; $\gamma, \alpha, \beta$ are coefficients and we describe their parameter tuning in §4.

$$\mathcal{R}(Y) = \mathcal{R}_a(Y) + \gamma \mathcal{R}_b(Y) - \alpha \mathcal{R}_f(Y) - \beta \mathcal{R}_s(Y) \tag{5}$$

## 3.2 Reinforcement Learning

In the following we seek to optimize a policy $P(Y|X)$ for generating extractive summaries so that the expected reward $\mathbb{E}_{P(Y|X)}[\mathcal{R}(Y)]$ is maximized. Taking derivatives of this objective with respect to model parameters $\theta$ involves repeatedly sampling summaries $\hat{Y} = (\hat{y}_1, \hat{y}_2, \cdots, \hat{y}_{|Y|})$ (illustrated in Eq. (6)). In this way reinforcement learning exploits the space of extractive summaries of a source document.

$$\nabla_\theta \mathbb{E}_{P(Y|X)}[\mathcal{R}(Y)]$$
$$= \mathbb{E}_{P(Y|X)}[\mathcal{R}(Y) \nabla_\theta \log P(Y|X)]$$
$$\approx \frac{1}{N} \sum_{n=1}^{N} \mathcal{R}(\hat{Y}^{(n)}) \nabla_\theta \log P(\hat{Y}^{(n)}|X) \tag{6}$$

To calculate $P(Y|X)$ and then sample $\hat{Y}$ from it, we use a bidirectional LSTM to encode a source document to a sequence of vectors: $(\mathbf{h}_1^D, \mathbf{h}_2^D, \cdots, \mathbf{h}_{|X|}^D) = \text{Bi-LSTM}(X)$. Whether to include the $t$-th source word in the summary ($\hat{y}_t$) thus can be decided based on $\mathbf{h}_t^D$. However, we also want to accommodate the previous $t$-1 sampling decisions ($\hat{y}_{1:t-1}$) to improve the fluency of the extractive summary. Following (Lei et al., 2016), we introduce a single-direction LSTM encoder whose hidden state $\mathbf{s}_t$ tracks the sampling decisions up to time step $t$ (Eq. 8). It represents the semantic meaning encoded in the current summary. To sample the $t$-th word, we concatenate the two vectors $[\mathbf{h}_t^D || \mathbf{s}_{t-1}]$ and use it as input to a feed-forward layer with sigmoid activation to estimate $\hat{y}_t \sim P(y_t|\hat{y}_{1:t-1}, X)$ (Eq. 7).

$$P(y_t|\hat{y}_{1:t-1}, X) = \sigma(\mathbf{W}^h[\mathbf{h}_t^D||\mathbf{s}_{t-1}] + b^h) \tag{7}$$
$$\mathbf{s}_t = \text{LSTM}([\mathbf{h}_t^D||\hat{y}_t], \mathbf{s}_{t-1}) \tag{8}$$
$$P(\hat{Y}|X) = \prod_{t=1}^{|Y|} P(\hat{y}_t|\hat{y}_{1:t-1}, X) \tag{9}$$

Note that Eq. (7) can be pretrained using goldstandard summary sequence $Y^* = (y_1^*, y_2^*, \cdots, y_{|Y|}^*)$ to minimize the word-level cross-entropy loss,

| System | R-1 | R-2 | R-L |
|---|---|---|---|
| LSA (Steinberger and Jezek, 2004) | 21.2 | 6.2 | 14.0 |
| LexRank (Erkan and Radev, 2004) | 26.1 | 9.6 | 17.7 |
| TextRank (Mihalcea and Tarau, 2004) | 23.3 | 7.7 | 15.8 |
| SumBasic (Vanderwende et al., 2007) | 22.9 | 5.5 | 14.8 |
| KL-Sum (Haghighi and Vanderwende, 2009) | 20.7 | 5.9 | 13.7 |
| Distraction-M3 (Chen et al., 2016b) | 27.1 | 8.2 | 18.7 |
| Seq2Seq w/ Attn (See et al., 2017) | 25.0 | 7.7 | 18.8 |
| Pointer-Gen w/ Cov (See et al., 2017) | 29.9 | 10.9 | 21.1 |
| Graph-based Attn (Tan et al., 2017) | 30.3 | 9.8 | 20.0 |
| **Extr+EntityQ** (this paper) | **31.4** | **11.5** | **21.7** |
| **Extr+KeywordQ** (this paper) | **31.7** | **11.6** | **21.5** |

Table 2: Results on the CNN test set (full-length F1 scores).

where we set $y_t^*$ as 1 if $(x_t, x_{t+1})$ is a bigram in the human abstract. For reinforcement learning, our goal is to optimize the policy $P(Y|X)$ using the reward function $\mathcal{R}(Y)$ (§3.1) during the training process. Once the policy $P(Y|X)$ is learned, we do not need the reward function (or any QA pairs) at test time to generate generic summaries. Instead we choose $\hat{y}_t$ that yields the highest probability $\hat{y}_t = \arg\max P(y_t|\hat{y}_{1:t-1}, X)$.

## 4 Experiments

All training, validation, and testing was performed using the CNN dataset (Hermann et al., 2015; Nallapati et al., 2016) containing news articles paired with human-written highlights (i.e., abstracts). We observe that a source article contains 29.8 sentences and an abstract contains 3.54 sentences on average. The train/valid/test splits contain 90,266, 1,220, 1,093 articles respectively.

### 4.1 Hyperparameters

The hyperparameters, tuned on the validation set, include the following: the hidden state size of the Bi-LSTM is 256; the hidden state size of the single-direction LSTM encoder is 30. Dropout rate (Srivastava, 2013), used twice in the sampling component, is set to 0.2. The minibatch size is set to 256. We apply early stopping on the validation set, where the maximum number of epochs is set to 50. Our source vocabulary contains 150K words; words not in the vocabulary are replaced by the $\langle\text{unk}\rangle$ token. We use 100-dimensional word embeddings, initialized by GloVe (Pennington et al., 2014) and remain trainable. We set $\beta = 2\alpha$ and select the best $\alpha \in \{10, 20, 50\}$ and $\gamma \in \{5, 6, 7, 8\}$ using the valid set (best value underlined). The maximum length of input is set to 100 words; $\delta$ is set to be 0.4 ($\approx$40 words). We use the Adam optimizer (Kingma and Ba, 2015) with an initial learning rate of 1e-4 and halve the learning rate if the objective worsens beyond a threshold ($> 10\%$). As mentioned we utilized a bigram based pretraining method. We found that this stabilized the training of the full model.

## 4.2 Results

We compare our methods with state-of-the-art published systems, including both extractive and abstractive approaches (their details are summarized below). We experiment with two variants of our approach. "EntityQ" uses QA pairs whose answers are named entities. "KeywordQ" uses pairs whose answers are sentence root words. According to the R-1, R-2, and R-L scores (Lin, 2004) presented in Table 2, both methods are superior to the baseline systems on the benchmark dataset, yielding 11.5 and 11.6 R-2 F-scores, respectively.

- **LSA** (Steinberger and Jezek, 2004) uses the latent semantic analysis technique to identify semantically important sentences.

- **LexRank** (Erkan and Radev, 2004) is a graph-based approach that computes sentence importance based on the concept of eigenvector centrality in a graph representation of source sentences.

- **TextRank** (Mihalcea and Tarau, 2004) is an unsupervised graph-based ranking algorithm inspired by algorithms PageRank and HITS.

- **SumBasic** (Vanderwende et al., 2007) is an extractive approach that assumes words occurring frequently in a document cluster have a higher chance of being included in the summary.

- **KL-Sum** (Haghighi and Vanderwende, 2009) describes a method that greedily adds sentences to the summary so long as it decreases the KL divergence.

- **Distraction-M3** (Chen et al., 2016b) trains the summarization model to not only attend to specific regions of input documents, but also distract the attention to traverse different content of the source document.

- **Pointer-Generator** (See et al., 2017) allows the system to not only copy words from the source text via pointing but also generate novel words through the generator.

- **Graph-based Attention** (Tan et al., 2017) introduces a graph-based attention mechanism to enhance the encoder-decoder framework.

|  | K1 | K2 | K3 | K4 | K5 |
|---|---|---|---|---|---|
| # Uniq Entities | 23.7K | 37.0K | 46.1K | 50.3K | 50.3K |
| Train Acc (%) | 46.1 | 37.2 | 34.2 | 33.6 | 34.8 |
| Valid Acc (%) | 12.8 | 14.0 | 14.7 | 15.7 | 15.4 |
| Valid R-2 F (%) | 11.2 | 11.1 | 11.2 | 11.1 | 10.8 |
| # Uniq Keywds | 7.3K | 10.4K | 12.5K | 13.7K | 13.7K |
| Train Acc (%) | 30.5 | 28.2 | 27.6 | 27.5 | 27.5 |
| Valid Acc (%) | 19.3 | 22.5 | 22.2 | 23.0 | 21.9 |
| Valid R-2 F (%) | 11.2 | 11.1 | 10.8 | 11.0 | 10.8 |

Table 3: Train/valid accuracy and R-2 F-scores when using varying numbers of QA pairs (K=1 to 5) in the reward func.

In Table 3, we vary the number of QA pairs used per article in the reward function ($K$=1 to 5). The summaries are encouraged to contain comprehensive content useful for answering *all* questions. When more QA pairs are used (K1→K5), we observe that the number of answer tokens has increased and almost doubled: 23.7K (K1)→50.3K (K5) for entities as answers, and 7.3K→13.7K for keywords. The enlarged answer space has an impact on QA accuracies. When using entities as answers, the training accuracy is 34.8% (Q5) and validation is 15.4% (Q5), and there appears to be a considerable gap between the two. In contrast, the gap is quite small when using keywords as answers (27.5% and 21.9% for Q5), suggesting that using sentence root words as answers is a more viable strategy to create QA pairs.

Comparing to QA studies (Chen et al., 2016a), we remove the constraint that requires answer entities (or keywords) to reside in the source documents. Adding this constraint improves the QA accuracy for a standard QA system. However, because our system does not perform QA during testing (the question-answer pairs are not available for the test set) but only generate generic summaries, we do not enforce this requirement and report no testing accuracies. We observe that the R-2 scores only present minor changes from K1 to K5. We conjecture that more question-answer pairs do not make the summaries contain more comprehensive content because the input and the summary are relatively short; $K$=1 yields the best results.

In Table 4, we present example system and reference summaries. Our extractive summaries can be overlaid with the source documents to assist people with browsing through the documents. In this way the summaries stay true to the original and do not contain information that was not in the source documents.

**Future work.** We are interested in investigating

Source Document

It was all set for a fairytale **ending for record breaking jockey AP Mc-Coy**. In the end it was a different but familiar name who **won the Grand National on** Saturday.

25-1 outsider Many Clouds, who had shown little form going into the race, won by a length and a half, **ridden by jockey Leighton Aspell**.

**Aspell won last year's Grand National** too, making him **the first jockey since the 1950s to ride back-to-back winners on different horses**.

"It feels wonderful, I asked big questions," Aspell said...

Abstract

25-1 shot Many Clouds wins Grand National
Second win a row for jockey Leighton Aspell
First jockey to win two in a row on different horses since 1950s

Table 4: Example system summary and human abstract. The summary words are shown in bold in the source document.

approaches that automatically group selected summary segments into clusters. Each cluster can capture a unique aspect of the document, and clusters of text segments can be color-highlighted. Inspired by the recent work of Narayan et al. (2018), we are also interested in conducting the usability study to test how well the summary highlights can help users quickly answer key questions about the documents. This will provide an alternative strategy for evaluating our proposed method against both extractive and abstractive baselines.

## 5 Conclusion

In this paper we explore a new training paradigm for extractive summarization. Our system converts human abstracts to a set of question-answer pairs. We use reinforcement learning to exploit the space of extractive summaries and promote summaries that are concise, fluent, and adequate for answering questions. Results show that our approach is effective, surpassing state-of-the-art systems.

## Acknowledgments

We thank the anonymous reviewers for their valuable suggestions. This work is in part supported by an unrestricted gift from Bosch Research. Kristjan Arumae gratefully acknowledges a travel grant provided by the National Science Foundation.

## References

Ziqiang Cao, Furu Wei, Wenjie Li, and Sujian Li. 2018. Faithful to the original: Fact aware neural abstractive summarization. In *Proceedings of the AAAI Conference on Artificial Intelligence (AAAI)*.

Danqi Chen, Jason Bolton, and Christopher D. Manning. 2016a. A thorough examination of the cnn/daily mail reading comprehension task. In *Proceedings of the 54th Annual Meeting of the Association for Computational Linguistics (ACL)*.

Qian Chen, Xiaodan Zhu, Zhen-Hua Ling, Si Wei, and Hui Jiang. 2016b. Distraction-based neural networks for document summarization. In *Proceedings of the Twenty-Fifth International Joint Conference on Artificial Intelligence (IJCAI)*.

Yen-Chun Chen and Mohit Bansal. 2018. Fast abstractive summarization with reinforce-selected sentence rewriting. In *Proceedings of the Annual Meeting of the Association for Computational Linguistics*.

Jianpeng Cheng and Mirella Lapata. 2016. Neural summarization by extracting sentences and words. In *Proceedings of ACL*.

Eunsol Choi, Daniel Hewlett, Jakob Uszkoreit, Illia Polosukhin, Alexandre Lacoste, and Jonathan Berant. 2017. Coarse-to-fine question answering for long documents. In *Proceedings of the Annual Meeting of the Association for Computational Linguistics (ACL)*.

Hoa Trang Dang and Karolina Owczarzak. 2008. Overview of the TAC 2008 update summarization task. In *Proceedings of Text Analysis Conference*.

Hal Daumé III and Daniel Marcu. 2006. Bayesian query-focused summarization. In *Proceedings of the 44th Annual Meeting of the Association for Computational Linguistics (ACL)*.

Günes Erkan and Dragomir R. Radev. 2004. LexRank: Graph-based lexical centrality as salience in text summarization. *Journal of Artificial Intelligence Research* .

Dan Gillick and Benoit Favre. 2009. A scalable global model for summarization. In *Proceedings of the NAACL Workshop on Integer Linear Programming for Natural Langauge Processing*.

Jiatao Gu, Daniel Jiwoong Im, and Victor O.K. Li. 2018. Neural machine translation with gumbel-greedy decoding. In *Proceedings of the Thirty-Second AAAI Conference on Artificial Intelligence (AAAI)*.

Aria Haghighi and Lucy Vanderwende. 2009. Exploring content models for multi-document summarization. In *Proceedings of the North American Chapter of the Association for Computational Linguistics (NAACL)*.

Karl Moritz Hermann, Tomas Kocisky, Edward Grefenstette, Lasse Espeholt, Will Kay, Mustafa Suleyman, and Phil Blunsom. 2015. Teaching machines to read and comprehend. In *Proceedings of Neural Information Processing Systems (NIPS)*.

Diederik P. Kingma and Jimmy Ba. 2015. Adam: A method for stochastic optimization. In *Proceedings of the International Conference on Learning Representations (ICLR)*.

Tao Lei, Regina Barzilay, and Tommi Jaakkola. 2016. Rationalizing neural predictions. In *Proceedings of the Conference on Empirical Methods in Natural Language Processing (EMNLP)*.

Chen Li, Fei Liu, Fuliang Weng, and Yang Liu. 2013. Document summarization via guided sentence compression. In *Proceedings of the 2013 Conference on Empirical Methods in Natural Language Processing (EMNLP)*.

Jiwei Li, Will Monroe, Tianlin Shi, Sebastien Jean, Alan Ritter, and Dan Jurafsky. 2017. Adversarial learning for neural dialogue generation. In *Proceedings of the Conference on Empirical Methods in Natural Language Processing (EMNLP)*.

Chin-Yew Lin. 2004. ROUGE: a package for automatic evaluation of summaries. In *Proceedings of ACL Workshop on Text Summarization Branches Out*.

Rada Mihalcea and Paul Tarau. 2004. TextRank: Bringing order into text. In *Proceedings of EMNLP*.

Nasrin Mostafazadeh, Nathanael Chambers, Xiaodong He, Devi Parikh, Dhruv Batra, Lucy Vanderwende, Pushmeet Kohli, and James Allen. 2016. A corpus and cloze evaluation for deeper understanding of commonsense stories. In *Proceedings of the North American Chapter of the Association for Computational Linguistics (NAACL)*.

Ramesh Nallapati, Bowen Zhou, Cicero dos Santos, Caglar Gulcehre, and Bing Xiang. 2016. Abstractive text summarization using sequence-to-sequence RNNs and beyond. In *Proceedings of the 20th SIGNLL Conference on Computational Natural Language Learning (CoNLL)*.

Shashi Narayan, Shay B. Cohen, and Mirella Lapata. 2018. Ranking sentences for extractive summarization with reinforcement learning. In *Proceedings of the 16th Annual Conference of the North American Chapter of the Association for Computational Linguistics: Human Language Technologies (NAACL-HLT)*.

Ani Nenkova and Kathleen McKeown. 2011. Automatic summarization. *Foundations and Trends in Information Retrieval* .

Romain Paulus, Caiming Xiong, and Richard Socher. 2017. A deep reinforced model for abstractive summarization. In *Proceedings of the Conference on Empirical Methods in Natural Language Processing (EMNLP)*.

Jeffrey Pennington, Richard Socher, and Christopher D. Manning. 2014. GloVe: Global vectors for word representation. In *Proceedings of the Conference Empirical Methods in Natural Language Processing (EMNLP)*.

Pranav Rajpurkar, Jian Zhang, Konstantin Lopyrev, and Percy Liang. 2016. SQuAD: 100,000+ questions for machine comprehension of text. In *Proceedings of the Conference on Empirical Methods in Natural Language Processing (EMNLP)*.

Marc'Aurelio Ranzato, Sumit Chopra, Michael Auli, and Wojciech Zaremba. 2016. Sequence level training with recurrent neural networks. In *Proceedings of the International Conference on Learning Representations (ICLR)*.

Matthew Richardson, Christopher J.C. Burges, and Erin Renshaw. 2013. MCTest: A challenge dataset for the open-domain machine comprehension of text. In *Proceedings of Empirical Methods in Natural Language Processing (EMNLP)*.

Alexander M. Rush, Sumit Chopra, and Jason Weston. 2015. A neural attention model for sentence summarization. In *Proceedings of the Conference on Empirical Methods in Natural Language Processing (EMNLP)*.

Abigail See, Peter J. Liu, and Christopher D. Manning. 2017. Get to the point: Summarization with pointer-generator networks. In *Proceedings of the Annual Meeting of the Association for Computational Linguistics (ACL)*.

Kaiqiang Song and Fei Liu. 2018. Structure-infused copy mechanisms for abstractive summarization. In *Proceedings of the International Conference on Computational Linguistics (COLING)*.

Nitish Srivastava. 2013. *Improving Neural Networks with Dropout*. Master's thesis, University of Toronto, Toronto, Canada.

Josef Steinberger and Karel Jezek. 2004. Using latent semantic analysis in text summarization and summary evaluation. In *Proceedings of ISIM*.

Jiwei Tan, Xiaojun Wan, and Jianguo Xiao. 2017. Abstractive document summarization with a graph-based attentional neural model. In *Proceedings of the Annual Meeting of the Association for Computational Linguistics (ACL)*.

Lucy Vanderwende, Hisami Suzuki, Chris Brockett, and Ani Nenkova. 2007. Beyond SumBasic: Task-focused summarization with sentence simplification and lexical expansion. *Information Processing and Management* 43(6):1606–1618.

Jason Weston, Antoine Bordes, Sumit Chopra, Sasha Rush, Bart van Merrienboer, Armand Joulin, and Tomas Mikolov. 2016. Towards AI-complete question answering: A set of prerequisite toy tasks. In *Proceedings of the International Conference on Learning Representations (ICLR)*.

Xingxing Zhang and Mirella Lapata. 2017. Sentence simplification with deep reinforcement learning. In *Proceedings of the Conference on Empirical Methods in Natural Language Processing (EMNLP)*.

# Graph-based Filtering of Out-of-Vocabulary Words
# for Encoder-Decoder Models

**Satoru Katsumata, Yukio Matsumura*, Hayahide Yamagishi* and  Mamoru Komachi**
Tokyo Metropolitan University
{katsumata-satoru, matsumura-yukio, yamagishi-hayahide}@ed.tmu.ac.jp,
komachi@tmu.ac.jp

## Abstract

Encoder-decoder models typically only employ words that are frequently used in the training corpus to reduce the computational costs and exclude noise. However, this vocabulary set may still include words that interfere with learning in encoder-decoder models. This paper proposes a method for selecting more suitable words for learning encoders by utilizing not only frequency but also co-occurrence information, which we capture using the HITS algorithm. We apply our proposed method to two tasks: machine translation and grammatical error correction. For Japanese-to-English translation, this method achieves a BLEU score that is 0.56 points more than that of a baseline. Furthermore, it outperforms the baseline method for English grammatical error correction, with an $F_{0.5}$-measure that is 1.48 points higher.

## 1 Introduction

Encoder-decoder models (Sutskever et al., 2014) are effective in tasks such as machine translation (Cho et al., 2014; Bahdanau et al., 2015) and grammatical error correction (Yuan and Briscoe, 2016). Vocabulary in encoder-decoder models is generally selected from the training corpus in descending order of frequency, and low-frequency words are replaced with an unknown word token <unk>. The so-called out-of-vocabulary (OOV) words are replaced with <unk> to not increase the decoder's complexity and to reduce noise. However, naive frequency-based OOV replacement may lead to loss of information that is necessary for modeling context in the encoder.

This study hypothesizes that vocabulary constructed using unigram frequency includes words that interfere with learning in encoder-decoder models. That is, we presume that vocabulary selection that considers co-occurrence information selects fewer noisy words for learning robust encoders in encoder-decoder models. We apply the hyperlink-induced topic search (HITS) algorithm to extract the co-occurrence relations between words. Intuitively, the removal of words that rarely co-occur with others yields better encoder models than ones that include noisy low-frequency words.

This study examines two tasks, machine translation (MT) and grammatical error correction (GEC) to confirm the effect of decreasing noisy words, with a focus on the vocabulary of the encoder side, because the vocabulary on the decoder side is relatively limited. In a Japanese-to-English MT experiment, our method achieves a BLEU score that is 0.56 points more than that of the frequency-based method. Further, it outperforms the frequency-based method for English GEC, with an $F_{0.5}$-measure that is 1.48 points higher.

The main contributions of this study are as follows:

1. The simple but effective preprocessing method we propose for vocabulary selection improves encoder-decoder model performance.

2. This study is the first to address noise reduction in the source text of encoder-decoder models.

## 2 Related Work

There is currently a growing interest in applying neural models to MT (Sutskever et al., 2014; Cho et al., 2014; Bahdanau et al., 2015; Wu

---

*Both authors equally contributed to the paper.



*Proceedings of ACL 2018, Student Research Workshop*, pages 112–119
Melbourne, Australia, July 15 - 20, 2018. ©2018 Association for Computational Linguistics

et al., 2016) and GEC (Yuan and Briscoe, 2016; Xie et al., 2016; Ji et al., 2017); hence, this study focuses on improving the simple attentional encoder-decoder models that are applied to these tasks.

In the investigation of vocabulary restriction in neural models, Sennrich et al. (2016) applied byte pair encoding to words and created a partial character string set that could express all the words in the training data. They increased the number of words included in the vocabulary to enable the encoder-decoder model to robustly learn contextual information. In contrast, we aim to improve neural models by using vocabulary that is appropriate for a training corpus—not to improve neural models by increasing their vocabulary.

Jean et al. (2015) proposed a method of replacing and copying an unknown word token with a bilingual dictionary in neural MT. They automatically constructed a translation dictionary from a training corpus using a word-alignment model (GIZA++), which finds a corresponding source word for each unknown target word token. They replaced the unknown word token with the corresponding word into which the source word was translated by the bilingual dictionary. Yuan and Briscoe (2016) used a similar method for neural GEC. Because our proposed method is performed as preprocessing, it can be used simultaneously with this replace-and-copy method.

Algorithms that rank words using co-occurrence are employed in many natural language processing tasks. For example, TextRank (Mihalcea and Tarau, 2004) uses PageRank (Brin and Page, 1998) for keyword extraction. TextRank constructs a word graph in which nodes represent words, and edges represent co-occurrences between words within a fixed window; TextRank then executes the PageRank algorithm to extract keywords. Although this is an unsupervised method, it achieves nearly the same precision as one state-of-the-art supervised method (Hulth, 2003). Kiso et al. (2011) used HITS (Kleinberg, 1999) to select seeds and create a stop list for bootstrapping in natural language processing. They reported significant improvements over a baseline method using unigram frequency. Their graph-based algorithm was effective at extracting the relevance between words, which cannot be grasped with a simple unigram frequency. In this study, we use HITS

---

**Algorithm 1** HITS

**Require:** hubness vector $i_0$
**Require:** adjacency matrix $A$
**Require:** iteration number $\tau$
**Ensure:** hubness vector $i$
**Ensure:** authority vector $p$
1: **function** HITS($i_0$, $A$, $\tau$)
2:     $i \leftarrow i_0$
3:     **for** $t = 1, 2, ..., \tau$ **do**
4:         $p \leftarrow A^{\mathrm{T}} i$
5:         $i \leftarrow A p$
6:         normalize $i$ and $p$
7:     **return** $i$ and $p$
8: **end function**

---

to retrieve co-occurring words from a training corpus to reduce noise in the source text.

## 3 Graph-based Filtering of OOV Words

### 3.1 Hubness and authority scores from HITS

HITS, which is a web page ranking algorithm proposed by Kleinberg (1999), computes hubness and authority scores for a web page (node) using the adjacency matrix that represents the web page's link (edge) transitions. A web page with high authority is linked from a page with high hubness scores, and a web page with a high hubness score links to a page with a high authority score. Algorithm 1 shows pseudocode for the HITS algorithm. Hubness and authority scores converge by setting the iteration number $\tau$ to a sufficiently large value.

### 3.2 Vocabulary selection using HITS

In this study, we create an adjacency matrix from a training corpus by considering a word as a node and the co-occurrence between words as an edge. Unlike in web pages, co-occurrence between words is nonbinary; therefore, several co-occurrence measures can be used as edge weights. Section 3.3 describes the co-occurrence measures and the context in which co-occurrence is defined.

The HITS algorithm is executed using the adjacency matrix created in the way described above. As a result, it is possible to obtain a score indicating importance of each word while considering contextual information in the training corpus.

Figure 1 shows a word graph example. A word that obtains a high score in the HITS algorithm is considered to co-occur with a variety of words. Figure 1 demonstrates that second order co-occurrence scores (the scores of words co-occurring with words that co-occur with various words (Schütze, 1998)) are also high.

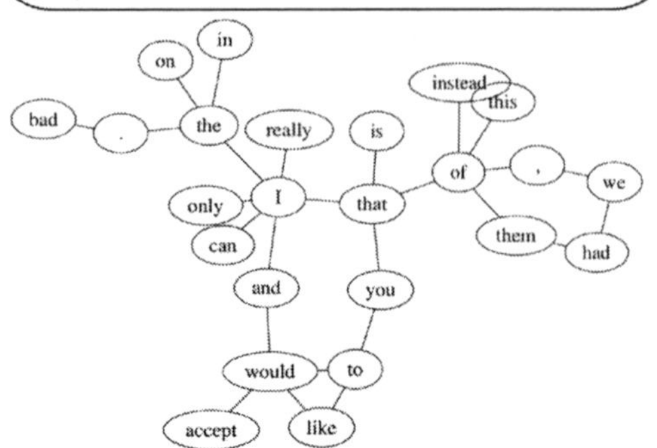


Figure 1: An example word graph created for ten sentences in the training corpus used for GEC[1].

In this study, words with high hubness scores are considered to co-occur with an important word, and low-scoring words are excluded from the vocabulary. Using this method appears to generate a vocabulary that includes words that are more suitable for representing a context vector for encoder models.

### 3.3 Word graph construction

To acquire co-occurrence relations, we use a combination of each word and its peripheral words. Specifically, we combine the target word with surrounding words within window width $N$ and count the occurrences. When defining the context in this way, because the adjacency matrix becomes symmetric, the same hubness and authority scores can be obtained. Figure 2 shows an example of co-occurrence in which $N$ is set to two.

We use raw co-occurrence frequency (Freq) and positive pointwise mutual information (PPMI) between words as the $(x, y)$ element $A_{xy}$ of the adjacency matrix. However, naive PPMI reacts sensitively to low-frequency words in a training corpus. To account for high-frequency, we weight the PMI by the logarithm of the number of co-occurrences and use PPMI based on this weighted PMI (Equa-

---

Co-occurrence: (define, the), (define, problem), (define, to), (define, have)

Figure 2: An example of co-occurrence context.

tion 2).

$$A_{xy}^{freq} = |x, y| \tag{1}$$

$$A_{xy}^{ppmi} = \max(0, \mathrm{pmi}(x, y) + \log_2 |x, y|) \tag{2}$$

Equation 3 is the PMI of target word $x$ and co-occurrence word $y$. $M$ is the number of tokens of the combination, $|x, *|$ and $|*, y|$ are the number of token combinations when fixing target word $x$ and co-occurrence word $y$, respectively.

$$\mathrm{pmi}(x, y) = \log_2 \frac{M \cdot |x, y|}{|x, *||*, y|} \tag{3}$$

## 4  Machine Translation

### 4.1  Experimental setting

In the first experiment, we conduct a Japanese-to-English translation using the Asian Scientific Paper Excerpt Corpus (ASPEC; Nakazawa et al., 2016). We follow the official split of the train, development, and test sets. As training data, we use only the first 1.5 million sentences sorted by sentence alignment confidence to obtain a Japanese–English parallel corpus (sentences of more than 60 words are excluded). Our training set consists of 1,456,278 sentences, development set consists of 1,790 sentences, and test set consists of 1,812 sentences. The training set has 247,281 Japanese word types and 476,608 English word types.

The co-occurrence window width $N$ is set to two. For combinations that co-occurred only once within the training corpus, we set the value of element $A_{xy}$ of the adjacency matrix to zero. The iteration number $\tau$ of the HITS algorithm is set to 300. As mentioned in Section 1, we only use the proposed method on the encoder side.

For this study's neural MT model[2], we implement global dot attention (Luong et al., 2015). We train a baseline model that uses vocabulary that is determined by its frequency in the training corpus. Vocabulary size is set to 100K on the encoder side and 50K on the decoder side. Additionally, we

---

[1]In this study, singleton words and their co-occurrences are excluded from the graph.

[2]https://github.com/yukio326/nmt-chainer

| | baseline | HITS (Freq) | HITS (PPMI) |
|---|---|---|---|
| BLEU (50K) | 22.24 | - | 22.40 |
| BLEU (100K) | 22.21 | 22.25 | **22.77** |
| $p$-value | - | 0.35 | 0.01 |

Table 1: BLEU scores for Japanese-to-English translation[3]. The parentheses indicate vocabulary size of the encoder.

| | COMMON outputs | | DIFF outputs | |
|---|---|---|---|---|
| | baseline | PPMI | baseline | PPMI |
| BLEU | 22.33 | **22.98** | 21.44 | **21.98** |

Table 2: BLEU scores of the COMMON and DIFF outputs.

conduct an experiment of varying vocabulary size of the encoder to 50K in the baseline and PPMI to investigate the effect of vocabulary size. Unless otherwise noted, we conduct an analysis of the model using the vocabulary size of 100K. The number of dimensions for each of the hidden and embedding layers is 512. The mini-batch size is 150. AdaGrad is used as an optimization method with an initial learning rate of 0.01. Dropout is applied with a probability of 0.2.

For this experiment, a bilingual dictionary is prepared for postprocessing unknown words (Jean et al., 2015). When the model outputs an unknown word token, the word with the highest attention score is used as a query to replace the unknown token with the corresponding word from the dictionary. If not in the dictionary, we replace the unknown word token with the source word (unk_rep). This dictionary is created based on word alignment obtained using fast_align (Dyer et al., 2013) on the training corpus.

We evaluate translation results using BLEU scores (Papineni et al., 2002).

### 4.2 Results

Table 1 shows the translation accuracy (BLEU scores) and $p$-value of a significance test ($p < 0.05$) by bootstrap resampling (Koehn, 2004). The PPMI model improves translation accuracy by 0.56 points in Japanese-to-English translation, which is a significant improvement.

Next, we examine differences in vocabulary by comparing each model with the baseline. Compared to the vocabulary of the baseline in 100K setting, Freq and PPMI replace 16,107 and 17,166

types, respectively; compared to the vocabulary of the baseline in 50K setting, PPMI replaces 4,791 types.

### 4.3 Analysis

According to Table 1, the performance of Freq is almost the same as that of the baseline. When examining the differences in selected words in vocabulary between PPMI and Freq, we find that PPMI selects more low-frequency words in the training corpus compared to Freq, because PPMI deals with not only frequency but also co-occurrence.

The effect of unk_rep is almost the same in the baseline as in the proposed method, which indicates that the proposed method can be combined with other schemes as a preprocessing step.

As a comparison of the vocabulary size 50K and 100K, the BLEU score of 100K is higher than that of 50K in PPMI. Moreover, the BLEU scores are almost the same in the baseline. We suppose that the larger the vocabulary size of encoder, the more noisy words the baseline includes, while the PPMI filters these words. That is why the proposed method works well in the case where the vocabulary size is large.

To examine the effect of changing the vocabulary on the source side, the test set is divided into two subsets: COMMON and DIFF. The former (1,484 sentences) consists of only the common vocabulary between the baseline and PPMI, whereas the latter (328 sentences) includes at least one word excluded from the common vocabulary.

Table 2 shows the translation accuracy of the COMMON and DIFF outputs. Translation performance of both corpora is improved.

In order to observe how PPMI improves COMMON outputs, we measure the similarity of the baseline and PPMI output sentences by counting the exact same sentences. In the COMMON outputs, 72 sentence pairs (4.85%) are the same, whereas 9 sentence pairs are the same in the DIFF outputs (2.74%). Surprisingly, even though it uses the same vocabulary, PPMI often outputs different but fluent sentences.

Table 3 shows an example of Japanese-to-English translation. The outputs of the proposed method (especially PPMI) are improved, despite the source sentence being expressed with common vocabulary; this is because the proposed method yielded a better encoder model than the baseline.

---

[3]BLEU score for postprocessing (unk_rep) improves by 0.46, 0.44, and 0.46 points in the baseline, Freq, and PPMI, respectively.

| src | 有用物質の分離・抽出，反応性向上，新材料創製，廃棄物処理，分析等の分野がある。 |
| --- | --- |
| baseline | there are fields such as separation , extraction , extraction , improvement of new material creation , waste treatment , analysis , etc . |
| Freq | there are separation and extraction of useful substances , the improvement of reactivity , new material creation , waste treatment and analysis . |
| PPMI | there are the fields such as separation and extraction of useful materials , the reaction improvement , new material creation , waste treatment , analysis , etc ... |
| ref | the application fields are separation and extraction of useful substances , reactivity improvement , creation of new products , waste treatment , and chemical analysis . |

Table 3: An example of Japanese-to-English translation on a source sentence from COMMON.

| | baseline | | PPMI | |
| --- | --- | --- | --- | --- |
| | 50K | 150K | 50K | 150K |
| Precision | 48.09 | 46.53 | **49.45** | 49.23 |
| Recall | 8.30 | 8.50 | 8.61 | **9.02** |
| $F_{0.5}$ | 24.55 | 24.55 | 25.37 | **26.03** |

Table 4: $F_{0.5}$ results on the CoNLL-14 test set[4].

| | COMMON outputs | | DIFF outputs | |
| --- | --- | --- | --- | --- |
| | baseline | PPMI | baseline | PPMI |
| P | 48.26 | 60.07 | 9.40 | 17.32 |
| R | 0.01 | 0.01 | 0.01 | 0.02 |
| $F_{0.5}$ | 0.04 | 0.04 | 0.04 | 0.08 |

Table 5: $F_{0.5}$ of COMMON and DIFF outputs.

## 5  Grammatical Error Correction

### 5.1  Experimental setting

The second experiment addresses GEC. We combine the FCE public dataset (Yannakoudakis et al., 2011), NUCLE corpus (Dahlmeier et al., 2013), and English learner corpus from the Lang-8 learner corpus (Mizumoto et al., 2011) and remove sentences longer than 100 words to create a training corpus. From the Lang-8 learner corpus, we use only the pairs of erroneous and corrected sentences. We use 1,452,584 sentences as a training set (502,908 types on the encoder side and 639,574 types on the decoder side). We evaluate the models' performances on the standard sets from the CoNLL-14 shared task (Ng et al., 2014) using CoNLL-13 data as a development set (1,381 sentences) and CoNLL-14 data as a test set (1,312 sentences)[4]. We employ $F_{0.5}$ as an evaluation measure for the CoNLL-14 shared task.

We use the same model as in Section 4.1 as a neural model for GEC. The models' parameter settings are similar to the MT experiment, except for the vocabulary and batch sizes. In this experiment, we set the vocabulary size on the encoder and decoder sides to 150K and 50K, respectively. Ad-

| src | Genetic refers the chance of inheriting a disorder or disease . |
| --- | --- |
| baseline | Genetic refers the chance of inheriting a disorder or disease . |
| PPMI | Genetic refers **to** the chance of inheriting a disorder or disease . |
| gold | Genetic **risk** refers **to** the chance of inheriting a disorder or disease . |

Table 6: An example of GEC using a source sentence from COMMON.

ditionally, we conduct the experiment of changing vocabulary size of the encoder to 50K to investigate the effect of the vocabulary size. Unless otherwise noted, we conduct an analysis of the model using the vocabulary size of 150K. The mini-batch size is 100.

### 5.2  Result

Table 4 shows the performance of the baseline and proposed method. The PPMI model improves precision and recall; it achieves a $F_{0.5}$-measure 1.48 points higher than the baseline method.

In setting the vocabulary size of encoder to 150K, PPMI replaces 37,185 types from the baseline; in the 50K setting, PPMI replaces 10,203 types.

### 5.3  Analysis

The $F_{0.5}$ of the baseline is almost the same while the PPMI model improves the score in the case where the vocabulary size increases. Similar to MT, we suppose that the PPMI filters noisy words.

As in Section 4.3, we perform a follow-up experiment using two data subsets: COMMON and DIFF, which contain 1,072 and 240 sentences, respectively.

Table 5 shows the accuracy of the error correction of the COMMON and DIFF outputs. Precision increases by 11.81 points, whereas recall remains the same for the COMMON outputs.

In GEC, approximately 20% of COMMON's output pairs differ, which is caused by the dif-

---

[4]We do not consider alternative answers suggested by the participating teams.

|  | MT | | GEC | |
|---|---|---|---|---|
|  | baseline | PPMI | baseline | PPMI |
| tokens | 52,700 | 27,364 | 126,884 | 70,003 |
| Ave. tokens | 3.07 | 1.59 | 3.36 | 1.85 |

Table 7: Number of words included only in either the baseline or PPMI vocabulary.

ferences in the training environment. Unlike MT, we can copy OOV in the target sentence from the source sentence without loss of fluency; therefore, our model has little effect on recall, whereas its precision improves because of noise reduction.

Table 6 shows an example of GEC. The proposed method's output improves when the source sentence is expressed using common vocabulary.

## 6 Discussion

We described that the proposed method has a positive effect on learning the encoder. However, we have a question; what affects the performance? We conduct an analysis of this question in this section.

First, we count the occurrence of the words included only in the baseline or PPMI in the training corpus. We also show the number of the tokens per types ("Ave. tokens") included only in either the baseline or PPMI vocabulary.

The result is shown in Table 7. We find that the proposed method uses low-frequency words instead of high-frequency words in the training corpus. This result suggests that the proposed method works well despite the fact that the encoder of the proposed method encounters more <unk> than the baseline. This is because the proposed method excludes words that may interfere with the learning of encoder-decoder models.

Second, we conduct an analysis of the POS of the words in GEC to find why increasing OOV improves the learning of encoder-decoder models. Specifically, we apply POS tagging to the training corpus and calculate the occurrence of the POS of the words only included in the baseline or PPMI. We use NLTK as a POS tagger.

Table 8 shows the result. It is observed that NOUN is the most affected POS by the proposed method and becomes often represented by <unk>. NOUN words in the vocabulary of the baseline contain some non-English words, such as Japanese or Korean. These words should be treated as OOV but the baseline fails to exclude them using only the frequency. According to Table 8, NUM is also

| POS | baseline | PPMI | ALL |
|---|---|---|---|
| NOUN | 92,693 | 44,472 | 4,644,478 |
| VERB | 11,066 | 10,099 | 3,597,895 |
| PRON | 127 | 107 | 1,869,422 |
| ADP | 626 | 685 | 1,836,193 |
| DET | 128 | 202 | 1,473,391 |
| ADJ | 13,855 | 12,270 | 1,429,056 |
| ADV | 2,032 | 1,688 | 931,763 |
| PRT | 319 | 75 | 615,817 |
| CONJ | 62 | 28 | 537,346 |
| PUNCT | 110 | 11 | 223,573 |
| NUM | 5,585 | 299 | 207,487 |
| OTHER | 281 | 67 | 5,209 |
| Total | 126,884 | 70,003 | 17,371,630 |

Table 8: Number of the POS of words only included in the baseline or PPMI.

affected by the proposed method. NUM words of the baseline include a simple numeral such as "119", in addition to incorrectly segmented numerals such as "514&objID". This word appears 25 times in the training corpus owing to the noisy nature of Lang-8. We suppose that the proposed method excludes these noisy words and has a positive effect on training.

## 7 Conclusion

In this paper, we proposed an OOV filtering method, which considers word co-occurrence information for encoder-decoder models. Unlike conventional OOV handling, this graph-based method selects the words that are more suitable for learning encoder models by considering contextual information. This method is effective for not only machine translation but also grammatical error correction.

This study employed a symmetric matrix (similar to skip-gram with negative sampling) to express relationships between words. In future research, we will develop this method by using vocabulary obtained by designing an asymmetric matrix to incorporate syntactic relations.

### Acknowledgments

We thank Yangyang Xi of Lang-8, Inc. for allowing us to use the Lang-8 learner corpus. We also thank Masahiro Kaneko and anonymous reviewers for their insightful comments. We thank Roam Analytics for a travel grant to support the presentation of this paper.

## References

Dzmitry Bahdanau, Kyunghyun Cho, and Yoshua Bengio. 2015. Neural machine translation by jointly learning to align and translate. In *Proc. of ICLR*.

Sergey Brin and Lawrence Page. 1998. The anatomy of a large-scale hypertextual web search engine. *Comput. Netw. ISDN Syst.* 30(1-7):107–117. https://doi.org/10.1016/S0169-7552(98)00110-X.

Kyunghyun Cho, Bart van Merrienboer, Caglar Gulcehre, Dzmitry Bahdanau, Fethi Bougares, Holger Schwenk, and Yoshua Bengio. 2014. Learning phrase representations using RNN encoder–decoder for statistical machine translation. In *Proc. of EMNLP*. pages 1724–1734. http://www.aclweb.org/anthology/D14-1179.

Daniel Dahlmeier, Hwee Tou Ng, and Siew Mei Wu. 2013. Building a large annotated corpus of learner English: The NUS corpus of learner English. In *Proc. of BEA*. pages 22–31. http://www.aclweb.org/anthology/W13-1703.

Chris Dyer, Victor Chahuneau, and Noah A. Smith. 2013. A simple, fast, and effective reparameterization of IBM model 2. In *Proc. of NAACL-HLT*. pages 644–648. http://www.aclweb.org/anthology/N13-1073.

Anette Hulth. 2003. Improved automatic keyword extraction given more linguistic knowledge. In *Proc. of EMNLP*. pages 216–223. http://www.aclweb.org/anthology/W03-1028.

Sébastien Jean, Orhan Firat, Kyunghyun Cho, Roland Memisevic, and Yoshua Bengio. 2015. Montreal neural machine translation systems for WMT15. In *Proc. of WMT*. pages 134–140. http://aclweb.org/anthology/W15-3014.

Jianshu Ji, Qinlong Wang, Kristina Toutanova, Yongen Gong, Steven Truong, and Jianfeng Gao. 2017. A nested attention neural hybrid model for grammatical error correction. In *Proc. of ACL*. pages 753–762. http://aclweb.org/anthology/P17-1070.

Tetsuo Kiso, Masashi Shimbo, Mamoru Komachi, and Yuji Matsumoto. 2011. HITS-based seed selection and stop list construction for bootstrapping. In *Proc. of ACL*. pages 30–36. http://www.aclweb.org/anthology/P11-2006.

Jon M. Kleinberg. 1999. Authoritative sources in a hyperlinked environment. *J. ACM* 46(5):604–632. https://doi.org/10.1145/324133.324140.

Philipp Koehn. 2004. Statistical significance tests for machine translation evaluation. In *Proc. of EMNLP*. pages 388–395. http://www.aclweb.org/anthology/W04-3250.

Thang Luong, Hieu Pham, and Christopher D. Manning. 2015. Effective approaches to attention-based neural machine translation. In *Proc. of EMNLP*. pages 1412–1421. http://aclweb.org/anthology/D15-1166.

Rada Mihalcea and Paul Tarau. 2004. TextRank: Bringing order into texts. In *Proc. of EMNLP*. pages 404–411. http://www.aclweb.org/anthology/W04-3252.

Tomoya Mizumoto, Mamoru Komachi, Masaaki Nagata, and Yuji Matsumoto. 2011. Mining revision log of language learning sns for automated Japanese error correction of second language learners. In *Proc. of IJCNLP*. pages 147–155. http://www.aclweb.org/anthology/I11-1017.

Toshiaki Nakazawa, Manabu Yaguchi, Kiyotaka Uchimoto, Masao Utiyama, Eiichiro Sumita, Sadao Kurohashi, and Hitoshi Isahara. 2016. ASPEC: Asian scientific paper excerpt corpus. In *Proc. of LREC*. pages 2204–2208.

Hwee Tou Ng, Siew Mei Wu, Ted Briscoe, Christian Hadiwinoto, Raymond Hendy Susanto, and Christopher Bryant. 2014. The CoNLL-2014 shared task on grammatical error correction. In *Proc. of CoNLL Shared Task*. pages 1–14.

Kishore Papineni, Salim Roukos, Todd Ward, and Wei-Jing Zhu. 2002. BLEU: a method for automatic evaluation of machine translation. In *Proc. of ACL*. pages 311–318. http://www.aclweb.org/anthology/P02-1040.

Hinrich Schütze. 1998. Automatic word sense discrimination. *Computational Linguistics* 24(1):97–123. http://dl.acm.org/citation.cfm?id=972719.972724.

Rico Sennrich, Barry Haddow, and Alexandra Birch. 2016. Neural machine translation of rare words with subword units. In *Proc. of ACL*. pages 1715–1725. http://www.aclweb.org/anthology/P16-1162.

Ilya Sutskever, Oriol Vinyals, and Quoc V Le. 2014. Sequence to sequence learning with neural networks. In *Proc. of NIPS*. pages 3104–3112.

Yonghui Wu, Mike Schuster, Zhifeng Chen, Quoc V Le, Mohammad Norouzi, Wolfgang Macherey, Maxim Krikun, Yuan Cao, Qin Gao, Klaus Macherey, et al. 2016. Google's neural machine translation system: Bridging the gap between human and machine translation. *arXiv preprint arXiv:1609.08144* .

Ziang Xie, Anand Avati, Naveen Arivazhagan, Dan Jurafsky, and Andrew Y Ng. 2016. Neural language correction with character-based attention. *arXiv preprint arXiv:1603.09727* .

Helen Yannakoudakis, Ted Briscoe, and Ben Medlock. 2011. A new dataset and method for automatically grading ESOL texts. In *Proc. of ACL-HLT*. pages 180–189. http://www.aclweb.org/anthology/P11-1019.

Zheng Yuan and Ted Briscoe. 2016. Grammatical error correction using neural machine translation. In *Proc. of NAACL-HLT*. pages 380–386. http://www.aclweb.org/anthology/N16-1042.

# Exploring Chunk Based Templates for Generating a subset of English Text


**Nikhilesh Bhatnagar**
LTRC, IIIT Hyderabad

**Manish Shrivastava**
LTRC, IIIT Hyderabad

**Radhika Mamidi**
LTRC, IIIT Hyderabad



## Abstract

Natural Language Generation (NLG) is a research task which addresses the automatic generation of natural language text representative of an input non-linguistic collection of knowledge. In this paper, we address the task of the generation of grammatical sentences in an isolated context given a partial bag-of-words which the generated sentence must contain. We view the task as a search problem (a problem of choice) involving combinations of smaller chunk based templates extracted from a training corpus to construct a complete sentence. To achieve that, we propose a fitness function which we use in conjunction with an evolutionary algorithm as the search procedure to arrive at a potentially grammatical sentence (modeled by the fitness score) which satisfies the input constraints.


## 1 Introduction

One of the reasons why NLG is a challenging problem is because there are many ways in which a given content can be represented. These are represented by the stylistic constraints which address syntactic and pragmatic choices (largely) independent of the information conveyed.

Classically, there are two major subtasks recognized in NLG: Strategic Generation and Tactical Generation (Sentence Planning and Surface Realization)[1](Reiter and Dale, 2000). Strategic Generation - "what to say" deals with identifying the relevant information to present to the audience and Tactical Generation - "how to say" addresses the

---

[1]Because we follow a template based approach, there is some overlap between the Content Determination and Aggregation steps.

problems of linguistic representation of the input concepts. In this work, we address the problem of tactical generation, with a focus on the grammaticality of the generated sentences. We formulate our task as follows: to generate syntactically correct sentences given a set of constraints such as a bag-of-words, partial ordering, etc.

So, for example, given a bag of words such as "man", "plays", "football" and length constraints, a sentence like "The man plays football in October." would be acceptable.

Our approach involves a corpus derived formulation of template based generation. Templates are instances of canned text with a slot-filler structure ("gaps") which can be filled with the appropriate information thus realizing the sentence. Since they are a manual resource, it is rather expensive and hard to generalize over different types or domains of text.

Thus, it is desirable to be able to automatically extract templates from a corpus. Also, to increase the syntactic coverage, we use sub-sentence level (smaller) templates to generate a sentence.

## 2 Background and Related Work

Traditionally, template based systems are used in scenarios where the output text is structurally very well defined and/or requires very high quality text as output with little variance. This work is inspired from (Van Deemter et al., 2005) who point out that template based systems and "real" NLG systems are "Turing equivalent" meaning that at least in terms of expressiveness, there is no theoretical disparity between the two. (Rudnicky and Oh, 2002) use language models to generate text. In recent years, (Kondadadi et al., 2013) present a hybrid NLG system which generates text by ranking tagged clusters of templates. NaturalOWL (Galanis and Androutsopoulos, 2007) use templates for




*Proceedings of ACL 2018, Student Research Workshop*, pages 120–126
Melbourne, Australia, July 15 - 20, 2018. ©2018 Association for Computational Linguistics

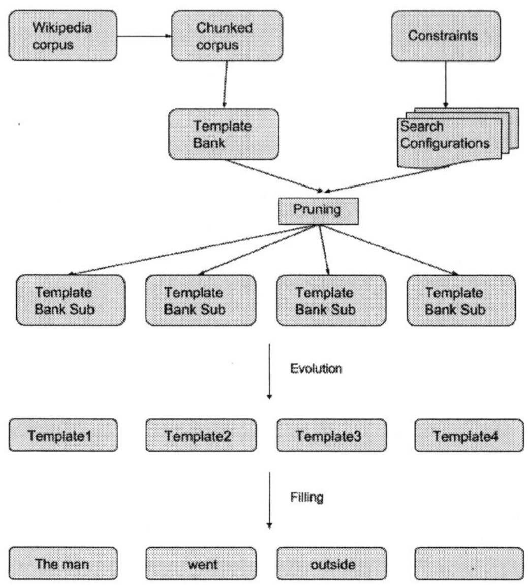

Figure 1: System architecture

their sentence plans and rules to manipulate them.

## 3   Core Assumptions and Motivation

As an extension of our previous work (Bhatnagar and Mamidi, 2016), in this work, we adopt a simplistic model of language - a sequence of linguistic units. Given a set of such units, each possible sentence is contained in the search space of all possible permutations. Thus, given a grammaticality fitness function, pruning and vocabulary reduction is essential to be able to tractably search this space.

Since templates are based on canned text, templates are locally grammatical. The core idea is to effectively use the local grammaticality guarantee of a corpus extracted template to combine, rather than construct the component templates to generate a sentence. These templates themselves contain individual tokens, effectively considering templates as a unit of sentence construction instead of tokens. The obvious trade-off is that since there are a lot more templates than tokens, which results in a much larger search space. However, if appropriate abstractions are used, perhaps the vocabulary problem can be mitigated somewhat.

The task is then twofold: how to determine which templates to combine (pruning) and constraining that with a measure of grammaticality of the generated sentence (fitness).

## 4   Templates and Sentence Representation

We use chunks as a basis for the linear templates because chunks are linguistically sound and hence the vocabulary increase is lesser compared to unconstrained spans of text. In general, an extended feature has syntactic identifiers added to the feature space. This is to better inform syntactic behavior of the template even though it increases the feature space a little. Abstracted features have multiple features clustered together which reduces the feature space. We describe the extension process below.

### 4.1   Abstraction

The chunks should be abstracted in such a way so as to have a minimal impact on their syntactic combination behavior.

All punctuation and stopwords are not abstracted because they are highly relevant, syntactically. Following are the mappings applied to the chunks:

1. Named Entity Abstraction (NE): Each NE is mapped to a unique symbol corresponding to its category.
2. POS Abstraction (POS): POS categories such as "CD", "FW" and "SYM" and continuous "NNP" and "NNPS" sequences are mapped to their corresponding POS tags.
3. Cluster Abstraction (WC): Each token (except punctuation and stopwords), is mapped to the cluster ID of its syntatico-semantic cluster. Since a token can have multiple POS categories which in turn effect its syntactic behavior, we consider a token with different POS categories as distinct while clustering. The clusters are obtained by computing the KMeans cluster for token-POS pairs with euclidean distance of L2-normed vector embeddings.

### 4.2   Extended Categories

We extend the POS and chunk tag categories to better inform template combinations:

1. Extended POS (EPOS): Each punctuation, stopword and NE is assigned its own unique POS category.
2. Extended Chunk Tags (ECTag): Since the "O" (outside) chunk tag is a "default" category, it contributes a lot of syntactic confusion, we assign a separate chunk tag for all

Table 1: Template Example

| Chunk Feature | Chunk | Template | Template Feature |
| --- | --- | --- | --- |
| Chunk Tag | "NP" | "NP" | Extended Chunk Tag (ECTag) |
| Tokens | "a", "popular", "wrestler" | "a", "JJ213", "NN5266" | Tok-POS cluster (WC) |
| POS | "DT", "JJ", "NN" | "DT", "JJ", "NN" | Extended POS (EPOS) |
| Head token | "wrestler" | "NN5266" | Head Tok-POS cluster (HWC) |
| Head POS | "NN" | "NN" | Head Extended POS (HEPOS) |
| | | "a" and "NN5266" | Junction Tok-POS clusters (WCJ) |
| | | "DT", "NN" | Junction Extended POS (EPOSJ) |
| | | "a_BLANK_BLANK" | "Blank" Construction Feature (BlankCo) |
| | | "a_JJ_NN" | Extended POS Construction Feature (EPOSCo) |

chunks tagged "O" which contain sentence endings (".", ",", or "!") or brackets ("(" or ")"). In addition, chunk tags for chunks containing wh-words (POS tags "WDT", "WP", "WP$" or "WRB") are marked (eg. "NP" becomes "WNP").

### 4.3 Template features

A template is created after applying abstractions to a chunk and extending its syntactic categories. The template, however has two more feature types:

1. Junction Features (WCJ, EPOSJ): Junction features are comprised of the leftmost and rightmost features of the template. These features are used to predict if two templates "glue" together well at the point of contact (the junction). Both factors (tok-pos clusters and extended POS category) are applicable.
2. Head Features (HWC, HEPOS): Head features represent the "external" features for a chunk used to compute a global grammaticality component. Both factors - extended POS and tok-pos clusters are applicable.
3. Construction features (BlankCo, EPOSCo): Construction features represent the chunk as a syntactic construction or a layout, encoding the positional combination of the components comprising it. It is constructed by creating a feature for the ordered tuple of tokens comprising the chunk where all tokens are mapped to a single "blank" symbol or its extended POS except punctuations and stopwords. Two factors (single "blank" and extended POS) are applicable.

Table 1 shows an example chunk and its corresponding derived template. A sentence is represented as a sequence of templates described above.

## 5 Scoring the template combinations

It should be noted that this score is not equivalent to a syntactic correctness score, but rather a subset of it. This is because here we are dealing with configurations of untampered templates whose local syntactic correctness still holds and the syntactic incorrectness is a matter of their combinatorial configuration while a grammaticality score needs to deal with "broken" chunks as well.

The fitness score $F$ is a linear combination of length-normalized total log-probabilities $TP$ of different sequences derived from the sentence computed using an NGram language model. The total probability of an NGram model is defined as:

$$TP(s) = P(w_1|bos)P(w_2|w_1 bos)... \\ ..P(eos|w_k w_{k-1}...w_{k-n+1}) \quad (1)$$

where $n$ is the order of the language model, $s$ is a sequence and $w_i$ is the $i^{th}$ element in $s$. $F$ is a weighted sum of length-normalized total log-probabilities of five different sequences:

$$nTP(s) = log_{10}(TP(s))/(l_s + 1) \quad (2)$$

$$F(s) = \alpha_c nTP(ec) + \alpha_{co} nTP(co)/2 \\ + \alpha_j nTP(j)/2 + \alpha_h nTP(h)/2 \quad (3) \\ + \alpha_l nTP(l)/2$$

where $nTP(s)$ is the length normalized total log-probability for the sequence $s$ where $l_s$ is the number of elements in that sequence. $ec, co, j, h$ and $l$ represent the sequences in chunk score, construction score, junction score, head score and lexical score. $\alpha_i$ are the weight for each component score which are discussed:

1. Extended Chunk Score $nTP(ec)$ - This score is calculated using the extended chunk tags (ECTags) for the sentence. It is useful in determining the global syntactic structure.

Table 2: A sentence and sequences used to compute the fitness

| Template Feature Sequence | Sentence |
|---|---|
| | NP[Sand] VP[blows] PP[in] NP[the strong wind] .[.] |
| | NP[NN969/NN] VP[VBZ29/VBZ] PP[in/in] NP[the/the JJ347/JJ NN628/NN] .[./.] |
| Extended Chunk Tags (ECTags) | NP VP PP NP . |
| Blank Construction (BlankCo) | BLANK BLANK in the_BLANK_BLANK . |
| Extended POS Construction (EPOSCo) | NN VBZ in the_JJ_NN . |
| Tok-POS Junction (WCJ) | (bos, NN969), (NN969, VBZ29), (VBZ29, in), (in, the), (NN628, .), (., eos) |
| Extended POS Junction (EPJ) | (bos, NN), (NN, VBZ), (VBZ, in), (in, the), (NN, .), (., eos) |
| Head Tok-POS (HWC) | NN969 VBZ29 in NN628 . |
| Head Extended POS (HEPOS) | NN VBZ in NN . |
| Tok-POS Sequence (WCs) | NN969 VBZ29 in the JJ347 NN628 . |
| Extended POS Sequence (EPOSs) | NN VBZ in the JJ NN . |

2. Construction Score $nTP(co)$ - This score is calculated using blank construction layout (BlackCo) and extended POS construction layout (EPOSCo). It is useful in augmenting the overall grammaticality of the sentence as it encodes the syntactic layout of the chunk as a whole.

3. Junction Score $JP(j)$ - This score is calculated as the sum of the bigram probability of the left junction of the right template conditioned on the right junction of the left template for both tok-pos clusters (WC) and extended POS (EPOS) for all junctions in the sentence. This score represents a local view of inter-template cohesiveness. It represents how a sentence "glues" together.

4. Head Score $nTP(h)$ - This score is calculated using head tok-pos clusters (HWC) and head extended POS (HEPOS). Counter to the junction score, it represents a more semantic view of the chunk interactions. This is because generally a chunk head is often the primary content word in that chunk.

5. Lexical Score $nTP(l)$ - This score is computed using the tok-pos clusters (WC) and extended POS (EPOS). This score represents a baseline grammaticality score on a lexical level.

A sentence with all the sequences are fed to the fitness function are shown in table 2.

## 6 Parameters for pruning the search space

The search space is the space of all permutations of the templates to form the sentence. Such a search space is huge. We observe that depending on the particular constraints described in section 7, we can prune the permutation search space. This is done by finding a subset of the template bank that can occur at each position in the template sequence. The subsets are represented by a set of constraints which we call a search configuration. Thus, say, if a sentence is determined to have 5 templates, there will be a search configuration computed for each template slot, in accordance with the global constraints for the sentence. Described below is the specification of a search configuration:

1. Length The templates must contain exactly the specified number of tokens (tok-pos clusters) in it.
2. Extended chunk tag (ECtag) The templates must have the specified extended chunk tag.
3. Tok-POS clusters and extended POS tags (WC-EPOS) All the specified tok-pos clusters and their corresponding extended POS tags must be present in the templates.

Note that neither of the above constraints needs to be specified for a search configuration, in which case all templates can be considered to fill that position. We use memoization to make the pruning computationally feasible.

Eg. if a search configuration has a length of 5, no preference specified for the extended search tag and (cluster("run"/NN), "NN") in the tok-pos (WC-EPOS) list, all templates containing 5 tokens which also contain the cluster for run used as an "NN" are valid for that configuration.

## 7 Search

To search the very large permutation space, we use a population based searching method which uses only mutation as the genetic operator for generating new solutions. Following are the components of the evolutionary search:

## 7.1 Population Selection

The search can be parametrized by specifying a collection of sentence level constraints which have their own individual sub-constraints. These constraints are different from search configurations as defined in section 6 as these constraints operate on a sentence level, while search configurations, which are derived from these constraints operate on a template level. The sentence level constraints are listed below:

1. Number of tokens: The number of tokens in the generated sentence must be in a specified range. A maximum value is required.
2. Number of templates: The number of templates in the generated sentence must be in the specified range.
3. Chunk specifications (inclusion): For each chunk specification, at least one template must be present in the sentence which follows it and it must satisfy all the sub-constraints such as extended chunk tag and constituent tok-pos clusters.
4. Position Chunk specifications: This is a chunk constraint like the one described above, with the additional constraint of a fixed position.
5. Ordered Chunk specifications: These are list of chunk constraints with the additional constraint that they be in order in the generated sentence.
6. Tok-pos specifications (inclusion): The sentence must contain the specified tok-pos clusters.
7. Ordered Tok-pos specifications: The specified tok-pos clusters must occur in the same order in the sentence.

Note that every constraint and sub-constraint can be left empty which means that there could be no specification for the extended chunk tag for a chunk constraint. Based on these sentence level constraints, search configurations for each template position are derived.

### 7.1.1 Sentence level constraints to template level SearchConfigs

Based on the number of templates selected between the range given, it distributes the total length specified between all the templates randomly. Then, it arranges the Chunks, Ordered-Chunks and PositionFixedChunks and distributes the token level constraints (OrderedTokPOSs and TokPOSConstraints) to the templates. Now, all three parameters of the SearchConfigs have been minimally inferred and the search space can now be pruned.

### 7.1.2 Sampling from the pruned space

Since we are dealing with naturally occurring text, the distribution of the templates grouped by extended chunk tags follows a Zipf curve meaning that almost 40% of the time, an "NP" is selected and a "." almost never gets a chance even though both templates are prominent in the set of templates having the same chunk tag as them. This drastically hampers the chances of getting structural variance in the templates constructed. To remedy this, we assign weights to the set of templates with a dampening exponent of 0.4 which makes the distribution more uniform, yet preserves the selectional biases.

1. Dampen the Zipf for selection of extended chunk tag
2. Dampen the Zipf for selection of templates given an extended chunk tag
3. Obtain the distribution for selection of templates by multiplying probabilities taken from the above two distribution.

This results in a damped Zipf curve for the selection of templates which allows for much more variance in the extended chunk tags of the generated sentences.

## 7.2 Mutation

To perform mutation, we randomly select a template to mutate and using the dampened distribution obtained, we sample a template from the subspace corresponding to the search configuration of that template position.

## 7.3 Selection and Evolution Strategy

We use elitist selection (pick the top k organisms) with enforced variability. We enforce that at least 8% and 15% of the population have unique blank construction layout and extended POS construction layout respectively. Following are the steps for evolving the population.

1. Initialize population given a set of Constraints and sample a population of size 1000
2. Mutate the first half of the population and assign it to the second half.
3. compute fitnesses for all organisms and sort population based on fitness score

4. Retain organisms such that the variability constraints are met.

5. Re-initialize 25% of the population so that different search configurations are searched.

6. Repeat 1 to 5 until 100 generations.

This evolution run gives a population consisting of grammatical configurations which adhere to the constraints given as input. There are still possibly word clusters remaining which need to be filled since sentences which are generated are comprised of templates which contain clusters, not word forms. We fill these cluster slots with the tokens we gave in the initial bag-of-words constraints. To do that, we run a random search on the best generated sentence and fill the cluster slots which maximizes the token and head token perplexity.

## 8 Experiment Setup

Following are the steps we took to conduct our experiments:

1. We tokenized, POS tagged, NER tagged, and chunked and abstracted the English Wikipedia corpus using Stanford CoreNLP (Manning et al., 2014), spaCy (Honnibal and Montani, 2017) and LM-LSTM-CRF (Liu et al., 2018) to extract the templates.

2. The number of clusters, $k$ was chosen to be 7500.

3. We used lexvec(Salle et al., 2016) pretrained vectors for clustering.

4. The weights for the fitness function were empirically chosen to be 75, 10, 10, 5 and 2.

## 9 Results

Following are the top sentences generated with the following constraints:

1. "cat" should be present:
   the heated water plant is likewise formed entirely of cat .

2. "what" as the first token and sentence contains a "?":
   what does the right thing do ?

3. "the" in position=0 and "." in sentence:
   the mid product can readily be used in polynomial practices .

4. "and", "ate" and "ran" in sentence:
   the division ate a plant of cape , ran a principal prying need and stockpiled superconductivity .

5. "on" and "in" in sentence:
   PERSON bumped ORG in DATE on spirits

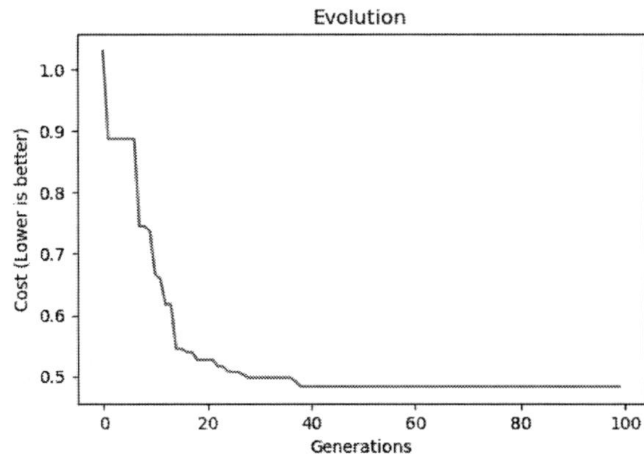

Figure 2: Evolution

of error .

6. "influential", "large" and "red" in sentence:
   large influential player vocals defined red to the convenience of the detector .

We show the generation improvements for the first sentence. As we can see, the algorithm is able to generate a question with minimal supervision. Also, in sentence 5, multiple PPs can be seen.

Some level of supervision is necessary to drive the required syntax and content words to generate predictable outputs. We observe that there is a bias in the model e.g. usage of "the" in the starting noun phrase, and chaining verb phrases and prepositional phrases. Hence, to generate a question, one has to specify the position of the wh word, otherwise the sentences often start with a noun phrase.

Computationally, the search time increases with increasing sentence lengths. On a reasonably modern machine, our implementation generated the above sentences in about 150 seconds while using 2.2 GB of memory.[2]

## 10 Future Work

As a future work, detailed qualitative analysis and minimum constraints needed to generate specific linguistic structures can be done. Also, automatic extraction of content words and other relevant constraints can be explored for generation.

## 11 Acknowledgements

The authors would like to thank Prof. Owen Rambow for helping gain insight into the problem.

---

[2]The code used for this research will be made available on https://github.com/tingc9/LinearTemplatesSRW

# References

Nikhilesh Bhatnagar and Radhika Mamidi. 2016. Experiments in linear template combination using genetic algorithms. *22nd Himalayan Languages Symposium.*

Dimitrios Galanis and Ion Androutsopoulos. 2007. Generating multilingual descriptions from linguistically annotated owl ontologies: the naturalowl system. In *Proceedings of the Eleventh European Workshop on Natural Language Generation*, pages 143–146. Association for Computational Linguistics.

Matthew Honnibal and Ines Montani. 2017. spacy 2: Natural language understanding with bloom embeddings, convolutional neural networks and incremental parsing. *To appear.*

Ravi Kondadadi, Blake Howald, and Frank Schilder. 2013. A statistical nlg framework for aggregated planning and realization. In *ACL (1)*, pages 1406–1415.

L. Liu, J. Shang, F. Xu, X. Ren, H. Gui, J. Peng, and J. Han. 2018. Empower Sequence Labeling with Task-Aware Neural Language Model. In *AAAI.*

Christopher D. Manning, Mihai Surdeanu, John Bauer, Jenny Finkel, Steven J. Bethard, and David McClosky. 2014. The Stanford CoreNLP natural language processing toolkit. In *Association for Computational Linguistics (ACL) System Demonstrations*, pages 55–60.

Ehud Reiter and Robert Dale. 2000. *Building natural language generation systems.* Cambridge university press.

Alexander I Rudnicky and Alice H Oh. 2002. Dialog annotation for stochastic generation.

Alexandre Salle, Marco Idiart, and Aline Villavicencio. 2016. Matrix factorization using window sampling and negative sampling for improved word representations. *CoRR*, abs/1606.00819.

Kees Van Deemter, Emiel Krahmer, and Mariët Theune. 2005. Real versus template-based natural language generation: A false opposition? *Computational Linguistics*, 31(1):15–24.

# Trick Me If You Can: Adversarial Writing of Trivia Challenge Questions


**Eric Wallace**
University of Maryland, College Park
ewallac2@umd.edu

**Jordan Boyd-Graber**
University of Maryland, College Park
jbg@umiacs.umd.edu



## Abstract

Modern question answering systems have been touted as approaching human performance. However, existing question answering datasets are imperfect tests. Questions are written with humans in mind, not computers, and often do not properly expose model limitations. To address this, we develop an adversarial writing setting, where humans interact with trained models and try to break them. This annotation process yields a challenge set, which despite being easy for trivia players to answer, systematically stumps automated question answering systems. Diagnosing model errors on the evaluation data provides actionable insights to explore in developing robust and generalizable question answering systems.


## 1 Introduction

Proponents of modern machine learning systems have claimed human parity on difficult tasks such as question answering.[1] Datasets such as SQuAD and TriviaQA (Rajpurkar et al., 2016; Joshi et al., 2017) have certainly advanced the state of the art, but are they providing the right examples to measure how well machines can answer questions?

Many of the existing question answering datasets are written and evaluated with humans in mind, not computers. Though the way computers solve NLP tasks is fundamentally different than humans. They train on hundreds of thousands of questions, rather than looking at small groups of them in isolation. This allows models to pick up on superficial patterns that may occur in data crawled from the internet (Chen et al., 2016) or

from biases in the crowd-sourced annotation process (Gururangan et al., 2018). Additionally, because existing test sets do not provide specific diagnostic information for improving models, it can be difficult to get proper insight into a system's capabilities or its limitations. Unfortunately, when rigorous evaluations are not performed, strikingly simple model limitations can be overlooked (Belinkov and Bisk, 2018; Ettinger et al., 2017; Jia and Liang, 2017).

To address this lacuna, we ask trivia enthusiasts—who write new questions for scholastic and open circuit tournaments—to create examples that specifically challenge Question Answering (QA) systems. We develop a user interface (Section 2) that allows question writers to adversarially craft these questions. This interface provides a model's predictions and its evidence from the training data to facilitate a model-driven annotation process.

Humans find the resulting challenge questions *easier* than regular questions (Section 3), but strong QA models struggle (Section 4). Unlike many existing QA test sets, our questions highlight specific phenomena that humans can capture but machines cannot (Section 5). We release our QA challenge set to better evaluate models and systematically improve them.[2]

## 2 A Model-Driven Annotation Process

This section introduces our framework for tailoring questions to challenge computers, the surrounding community of trivia enthusiasts that create thousands of questions annually, and how we expose QA algorithms to this community to help them craft questions that challenge computers.

---

[1] https://rajpurkar.github.io/SQuAD-explorer/

[2] www.qanta.org




*Proceedings of ACL 2018, Student Research Workshop*, pages 127–133
Melbourne, Australia, July 15 - 20, 2018. ©2018 Association for Computational Linguistics

The protagonist of this opera describes the future day when her lover will arrive on a boat in the aria "Un Bel Di" or "One Beautiful Day." The only baritone role in this opera is the consul Sharpless who reads letters for the protagonist, who has a maid named Suzuki. That protagonist blindfolds her child Sorrow before stabbing herself when her lover B.F. Pinkerton returns with a wife. For 10 points, name this Giacomo Puccini opera about an American lieutenants affair with the Japanese woman Cio-Cio San.

**ANSWER**: Madama Butterfly

Figure 1: An example Quiz Bowl question. The question becomes progressively easier to answer later on; thus, more knowledgeable players can answer after hearing fewer clues.

## 2.1 The Quiz Bowl Community: Writers of Questions

The "gold standard" of academic competitions between universities and high schools is Quiz Bowl. Unlike other question answering formats such as Jeopardy! or TriviaQA (Joshi et al., 2017), Quiz Bowl questions are designed to be interrupted. This allows more knowledgeable players to "buzz in" before their opponent knows the answer. This style of play requires questions to be structured "pyramidally": questions start with difficult clues and get progressively easier (Figure 1).

However, like most existing QA datasets, Quiz Bowl questions are written with humans in mind. Unfortunately, the heuristics that question writers use to select clues do not always apply to computers. For example, humans are unlikely to memorize every song in every opera by a particular composer. This, however, is trivial for a computer. In particular, a simple baseline QA system easily solves the example in Figure 1 from seeing the reference to "Un Bel Di". Other questions contain uniquely identifying "trigger words". For example, "Martensite" only appears in questions on Steel. For these types of examples, a QA system needs to understand no additional information other than an if–then rule. Surprisingly, this is true for many different answers: in these cases, QA devolves into trivial pattern matching. Consequently, information retrieval systems are strong baselines for this task, even capable of defeating top high

school and collegiate players. Well-tuned neural based QA systems (Yamada et al., 2018) can give small improvements over the baselines and have even defeated teams of expert humans in live Quiz Bowl events.

Although, other types of Quiz Bowl questions are fiendishly difficult for computers. Many questions have complicated coreference patterns (Guha et al., 2015), require reasoning across multiple types of knowledge, or involve wordplay. Given that these difficult types of question truly challenge models, how can we generate and analyze more of them?

## 2.2 Adversarial Question Writing

One approach to evaluate models beyond a typical test set is through adversarial examples (Szegedy et al., 2013) and other types of intentionally difficult inputs. However, language data is hard to modify (e.g., replacing word tokens) without changing the meaning of the input. Past work side-steps this difficulty by modifying examples in a simple enough manner to preserve meaning (Jia and Liang, 2017; Belinkov and Bisk, 2018). Though it is hard to generate complex examples that expose richer phenomena through automatic means. Instead, we propose to use human adversaries in a process we call *adversarial writing*.

In this setting, question writers are tasked with generating *challenge questions* that break existing QA systems but are still answerable by humans. To facilitate this breaking process, we expose model predictions and interpretation methods to question writers through a user interface. This allows writers to see what changes should be made to confuse the system and visualize the resulting effects. For example, our system highlights the revealing "Un Bel Di" clue in bright red.

This results in a small, model-driven challenge set that is explicitly designed to expose a model's limitations. While the regular held-out test set for Quiz Bowl provides questions that are likely to be asked in an actual tournament, these challenge questions highlight rare and difficult QA phenomena that models can't handle.

## 2.3 User Interface

The interface (Figure 2) provides the top five predictions (Guesses) from a simple non-neural model, the baseline system from a NIPS 2017 competition that used Quiz Bowl as a shared task (Boyd-Graber et al., 2018). This model uses

Figure 2: The writer inputs a question (top right), the system provides guesses (left), and explains why it's making those guesses (bottom right). The writer can then adapt their question to "trick" the model.

an inverted index built using the shared task training data (which consists of Quiz Bowl questions and Wikipedia pages).

We select an information retrieval model as it enables us to extract meaningful reasoning behind the model's predictions. In particular, the Elasticsearch Highlight API (Gormley and Tong, 2015) visually highlights words in the *Evidence* section of the interface. This helps users understand which words and phrases are present in the training data and may be revealing the answer. Though the users never see outputs from a neural system, the questions they write are quite challenging for them (Section 4).

## 2.4 Farmed from the Maddeningly Smart Crowd

In contrast to crowd-sourced datasets, our data comes from the fecund pool of thousands of questions written annually for Quiz Bowl tournaments (Jennings, 2006). We connect with the question writers of these tournaments, who find the adversarial writing process useful to help write high quality, original questions.

The current dataset (we intend to have twice-yearly competitions to continually collect data) consists of 651 questions made of 3219 sentences. A few of the writers have indicated that they plan to use their question submissions in an upcoming tournament. We will release these questions after those respective tournaments have completed.

## 3 Validating Written Questions

We next verify the validity of the challenge questions. We do not want to collect questions that are a jumble of random characters or contain insufficient information to discern the answer. Thus, we first automatically filter out invalid questions based on length, the presence of vulgar statements, or repeated submissions (including re-submissions from the Quiz Bowl training or evaluation data). Next, we manually verify all of the resulting questions appear legitimate and that no obviously invalid questions made it into the challenge set.

We further wish to investigate not only the validity, but also the *difficulty* of the challenge questions according to human Quiz Bowl players. To do so, we play a portion of the submitted questions in a live Quiz Bowl event, using intermediate and expert players (current and former collegiate Quiz Bowl players) as the human baseline. We sample 60 challenge questions from categories that match typical tournament distributions. As a baseline, we additionally select 60 unreleased high school tournament questions (to ensure no player has seen them before).

When answering in Quiz Bowl, a player must interrupt the question with a buzz. The earlier that a player buzzes, the less of a chance their opponent has to answer the question before them. To capture this, we consider two metrics to evaluate performance, the average buzz position (as a percentage of the question seen) and the corresponding answer accuracy. We randomly shuffle the baseline and challenge questions, play them, and record these two metrics. On average for the challenge set, humans buzz with 41.6% of the question remaining and an accuracy of 89.7%. On the baseline questions, humans buzz with 28.3% of the question remaining and an accuracy of 84.2%. The difference in accuracy between the two types of questions is not significantly different ($p = 0.16$ using Fisher's exact test), but the buzzing position is significantly earlier for the challenge questions (a two-sided t-test yields $p = 0.0047$). Humans find the challenge questions *easier* on average than the regular test examples (they buzz much earlier). We expect human performance to be comparable on the questions not played, as all questions went through the same submission and post-processing stages.

## 4   Models and Experiments

In this section, we evaluate numerous QA systems on the challenge questions. We consider a diverse set of models: ones based on recurrent networks, feed-forward networks, and IR systems to properly explore the difficulty of the examples.

We consider two neural models: a recurrent neural network (RNN) and Deep Averaging Network (Iyyer et al., 2015, DAN). The two models treat the problem as text classification and predict which of the answer entities the question is about. The RNN is a bidirectional GRU (Cho et al., 2014) and the DAN uses fully connected layers with a word vector average as input.

To train the systems, we collect the data used at the 2017 NIPS Human-Computer Question Answering competition (Boyd-Graber et al., 2018). The dataset consists of about 70,000 questions with 13,500 answer options. We split the data into validation and test sets to provide baseline evaluations for the models. We also report results on the baseline system (IR) shown to users during the writing process. For evaluation, we report the accuracy as a function of the question position (to capture the incremental nature of the game). The accuracy varies as the words are fed in (mostly improving, but occasionally degrading).

The buzz position of all models significantly degrades on the challenge set. We compare the accuracy on the original test set (Test Questions) to the challenge questions in Figure 3.

For both the challenge and original test data, the questions begin with abstract clues that are difficult to answer (accuracy at or below 10%). However, during the crucial middle portions of the questions (after revealing 25% to 75%), where buzzes in Quiz Bowl matches most frequently occur, the accuracy on original test questions rises significantly quicker than the challenge ones. For both questions, the accuracy rises towards the end as the "give-away" clues arrive. Despite users never observing the output of a neural system, the two neural models decreased more in absolute accuracy than the IR system. The DAN model had the largest absolute accuracy decrease (from 54.1% to 32.4% on the full question), likely because a vector average isn't capable of capturing the difficult wording of the challenge questions.

The human results are displayed on the left of Figure 3 and show a different trend. For both question types, human accuracy rises very quickly after about 50% of the question has been seen. We suspect this occurs because the "give-aways", which often contain common sense or simple knowledge clues, are easy for humans but quite difficult for computers. The reverse is true for the early clues. They contain quotes and entities that models can retrieve but humans struggle to remember.

## 5   Challenge Set Reveals Model Limitations

In this section, we conduct an analysis of the challenge questions to better understand the source of their difficulty. We harvest recurring patterns using the user edit logs and corresponding model predictions, grouping the questions into linguistically-motivated clusters (Table 1).

These groups provide an informative analysis of model errors on a diverse set of phenomena. In our dataset, we additionally provide the most similar training questions for each challenge question.

A portion of the examples contain clues that are unseen during training time. Many of these clues are quite interesting, for example, the common knowledge clue "this man is on the One Dollar Bill". However, because we experiment with systems that are not able to capture open-domain information, we do not investigate these examples further as they trivially break systems.

### 5.1   Understanding Changes in Language

The first categories of challenge questions contain previously seen clues that have been written in a misleading manner. Table 1 shows snippets of ex-

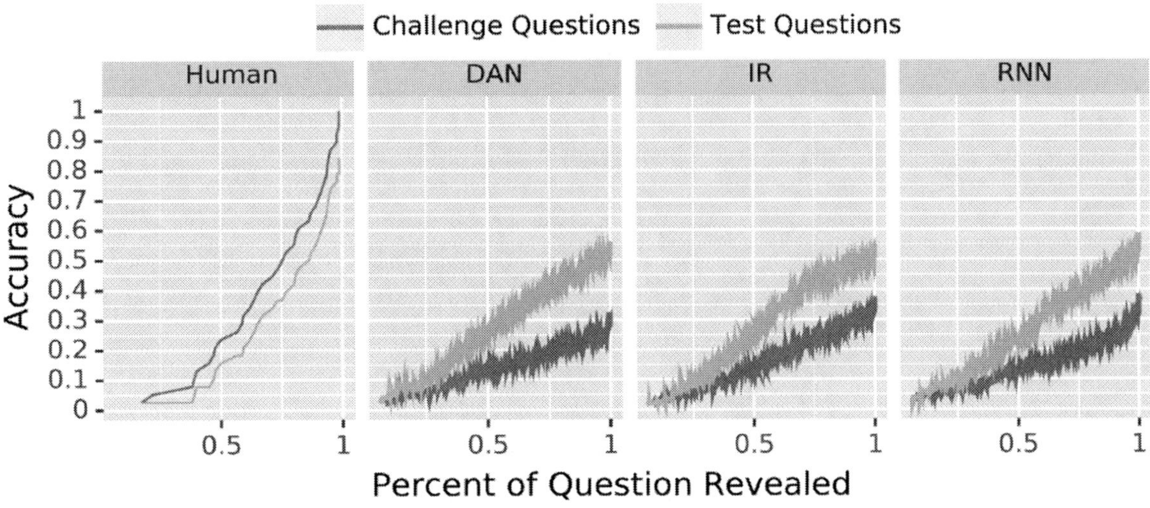


Figure 3: Both types of questions (challenge questions and original test set questions) begin with abstract clues the models are unable to capture, but the challenge questions are significantly harder during the crucial middle portions (0.25 to 0.75) of the question. The human results (displayed on the left of the figure) show their performance on a sample of the challenge questions and a separate test set.

emplar challenge questions for each category.

**Paraphrases** A common adversarial writing strategy is to paraphrase clues to remove exact n-gram matches from the training data. This renders an IR system useless but also hurts neural models.

**Entity Type Distractors** One key component for QA is determining the answer type that is desired from the question. Writers often take advantage of this by providing clues that lead the system into selecting a wrong answer type. For example, in the second question of Table 1, the "lead in" implies the answer may be an actor. This triggers the model to answer Don Cheadle despite previously seeing the Bill Clinton "Saxophone" clue.

### 5.2 Composing Existing Knowledge

The other categories of challenge questions require composing knowledge from multiple existing clues. Table 2 shows snippets of exemplar challenge questions for each category.

**Triangulation** In these questions, entities that have a first order relationship to the correct answer are given. The system must then triangulate the correct answer by "filling in the blank". For example, in the first question of Table 2, the place of death and the brother of the entity are given. The training data contains a clue about the place of death (The Battle of Thames) reading "though

stiff fighting came from their Native American allies under Tecumseh, who died at this battle". The system must connect these two clues to answer.

**Operator** One extremely difficulty question type requires applying a mathematical or logical operator to the text. For example, the training data contains a clue about the Battle of Thermopylae reading "King Leonidas and 300 Spartans died at the hands of the Persians" and the second question in Table 2 requires one to add 150 to the number of Spartans.

**Multi-Step Reasoning** The final type of questions requires a model to make multiple reasoning steps between entities. For example, in the last question of Table 2, a model needs to make a reasoning step first from the "I Have A Dream" speech to the Lincoln Memorial and an additional step to reach president Abraham Lincoln.

## 6 Related Work

Creating evaluation datasets to get fine-grained analysis of particular linguistics features or model attributes has been explored in past work. The LAMBADA dataset tests a model's ability to understand the broad contexts present in book passages (Paperno et al., 2016). Linzen et al. (2016) create a dataset to evaluate if language models can learn subject-verb number agreement. The most closely

| Set | Question | Answer | Rationale |
|---|---|---|---|
| Training | Name this sociological phenomenon, the *taking of one's own life*. | Suicide | Paraphrase |
| Challenge | Name this *self-inflicted method of death*. | Arthur Miller | |
| Training | Clinton played the *saxophone on The Arsenio Hall Show* | Bill Clinton | Entity Type Distractor |
| Challenge | He was edited to appear in the film "Contact"... For ten points, name this American president who played the *saxophone on an appearance on the Arsenio Hall Show*. | Don Cheadle | |

Table 1: Snippets from challenge questions show the difficulty in retrieving previously seen evidence. *Training* questions indicate relevant snippets from the training data. *Answer* displays the RNN Reader's answer prediction (always correct on Training, always incorrect on Challenge).

| Question | Prediction | Answer | Rationale |
|---|---|---|---|
| This man, who died at the Battle of the Thames, experienced a setback when his brother Tenskwatawa's influence over their tribe began to fade | Battle of Tippecanoe | Tecumseh | Triangulation |
| This number is one hundred and fifty more than the number of Spartans at Thermopylae. | Battle of Thermopylae | 450 | Operator |
| A building dedicated to this man was the site of the "I Have A Dream" speech | Martin Luther King Jr. | Abraham Lincoln | Multi-Step Reasoning |

Table 2: Snippets from challenge questions show examples of composing existing evidence. *Answer* displays the RNN Reader's answer prediction. For these examples, connecting the training and challenge clues is quite simple for humans but very difficult for models.

related work to ours is Ettinger et al. (2017) who also consider using humans as adversaries. Our work differs in that we use model interpretation methods to facilitate breaking a specific system.

Other methods have found very simple input modifications can break neural models. For example, adding character level noise drastically reduces machine translation quality (Belinkov and Bisk, 2018), while paraphrases can fool natural language inference systems (Iyyer et al., 2018). Jia and Liang (2017) placed distracting sentences at the end of paragraphs and caused QA systems to incorrectly pick up on the misleading information. These types of input modifications can evaluate one specific type of phenomenon and are complementary to our approach.

## 7   Conclusion

It is difficult to automatically expose the limitations of a machine learning system, especially when that system reaches very high performance metrics on a held-out evaluation set. To address this, we have introduced a human driven evaluation setting, where users try to break a trained system. By facilitating this process with interpretation methods, users can understand what a model is doing and how to create challenging examples for it. An analysis of the resulting data can reveal unknown model limitations and provide insight into improving a system.

## Acknowledgments

We thank all of the Quiz Bowl players and writers who helped make this work possible. We also thank the anonymous reviewers and members of the UMD "Feet Thinking" group for helpful comments. JBG is supported by NSF Grant IIS-1652666. Any opinions, findings, conclusions, or recommendations expressed here are those of the authors and do not necessarily reflect the view of the sponsor.

# References


Yonatan Belinkov and Yonatan Bisk. 2018. Synthetic and natural noise both break neural machine translation. In *Proceedings of the International Conference on Learning Representations*.

Jordan Boyd-Graber, Shi Feng, and Pedro Rodriguez. 2018. *Human-Computer Question Answering: The Case for Quizbowl*, Springer.

Danqi Chen, Jason Bolton, and Christopher D. Manning. 2016. A thorough examination of the cnn/daily mail reading comprehension task. *Proceedings of the Association for Computational Linguistics* .

Kyunghyun Cho, Bart van Merrienboer, Caglar Gulcehre, Dzmitry Bahdanau, Fethi Bougares, Holger Schwenk, and Yoshua Bengio. 2014. Learning phrase representations using rnn encoder-decoder for statistical machine translation .

Allyson Ettinger, Sudha Rao, Hal Daumé III, and Emily M. Bender. 2017. Towards linguistically generalizable nlp systems: A workshop and shared task .

Clinton Gormley and Zachary Tong. 2015. *Elasticsearch: The Definitive Guide*. " O'Reilly Media, Inc.".

Anupam Guha, Mohit Iyyer, Danny Bouman, and Jordan Boyd-Graber. 2015. Removing the training wheels: A coreference dataset that entertains humans and challenges computers. In *North American Association for Computational Linguistics*.

Suchin Gururangan, Swabha Swayamdipta, Omer Levy, Roy Schwartz, Samuel R. Bowman, and Noah A. Smith. 2018. Annotation artifacts in natural language inference data .

Mohit Iyyer, Varun Manjunatha, Jordan Boyd-Graber, and Hal Daumé III. 2015. Deep unordered composition rivals syntactic methods for text classification. In *Proceedings of the Association for Computational Linguistics*.

Mohit Iyyer, John Wieting, Kevin Gimpel, and Luke Zettlemoyer. 2018. Adversarial example generation with syntactically controlled paraphrase networks. In *Conference of the North American Chapter of the Association for Computational Linguistics*.

Ken Jennings. 2006. *Brainiac: adventures in the curious, competitive, compulsive world of trivia buffs*. Villard. http://books.google.com/books?id=tXi_rfgUWCcC.

Robin Jia and Percy Liang. 2017. Adversarial examples for evaluating reading comprehension systems. In *Proceedings of Empirical Methods in Natural Language Processing*.

Mandar Joshi, Eunsol Choi, Daniel S. Weld, and Luke Zettlemoyer. 2017. Triviaqa: A large scale distantly supervised challenge dataset for reading comprehension. In *Proceedings of the Association for Computational Linguistics*.

Tal Linzen, Emmanuel Dupoux, and Yoav Goldberg. 2016. Assessing the ability of lstms to learn syntax-sensitive dependencies 4:521–535.

Denis Paperno, Germán Kruszewski, Angeliki Lazaridou, Quan Ngoc Pham, Raffaella Bernardi, Sandro Pezzelle, Marco Baroni, Gemma Boleda, and Raquel Fernández. 2016. The LAMBADA dataset: Word prediction requiring a broad discourse context .

Pranav Rajpurkar, Jian Zhang, Konstantin Lopyrev, and Percy Liang. 2016. Squad: 100,000+ questions for machine comprehension of text .

Christian Szegedy, Wojciech Zaremba, Ilya Sutskever, Joan Bruna, Dumitru Erhan, Ian J. Goodfellow, and Rob Fergus. 2013. Intriguing properties of neural networks .

Ikuya Yamada, Ryuji Tamaki, Hiroyuki Shindo, and Yoshiyasu Takefuji. 2018. Studio ousia's quiz bowl question answering system. *arXiv preprint arXiv:1803.08652* .

# Alignment Analysis of Sequential Segmentation of Lexicons to Improve Automatic Cognate Detection


**Pranav A**

Big Data Institute

Hong Kong University of Science and Technology

Hong Kong

`cs.pranav.a@gmail.com`



## Abstract

Ranking functions in information retrieval are often used in search engines to recommend the relevant answers to the query. This paper makes use of this notion of information retrieval and applies onto the problem domain of cognate detection. The main contributions of this paper are: (1) positional segmentation, which incorporates the sequential notion; (2) graphical error modelling, which deduces the transformations. The current research work focuses on classification problem; which is distinguishing whether a pair of words are cognates. This paper focuses on a harder problem, whether we could predict a possible cognate from the given input. Our study shows that when language modelling smoothing methods are applied as the retrieval functions and used in conjunction with positional segmentation and error modelling gives better results than competing baselines, in both classification and prediction of cognates.


## 1 Introduction

Cognates are a collection of words in different languages deriving from the same origin. The study of cognates plays a crucial role in applying comparative approaches for historical linguistics, in particular, solving language relatedness and tracking the interaction and evolvement of multiple languages over time. A cognate instance in Indo-European languages is given as the word group: *night* (English), *nuit* (French), *noche* (Spanish) and *nacht* (German).

The existing studies on cognate detection involve experiments which distinguish between a pair of words whether they are cognates or non-

cognates (Ciobanu and Dinu, 2014; List, 2012a). These studies do not approach the problem of predicting the possible cognate of the target language, if the cognate of the source language is given. For example, given the word *nuit*, could the algorithm predict the appropriate German cognate within the huge German wordlist? This paper tackles this problem by incorporating heuristics of the probabilistic ranking functions from information retrieval. Information retrieval addresses the problem of scoring a document with a given query, which is used in every search engine. One can view the above problem as the construction of a suitable search engine, through which we want to find the cognate counterpart of a word (query) in a lexicon of another language (documents).

This paper deals with the intersection between the areas of information retrieval and approximate string similarity (like the cognate detection problem), which is largely under-explored in the literature. Retrieval methods also provide a variety of alternative heuristics which can be chosen for the desired application areas (Fang et al., 2011). Taking such advantage of the flexibility of these models, the combination of approximate string similarity operations with an information retrieval system could be beneficial in many cases. We demonstrate how the notion of information retrieval can be incorporated into the approximate string similarity problem by breaking a word into smaller units. Regarding this, Nguyen et al. (2016) has argued that segmented words are a more practical way to query large databases of sequences, in comparison with conventional query methods. This further encourages the heuristic attempt at imposing an information retrieval model on the cognate detection problem in this paper.

Our main contribution is to design an information retrieval based scoring function (see section 4) which can capture the complex morphological




*Proceedings of ACL 2018, Student Research Workshop*, pages 134–140

Melbourne, Australia, July 15 - 20, 2018. ©2018 Association for Computational Linguistics

shifts between the cognates. We tackled this by proposing a shingling (chunking) scheme which incorporates positional information (see section 2) and a graph-based error modelling scheme to understand the transformations (see section 3). Our test harness focuses not only on distinguishing between a pair of cognates, but also the ability to predict the cognate for a target language (see section 5).

## 2 Positional Character-based Shingling

This section examines on converting a string into a shingle-set which includes the encodings of the positional information. In this paper, we notify, $S$ as the shingle-set of cognate from the source language and $T$ as the shingle-set of cognate for the target language. The similarity between these split-sets is denoted by $S \cap T$. An example of cognate from the source language, $S$ (Romanian) could be shingle set of the word *rosmarin* and $T$ (Italian) could be *romarin*.

**K-gram shingling:** Usually, set based string similarity measures are based on comparing overlap between the shingles of two strings. Shingling is a way of viewing a string as a document by considering $k$ characters at a time. For example, the shingle of the word *rosmarin* is created with $k = 2$ as: $S = \{\langle s \rangle r,\ ro,\ os,\ sm,\ ma,\ ar,\ ri,\ in,\ n \langle /s \rangle\}$. Here, $\langle s \rangle$ is the start sentinel token and $\langle /s \rangle$ is the stop sentinel token. For the sake of simplicity, we have ignored sentinel tokens; which transforms into: $S = \{r,\ ro,\ os,\ sm,\ ma,\ ar,\ ri,\ in,\ n\}$. This method splits the strings into smaller $k$-grams without any positional information.

### 2.1 Positional Shingling from 1 End

We argue that the unordered *k-grams* splitting could lead to an inefficient matching of strings since a shingle set is visualized as the bag-of-words method. Given this, we propose a positional k-gram shingling technique, which introduces position number in the splits to incorporate the notion of the sequence of the tokens. For example, the word *rosmarin* could be position-wise split with $k = 2$ as: $S = \{1r,\ 2ro,\ 3os,\ 4sm,\ 5ma,\ 6ar,\ 7ri,\ 8in,\ 9n\}$.

Thus, the member *4sm* means that it is the fourth member of the set. The motivation behind this modification is that it retains the positional information which is useful in probabilistic retrieval ranking functions.

## 2.2 Positional Shingling from 2 Ends

The main disadvantage of the positional shingling from single end is that any mismatch can completely disturb the order of the rest, leading to low similarity. For example, if the query is *rosmarin* with cognate *romarin*, the corresponding split sets would be $\{1r,\ 2ro,\ 3os,\ 4sm,\ 5ma,\ 6ar,\ 7ri,\ 8in,\ 9n\}$ and $\{1r,\ 2ro,\ 3om,\ 4ma,\ 5ar,\ 6ri,\ 7in,\ 8n\}$. The order of the members after *2ro* is misplaced, thus this will lead to low similarity between two cognates. Only $\{1r,\ 2ro\}$ is common between the cognates. Considering this, we propose positional shingling from both ends, which is robust against such displacements.

We attach a position number to the left if the numbering begins from the start, and to the right if the numbering begins from the end. Then the smallest position number is selected between the two position numbers. If the position numbers are equal, then we select the left position number as a convention. Figure 1 gives an exemplification of this algorithm illustrated with splits of *romarin* and *rosmarin*.

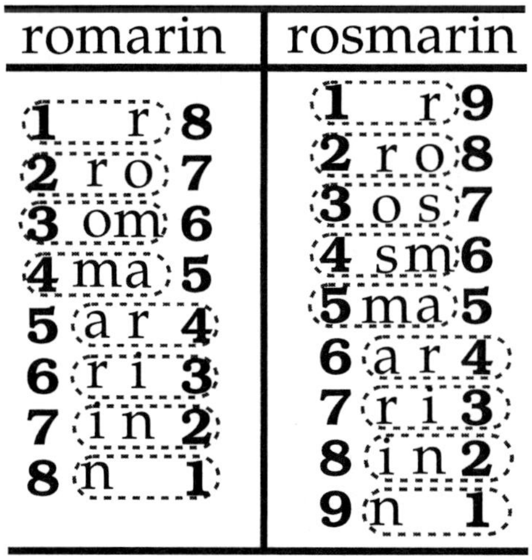

| romarin | rosmarin |
|---|---|
| **1** r **8** | **1** r **9** |
| **2** ro **7** | **2** ro **8** |
| **3** om **6** | **3** os **7** |
| **4** ma **5** | **4** sm **6** |
| **5** ar **4** | **5** ma **5** |
| **6** ri **3** | **6** ar **4** |
| **7** in **2** | **7** ri **3** |
| **8** n **1** | **8** in **2** |
| | **9** n **1** |

Figure 1: The process of positional tokenisation from both ends. On the left, algorithm segments the Romanian word *romarin* into the split-set $\{1r,\ 2ro,\ 3om,\ 4ma,\ ar4,\ ri3,\ in2,\ n1\}$. On the right, the algorithm segments *rosmarin* into $\{1r,\ 2ro,\ 3os,\ 4sm,\ 5ma,\ ar4,\ ri3,\ in2,\ n1\}$.

In Figure 1, split sets of *rosmarin* and *romarin* are shown. After taking intersection of them, we get $\{1r,\ 2ro,\ ar4,\ ri3,\ in2,\ n1\}$, indicating a higher similarity.

135

## 3  Graphical Error Modelling

Once shingle sets are created, common overlap set measures like set intersection, Jaccard (Järvelin et al., 2007), XDice (Brew et al., 1996) or TF-IDF (Wu et al., 2008) could be used to measure similarities between two sets. However, these methods only focus on similarity of the two strings. For cognate detection, it is crucial to understand how substrings are transformed from source language to target language. This section discusses on how to view this "dissimilarity" by creating a graphical error model.

Algorithm 1 explicates the process of graphical error modelling. For illustration purposes, we visualize the procedure via a Romanian-Italian cognate pair (*mesia*, *messia*). If the source language is Romanian, then $S = \{1m, 2me, 3es, si3, ia2, a1\}$, which is the split-set of *mesia*. Let the target language by Italian. Then the split-set of the Italian word *messia*, denoted as $T$, will be $\{1m, 2me, 3es, 4ss, si3, ia2, a1\}$. Thus $|S \cap T|$ is the number of common terms. Thus the term matches are, $S \cap T = \{1m, 2me, 3es, si3, ia2, a1\}$. We are interested in examining the "dissimilarity", which are the leftover terms in the sets. That means, we need to infer a certain pattern from leftover sets, which are $S - \{S \cap T\}$ and $T - \{S \cap T\}$. Thus we can draw mappings to gather information of the corrections. Let *top* and *bottom* be the **ordered sets** referring to $S - \{S \cap T\}$ and $T - \{S \cap T\}$ respectively. Referring to the example, $T - S \cap T = \{4ss\}$, a *bottom* set. Similarly, $S - S \cap T = \{\}$, a *top* set. Then we follow instructions given in algorithm 1.

---

**Algorithm 1**: Graphical Error Model

---

**Graphical Error Model** takes two split sets generated by the shingling variants, namely *top* and *bottom*. The objective is to output a graphical structure showing connections between members of the *top* and the *bottom* sets.

1. **Initialization of the *top* and *bottom*:** If the given sets *top* and *bottom* are empty, we initialize them by inserting an empty token ($\phi$) into those sets.

   **Running example:** This step transforms *top* set as $\{\phi\}$ and *bottom* as $\{4ss\}$.

2. **Equalization of the set cardinalities:** The cardinalities of the sets *top* and *bottom* made equal by inserting empty tokens ($\phi$) into the middle of the sets.

**Running example:** The set cardinalities of *top* and *bottom* were already equal. Thus the output of this step are *top* set as $\{\phi\}$ and *bottom* as $\{4ss\}$.

3. **Inserting the mappings of the set members into the graph:** The empty graph is initialized as $graph = \{\}$. The directed edges are generated, originating from every set member of *top* to every set member of *bottom*. This results in a complete directed bipartite graph between *top* and *bottom* sets. Each edge is assigned a probability $P(e)$ which is discussed in a later section.

   **Running example:** The output of this step would be complete directed bipartite graph between *top* and *bottom* sets which is $\{\phi \rightarrow 4ss\}$

One more example is provided in figure 2.

---

**Intuition:**  The edges created as the result of this graph could be used for probabilistic calculations which are detailed more in section 4.2. Intuitively, $\phi \rightarrow 4ss$ means that if the letter $s$ is added at position 4 of the word of the source *mesia*, then one could get the target word *messia*.

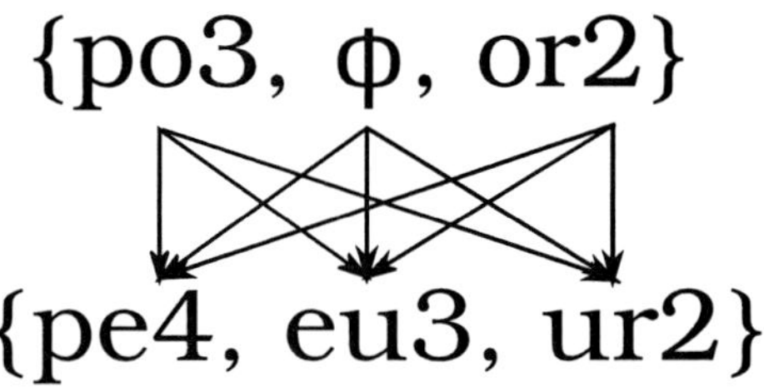


Figure 2: The figure shows the bipartite graph output of the algorithm when the source cognate is *stupor* and the target cognate is *stupeur*.

## 4  Evaluation Function

The design of our evaluation function focuses on two main properties: set based similarity (see section 4.1) and probabilistic calculation through graphical model (see section 4.2)

### 4.1  Similarity Function

Usually, the computation of similarity between two sets is done by metrics like Jaccard, Dice and XDice (Brew et al., 1996). Dynamic programming based methods like edit distance and LCSR (Longest Common Subsequence Ratio,

(Melamed, 1999)) are also often used to calculate similarity between two strings. Ranking functions incorporate more complex but necessary features which are needed to distinguish between the documents.

In this paper, we use BM25 and a Dirichlet smoothing based ranking function to compute the similarity. BM25 considers term-frequency, inverse document frequency and length normalization based penalization features for similarity calculations. Dirichlet smoothing function (Robertson and Zaragoza, 2009) makes use of language modelling features and tunable parameter which aids in Bayesian smoothing of unseen shingles in the split sets (Blei et al., 2003).

## 4.2 Error Modelling Function

The information of the common morphological transformations for cognates between two different languages helps in determining if a pair of words could be cognates. Based on the graphs of cognate pairs between Italian and Romanian (section 3), which models the morphological shifts between the cognates in the two languages, we define an error modelling function on any pair of words from the two languages. The split set from the source language is denoted by $S$ and target language by $T$, then probabilistic function would be:

$$\pi(S, T) = \frac{1}{|G(S,T)|} \sum_{e \in G(S,T)} P(e)^q$$

where $G(S,T)$ is the constructed graph of $S$ and $T$, the strength parameter is called $q$ here with the range of $(0, \infty)$, and $P(e)$ is the probability of edge $e$ to occur in between two cognates, which is estimated by its frequency of being observed in the graphs of cognate pairs in the training set.

Figure 3 illustrates the aggregation of edges in the graph and figure 4 shows the final output of the error modelling function after normalizing.

$\pi(S, T)$ is called the error modelling function defined for the word pair, which is an intuitive calculation of probabilty between a pair of cognates through estimating their transformations. $q$ is a tunable parameter that controls the effect of the probabilistic frequencies $P(e)$ observed in the training set, often useful in avoiding overfitting. $\frac{1}{|G(S,T)|}$ is the normalization factor to allow us to compare the quantity across different word pairs.

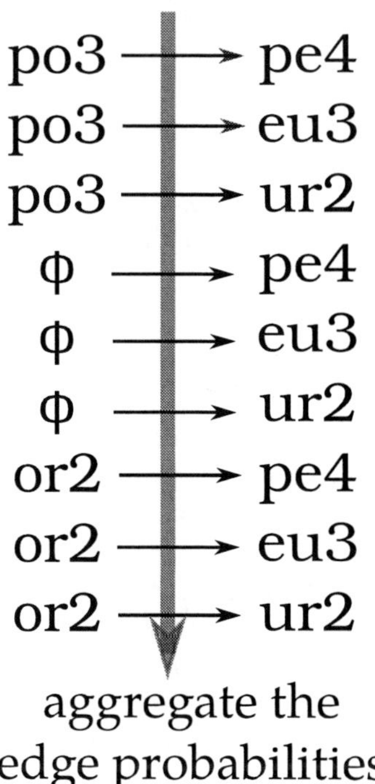



Figure 3: From the graph created in figure 2, we calculate the probabilities of each edge (by computing frequencies and smoothing) and then aggregate all the probabilities of edges in the graph.

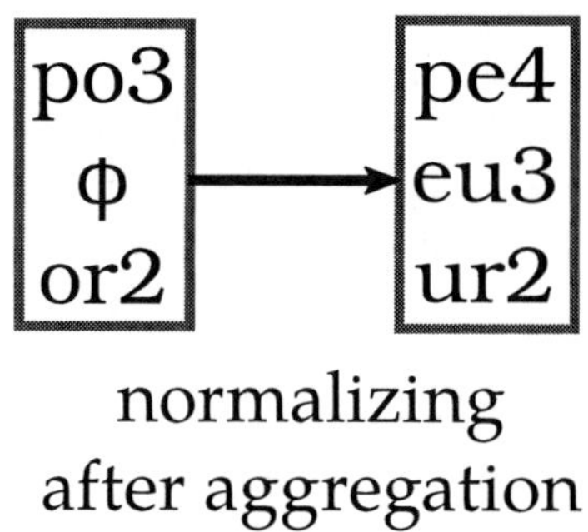



Figure 4: After aggregating, we normalize the sum and the graph conversion score is outputted.

## 4.3 Combining Error Modelling and Similarity Function metrics

In this subsection, we merge the notion of similarity and dissimilarity together. We combine a set-based similarity function (discussed in section 4.1) and the error modelling function (discussed in section 4.2) into a score function by a weighted sum of them, which is,

$$score(S,T) = \lambda \times sim(S, T) + (1 - \lambda) \times \pi(S, T)$$

where $\lambda \in [0, 1]$ is a weight based hyperparameter, $sim(S,T)$ is a set-based similarity between $S$ and

$T$, and $\pi(S,T)$ is the graphical error modelling function defined above.

## 5 Test Harness

Table 1 summarizes the results of the experimental setup. The elements of test harness are mentioned as following:

### 5.1 Setup Description

**Dataset:** The experiments in this paper are performed on the dataset used by Ciobanu *et al* (2014). The dataset consists 400 pairs of cognates and non-cognates for Romanian-French (Ro - Fr), Romanian-Italian (Ro - It), Romanian-Spanish (Ro - Es) and Romanian-Portuguese (Ro - Pt). The dataset is divided into a 3:1 ratio for training and testing purposes. Using cross-validation, hyperparameters and thresholds for all the algorithms and baselines were tuned accordingly in a fair manner.
**Experiments:** Two experiments are included in test harness.

1. We provide a pair of words and the algorithms would aim to detect whether they are cognates. Accuracy on the test set is used as a metric for evaluation.

2. We provide a source cognate as the input and the algorithm would return a ranked list as the output. The efficiency of the algorithm would depend on the rank of the desired target cognate. This is measured by MRR (Mean Reciprocal Rank), which is defined as, $MRR = \sum_{i=1}^{|dataset|} \frac{1}{rank_i}$, where $rank_i$ is the rank of the true cognate in the ranked list returned to the $i^{th}$ query.

### 5.2 Baselines

**String Similarity Baselines:** It is intuitive to compare our methods with the prevalent string similarity baselines since the notions behind cognate detection and string similarity are almost similar. Edit Distance is often used as the baseline in the cognate detection papers (Melamed, 1999). This computes the number of operations required to transform from source to target cognate. We have also incorporated XDice (Brew et al., 1996), which is a set based similarity measure that operates between shingle set between two strings. Hidden alignment conditional random fields (CRF) are often used in transliteration which serves as the generative sequential model to compute the probabilities between the cognates, which is analogous

to learnable edit distance (McCallum et al., 2012). Among these baselines, CRF performs the best in accuracy and MRR.
**Orthographic Cognate Detection:** Papers related to this notion usually take alignment of substrings which in classifier like support vector machines (Ciobanu and Dinu, 2015, 2014) or hidden markov models (Bhargava and Kondrak, 2009). We included Alina *et al* as the baseline (2014), which employs the dynamic programming based methods for sequence alignment following which features were extracted from the mismatches in the word alignments. These features are plugged into the classifier like SVM which results in decent performance on accuracy with an average of 84%, but only 16% on MRR. This result is due to the fact that a large number of features leads to overfitting and scoring function is not able to distinguish the appropriate cognate.
**Phonetic Cognate Detection:** Research in automatic cognate identification using phonetic aspects involve computation of similarity by decomposing phonetically transcribed words (Kondrak, 2000), acoustic models (Mielke, 2012), phonetic encodings (Rama, 2015), aligned segments of transcribed phonemes (List, 2012b). We implemented Rama's research (2015), which employs a Siamese convolutional neural network to learn the phonetic features jointly with language relatedness for cognate identification, which was achieved through phoneme encodings. Although it performs well on accuracy, it shows poor results with MRR, possibly the reason as same as SVM performance.

### 5.3 Ablation experiments

We experiment with the variables like length of substrings, ranking functions, shingling techniques, and graphical error model, which are detailed in the Table 1. Amongst the shingling techniques, we found that character bigrams with 2-ended positioning give better results. Adding trigrams to the database does not give major effect on the results. The results clearly indicate that adding graphical error model features greatly improve the test results. Amongst the ranking functions, Dirichlet smoothing tends to give better results, possibly due to the fact that it requires fewer parameters to tune and is able to capture the sequential data (like substrings) better than other ranking functions (Fang et al., 2011). The hy-

| Algorithms | Ro - It | | Ro - Fr | | Ro - Es | | Ro - Pt | |
|---|---|---|---|---|---|---|---|---|
| | Acc | MRR | Acc | MRR | Acc | MRR | Acc | MRR |
| Edit Distance (Melamed, 1999) | 0.53 | 0.11 | 0.52 | 0.13 | 0.58 | 0.15 | 0.54 | 0.13 |
| XDice (Brew et al., 1996) | 0.54 | 0.19 | 0.53 | 0.14 | 0.59 | 0.16 | 0.53 | 0.14 |
| SVM with Orthographic Aligment (Ciobanu and Dinu, 2014) | 0.81 | 0.18 | 0.87 | 0.15 | 0.86 | 0.16 | 0.73 | 0.14 |
| Phonetic Encodings in CNN (Rama, 2016) | 0.69 | 0.21 | 0.78 | 0.17 | 0.77 | 0.19 | 0.66 | 0.15 |
| Hidden alignment CRF (McCallum et al., 2012) | 0.84 | 0.51 | 0.85 | 0.48 | 0.84 | 0.50 | 0.71 | 0.45 |

| Shingling Technique | Ranking Function | Ro - It | | Ro - Fr | | Ro - Es | | Ro - Pt | |
|---|---|---|---|---|---|---|---|---|---|
| Bigram, 0-ended | TF-IDF | 0.54 | 0.18 | 0.52 | 0.14 | 0.59 | 0.15 | 0.55 | 0.11 |
| Bigram, 1-ended | TF-IDF | 0.59 | 0.19 | 0.54 | 0.18 | 0.60 | 0.18 | 0.57 | 0.12 |
| Bigram, 2-ended | TF-IDF | 0.64 | 0.25 | 0.63 | 0.21 | 0.68 | 0.22 | 0.65 | 0.17 |
| (Bi + Tri)-gram, 2-ended | TF-IDF | 0.64 | 0.25 | 0.64 | 0.21 | 0.57 | 0.22 | 0.65 | 0.18 |
| Bigram, 2-ended | BM25 | 0.84 | 0.40 | 0.87 | 0.37 | 0.86 | 0.34 | 0.73 | 0.35 |
| Bigram, 2-ended | Dirichlet | 0.84 | 0.41 | 0.86 | 0.38 | 0.86 | 0.39 | 0.74 | 0.36 |
| Bigram, 2-ended | BM25 + Graphical Error Model | 0.87 | 0.64 | 0.89 | 0.51 | 0.86 | 0.54 | 0.78 | 0.55 |
| Bigram, 2-ended | Dirichlet + Graphical Error Model | **0.88** | **0.67** | **0.89** | **0.59** | **0.87** | **0.60** | **0.80** | **0.58** |

Table 1: Results on the test dataset. The upper half denotes the baselines used and the lower half describes our ablation experiments. For the experiment 1, we evaluate using the accuracy (Acc) metric. We used MRR (Mean Reciprocal Rank) for describing the second experiment. Higher scores signify the better performance. The maximum value possible is 1.0. It is worth noting that for the classification problem (experiment 1), our algorithm has slight improvement. However for the recommendation problem (experiment 2), our algorithm shows massive improvement. The thresholds, hyper-parameters, source code and sample Python notebooks are available at our github repository: `https://github.com/pranav-ust/cognates`

perparameter $\lambda$ mentioned in the section 4.3, was tuned around 0.6, which shows the 60% contribution by the similarity function and 40% contribution by the dissimilarity. Overall, the combination of bigrams with 2-ended positional shingling, graphical error modelling with Dirichlet ranking function gives the best performance with an average of 86% on accuracy metric and 60% on MRR.

## 6 Conclusions

We approach towards the harder problem where the algorithm aims to find a target cognate when a source cognate is given. Positional shingling outperformed non-positional shingling based methods, which demonstrates that inclusion of positional information of substrings is rather important. Addition of graphical error model boosted the test results which shows that it is crucial to add dissimilarity information in order to capture the transformations of the substrings. Methods whose scoring functions rely only on complex machine learning algorithms like CNN or SVM tend to give worse results when searching for a cognate.

## Acknowledgements

This work would not be possible without the support from my parents. I would like to thank the NLP community for providing me open-sourced resources to help an underprivileged and naive student like me. Finally, I would like to thank the reviewers, mentors, and organizers for ACL-SRW for supporting student research. Special thanks to my classmate Chun Sik Chan and SRW mentor Sam Bowman for providing excellent critiques for this paper, and Alina Ciobanu for providing the dataset.

## References

Aditya Bhargava and Grzegorz Kondrak. 2009. Multiple word alignment with profile hidden markov models. In *Proceedings of Human Language Technologies: The 2009 Annual Conference of the North American Chapter of the Association for Computational Linguistics, Companion Volume: Student Research Workshop and Doctoral Consortium*, pages 43–48. Association for Computational Linguistics.

David M. Blei, Andrew Y. Ng, and Michael I. Jordan. 2003. Latent dirichlet allocation. *J. Mach. Learn. Res.*, 3:993–1022.

Chris Brew, David Mckelvie, and Buccleuch Place. 1996. Word-pair extraction for lexicography.

Alina Maria Ciobanu and Liviu P Dinu. 2014. Automatic detection of cognates using orthographic alignment. In *ACL (2)*, pages 99–105.

Alina Maria Ciobanu and Liviu P Dinu. 2015. Automatic discrimination between cognates and borrowings. In *Proceedings of the 53rd Annual Meeting of the Association for Computational Linguistics and the 7th International Joint Conference on Natural Language Processing (Volume 2: Short Papers)*, volume 2, pages 431–437.

Hui Fang, Tao Tao, and Chengxiang Zhai. 2011. Diagnostic evaluation of information retrieval models. *ACM Trans. Inf. Syst.*, 29(2):7:1–7:42.

Anni Järvelin, Antti Järvelin, and Kalervo Järvelin. 2007. s-grams: Defining generalized n-grams for information retrieval. *Information Processing & Management*, 43(4):1005–1019.

Grzegorz Kondrak. 2000. A new algorithm for the alignment of phonetic sequences. In *Proceedings of the 1st North American chapter of the Association for Computational Linguistics conference*, pages 288–295. Association for Computational Linguistics.

Johann-Mattis List. 2012a. Lexstat: Automatic detection of cognates in multilingual wordlists. In *Proceedings of the EACL 2012 Joint Workshop of LINGVIS & UNCLH*, EACL 2012, pages 117–125, Stroudsburg, PA, USA. Association for Computational Linguistics.

Johann-Mattis List. 2012b. Lexstat: Automatic detection of cognates in multilingual wordlists. In *Proceedings of the EACL 2012 Joint Workshop of LINGVIS & UNCLH*, pages 117–125. Association for Computational Linguistics.

Andrew McCallum, Kedar Bellare, and Fernando Pereira. 2012. A conditional random field for discriminatively-trained finite-state string edit distance. *arXiv preprint arXiv:1207.1406*.

I. Dan Melamed. 1999. Bitext maps and alignment via pattern recognition. *Comput. Linguist.*, 25(1):107–130.

Jeff Mielke. 2012. A phonetically based metric of sound similarity. *Lingua*, 122(2):145–163.

Ken Nguyen, Xuan Guo, and Y Pan. 2016. *Multiple Biological Sequence Alignment: Scoring Functions, Algorithms and Applications*.

Taraka Rama. 2015. Automatic cognate identification with gap-weighted string subsequences. In *Proceedings of the 2015 Conference of the North American Chapter of the Association for Computational Linguistics: Human Language Technologies.*, pages 1227–1231.

Taraka Rama. 2016. Siamese convolutional networks based on phonetic features for cognate identification. *CoRR*, abs/1605.05172.

Stephen Robertson and Hugo Zaragoza. 2009. The probabilistic relevance framework: Bm25 and beyond. *Found. Trends Inf. Retr.*, 3(4):333–389.

Ho Chung Wu, Robert Wing Pong Luk, Kam Fai Wong, and Kui Lam Kwok. 2008. Interpreting tf-idf term weights as making relevance decisions. *ACM Trans. Inf. Syst.*, 26(3):13:1–13:37.

# Mixed Feelings: Natural Text Generation with Variable, Coexistent Affective Categories

**Lee Kezar**

Mathematics and Computer Science Department, Rhodes College

Memphis, Tennessee, USA

`kezarlee@gmail.com`

## Abstract

Conversational agents, having the goal of natural language generation, must rely on language models which can integrate emotion into their responses. Recent projects outline models which can produce emotional sentences, but unlike human language, they tend to be restricted to one affective category out of a few (e.g. Zhao et al. (2018)). To my knowledge, none allow for the intentional coexistence of multiple emotions on the word or sentence level. Building on prior research which allows for variation in the intensity of a singular emotion (Ghosh et al., 2017), this research proposal outlines an LSTM (Long Short-Term Memory) language model which allows for variation in multiple emotions simultaneously.

## 1 Introduction

In closing her landmark paper on affective computing, Rosalind Picard charges researchers of artificial intelligence with a task. She writes, "Computers that will interact naturally and intelligently with humans need the ability to at least recognize and express affect" (Picard, 1995). While Picard herself has since spent her time primarily studying the physiology behind emotion and health, there is also a strong relationship between linguistics and emotion. The task for computer scientists who study this relationship is to symbolize and express emotion through verbal language alone.

Although this goal easy to articulate, accomplishing it has proven to be quite challenging. However, in the same way AI researchers acquired valuable insight from reviewing models of cellular neuroscience to produce an artificial neural network, perhaps we can demystify affect generation by reviewing psychological models which build on neuro-biological findings in regards to human emotion.

### 1.1 Need for Affective Mixing

I will now summarize two key ideas from these findings: emotion/language dynamic and classification of emotion.

First, emotion usually precedes language. In describing phenomenal consciousness as it pertains to emotion, Carroll Izard wrote that "an emotion feeling remains functional and motivational without being symbolized and made accessible in reflective consciousness via language" (Izard, 2009). One might support this claim by noting how complex emotional qualia feels and how rather limited language can be. For example, how accurate is it to say that "Alice is happy"? To what extent is she happy? Is it the same happiness that she feels when being in good company, or in favorable weather? Do they only differ in magnitude, or also along some other dimension? Or as a second example, can you recall a moment where you couldn't describe how you were feeling, but felt it nonetheless? Clearly, emotion is rather difficult to express in simple words. Yet, recent affective generation techniques tend to presume that they fall neatly into one of five or six discrete categories (Zhao et al., 2018). Recently, researchers added nuance to affect generation via variation in intensity (Ghosh et al., 2017), but to my knowledge no model adds nuance along extra dimensions, such as other emotions.

Second, emotion is usually the conflation of two distinct phenomena: "basic emotions" and "dynamic emotion-cognition interactions" (Izard, 2009). The basic emotions are linked to old evolutionary stimuli and are more automatic (e.g. fear



*Proceedings of ACL 2018, Student Research Workshop*, pages 141–145
Melbourne, Australia, July 15 - 20, 2018. ©2018 Association for Computational Linguistics

as a response mechanism to avoid danger). That is to say, basic emotions have little involvement with cognition. Emotion schemas, on the other hand, result directly from interactions between cognition and emotion. This type of emotion is underscored by research which casts emotion and cognition as interdependent processes (Storbeck and Clore, 2007), closely mirroring Picard's insistence that intelligence is comprised of emotion.

The categorizations usually found in lexicons (e.g. Linguistic Inquiry and Word Count or LIWC) treat words as stimuli which humans respond to with emotions. This model aligns closely with basic emotions, and supposes language precedes emotion. However, in actuality humans tend to incorporate cognitive processes such as memory and perspective-taking, allowing us to have multiple emotions simultaneously. If we are to use this as inspiration for generating affective text algorithmically, we might then permit the AI to intentionally express multiple emotions.

## 1.2 Project Overview

Having established this need for emotional intelligence in AI (including natural language processing), and reviewed psychological research in this area, we might conclude that emotions should not be modeled as singular, discrete categories but continuous and constantly mixing.

This project aims to create an algorithm which is capable of taking some priming text and the desired affective state which can vary along different emotional dimensions simultaneously, and produce a corresponding utterance. This algorithm is primarily meant for conversational agents, but could be adapted for other purposes.

## 1.3 Use Cases

Mixing emotions are not only more realistic to human emotion, since they allow for significantly more flexibility in expression, but also more helpful for specific applications. I will introduce three such applications here.

First, the ability to mix emotions in a continuous fashion allows for conversational agents to gradually and imperceptibly shift the tone of a conversation toward a new tone. Human tendency to mirror the emotions of others through empathy would make this an effective strategy to improve attitude and emotional outlook.

Second, mixing emotions in this way also allows for an extra layer of nuance in conversational practice, as we are affected by emotional language as often as we produce it. For example, in simulating a realistic conversation, the deliverance of emotionally-charged statements should cause the computer to respond appropriately. However, models which treat emotion as discrete categories would "overreact" and abruptly switch from one emotion to another.

Third, realistic personality can be introduced as a tendency to hover near or avoid specific points. Naturally, the conversational agent will vary in emotion, but ultimately return to some default state. For example, if an agent were to express optimistic personality, it might impose some minimum on the *joy* vector, and a maximum on the *sadness* and *anger* vectors. This is not possible with models that suppose emotions are discrete categories.

## 1.4 Algorithm Overview

We can encapsulate this goal with a broad formula

$$g(p, e) = w \tag{1}$$

where $p$ is the priming text, $e$ is a quadruple of values such that

$$e_x \in \mathbb{R} \mid x \in \{\text{j}, \text{s}, \text{f}, \text{a}\}, 0 \leq e_x \leq 1 \tag{2}$$

which correspond to the intensity of *joy, sadness, fear, anger*, respectively; and $w$ is an array of words and punctuation which represent the algorithm's response to $p$ with emotional state $e$. The emotional categories are selected to correspond with the DepecheMood database, which I will describe in section 3.2. The priming text can be a sentence fragment which the user seeks to complete or a natural sentence which the algorithm is meant to respond to.

The purpose for $g$ is to be embedded into a conversational setting with improvements on parsing and production. I will not detail what this embedding looks like for sake of brevity and coherency.

An example set of sentences generated across a gradient beginning at high happiness ($e_j \approx 1$), low fear ($e_f \approx 0$) and ending at moderate happiness ($e_j \approx 0.5$), high fear ($e_f \approx 1$) might look like this:

- I am happy to go to work today

- I am content to go …

- I am hesitant to go …

- I am worried to go …

- I am nervous to go …

- I am anxious to go …

since anxiety is, in a sense, the combination of fear and partial excitement or happiness.

## 2   Related Work

In the last two years, different models have been used to create conversational agents which can express affect. Namely, the Emotional Chatting Machine (ECM) (Zhao et al., 2018) and Affect-LM (Ghosh et al., 2017). These models are motivated by the psychological finding that agents with subtle expressivity can improve the affective state of the user (Prendinger et al., 2005). These projects utilize an array of emotional categories including *liking, happiness, sadness, disgust, anger*, and *anxiety*.

To accomplish this, different language models which utilize machine learning algorithms have been crafted and tested for accuracy and grammaticality. The most popular include feed-forward neural networks, recurrent neural networks (RNNs), and long short-term memory (LSTM) neural networks (Sundermeyer et al., 2015). Among these, the LSTM model is notably superior for establishing long-term dependencies in text, and reducing the vanishing gradient problem found in RNNs. This is the method used by (Ghosh et al., 2017), with an additional network for including emotionally-charged words of the desired strength. Importantly, they accommodated and tested for loss in grammaticality, which was predicted for expressions of intense emotion but not low emotions, where standard LSTMs typically suffice.

## 3   Model

### 3.1   LSTM Language Model

The LSTM Language Model allows for the use of all prior words as evidence in predicting the next best word, $w_t$. We can write this prediction as a probability like so:

$$p(w_1^M) = \prod_{i=1}^{M} p(w_i|w_1^{i-1}) \tag{3}$$

for a sequence of $M$ words. We can utilize the LSTM as a function $l$ of the prior words $w_1^{i-1}$ to calculate $p(w_i)$. An additional bias term $b_i$ corresponding to unigram occurrence of $w_i$ may be included to favor more common words, as in Ghosh et al. (2017). The output layer of $l$ summed with this bias term then pass through a softmax activation function to normalize the outputs, producing

$$p(w_i|w_1^{i-1}) = \text{softmax}(l(w_1^{i-1}) + b_i) \tag{4}$$

The algorithm would simply repeat this calculation, each step incrementing $i$ and selecting the most probable word, until a period is produced indicating the end of the sentence and completion of the algorithm.

### 3.2   Incorporating Affective Data

The DepecheMood lexicon contains affective data for over 13,500 words, each rated along a continuous interval $[0, 1]$ for eight affective dimensions: {*Fear, Amusement, Anger, Annoyance, Indifference, Happiness, Inspiration, Sadness*} (Staiano and Guerini, 2014). As a comical American example, DepecheMood rates the word "president" as $\{0.2, 0.346, 0.626, 1.0, 0.528, 0.341, 0.0, 0.115\}$ respectively – that is, moderately infuriating, never inspiring, and completely annoying.

For this project, I would use the more typical categories of *joy, sadness, fear*, and *anger*. This lexicon contrasts other popular lexicons with affective data, e.g. LIWC, in that these ratings are *continuous* along $[0, 1]$. This property allows for more precise matching to the affective state, and movement along a gradient between the four dimensions.

In addition to the bias term from the previous section, we would account for affect by introducing a third term $d(w_i, e)$ which favors words most affectively similar to the desired output.

Graphically, this equation maps the vocabulary $V$ into four-dimensional space corresponding to each word's emotional valences, and calculates the distance between $e$, a point in this space, and each word $w_i \in V$. This inverse distance function can be written as such:

$$d(w_i, e) = \text{softmax} \left( \frac{1}{\sqrt{\sum_{j=1}^{|e|} (w_{ij} - e_j)^2}} \right) \tag{5}$$

where $j$ enumerates each of the four affective dimensions, $w_{ij}$ is the intensity along that dimension $e_j$ is the target intensity.

### 3.3 Optimizing $d(w_i, e)$

In its current form, this function requires a calculation for each $w_i \in V$ which is has a subideal time complexity of O($n$). We can reduce this to O($\log n$) by estimating $e$ to its nearest neighbor in $V$ (a O($\log n$) operation, as I will soon explain), whose distances to every other word can be precomputed and accessed via a hash table O(1). This replacement can be done without loss of accuracy due to the density of the data set.

To find $e$ nearest neighbor in $V$, we can utilize a modified QuadTree algorithm to reduce the search space to some arbitrary $n$ much smaller than 13,500. To briefly review, this algorithm organizes a set of data points into a hierarchical tree with leaf nodes containing a list of less than $n$ points (Finkel and Bentley, 1974). Querying this tree to find nearby data points has been empirically shown to take on average O($\log n$) time, a modest improvement over O($n$).

### 3.4 Avoiding Over-Emphasis

As Zhao et al. (2018) noted in their ECM project, "emotional responses are relatively short lived and involve changes." These changes, which the authors call "emotion dynamics", involve modeling emotions as quantities which decays at each step. This avoids the problem of over-emphasizing the input $e$ by repeatedly expressing the same state, unintentionally compounding its strength. Their implementation of this decay involves updating $e_j$ in (5) by subtracting $w_{ij}$ for each dimension $j$. Therefore, upon completion, $e$ would be close to $[0, 0, 0, 0]$.

Preliminary experimentation would certainly need to reveal the appropriate weights for $g$, $d$, and $b_i$ such that precision of emotion does not sacrifice grammaticality.

## 4 Implementation, Training, and Review

For the LSTM, we would follow the suggestion of Sundermeyer et al. (2012) and implement a network using TensorFlow[1] with two hidden layers of 200 nodes: the first being a projection layer of standard neural network units and the second being hidden layer of LSTM units. The output layer would also have 200 nodes.

The same authors later suggest training the network using the cross-entropy error criterion, using the function

$$F(A) = -\sum_{i=1}^{M} \log p_A(w_i | w_{i-n+1}^{i-1}) \tag{6}$$

where $M$ is the size of the training corpus (Sundermeyer et al., 2015). For a stochastic gradient descent algorithm, we can obtain a gradient using epochwise backpropogation through time (BPTT) on the first pass, and update the weights on the second pass as specified in Sundermeyer et al. (2014).

The training corpus for this algorithm would need only be some collection of natural dialogue. This can be catered to the environment it will be used in, but for our purposes the Ubuntu Dialogue Corpus will be used for its generality, accessibility, dyadic nature, and size (Lowe et al., 2016).

Additional funds have been secured to utilize Amazon's Mechanical Turk to analyze loss in grammaticality and verify the manipulation of $e$ by simply assessing sentences along a Likert scale and comparing this data to the intended affect. I predict that certain categories and combinations will be harder to express in text than others, resulting in higher variability and weaker correlations. For example, *anger* and *sadness* (an approximation of *remorse*) may be rather easy to express, but *joy* and *sadness* may be difficult. Visualizing these strengths and weaknesses will be an interesting reflection of the English language.

## 5 Conclusion

In this research proposal, I have given a brief overview of a natural language generation algorithm which is capable of producing utterances expressive of multiple emotional dimensions simultaneously. The DepecheMood lexicon enables the

---

[1]http://www.tensorflow.org

mapping of words into $n$-dimensional space, allowing us to prefer words which minimize the distance between it and the target affective state along the four emotional dimensions.

After clarifying implementation details such as LSTM node construction, neural architecture, and use of the training corpus, this algorithm has the potential to add further nuance to our current models of generating affect which are consistent with psychological and neuro-biological findings.

## References


R. A. Finkel and J. L. Bentley. 1974. Quad trees: A data structure for retrieval on composite keys. *Acta Informatica*, 4(1):1–9.

Sayan Ghosh, Mathieu Chollet, Eugene Laksana, Louis-Philippe Morency, and Stefan Scherer. 2017. Affect-lm: A neural language model for customizable affective text generation. *ACL*, pages 634–642.

Carroll E. Izard. 2009. Emotion theory and research: Highlights, unanswered questions, and emerging issues. *Annual Review of Psychology*, 60:1–25.

Ryan Lowe, Nissan Pow, Iulian V. Serban, and Joelle Pineau. 2016. The ubuntu dialogue corpus: A large dataset for research in unstructured multi-turn dialogue systems.

Rosalind W. Picard. 1995. Affective computing. Technical report, Massachusetts Institute of Technology, Perceptual Computing Section.

Helmut Prendinger, Junichiro Mori, and Mitsuru Ishizuka. 2005. Using human physiology to evaluate subtle expressivity of a virtual quizmaster in a mathematical game. *Human-Computer Studies*, 2:231–245.

Jacopo Staiano and Marco Guerini. 2014. Depechemood: a lexicon for emotion analysis from crowd-annotated news.

Justin Storbeck and Gerald L. Clore. 2007. On the interdependence of cognition and emotion. *Cognitive Emotion*, 21(6):1212–1237.

Martin Sundermeyer, Hermann Ney, and Ralf Schlter. 2012. Lstm neural networks for language modeling. In *Interspeech*.

Martin Sundermeyer, Hermann Ney, and Ralf Schlter. 2014. Rwthlm-the rwth aachen university neural network language modeling toolkit. In *Interspeech*, pages 2093–2097.

Martin Sundermeyer, Hermann Ney, and Ralf Schlter. 2015. From feedforward to recurrent lstm neural networks for language modeling. *IEEE/ACM Transactions on Audio, Speech, and Language Processing*, 23(3).

Hao Zhao, Minlie Huang, Tianyang Zhang, Xiaoyan Zhu, and Bing Liu. 2018. Emotional chatting machine: Emotional conversation generation with internal and external memory.

# Automatic Spelling Correction for Resource-Scarce Languages using Deep Learning


**Pravallika Etoori**
LTRC, KCIS
IIIT Hyderabad
e.pravallika@
research.iiit.ac.in

**Manoj Chinnakotla**
Microsoft
Bellevue, USA
manojc@microsoft.com

**Radhika Mamidi**
LTRC, KCIS
IIIT Hyderabad
radhika.mamidi@
iiit.ac.in



## Abstract

Spelling correction is a well-known task in Natural Language Processing (NLP). Automatic spelling correction is important for many NLP applications like web search engines, text summarization, sentiment analysis etc. Most approaches use parallel data of noisy and correct word mappings from different sources as training data for automatic spelling correction. Indic languages are resource-scarce and do not have such parallel data due to low volume of queries and non-existence of such prior implementations. In this paper, we show how to build an automatic spelling corrector for resource-scarce languages. We propose a sequence-to-sequence deep learning model which trains end-to-end. We perform experiments on synthetic datasets created for Indic languages, Hindi and Telugu, by incorporating the spelling mistakes committed at character level. A comparative evaluation shows that our model is competitive with the existing spell checking and correction techniques for Indic languages.


## 1 Introduction

Spelling correction is important for many of the potential NLP applications such as text summarization, sentiment analysis, machine translation (Belinkov and Bisk, 2017). Automatic spelling correction is crucial in search engines as spelling mistakes are very common in user-generated text. Many websites have a feature of automatically giving correct suggestions to the misspelled user queries in the form of *Did you mean?* suggestions or automatic corrections. Providing suggestions makes it convenient for users to accept a proposed correction without retyping or correcting the query

manually. This task is approached by collecting similar intent queries from user logs (Hasan et al., 2015; Wilbur et al., 2006; Ahmad and Kondrak, 2005). The training data is automatically extracted from event logs where users re-issue their search queries with potentially corrected spelling within the same session. Example query pairs are *(house lone, house loan), (ello world, hello world), (mobilephone, mobile phone)*. Thus, large amounts of data is collected and models are trained using techniques like Machine Learning, Statistical Machine Translation etc.

The task of spelling correction is challenging for resource-scarce languages. In this paper, we consider Indic languages, Hindi and Telugu, because of their resource scarcity. Due to lesser query share, we do not find the same level of parallel alteration data from logs. We also do not have many language resources such as Parts of Speech (POS) Taggers, Parsers etc. to linguistically analyze and understand these queries. Due to lack of relevant data, we create synthetic dataset using highly probable spelling errors and real world errors in Hindi and Telugu given by language experts. Similarly, synthetic dataset can be created for any resource-scarce language incorporating the real world errors. Deep Learning techniques have shown enormous success in sequence to sequence mapping tasks (Sutskever et al., 2014). Most of the existing spell-checkers for Indic languages are implemented using rule-based techniques (Kumar et al., 2018). In this paper, we approach the spelling correction problem for Indic languages with Deep learning. This model can be employed for any resource-scarce language. We propose a character based Sequence-to-sequence text Correction Model for Indic Languages (SCMIL) which trains end-to-end.

Our main contributions in this paper are summarized as follows:

- We propose a character based recurrent




*Proceedings of ACL 2018, Student Research Workshop*, pages 146–152
Melbourne, Australia, July 15 - 20, 2018. ©2018 Association for Computational Linguistics

sequence-to-sequence architecture with a Long Short Term Memory (LSTM) encoder and a LSTM decoder for spelling correction of Indic languages.

- We create synthetic datasets[1] of noisy and correct word mappings for Hindi and Telugu by collecting highly probable spelling errors and inducing noise in clean corpus.

- We evaluate the performance of SCMIL by comparing with various approaches such as Statistical Machine Translation (SMT), rule-based methods, and various deep learning models, for this task.

## 2 Related Work

Significant work has been done in the field of Spell checking for Indian languages. There are spell-checkers available for Indian languages like Hindi, Marathi, Bengali, Telugu, Tamil, Oriya, Malayalam, Punjabi.

Dixit et al. (2005) designed a rule-based spell-checker for Marathi, a major Indian Language. This is the first initiative for morphology-based spell checking for Marathi. The spell-checker is based on the rules of morphology and the rules of orthography.

A spell-checker is designed for Telugu (Rao, 2011), an agglutinating Indian language which has a very complex morphology. This spell-checker is based on Morphological Analysis and Sandhi splitting rules. It consists of two parts: a set of routines for scanning the text (Morphological Analyzer and sandhi splitting rules) and identifying valid words, and an algorithm for comparing the unrecognized words and word parts against a known list of variantly spelled words and word parts.

Another Hindi Spell-checker (Sharma and Jain, 2013) uses a dictionary with word, frequency pairs as language model. Error detection is done by dictionary look-up. Error correction is performed using Damerau-Levenshtein edit distance and n-gram technique. These candidates are ranked by sorting in increasing order of edit distance. Words at same edit distance are sorted in order of their frequencies.

HINSPELL(Singh et al., 2015) is a spell-checker designed for Hindi which is implemented using a hybrid approach. Error is detected by dictionary look-up. Error correction is done by using Minimum Edit Distance technique where the closest words in the dictionary to the error word are obtained. These obtained words are given priority using a weightage algorithm and Statistical Machine Translation (SMT).

Ambili et al. (2016) designed a Malayalam spell-checker that detects the error by a dictionary look-up approach and error correction is done through N-gram based technique. If a word is not present in the dictionary, it is identified as an error and N-gram based technique corrects error by finding similarity between words and computing a similarity coefficient.

Recently, Ghosh and Kristensson (2017) proposed a Deep Learning model for text correction and completion in keyboard decoding for English. This is a first attempt at text correction using Deep Neural Networks which gave promising results.

Sakaguchi et al. (2017) approached the problem of Spell Correction using semi-character Recurrent Neural Networks on English data.

Studies of spell checking techniques for Indian Languages (Kumar et al., 2018; Gupta and Mathur, 2012) show that the existing spell-checkers have two major steps: Error detection and error correction. Error detection is done by dictionary look-up. Error correction consists of two steps: the generation of candidate corrections and the ranking of candidate corrections. The most studied spelling correction algorithms are: edit distance, similarity keys, rule-based techniques, n-gram-based techniques, probabilistic techniques, neural networks, and noisy channel model. All of these methods can be thought of as calculating a distance between the misspelled word and each word in the dictionary or index. The shorter the distance the higher the dictionary word is ranked.

While there have been a few attempts to design spell-checkers for English and few other languages using Machine Learning, to the best of our knowledge, no such prior work has been attempted for Indian languages.

## 3 Model Description

We address the spelling correction problem for Indic languages by having a separate corrector network as an encoder and an implicit language model as a decoder in a sequence-to-sequence at-

---

[1] https://github.com/PravallikaRao/SpellChecker

tention model that trains end-to-end.

## 3.1 Sequence-to-sequence Model

Sequence-to-sequence (seq2seq) models (Sutskever et al., 2014; Cho et al., 2014) have enjoyed great success in a variety of tasks such as machine translation, speech recognition, image captioning, and text summarization. A basic sequence-to-sequence model consists of two neural networks: an encoder that processes the input and a decoder that generates the output. This model has shown great potential in input-output sequence mapping tasks like machine translation. An input side encoder captures the representations in the data, while the decoder gets the representation from the encoder along with the input and outputs a corresponding mapping to the target language. Intuitively, this architectural set-up seems to naturally fit the regime of mapping noisy input to de-noised output, where the corrected prediction can be treated as a different language and the task can be treated as Machine Translation.

## 3.2 System Architecture

The Recurrent Neural Network (RNN) (Rumelhart et al., 1986; Werbos, 1990) is a natural generalization of feed-forward neural networks to sequences. Given a sequence of inputs $(x_1, \ldots, x_T)$, a standard RNN computes a sequence of outputs $(y_1, \ldots, y_T)$ by iterating the following equation:

$$h_t = sigm(W^{hx}x_t + W^{hh}h_{t-1}) \tag{1}$$

$$y_t = W^{yh}h_t \tag{2}$$

The RNN can easily map sequences to sequences whenever the alignment between the inputs the outputs is known ahead of time. In fact, recurrent neural networks, long short-term memory networks (Hochreiter and Schmidhuber, 1997), and gated recurrent neural networks (Chung et al., 2014) have become standard approaches in sequence modelling and transduction problems such as language modelling and machine translation.

RNNs struggle to cope with long-term dependency in the data due to vanishing gradient problem (Hochreiter, 1998). This problem is solved using Long Short Term Memory (LSTM) recurrent neural networks.

SCMIL has the similar underlying architecture of sequence-to-sequence models. The encoder and decoder in SCMIL operate at character level.

**Encoder**: In SCMIL, the encoder is a character based LSTM. With LSTM as encoder, the input sequence is modeled as a list of vectors, where each vector represents the meaning of all characters in the sequence read so far.

**Decoder**: The decoder in SCMIL is a character level LSTM recurrent network with attention. The output from the encoder is the final hidden state of the character based LSTM encoder. This becomes the input to the LSTM decoder.

By letting the decoder have an attention mechanism (Bahdanau et al., 2014), the encoder is relieved from the burden of having to encode all information in the source sequence into a fixed-length vector. With attention, the information can be spread throughout the sequence of annotations, which can be selectively retrieved by the decoder accordingly. The attention mechanism computes a fixed-size vector that encodes the whole input sequence based on the sequence of all the outputs generated by the encoder as opposed to the plain encoder-decoder model which looks only at the last state generated by the encoder for all the slices of the decoder.

Thus, SCMIL is a sequence-to-sequence attention model with Bidirectional RNN encoder and attention decoder which is trained end-to-end having a character based representation on both encoder and decoder sides.

## 3.3 Training details

All the code is written in Python 2.7 using tf-seq2seq (Britz et al., 2017), a general-purpose encoder-decoder framework for Tensorflow (Abadi et al., 2016) deep learning library version 1.0.1. Both the encoder and the decoder are jointly trained end-to-end on the synthetic datasets we created. SCMIL has a learning rate of 0.001, batch size of 100, sequence length of 50 (characters) and number of training steps 10,000. The size of the encoder LSTM cell is 256 with one layer. The size of the decoder LSTM cell is 256 with two layers. We use Adam optimization (Kingma and Ba, 2014) for training SCMIL. The character embedding dimension are fixed to 256 and the dropout rate to 0.8.

## 4 Experiments and Results

We performed experiments with SCMIL and other models using synthetic datasets which we created for the Indic languages: Hindi and Telugu. Hindi is the most prominent Indian language and the third most spoken language in the world. Telugu is the most widely spoken Dravidian language in the world and third most spoken native language in India.

### 4.1 Dataset details

Due to lack of data with error patterns in Indic languages, we have built a synthetic dataset that SCMIL is trained on. Initially, we create data lists for Hindi and Telugu. For this, we have extracted a corpus of most frequent Hindi words[2] and most frequent Telugu words[3]. We have also extracted Hindi movie names and Telugu movie names of the movies released between the years 1930 and 2018 from Wikipedia which constitute phrases in the data lists. Thus, the Hindi and Telugu data lists consist of words and phrases consisting maximum of five words.

For each data instance in the data list, multiple noisy words are generated by introducing error. The type of errors include insertion, deletion, substitution of one character, and word fusing. Spaces between words are randomly dropped in phrases to simulate the word fusing problem. The list of errors for Hindi and Telugu is created by collecting the highly committed spelling errors users make in each of these languages. We created this error list from linguistic resources and with help from language experts. The language experts analyzed Hindi and Telugu usage and listed the most probable errors. These errors are based on observations on real data and lexicon of Hindi and Telugu. Thus, the synthetic datasets are made as close as possible to real world user-generated data.

Table 2 shows the example of generation of noisy words corresponding to a correct word considering a Hindi word. Thus, the pairs of noisy word and original word constitute the parallel data for training. Table 1 gives the details about size of the synthetic datasets for Hindi and Telugu.

### 4.2 Baseline Methods

We perform experiments on various models. The datasets are divided into train, dev, test partitions

randomly in the ratio 80:10:10 respectively. In all our results, the models learn over the train partition, get tuned over the dev partition, and are evaluated over the test partition.

We train a SMT model using Moses (Koehn et al., 2007) on Hindi and Telugu synthetic datasets. This is our main baseline model. The standard set of features is used, including a phrase model, length penalty, jump penalty and a language model. This SMT model is trained at the character-level. Hence, the system learns mappings between character-level phrases. Moses framework allows us to easily conduct experiments with several settings and compare with SCMIL.

Other baselines are character based sequence-to-sequence attention models: CNN-GRU and GRU-GRU. All the models compared in this set of experiments look at batch sizes of 100 inputs and a maximum sequence size of 50 characters with a learning rate of 0.001 and run for 10000 steps. Throughout, the size of GRU cell is 256 with one layer. The CNN consists of 5 filters with sizes varying in the range of [2,3,4]. These multiple filters of particular widths produce the feature map, which is then concatenated and flattened for further processing.

### 4.3 Results and Analysis

Table 3 shows the accuracies reported by SCMIL and SMT methods. To check if Moses performs better on larger training data, we increased the size of Hindi synthetic dataset to 20567 and performed SMT. The accuracy value was 62% which is almost equivalent to the accuracy on original synthetic dataset. SCMIL outperforms Moses, an SMT technique by a huge margin. In Table 3, we find that SCMIL performs better than other sequence-to-sequence models with different convolutional and recurrent encoder-decoder combinations. These accuracies are on test set over the entire sequence. Thus, the results show that SCMIL performs better than all other baseline models. Our results support the conclusion by Britz et al. (2017) that LSTMs outperform GRUs.

The rule-based spell-checker for Hindi, HINSPELL (Singh et al., 2015) reported an accuracy of 77.9% on a data of 870 misspelled words randomly collected from books, newspapers and people etc. Te data used in Singh et al. (2015) and the HINSPELL system are not available. Hence, we

---

[2] https://ltrc.iiit.ac.in/download.php
[3] https://en.wiktionary.org/Frequency_lists/Telugu

| Language | High Frequency Words | Movie names | Size of parallel corpus |
|---|---|---|---|
| Hindi | 15000 | 3021 | 108587 |
| Telugu | 10000 | 3689 | 92716 |

Table 1: Details of the synthetic datasets for Hindi and Telugu.

| Correct word | Noisy words |
|---|---|
| प्रेम कहानी (prem kahaanii) | प्रेमा कहानी (prema kahaanii) |
| | प्रेम कहनी (prem kahanii) |
| | प्रेमकहानी (premkahaanii) |
| | प्रेम कहानि (prem kahaani) |
| | प्रैम कहानी (praim kahaanii) |

Table 2: Example of noisy words generation for a Hindi word with corresponding transliterations.

| Model | Hindi(%) | Telugu(%) |
|---|---|---|
| Moses (SMT) | 62.8 | 64.7 |
| CNN-GRU | 74.4 | 79.7 |
| GRU-GRU | 77.6 | 84.3 |
| SCMIL | 85.4 | 89.3 |

Table 3: Accuracy of spelling correction on Hindi and Telugu synthetic datasets given by Moses, character-based deep learning models(CNN-GRU and GRU-GRU), and SCMIL.

implemented HINSPELL using Shabdanjali dictionary[4] consisting of 32952 Hindi word. This system when tested on our Hindi synthetic dataset, gave an accuracy is 72.3%. This accuracy being lower than the original HINSPELL accuracy can be accounted to larger size of testing data and inclusion of out-of-vocabulary words. Thus, SCMIL outperforms HINSPELL by reporting an accuracy of 85.4%.

In Table 4, we have shown predictions given by SCMIL on few Hindi inputs. The results show that errors are contextually learned by the model. It can also be seen that the model has learned the word fusing problem. Also, the error detection step is not required separately as SCMIL trains end-to-end and learns the presence of noise in the input based on context. The advantage of SCMIL over rule-based techniques is that it can handle out of vocabulary words as it is trained at character level. For example, the last entry in the Table 4, is the English word *bomb* spelled in Hindi. The model has learned it and corrected when misspelled in Hindi as *bombh*. Dictionary based techniques fail in such cases. The model fails in few cases when it corrects one character of the misspelled word instead of other like the example in fourth row of 4.

The slightly higher accuracy of SCMIL on Telugu data than on Hindi data might be due to the fact that the highly probable spelling errors used in data creation are slightly less in number for Telugu when compared to Hindi. This can be handled for any language with more errors by increasing size

of dataset which includes enough data instances capturing each kind of error.

## 5  Future Work

This paper is the initial approach to automatic spelling correction for Indic languages using Deep Learning and we have obtained results that are competitive with the existing techniques. SCMIL can be improved and extended in many ways.

SCMIL presently deals with spelling corrections at word level. It can be further extended to automatically make not only spelling corrections but also grammar corrections at phrase level/sentence level.

The synthetic dataset can be improved by collecting noisy words from different platforms like social media, blogs etc. and introducing these real world errors into clean corpus. This will improve the performance of the model on user-generated data. Further, for proper evaluation of the model, The model should be tested on real world user-generated parallel data.

One more potential improvement would be to change the training data from words and phrases to sentences. This will help in achieving context based spelling correction.

The spelling correction model can be extended to a text correction and completion model. Changing the decoder from character-level to word-level will add the functionality of auto completion. This will improve the scope of the model in various applications.

---

| Input | Prediction | Correct Output |
|---|---|---|
| राजसि (raajasi) | राजसी (raajasii) | राजसी (raajasii) |
| दोआँखें (dhoaankhei) | दो आँखें (dho aankhei) | दो आँखें (dho aankhei) |
| अंस (ans) | अंश (ansh) | अंश (ansh) |
| दशावतर (dhashaavatar) | दशवतर (dhashavatar) | दशावतार (dhashaavataar) |
| बॉम्भ (baambh) | बॉम्ब (baamb) | बॉम्ब (baamb) |
| बॉम्भ (baambh) | बॉम्ब (baamb) | बॉम्ब (baamb) |

Table 4: Qualitative evaluation of predictions by SCMIL on few Hindi inputs along with expected outputs and corresponding transliterations.

## 6 Summary and Conclusion

In this paper, we proposed SCMIL for automatic spelling correction in Indic languages which employs a recurrent sequence-to-sequence attention model to learn the spelling corrections from noisy and correct word pairs. We created a parallel corpus of noisy and correct spellings for training by introducing spelling errors in correct words. We validated SCMIL on these synthetic datasets created for Hindi and Telugu. We implemented spelling correction using Moses, a SMT system as a baseline model. We evaluated our system against existing techniques for Indic languages and showed favorable results. Finally, we discussed possible extensions to improve the scope of SCMIL and perform better evaluation.

SCMIL can be used in applications like search engines as we have shown that it automatically corrects the input text in Indic languages. Most of the deep learning models train on billions of data instances. On the contrary, SCMIL trains on a dataset of less than a million parallel instances and gives competitive results. This shows that our approach can be used for automatic spelling correction of any resource-scarce language.

## References


Martín Abadi, Paul Barham, Jianmin Chen, Zhifeng Chen, Andy Davis, Jeffrey Dean, Matthieu Devin, Sanjay Ghemawat, Geoffrey Irving, Michael Isard, et al. 2016. Tensorflow: A system for large-scale machine learning. In *OSDI*, volume 16, pages 265–283.

Farooq Ahmad and Grzegorz Kondrak. 2005. Learning a spelling error model from search query logs. In *Proceedings of the conference on Human Language Technology and Empirical Methods in Natural Language Processing*, pages 955–962. Association for Computational Linguistics.

Ambili, Panchami KS, and Neethu Subash. 2016. Automatic error detection and correction in malayalam. *International Journal of Science Technology and Engineering(IJSTE)*, 3(2).

Dzmitry Bahdanau, Kyunghyun Cho, and Yoshua Bengio. 2014. Neural machine translation by jointly learning to align and translate. *arXiv preprint arXiv:1409.0473*.

Yonatan Belinkov and Yonatan Bisk. 2017. Synthetic and natural noise both break neural machine translation. *arXiv preprint arXiv:1711.02173*.

D. Britz, A. Goldie, T. Luong, and Q. Le. 2017. Massive Exploration of Neural Machine Translation Architectures. *ArXiv e-prints*.

Denny Britz, Anna Goldie, Thang Luong, and Quoc Le. 2017. Massive exploration of neural machine translation architectures. *arXiv preprint arXiv:1703.03906*.

Kyunghyun Cho, Bart Van Merriënboer, Caglar Gulcehre, Dzmitry Bahdanau, Fethi Bougares, Holger Schwenk, and Yoshua Bengio. 2014. Learning phrase representations using rnn encoder-decoder for statistical machine translation. *arXiv preprint arXiv:1406.1078*.

Junyoung Chung, Caglar Gulcehre, KyungHyun Cho, and Yoshua Bengio. 2014. Empirical evaluation of gated recurrent neural networks on sequence modeling. *arXiv preprint arXiv:1412.3555*.

Veena Dixit, Satish Dethe, and Rushikesh K Joshi. 2005. Design and implementation of a morphology-based spellchecker for marathi, an indian language. *ARCHIVES OF CONTROL SCIENCE*, 15(3):301.

Shaona Ghosh and Per Ola Kristensson. 2017. Neural networks for text correction and completion in keyboard decoding. *arXiv preprint arXiv:1709.06429*.

Neha Gupta and Pratistha Mathur. 2012. Spell checking techniques in nlp: a survey. *International Journal of Advanced Research in Computer Science and Software Engineering*, 2(12).

Saša Hasan, Carmen Heger, and Saab Mansour. 2015. Spelling correction of user search queries through statistical machine translation. In *Proceedings of the 2015 Conference on Empirical Methods in Natural Language Processing*, pages 451–460.

Sepp Hochreiter. 1998. The vanishing gradient problem during learning recurrent neural nets and problem solutions. *International Journal of Uncertainty, Fuzziness and Knowledge-Based Systems*, 6(02):107–116.

Sepp Hochreiter and Jürgen Schmidhuber. 1997. Long short-term memory. *Neural computation*, 9(8):1735–1780.

Diederik P Kingma and Jimmy Ba. 2014. Adam: A method for stochastic optimization. *arXiv preprint arXiv:1412.6980*.

Philipp Koehn, Hieu Hoang, Alexandra Birch, Chris Callison-Burch, Marcello Federico, Nicola Bertoldi, Brooke Cowan, Wade Shen, Christine Moran, Richard Zens, et al. 2007. Moses: Open source toolkit for statistical machine translation. In *Proceedings of the 45th annual meeting of the ACL on interactive poster and demonstration sessions*, pages 177–180. Association for Computational Linguistics.

Rakesh Kumar, Minu Bala, and Kumar Sourabh. 2018. A study of spell checking techniques for indian languages. *JK Research Journal in Mathematics and Computer Sciences*, 1(1).

Uma Maheshwar Rao. 2011. Telugu spell-checker. *International Telugu Internet Conference Proceedings*.

David E Rumelhart, Geoffrey E Hinton, and Ronald J Williams. 1986. Learning representations by back-propagating errors. *nature*, 323(6088):533.

Keisuke Sakaguchi, Kevin Duh, Matt Post, and Benjamin Van Durme. 2017. Robsut wrod reocginiton via semi-character recurrent neural network. In *AAAI*, pages 3281–3287.

Amit Sharma and Pulkit Jain. 2013. Hindi spell checker. *Indian Institute of Technology Kanpur*.

Harsharndeep Singh et al. 2015. Design and implementation of hinspell-hindi spell checker using hybrid approach. *International Journal of Scientific Research and Management*, 3(2).

Ilya Sutskever, Oriol Vinyals, and Quoc V Le. 2014. Sequence to sequence learning with neural networks. In *Advances in neural information processing systems*, pages 3104–3112.

Paul J Werbos. 1990. Backpropagation through time: what it does and how to do it. *Proceedings of the IEEE*, 78(10):1550–1560.

W John Wilbur, Won Kim, and Natalie Xie. 2006. Spelling correction in the pubmed search engine. *Information retrieval*, 9(5):543–564.

# Automatic Question Generation using Relative Pronouns and Adverbs


**Payal Khullar**     **Konigari Rachna**     **Mukul Hase**     **Manish Shrivastava**

Language Technologies Research Centre
International Institute of Information Technology, Hyderabad
Gachibowli, Hyderabad, Telangana-500032

```
{payal.khullar@research., konigari.rachna@research.
    mukul.hase@student., m.shrivastava@}iiit.ac.in
```



## Abstract

This paper presents a system that automatically generates multiple, natural language questions using relative pronouns and relative adverbs from complex English sentences. Our system is syntax-based, runs on dependency parse information of a single-sentence input, and achieves high accuracy in terms of syntactic correctness, semantic adequacy, fluency and uniqueness. One of the key advantages of our system, in comparison with other rule-based approaches, is that we nearly eliminate the chances of getting a wrong wh-word in the generated question, by fetching the requisite wh-word from the input sentence itself. Depending upon the input, we generate both factoid and descriptive type questions. To the best of our information, the exploitation of wh-pronouns and wh-adverbs to generate questions is novel in the Automatic Question Generation task.


## 1   Introduction

Asking questions from learners is said to facilitate interest and learning (Chi, 1994), to recognize problem learning areas (Tenenberg and Murphy, 2005) to assess vocabulary (Brown et al., 2005) and reading comprehension (Mitkov, 2006); (Kunichika et al., 2004), to provide writing support (Liu et al., 2012), to support inquiry needs (Ali et al., 2010), etc. Manual generation of questions from a text for creating practice exercises, tests, quizzes, etc. has consumed labor and time of academicians and instructors since forever, and with the invent of a large body of educational material available online, there is a growing need to make this task scalable. Along with that, in the recent times, there is an increased demand to cre-

ate Intelligent tutoring systems that use computer-assisted instructional material or self-help practice exercises to aid learning as well as objectively check learner's aptitude and accomplishments. Inevitably, the task of Automatic Question Generation (QG) caught the attention of NLP researchers from across the globe. Automatic QG has been defined as "the task of automatically generating questions from various inputs like raw text, database or semantic representation" (Rus et al., 2008). Apart from its direct application in the educational domain, in general, the core NLP areas like Question Answering, Dialogue Generation, Information Retrieval, Summarization, etc. also benefit from large scale automatic Question Generation.

## 2   Related Work

Previous work on Automatic QG has focused on generating questions using question templates (Liu et al., 2012); (Mostow and Chen, 2009); (Sneiders, 2002), transformation rules based largely on case grammars (Finn, 1975), general-purpose, transformation rules (Heilman and Smith, 2009), tree manipulation rules (Heilman, 2011); (Ali et al., 2010); (Gates, 2008), discourse cues (Agarwal et al., 2011), queries (Lin, 2008), various scopes (Mannem et al., 2010), dependency parse information (Mazidi and Nielsen, 2015), topic information (Chali and Hasan, 2015), ontologies (Alsubait et al., 2015), etc. More recent approaches also apply neural methods (Subramanian et al., 2017); (Zhou et al., 2017); (Yuan et al., 2017); (Du et al.), etc. to generate questions.

In the current paper, we fetch relative pronouns and relative adverbs from complex English sentences and use dependency-based rules, grounded in linguistic theory of relative clause syntactic structure, to generate multiple relevant questions. The work follows in the tradition of question writing algorithm (Finn, 1975) and transformation




*Proceedings of ACL 2018, Student Research Workshop*, pages 153–158
Melbourne, Australia, July 15 - 20, 2018. ©2018 Association for Computational Linguistics

rules based approach (Heilman and Smith, 2009). However, while Finn's work was based largely around case grammars (Fillmore, 1968), our system exploits dependency parse information using the Spacy parser (Honnibal and Johnson, 2015), which provides us with a better internal structure of complex sentences to work with. The general-purpose transformation rules in Heilman's system do not work well on sentences with a highly complex structure, as we show in the section on comparison and evaluation. Although no other state-of-the art system focuses specifically on QG from relative pronouns and relative adverbs, a more recent Minimal Recursion semantics-based QG system (Yao et al., 2012) has a sub part that deals with sentences with a relative clause, but less comprehensively. We differ from their system in that, for one, we do not decompose the complex sentence into simpler parts to generate questions. The rules are defined for the dependencies between relative pronouns and relative adverbs and the rest of the sentence as a whole. Secondly, our system generates a different set and more number of questions per sentence than their system.

## 3  Why Relative Clauses?

In complex sentences, relative pronouns or relative adverbs perform the function of connecting or introducing the relative clause that is embedded inside the matrix clause. Examples of these in English include *who, whom, which, where, when, how, why*, etc. An interesting thing about both relative pronouns and relative adverbs is that they carry unique information on the syntactic relationship between specific parts of the sentence. For example, consider the following sentence in English:

*I am giving fur balls to John who likes cats.*

In this sentence, the relative pronoun *who* modifies the object of the root verb *give* of the matrix sentence. At the same time, it acts as the subject of the relative clause *likes cats*, which it links the matrix clause with. In this paper, we aim to exactly exploit this structural relationship to generate questions, thereby adding to the pool of questions that can be generated from a given sentence. One of the key benefits of using the information from relative pronouns and relative adverbs is that we are not likely to go wrong with the wh-word, as we fetch it from the relative clause itself to generate the question. This gives our system an edge

over other QG systems.

## 4  System Description

We split the complete QG task into the following sub parts - the input natural language sentence is first fed into the Spacy parser. Using the parse information, the system checks for the presence of one or more relative pronouns or adverbs in the sentence. Post that, it further checks for well-defined linguistic features in the sentence, such as tense and aspect type of the root and relative clause verb, head-modifier relationship between different parts of the sentence, etc. to accordingly send the information to the rule sets. Depending upon which rule in the rule sets the information is sent to, questions are generated. We define our rule sets in the next section.

## 5  Rule Sets

For each of the nine relative pronouns and relative adverbs in English (*who, whom, whose, which, that, where, when, why, how*) that we took into consideration, we defined three sets of rules. Each of the three rule sets further contains a total of ten rules, backed by linguistic principles. Each relative pronoun or relative adverb in the sentence is first checked for a set of requirements before getting fed into the rules. Depending upon the relative pronoun and relative adverb and the type of relative clause (restrictive or unrestrictive), questions are generated. We present an example of one out of the ten rules from each of the three rule sets in the next section.

### 5.1  Rule Set 1.

We know that the relative pronoun (RP) modifies the object of the root of the matrix sentence. Before feeding the sentence to the rule, we first check the sentence for the tense and aspect of the root verb and also for the presence of modals and auxiliary verbs (aux). Based on this information, we then accordingly perform do-insertion before Noun Phrase (NP) or aux/modal inversion. For a sentence of the following form, with an optional Preposition Phrase (PP) and RP *who* that precedes a relative clause (RC),

NP (aux) Root NP (PP)+ {RC}

The rule looks like this:

RP aux NP root NP Preposition?

Hence, for the example sentence introduced in the previous section, we get the following question

using the first rule:
*Who/Whom am I giving fur balls to?*

In representation of the rules, we follow the general linguistic convention which is to put round brackets on optional elements and '+' symbol for multiple possible occurrences of a word or phrase.

## 5.2 Rule Set 2.

The next understanding about the relative pronoun or adverb comes from the relative clause it introduces or links the matrix sentence with. The relative pronoun can sometimes act as the subject of the verb of relative clause. This forms the basis for rules in the second set.

After checking for dependency of the RP, which should be noun subject (n-subj) to the verb in the relative clause, we then check the tense and aspect of the relative clause verb and the presence of modals and auxiliary verbs. Based on this information, we then accordingly perform do-insertion or modal/auxiliary inversion. For a relative clause of the following form, with the relative pronoun *who*,

{matrix } RP (aux/modals)+ RC verb (NP) (PP)+

The rule looks like this:

RP do-insertion/aux/modal RC verb (NP) (Preposition)?

Taking the same example sentence, we get the following question using the second rule:
*Who likes cats?*

## 5.3 Rule Set 3.

The relative pronoun modifies or gives more information on the head of the noun phrase of the preceding sentence. This forms the basis to rules in the third set. Before feeding the sentence to this rule, we first check the tense of the relative clause verb along with its number agreement. We do this because English auxiliaries and copula carry tense and number features and we need this information to insert their correct form. For a sentence of the following form:

NP (aux/modals) Root NP RP (aux)+ RC verb (NP) (PP)+

The rule looks like this:

RP aux Head of NP?

Taking the first example sentence, from the previous sections, we get the following question using the fourth rule:
*Who is John?*

In a similar fashion, we define rules for all other relative pronouns and adverbs that we listed in the previous section.

## 6 Evaluation Criteria

There is no standard way to evaluate the output of a QG system. In the current paper, we go with manual evaluation, where 4 independent human evaluators, all non-native English speakers but proficient in English, give scores to questions generated from the system. The scoring schema is similar to one used by (Agarwal et al., 2011) albeit with some modifications. To judge syntactic correctness, the evaluators give a score of 3 when the questions are syntactically well-formed and natural, 2 when they have a few syntactic errors and 1 when they are syntactically unacceptable. Similarly, for semantic correctness, the raters give a score of 3 when the questions are semantically correct, 2 when they have a weird meaning and 1 when they are semantically unacceptable. Unlike (Agarwal et al., 2011), we test the fluency and semantic relatedness separately. The former tells us how natural the question reads. A question with many embedded clauses and adjuncts is syntactically acceptable, but disturbs the intended purpose of the question and, hence, should be avoided. For example, a question like *Who is that girl who works at Google which has its main office in America which is a big country?* is syntactically and semantically fine, but isn't as fluent as the question *Who is that girl who works at Google?* which is basically the same question but is more fluent. The evaluators give a score of 1 for questions that aren't fluent and 2 to the ones that are. Lastly, evaluators rate the questions for how unique they are. Adding this criteria is important because questions generated for academic purposes need to cover different aspects of the sentence. This is why if the generated questions are more or less alike, the evaluators give them a low score on distribution or variety. For a well distributed output, the score is 2 and for a less distributed one, it is 1. The evaluators give a score of 0 when there is no output for a given sentence. The scores obtained separately for syntactic correctness, semantic adequacy, fluency and distribution are used to compare the performance of the two systems.

## 7 Evaluation

We take sentences from the Wikipedia corpus. Out of a total of 25773127 sentences, 3889289 sentences have one or more relative pronoun or relative adverb in them. This means that sentences with relative clauses form roughly 20% of the corpus. To conduct manual evaluation, we take 300 sentences from the set of sentences with relative clauses, and run ours and Heilman's system on them. We give the questions generated per sentence for both the systems to 4 independent human evaluators who rate the questions on syntactic correctness, semantic adequacy, fluency and distribution.

## 8   Results

The results of our system and comparison with Heilman's is given in Figure 1. The ratings presented are average of ratings of all the evaluators. Our system gets 2.89/3.0 on syntactic correctness, 2.9/3.0 on semantic adequacy, 1.85/2.0 in fluency and 1.8/2.0 in distribution. On the same metrics, Heilman's system gets 2.56, 2.58, 1.3 and 1.1. The Cohen's kappa coefficient or the inter evaluator agreement is 0.6, 0.7, 0.7 and 0.7 on syntactic correctness, semantic adequacy, fluency and distribution respectively, which indicate reliability. The overall rating of our system is 9.44 out of 10 in comparison of Heilman's which is 7.54.

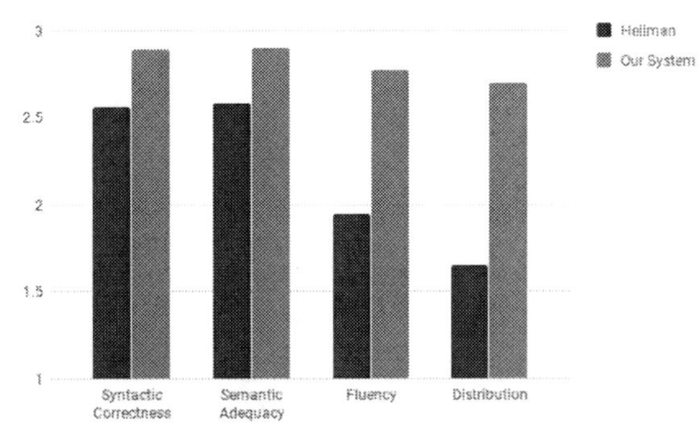

**Figure 1:** Evaluation scores: Our system performs better than Heilman's system on all of the given criteria; syntactic correctness, semantic adequacy, fluency and uniqueness.

## 9   Discussion

On all the four evaluation criteria that we used for comparison, our system performs better than Heilman's state-of-the-art rule based system, while generating questions from complex English sentences. Let us take a look at some specific input example cases to analyze the results. First of all, by fetching and modifying the wh-word from the sentence itself, we nearly eliminate the possibility of generating a sentence with a wrong wh-word. From the example comparison in Figure.2, we can see that the output of both the systems is the same. However, our system generates the correct wh-word for the generated question.

| Sentences | Heilman | Our System |
|---|---|---|
| Robert's elder brother plays badminton with the little girl who my mother teaches Mathematics to in the school which is state operated | Which is state operated? | What is state operated |

**Figure 2:** Wh-Word: Our system performs better than Heilman's system at fetching the correct Wh-word for the given input.

By exploiting the unique structural relationships between relative pronouns and relative adverbs with the rest of the sentence, we are able to cover different aspects of the same sentence. Also, by eliminating unwanted dependencies, we ensure that the system generates fluent questions. See Figure 3 for a reference example.

| Sentences | Heilman | Our System |
|---|---|---|
| Mary gave dark chocolates and flowers to Bart who works at Amazon which was known to be the biggest online store in Africa | Who did Mary give dark chocolates and flowers to? | Who did Mary give dark chocolates and flowers to? |
| | Who gave dark chocolates and flowers to Bart who works at Amazon which was known to be the biggest online store in Africa? | Who works at Amazon? |
| | What did Mary give to Bart who works at Amazon which was known to be the biggest online store in Africa? | Who is Bart? |
| | | What is the biggest online store in Africa? |
| | Did Mary give dark chocolates and flowers to Bart who works at Amazon which was known to be the biggest online store in Africa? | What is Amazon? |

**Figure 3:** Fluency: As compared to Heilman's system, our system generates more fluent questions for the given input.

Since Heilman's system does not look deeper into the internal structural dependencies between different parts of the sentence, it fails to generate reasonable questions for most cases of complex sentences. Our system, on the other hand, exploits such dependencies and is, therefore, able to handle complex sentences better. See Figure 4 for a reference example of this case. Lastly, there is a restriction put on the length of the input sentence in Heilman's system. Due to this, there is zero or no output at all for complex sentences that are very long. Our system, however, works well on such sentences also and gives reasonable output.

| Sentences | Heilman | Our System |
| --- | --- | --- |
| Using the findings , men can get a rough idea of their personal odds by answering questions that also include weight and race , experts said | Who said? | What also include weight and race? |
| | Did experts say? | What are questions that also include weight and race? |
| | | What can men get a rough idea of their personal odds by answering questions that also include weight and race? |

**Figure 4:** Complex Sentences: Our system is able to handle the given highly complex sentence better than Heilman's system.

## 10 Conclusion

This paper presented a syntax, rule-based system that runs on dependency parse information from the Spacy parser and exploits dependency relationship between relative pronouns and relative adverbs and the rest of the sentence in a novel way to automatically generate multiple questions from complex English sentences. The system is simple in design and can handle highly complex sentences. The evaluation was done by 4 independent human evaluators who rated questions generated from our system and Heilman's system on the basis of how syntactically correct, semantically adequate, fluent and well distributed or unique the questions were. Our system performed better than Heilman's system on all the aforesaid criterion. A predictable limitation of our system is that it is only meant to generate questions for sentences that contain at least one relative clause. Such sentences form about 20% of the tested corpus.

## 11 Acknowledgments

We acknowledge the support of Google LLC for this research, in the form of an International Travel Grant.

## References

Manish Agarwal, Rakshit Shah, and Prashanth Mannem. 2011. Automatic question generation using discourse cues. *Proceedings of the Sixth Workshop on Innovative Use of NLP for Building Educational Applications*, page 19.

Husam Ali, Yllias Chali, and Sadid A. Hasan. 2010. Automation of question generation from sentences. *Proceedings of QG2010: The Third Workshop on Question Generation*, pages 58–67.

Tahani Alsubait, Bijan Parsia, and Ulrike Sattler. 2015. Ontology-based multiple choice question generation. *KI - Knstliche Intelligenz*, 30(2):183188.

Jonathan C. Brown, Gwen A. Frishkoff, and Maxine Eskenazi. 2005. Automatic question generation for vocabulary assessment. *Proceedings of the conference on Human Language Technology and Empirical Methods in Natural Language Processing - HLT 05.*

Yllias Chali and Sadid A. Hasan. 2015. Towards topic-to-question generation. *Computational Linguistics*, 41.

M Chi. 1994. Eliciting self-explanations improves understanding,. *Cognitive Science*, 18(3):439477.

Xinya Du, Junru Shao, and Claire Cardie. Learning to ask: Neural question generation for reading comprehension. *Proceedings of the 55th Annual Meeting of the Association for Computational Linguistics*, 1.

Charles J. Fillmore. 1968. The case for case. *Emmon W. Bach and Robert T. Harms, editors, Universals in Linguistic Theory. Holt, Rinehart & Winston,* page 188.

Patrick J Finn. 1975. A question writing algorithm. *Journal of Reading Behavior*, 7(4).

Melinda D. Gates. 2008. Generating reading comprehension look back strategy questions from expository texts. *Masters thesis, Carnegie Mellon University.*

Michael Heilman. 2011. Automatic factual question generation from text.

Michael Heilman and Noah A. Smith. 2009. Question generation via overgenerating transformations and ranking.

Matthew Honnibal and Mark Johnson. 2015. An improved non-monotonic transition system for dependency parsing. In *Proceedings of the 2015 Conference on Empirical Methods in Natural Language Processing*, pages 1373–1378, Lisbon, Portugal. Association for Computational Linguistics.

Hidenobu Kunichika, Tomoki Katayama, Tsukasa IIirashima, and Akira Takeuchi. 2004. Automated question generation methods for intelligent english learning systems and its evaluation. *Proc. of ICCE2001*, page 11171124.

Chin-Yew Lin. 2008. Automatic question generation from queries.

Ming Liu, Rafael Calvo, and Vasile Rus. 2012. G-asks: An intelligent automatic question generation system for academic writing support. *Dialogue & Discourse*, 3(2):101124.

Prashanth Mannem, Rashmi Prasad, and Aravind Joshi. 2010. Question generation from paragraphs at upenn: Qgstec system discription. *Proceedings of QG2010: The Third Workshop on Question Generation.*

Karen Mazidi and Rodney D. Nielsen. 2015. Leveraging multiple views of text for automatic question generation. *Lecture Notes in Computer Science Artificial Intelligence in Education*, page 257266.

R. Mitkov. 2006. Comtuter-aided generation of multiple-choice tests. *International Conference on Natural Language Processing and Knowledge Engineering, 2003. Proceedings. 2003.*

J. Mostow and W Chen. 2009. Generating instruction automatically for the reading strategy of self questioning. *Proceeding of the Conference on Artificial Intelligence in Education*, pages 465–472.

Vasile Rus, Zhiqiang Cai, and Arthur Graesser. 2008. Question generation : Example of a multi-year evaluation campaign. *Online Proceedings of 1st Question Generation Workshop.*

Eriks Sneiders. 2002. Automated question answering using question templates that cover the conceptual model of the database. *Natural Language Processing and Information Systems Lecture Notes in Computer Science*, page 235239.

Sandeep Subramanian, Tong Wang, Xingdi Yuan, Saizheng Zhang, Adam Trischler, and Yoshua Bengio. 2017. Neural models for key phrase detection and question generation.

Josh Tenenberg and Laurie Murphy. 2005. Knowing what i know: An investigation of undergraduate knowledge and self-knowledge of data structures. *Computer Science Education*, 15(4):297315.

Xuchen Yao, Gosse Bouma, and Yi Zhang. 2012. Semantics-based question generation and implementation. *Dialogue & Discourse*, 3(2).

Xingdi Yuan, Tong Wang, Caglar Gulcehre, Alessandro Sordoni, Philip Bachman, Saizheng Zhang, Sandeep Subramanian, and Adam Trischler. 2017. Machine comprehension by text-to-text neural question generation. *Proceedings of the 2nd Workshop on Representation Learning for NLP.*

Qingyu Zhou, Nan Yang, Furu Wei, Chuanqi Tan, Hangbo Bao, and Ming Zhou. 2017. Neural question generation from text: A preliminary study. *Lecture Notes in Computer Science*, pages 662–671.

# Author Index

**Association for Computational Linguistics**
209 N. Eighth Street
Stroudsburg, Pennsylvania 18360

ISBN 978-1-5108-6707-9